HORRID CRIMES OF BYGONE CHESHIRE

HORRID CRIMES OF BYGONE CHESHIRE

Derek Yarwood

DB PUBLISHING

This one's for my whole family.

*With fond remembrance of
Eric Langton, former colleague,
long-time friend and all-round nice guy.*

First published 2017 by DB Publishing, an imprint of JMD Media Ltd, Nottingham, United Kingdom.

ISBN 9781780915531

Printed and bound in the UK

CONTENTS

Introduction

The title of this book was inspired by an 18th century Act of Parliament drawn up in response to an alarming increase in what was referred to in its preamble as 'the Horrid Crime of Murder'. Over the years the adjective that gave the phrase its potency has become so depreciated that, nowadays, it is more likely to be used, if at all, to describe bad weather or a particularly disagreeable meal. But back then it meant 'causing horror', 'dreadful', 'repulsive', 'frightening' and, not least, 'shocking'. It was that power to shock that characterised the historic cases re-visited in the following pages.

The stories, which cover both the 18th and 19th centuries, are not all about murder, though most of them are. Some relate to attempted murder; others to house-breaking and highway robbery — less serious offences, maybe, but each one featuring events for which any of the above definitions would be equally justified.

And, under the savage penal code in operation for much of that time-span, they were all subject to the death penalty and dealt with in a manner that, paradoxically, was also considered by a growing number of people as 'horrid' . . . in every sense of the word.

In presenting a detailed and, wherever possible, an officially authenticated study of the 17 cases revisited here, the book's dozen chapters shine a revealing light on a particularly dark age in Cheshire's criminal history — a period when hanging was prescribed for over 200 different offences — and on society's gradually changing attitude towards the treatment of offenders and, in particular, the vexatious issue of capital punishment.

It was an evolution that by 1830 had almost entirely erased the so-called 'Bloody Code' from the statute book and hanging was effectively reserved for murder. And, with the passing of the 1868 Capital Punishment Amendment Act, the unedifying spectacle of execution was finally removed from the public gaze and hidden away behind the walls of the county gaols.

Set in the context of the social and judicial conditions that impacted especially harshly on the lives of the poorest sections of the population, the book concludes with a behind-the-scenes look at the four brutal murder cases that resulted in the only private executions carried out at Chester following the 1868 Act.

During my extensive research I have received much valued help and support from a number of people, most of whom have given of their time and expertise freely and, in many instances, above and beyond my expectations.

I owe a special debt of gratitude to the ever-willing Search Room staff at the Cheshire Record Office — where I spent many long hours poring over age-old files and peering at electronic media to root out as much historic detail as possible — and especially with regard to access to illustrations from the Cheshire Image Bank.

The staff at the National Archives at Kew also provided invaluable assistance, particularly in relation to my efforts at understanding and transcribing fading old assize court files and other original source documents.

To Steve Caron and all at JMD Media/DB Publishing a big thank-you for enabling me to complete my Cheshire true-crime 'trilogy'. Also to Matthew Limbert for his cover artwork and pre-press guidance.

And of the many others who have helped me in their own individual ways, I wish to express my appreciation to the following (if I have missed anyone out, I apologise): Eamonn Andrews; Anthony Annakin-Smith; Vicki Bailey, Emily Dunn and Katherine Yates (Macclesfield Library); Janny Baxter (Stockport Museum); Mark Bevan; John Birchall; Tim Boddington (*macclesfieldcanal.org.uk*); Peter Boon (whose knowledge of the history of Congleton, and his comments on my necessarily brief references to it, were of great value); Peter Boughton (Grosvenor Museum); Peter Boumphrey; Will Brown (Museum Of Policing In Cheshire); Sylvia Buckley; James Button; Duncan Broady (Greater Manchester Police Museum); John Carsley; Richard Clark (who graciously allowed me to draw upon his authoritative *Capital Punishment UK* website); Tony Franks-Buckley; Jerry Harris; J. J. Heath-Caldwell; Christine Heathcote; Peter Higginbotham (for helping me better understand the operation of the Poor Laws and the role of the workhouse); Jane Hodkinson (Manchester Archives and Local Studies); Dr Carole Holme; Steve Howe; Roger Hull (Liverpool Record Office); Heather Jones; Liam Kelly (Findmypast); Colin Lynch; Dr Gordon S. Marino (for his contribution to my research into social conditions in Angel Meadow in the 19th century); Louise Martin; Margaret Myerscough (Stockport Heritage Library); Charlotte Nicholls (Stockport MBC); Dr Hugh Pihlens; Anna Rhodes; Ashleigh Talbot (*www.madametalbot.com*); Ron Thorn; Lavinia Whitfield; Tom Wigley and his colleagues at *hydonian.blogspot.co.uk*; Peter Wroe; and my wife Christine for her support and proof-reading skills. Any errors that remain are entirely my own.

Derek Yarwood,

Barnton, Spring 2017.

CHAPTER ONE

A Fate Worse Than Death

To unwary travellers crossing the windswept moorland on moonlit nights, the sudden appearance of black-shrouded corpses dangling in mid-air from a massive wooden gibbet would have been a sight to chill the blood, the sounds of creaking timbers and grating chains adding a ghostly soundtrack to the horror show. Even in daylight the mouldering bodies of the two executed men were a hellish vision that must have sent a shiver down the spine of any god-fearing soul who caught a glimpse of them.

Two hundred and eighty years ago, on wild and lonely Ettiley Heath, that was exactly the reaction this kind of gruesome display was designed to provoke. In 18th century England it was seen as both a shock-inducing deterrent to crime and a forceful reminder of the awesome power of the law.

In this particular scenario the menacing figures were convicted murderers Hugh Moss and William Hawthorn, who were 'posted' there in April 1736, after being found guilty at the Cheshire Assizes of robbing and killing an elderly widow in the nearby town of Sandbach. Following their joint execution, and in accordance with common custom in dealing with such aggravated offences, their bodies would have been wrapped in calico and coated in pitch (to preserve them for as long as possible), before being riveted into cages of hoop iron. They were then taken to the spot, about a mile-and-a-half west of the town, and suspended from the gibbet by chains to deliver their grim warning to the public.

In this hitherto anonymous corner of east Cheshire — with a history as featureless as the terrain and at this time home to only a few hardy farming folk — Moss and Hawthorn became at once its most notorious 'residents' and the most prominent landmark in the desolate countryside.

Erected, by order of the court, 'near some convenient highroad' close to the scene of the crime, the gibbet was sited for maximum impact. But to be sure that its stark message was visible over as wide an area as possible, it was also ordered that the crude structure — consisting of a single upright topped by a two-armed crossbeam — was built 20 feet high.

Though it had long been a feature of English judicial practice, it would be 15 years before gibbeting (or 'hanging in chains', as it was also called) was officially recognised in law. Ironically, it happened at a time when doubts were being voiced about its deterrent value. For it

This was how the Ettiley Heath gibbet would have looked as it towered above the landscape on the outskirts of Sandbach in 1736. Though not quite as tall, it was similar to the famous Combe Gibbet in Berkshire, the second replica of which is pictured here in 1923. It was first erected in 1676 to display the bodies of an adulterous couple convicted of murder.

Image courtesy of Hungerford Virtual Museum.

was a worrying surge in the number of murders, mainly in and around the capital, that prompted Parliament into passing the 1751 Murder Act. Acknowledging the need for stronger preventative measures, the Act's preamble explained that it had 'become necessary that some further Terror and peculiar Mark of Infamy be added to the Punishment of Death' for those guilty of 'the Horrid Crime of Murder'. The legislation, which came into force in June 1752, gave judges the option of committing the bodies of executed murderers into the possession of local surgeons — to be opened up for the advancement of anatomical and medical knowledge — as an alternative to gibbeting. The new power extended the principle that the humiliation of the worst offenders should continue beyond death for, as part of the punishment, it was ordered that the dissections were also to be carried out in public.

If hanging wasn't enough any more, there were now two fates worse than death. In addition, the Act also stipulated that only the remains of those murderers given over for dissection could be buried; those consigned to the gibbet were to be left suspended in their metal-bound winding-sheets to rot.

Judges were instructed to announce in open court the full extent of the sentence — including whether the convict's body was to be hung in chains or anatomised — 'in order to impress a just horror in the mind of the offender, and on the minds of such as shall be present, of the heinous crime of murder'.

Evidence from contemporary newspaper reports suggests that it was the Murder Act's new provision that impressed the greater horror in the minds of offenders; to them the anatomist's knife, rather than the gibbet, was the more dreadful prospect. This despite the belief, common at the time, that there was no hope of heaven and an afterlife without a proper Christian burial.

In 1736 the Ettiley gibbet — rising above the surrounding heathland like a huge capital 'T' — had been a perfect symbol for the

'Terror' that the earlier sanction was supposed to inspire: the 'letter of the law' writ large upon the landscape. And, effective or not, there is no doubt that it left its own 'peculiar Mark' on the minds of all those who encountered it.

The high profile villains who gave Ettiley Heath its unwelcome reputation were said to be 'labourers, late of Sandbach', though whether that was their occupation, or where they were from, is by no means certain as court documents of the day were surprisingly casual about such details. And in the case of Hugh Moss and William Hawthorn (also known as Lockett) the surviving records are disappointingly short of many key facts. From the Chester Assize Court files, preserved in the National Archives in Kew, however, it seems clear that the crime for which they paid with their lives was a burglary that went fatally wrong.

Judging by the amount of time they seem to have spent in Sandbach's many pubs, the pair had been employed on a part-time basis; and it was during one of their regular drinking sessions, on Tuesday 10 February 1736, that they hit upon their money-raising scheme. The name of the pub is not recorded, but its landlord was Richard Shaw who, in a statement he made at the inquest into Margaret Lowe's death — held by Cheshire Coroner John Baker two days later — said that the two men had arrived at his house at about four o'clock in the afternoon in company with a man named Wilkinson. It was one of the five inquest depositions that today provide the only detailed evidence about the case known to exist.

Shaw, whose main occupation was that of butcher, said that some time later the two accused claimed to be broke and he heard 'Lockett' mention that Mrs Lowe, who lived alone, was known to keep money in her house nearby. With little regard for secrecy, the pair continued to discuss their robbery plan. Shaw's statement, couched in the third person, as was the

Ettiley Heath today, looking south towards the last remaining area of open countryside, following the housing development that has taken place on the northern end of the heath.

Photograph by the author.

normal style adopted by legal clerks at the time, went on, 'He heard Lockett say he had no money but that he knew the widow Lowe had money and [that] he would have it.' He also heard Moss declare that he had no more money, either, but that 'he should have enough tomorrow'.

During the course of their stay, 'Lockett sent Moss to Margaret Lowe's' and, Shaw added, 'afterwards they both went to her house' — though quite how he knew that, he did not explain. Perhaps the talkative drinkers made it known that they had gone to beg for alms there, while at the same time checking out the lie of the land to see if robbery was a viable proposition. It was a theory that may have been given credence by the evidence of Susanna Snelson.

Early that evening the previously penniless Moss and Hawthorn/ Lockett were seen drinking with a third man in the widow Snelson's (again unidentified) ale house in Sandbach, presumably being treated by their companion, one Thomas Boswell. Mrs Snelson testified that the men were there until about 7pm. From their continuingly careless talk she was able to discern that the two of them had twice gone to Margaret Lowe's home 'or pretended to'. When they returned, she deposed, Lockett 'gave out scandalous words against her [Mrs Lowe], calling her a thief or to the like effect' and said that he would be 'revenged of her [*sic*] and several [other] threatening words to the like effect'. An indication, perhaps, that they *had* gone a-begging at the comfortably-off widow Lowe's and the old lady had sent them packing.

It wasn't until between three and four o'clock the next morning, however, that the robbers finally broke into Margaret Lowe's home (where, precisely, she lived is another detail missing from the records, though, as we shall see, there are one or two clues that point to a possible location). It appears the intruders were surprised to find her lying in bed in a downstairs room and, when she cried out, Moss apparently grabbed her by the throat. When that failed to silence her he beat her savagely with his bare hands.

After ransacking the house and stealing the £42 the woman had kept in a purse upstairs — it would have the spending power today of more than £8,000 — the robbers fled the scene and disappeared into the night. Though terminally injured, the widow Lowe seems to have summoned the strength to call out for help and soon a large number of her neighbours gathered in the street outside her house.

One of them was baker George Hopkin, who lived next-door. He deposed that he had arrived home late that night and noticed that, although it was around 3am, a light still burned in Margaret Lowe's house. So, when some little time later, he heard 'a great outcry in her house', he got up and went immediately to her front door. His deposition went on, 'He called out to her to open the door. [But] she replied from within that she could not, for they (as she expressed it) had throttled her.'

Farmer Joseph Beach was another neighbour roused from his bed by what he described as 'a great outcry in the street'. By the time he reached Mrs Lowe's, he said, there was already 'a great crowd of people outside'. He was told 'there had been thieves' at work there. When the concerned neighbours managed to gain access to the house, Beach helped search the premises and the immediate vicinity but found no trace of the intruders.

He said he questioned a barely conscious Mrs Lowe about what had happened and whether she could describe the thieves. In a weak voice she related how 'they had come to her bedside and said "Damn her, she lies here" and that she was inwardly crushed and, as she expressed it, they had "done her business" or words to that effect.'

She mentioned to Beach that she had £42 in cash in a purse in a desk upstairs, which she had no doubt the thieves had taken. Her instincts were correct. Beach and William Denton, a local shoemaker (the town was then renowned for producing quality boots and shoes), found the desk broken open. The purse was still there but it was empty.

Denton's wife Ann, in her deposition, recalled how, 'on hearing an outcry of thieves', she had gone with a lighted candle to Mrs Lowe's house and found her 'in great disorder'. She had tried to comfort her by 'telling her not to mind the loss of her money for that they had spared her life'. The old lady replied forlornly, 'They have not'. She was right about that, too.

Margaret Lowe's final hours were described by Joseph Beach. After being informed of her stolen savings, he stated, 'she wept and was after very sick and fainted, and continued very much disordered all the time he stayed in the house, and about eight o'clock that day [8am] she died.'

Later that day, 11 February, Beach went with Sarah Shaw, the wife of Richard, to the home of Thomas Wilkinson in Sandach to inquire if he was the man who had been drinking with Moss and Hawthorn at the Shaws' pub the previous day. He denied he had been there with them; he had been at the pub, he said, but left early.

The search for the robbers had now become a murder hunt. How Moss and Hawthorn were eventually tracked down is not possible to say; but their capture might have been accelerated by another of the dying comments of the victim herself. For she had told Ann Denton she had recognised 'the rogue' who had attacked her as a man she had seen at the home of one of her relations the previous Christmas.

After being secured in Chester Castle Gaol, the pair were set for trial at the county's Spring Assizes. Strictly speaking Chester, as an historic county palatine, didn't have 'assizes' at this time; instead it had its own Palatinate Court of Great Sessions and, while it was customarily referred to as 'the assizes', it was not until 1830 that its ancient judicial distinction was abolished and it was formally absorbed into the country's more familiar circuit court network.

Up to 1786, when the building was demolished under the Castle's last great re-development programme, the Court of Great Sessions sat in the magnificent 11th century Great Hall. Situated on the east side of the Lower Ward, and also known as Hugh Lupus's Hall, after the first great Earl of Chester, it was where he and his successors held their 'Parliament' in the immediate post-Conquest days when the earldom of Chester (Cheshire) was a largely independent province within the Norman-ruled kingdom. And it was there that the two Sandbach murder suspects were brought to the bar on Wednesday 21 April 1736.

Although the indictments show that it was Moss who struck the fatal blows, both men were charged with killing Margaret Lowe. As the murder was committed while they were engaged jointly in another felony (i.e. robbery), the law deemed them both equally responsible for her death.

Moss's indictment was a graphic testament to the brutality of his attack on the old woman. It alleged that he 'did make an assault on Margaret Lowe [and] with both hands on the head, neck, breast, shoulders and stomach did strike and beat . . . giving her several

mortal blows and bruises' from which, at about 7am [*sic*] on 11 February, she died. A second indictment accused Moss and Hawthorn of 'feloniously and burglariously' breaking and entering the deceased's home and stealing the £42 contents of her purse.

The medieval Great Hall at Chester Castle, in which the Court of Great Sessions ('Assizes') sat until 1876, and where, 140 years earlier, Hugh Moss and William Hawthorn were tried for murder.

The jury pronounced them guilty on both charges and the Judge, the Honourable John Verney, who had been appointed Chief Justice of Chester just over two years earlier, sentenced them to death. The copy of his order, entered in the Court's Crown Book (in which brief details of the day-to-day business of the court were entered), instructed that the convicts were to be taken on Wednesday 12 May to Boughton — the place overlooking the River Dee on the eastern outskirts of Chester where for centuries the county gallows was situated — 'and be then and there severally hanged by their necks till they are dead'.

Signed also by the 'Prothonotary', or Clerk of the Court, Roger Comberbach, the warrant went on, 'After their deaths [they are to] be without delay conveyed to Ettiley Heath . . . and there hung up upon a Gibbet twenty foot high . . . in Irons or Chains in the open air and so continue till they are rotted and consumed.'

The same Crown Book also contained several intriguing references to two other people who were obviously suspected of being in collusion with Moss and Hawthorn. In fact the pair, Thomas Bosson and Catherine Bosson (his wife, presumably), were arrested and committed to appear at the same Spring Assizes, also accused of the robbery and murder. The charges against the latter, it was noted on 21 April, were dismissed by the Grand Jury in their customary pre-trial consideration of the evidence, and she was set at liberty. But the entry revealed that the case against Thomas Bosson was 'continued till next session'. Interestingly, another reference in the Crown Book for that date, to the inquest on Margaret Lowe, seems to support the idea that more than two people were initially believed to have been involved in her murder. It stated that the dead woman had been 'murdered by William Lockett and *others*' (author's italics).

At the Autumn Assizes on Saturday 4 September, however, Thomas Bossen was formally discharged from the Court a free man, though he had probably been forced to remain in the foul subterranean cells at Chester Castle during the intervening five months. Following further investigation, there was insufficient evidence on which to try him. If the Bossons had played any part in the affair, it was obviously a minor one; it may have been limited, for example, to sheltering the killers after the murder — a couple with similar names were living in the nearby village of Warmingham during this period — or to supplying the information that led them to the widow Lowe's well-lined purse. We will never know.

Of greater significance is the loss of any solid evidence to identify Margaret Lowe's address, the scene of the crime in which the defenceless old woman was robbed of her life savings . . . and her life. For its time her home would have been a fairly substantial dwelling, as is borne out by a 'True and perfect Inventory of all and Singular the

Goods, Credits and Chattles' of the widow Lowe, the former Margaret Jellicoe, at her death. She died intestate and the inventory, filed at the Cheshire Record Office in Chester, was drawn up by the three men appointed to administer her estate: her brother and next-of-kin John Jellicoe of Stanthorne, near Winsford, John Johnson of Middlewich and George Walker of Woolstanwood, near Crewe, each of whom was described as a 'yeoman', a modest land-owning member of the middle class, ranked between husbandman and gentleman.

Dated 15 February 1736, the day Margaret Lowe was laid to rest in the graveyard of Sandbach Parish Church, it listed items in the 'house place' (living room), the parlour, the buttery and two bed chambers with a total value of £63 3s 7d (equivalent to over £12,000 today).

In the surviving court papers, Mrs Lowe's home was given merely as Sandbach; though, from a careful reading of the inquest depositions, several indicators to its possible location emerge. For instance, the witness statements consistently referred to a commotion 'in the street' outside her house; not in the road or the lane, but the street. In 1736 there were only two principal streets in Sandbach — High Street and Church Street — and the population was concentrated in its medieval core: the area between the Arclid Brook and High Town less than a third-of-a-mile away, and which also included the Parish Church of St. Mary, whose origins can be traced back as far as the 13th century, the old Town Hall and the ancient Market Square, focal point of the community probably since the 8th or 9th centuries, when the famous Sandbach Saxon Crosses are believed to have been first erected there.

Clearly, Margaret Lowe did not live in an isolated part of the town: the way in which a large crowd gathered so quickly outside her house once her cries were heard is testimony to that. Her next-door neighbour was a baker; a shoemaker worked nearby. As essential services their domestic businesses would surely have been in the town centre. That, of the two principle streets, it was Church Street where Mrs Lowe's home was situated, may be proved by the final clue among the depositions.

As we have seen, another close neighbour who gave evidence at the trial of Hugh Moss and William Hawthorn was Joseph Beach, a farmer. The only farm near the town centre at this time was 17th century Dingle Farm, which stood on rising ground to the north-east of the Parish Church and less than a hundred yards from Church Street. It is still there today, though much altered and hemmed in on all sides by modern housing. If, as Beach stated, he was awakened by 'a great outcry in the street', it is doubtful whether, had the disturbance been in High Street, he would have heard it quite so loudly separated by a

Modern Church Street, Sandbach: was this where Margaret Lowe's substantial cottage was situated?

Photograph by the author.

distance of more than 200 yards and the ridge of higher ground dominated by the Church — even in the dead of night.

Furthermore, it seems likely that the two pubs Moss and Hawthorn visited the previous evening were fairly close to the widow Lowe's house. In 1736 there were four coaching inns and hostelries clustered around the nearby Market Square, where they can still be found today: the Crown, parts of which date back to the 15th century, the Lower Chequer (1570), the Black Bear (1634) and the Market Tavern (circa 1680). The nearest was the Lower Chequer on Crown Bank, though that may not have been its name at that time (it was called originally the Church Inn). All were/are within a few minutes' walk of Church Street. Admittedly, this could also apply to High Street; but, of the two locations, Church Street, tucked away below the mound of St. Mary's, would seem a far less risky place than the town's busy main thoroughfare to attempt a burglary.

An equally frustrating omission from the evidence is the site of the gibbet on which Hugh Moss and William Hawthorn spent their last days on earth. The history books contain no references at all to the murderous events of that February night in 1736; only one newspaper, the *Chester Courant*, existed in Cheshire at that time (though its title then was *Adams's Weekly Courant*), and the relevant editions of that venerable publication, launched in 1732, are missing. In the paper's original four-page format there were more column inches devoted to international and national 'intelligence' and advertising than local news, and crimes were reported in only the barest detail; so they probably would not have been of great help in our search. And any folk-memories that once persisted in local tradition don't appear to have survived the passage of time, either.

Judge Verney's court order had laid down that the gibbet was to be erected 'near some convenient high road', which would suggest the main road between Sandbach and Middlewich (now the A533). That

A view, circa 1900, of the Lower Chequer inn on Crown Bank. Was this where Moss and Hawthorn made their plans to rob Margaret Lowe? Church Street, the most likely location for the widow Lowe's cottage, was just around the corner.

would have ensured that it was seen by the largest number of people, as this was the route taken by most travellers then as it is today. But on late 18th century maps that high road only appears to run through the northern-most edge of Ettiley Heath.

As a favoured spot for a gibbet was at a crossroads, perhaps an equally compelling case could be made for the intersection between the old north-south route across the heath — which roughly followed the line of what are now Station Road, Elworth Road and Hindheath Road (B5079) — and the main east-west route, which closely corresponded with modern Deans Lane and Moston Road. That would have put the gibbet site near the junction between Deans Lane and Elworth Road, in the heart of the heath. And — another consideration when siting gibbets — it would have been a tolerable distance from the nearest houses to the north and east of the heathland.

During the 16th century Ettiley Heath was on a regular pilgrimage trail between the diocese of Chester and Lichfield, early cathedral cities with strong historic links. Part of it ran from the main Sandbach-Middlewich road and crossed the heath along what would later become Elton Road before continuing on to Warmingham, where pilgrims were able to obtain rest and refreshment at a house run by nuns. An old property on Elton Road called Tollgate Cottage may indicate that the route was of some significance in later years, too. Could this be a fourth candidate for the gibbet site?

What the records also leave hanging in the air is whether Hugh Moss and William Hawthorn, the long-forgotten terrors of Ettiley Heath, served their 'suspended sentences' in full. While many remained in place — sometimes for years — long after their bones had been picked clean by the birds, it was not uncommon for the gibbeted bodies of condemned criminals to be spirited away in the night by family members and secretly buried in unmarked graves well before they were 'rotted and consumed'. Whatever the legal position was before, the Murder Act addressed this issue, too.

From 1752 anyone retrieving a cadaver from the gibbet or intercepting it on its way to the dissecting room risked being transported to the colonies for a minimum of seven years.

*   *   *

FOURTEEN years after Moss and Hawthorn were chained up together on distant Ettiley Heath, another double gibbet cast its sinister shadow over the Cheshire countryside on the west of the county. It was erected in Wirral to accommodate another pair of cowardly thugs after another callous murder.

The victim, an elderly man by the name of Bryan Molloy, was attacked in the summer of 1750 on the road between Chester and Parkgate. He was on his way home after joining the annual migration of Irish farm labourers travelling to England seeking employment in the harvesting season. Arriving at the then bustling Deeside port of Parkgate by packet-boat from Dublin at the beginning of May, most of them headed for London and the Home Counties, where the cattle farmers grew vast quantities of hay and relied on this massive influx of casual workers to harvest it.

Thousands took part in the seasonal 'invasion', which seems to have begun in the 1720s. In consequence large numbers of mainly impoverished strangers — mostly 'cottars', or peasants, from Galway, Roscommon and Mayo, apparently — passed through Chester on the journey south, often resorting to stealing, begging and dossing (usually uninvited) in stables and outhouses en route. They aroused great hostility among the locals, who saw their jobs being taken away by men willing to work for far lower wages; they were frequently involved in fights and riots and their presence was an added burden on the parish poor rates . . . and policing.

In 1753 Saunders Welch, the High Constable of the Holborn Division of Middlesex and later a county magistrate, wrote that 'the Irish imported into this kingdom of the lower class are those who annually come to harvest work and when that is over return with the savings of their labour to their own country'. In her book *London Life In The Eighteenth Century*, first published in 1925, Mary Dorothy George quotes him as saying that there were two distinct types. Those in the first group were 'useful, faithful good servants to the farmer' and, as such, deserved protection and encouragement. But the other group, he declared, comprised 'a set of fellows made desperate by their crimes . . . who come to London to perpetrate their outrages, and it may justly be asserted that most of the robberies, and the murders consequent upon them, have been committed by these outcasts from Ireland'.

Bryan Molloy, by all accounts, was one of the former class. Garrett Delaney and Edward Johnson, on the other hand, undoubtedly belonged to the latter. The robbery, and

The packet boats that carried Irish harvesters in their thousands on their seasonal trips between Dublin and the then thriving port of Parkgate in Wirral in the 18th and early 19th centuries.

consequent murder, of their fellow countryman was, indeed, an outrage perpetrated by desperate men.

Our story begins on the morning of Wednesday 29 August 1750, when Mr Molloy and his nephew David, who had also been working in London as a harvester, arrived at a public house in Boughton, Chester. After breakfast they planned to meet up with David Molloy's wife and children, who had accompanied him on his travels, and continue together on to Parkgate to catch the packet back to Ireland. But David Molloy's family were delayed and so his uncle decided to go on ahead alone. It was a decision that undoubtedly cost him his life.

Setting out to walk the 10 miles to Parkgate, the elder Molloy was soon joined by Delaney and Johnson and a third man, John Caffery, also an Irish harvester, all following the same route to their homeland. Traditionally, the migrant workers left England towards the end of the summer in time to take up similar employment in Ireland, where the harvest was later than in this country.

When they had got as far as Great Saughall, some three miles outside Chester, Delaney explained to their new companion that two friends were following behind and suggested that they all sat down beside the high road (now the A540 and known most commonly as 'the Parkgate road') to await for them. It was while they were resting there that Bryan Molloy was attacked, beaten with sticks and, as he lay insensible on the ground, knifed in the throat. His body was thrown into a ditch beside the road and the three men took off in the direction of Parkgate, taking with them the coarse linen shoulder bag Molloy had been carrying. Inside were a coat, a pair of breeches, a pair of stockings, a linen handkerchief, a snuff box, a leather belt and a leather purse containing two guinea-pieces (£2 2s) and a further 6s 6d in silver and copper.

Instead of making straight for the port, however, the Irishmen — unwisely as it turned out — went on a leisurely detour, pausing at two inns, the first at Great Saughall and the other at Shotwick. And it was while they enjoyed a meal and a pint of ale in the latter that they were apprehended — sublimely ignorant of the fact that they had been observed by a farm hand as they departed the murder scene.

Agricultural labourer John Morgan had been sitting in a field alongside the Parkgate road eating his lunch with two young helpers, a boy and a girl, when, he would confirm in court, he heard the sounds of a fight in the road close by. Hiding behind the field hedge that ran alongside the highway, he observed three men, two of whom he later identified as Delaney and Johnson. After throwing various objects into some gorse bushes they walked off. Suspecting foul play, Morgan went presently to the spot and stumbled upon the much bloodied body of a man sprawled in a ditch. He had a large wound in his neck and appeared to be dead.

Morgan and his young companions hurried back to their home village of Great Saughall to raise the alarm and when word reached Chester, two city constables were immediately dispatched to the area. Having been given excellent descriptions by the watching farm worker, they were able to run the fugitives to earth in double quick time at the appropriately-named Greyhound Inn, two miles away in Shotwick.

The following day (30 August), in the presence of the three suspects, local magistrate Thomas Salusbury began interviewing witnesses and the official picture of the events surrounding Bryan Molloy's violent death began to take shape. More details were filled in at the inquest at Great Saughall on the 31st and it is from these two sets of depositions, contained in the Chester Assize Court files held at the National Archives, that, more than 250 years later, we are able to piece together what happened that late summer's day on the Parkgate road. And, in the absence of any meaningful newspaper reports on the case, they are also our only guide to the evidence given at the subsequent trial.

In his inquest deposition David Molloy informed Coroner John Baker that he and his uncle arrived at Boughton around 6am on 29 August and stopped at the house of Cornelius McDougal, a pensioner and — he somehow felt it necessary to mention — 'a person with only one arm'. His uncle left the hostelry at about 10 o'clock that morning with a white bag over his shoulder. Among its contents were a grey cloth coat and a pair of blue cloth breeches. Garments of that description were shown to the witness and he identified them as belonging to his uncle who, he said, had bought them in Chelsea from a brewer's clerk for nine shillings while they had been working together in London.

Curiously, on the evening of 28 August, while on their way to Chester, Bryan Molloy had given his nephew two freshly-minted guineas and a few shillings to hold for him for safekeeping overnight. Whether he was worried about being robbed David Molloy did not say. But it must have given him an uneasy feeling the next day when, three hours behind his uncle and having handed the money back, he himself set off down the Parkgate road, then notorious as a haunt of highway robbers. Then, at some point along the way, he learned that an Irishman had just been robbed and murdered up ahead.

Borrowing a spare horse from two men he overtook on the road and, with his mood no doubt growing ever more anxious, young Molloy rode at a gallop to where the crime was reported to have taken place. And there, to his horror, he found the body of his uncle, now lifted from the ditch into which it had been unceremoniously dumped and placed at the roadside. Two men were standing guard over it. His uncle, said Molloy, had 'a large hole in the right side of his neck, between his ear and windpipe'.

In his statement to Salusbury, John Morgan recalled that he was having his lunch in the field alongside the Parkgate road at Great Saughall, some time between 11am and 2pm. His deposition went on, 'He heard the noise of blows as if given with a stick upon some person' and immediately afterwards he heard someone cry out "Murder!"'

Peering through the field hedge, Morgan saw a man cross the road and throw what he thought was a hat into some gorse bushes, then toss another object (which he did not recognise) into a field opposite. Looking over at the three suspects seated nearby, he said the man was wearing light-coloured clothes — 'the same coloured clothes as [worn by] the person now present and who calls himself Garrett Delaney'. A second man was dressed in darker clothing similar to that worn by the prisoner Johnson, he said. Concerned for the safety of the two children who were with him, Morgan waited until the three men had got out of sight before he emerged from his hiding place and, 'suspecting that some mischief had been done', he went into the high road where he had first seen Delaney. In a gorse bush he found a man's worsted cap, a hat and a stick. 'And upon searching further,' he deposed, '[he] found in a ditch in the high road a man bloody about his face and head, who appeared to be dead.'

The manner in which the three Irishmen came to be arrested was related by William Maddock, landlord of the Greyhound Inn. In his 30 August statement to Magistrate Salusbury he deposed that, returning home at about 4pm the previous day, he discovered three men eating in the pub. He identified them as Delaney, Johnson and Caffery. Half-an-hour later, the two Chester constables arrived and, drawing him to one side, told him confidentially that there had been a murder and that the three men in the pub matched the descriptions of the suspects.

With Maddock's assistance, the surprised strangers were overpowered and shackled. Their sticks were seized and on two of them, said Maddock, he 'thought there was blood'. He also noticed similar stains on one of Johnson's shoes. The three men also had with them 'a bundle' containing a grey coat and a pair of blue breeches. Johnson claimed they were his and had the effrontery to counsel Maddock's servant to take good care of them.

Earlier, Maddock told Salusbury, John Caffery had taken two shiny new guineas from his pocket and asked the ale seller to give him silver in exchange for one of them, which he did. The gold coin in question he handed to the magistrate. All three suspects denied any involvement in the robbery and murder. They said they had not even been on the Parkgate road that day. From Chester, they insisted, they had walked to Shotwick across the fields and along 'the Strand', the expanding sandy shoreline on the Wirral bank of the Dee estuary.

The Greyhound, Shotwick, pictured in 1896 (note the inn sign above the door). The robbers stopped off at the pub in their flight from the murder scene. It was a fatal mistake.

Image from Pubs of Wirral, Part Four — Pubs of South Wirral *by Ian Boumphrey. With permission.*

The progressive silting up of the estuary, which by the end of the 15th century had choked the commercial life out of the once thriving port of Chester, led to anchorages much more accessible to the larger vessels being established lower down the river. And

Shotwick was the first of the new 'outports' to enjoy the benefits of the trade lost to Chester, most notably the passenger traffic to and from Ireland. It was a period of prosperity that lasted a hundred years.

Completion in 1737 of the 'New Cut' — canalisation of the river close to the Welsh shore — created a deeper, more reliable channel and brought a brief revival of business to the port of Chester, but added to the problems on the Wirral side. And now the constantly shifting 'Sands o' Dee' had left Shotwick cut off from the sea at all but high tide by a broadening stretch of sandbanks, mudflats and marshland.

As this does not appear to have been the first time Delaney, Johnson and Caffery had visited these shores to help bring in the harvest, they would doubtless have known that many travellers between Chester and Parkgate preferred to take the 'seaside' route to avoid the miry, often impassable conditions caused by seasonal bad weather on the glorified cart-track that passed for a main road (it was not turnpiked until 1789) and the more-or-less perennial threat posed by highwaymen.

It was a journey not without its own risks, however; and the Chester coroners' records contain many instances of people drowning in the estuary after misjudging the tides surging in from the Irish Sea.

When on 30 August they, too, were examined by Thomas Salusbury, Johnson and Caffery stuck to their story about travelling from Chester 'sometimes by the Strand and sometimes through the fields'. Johnson said he had arrived in the city in company with Delaney and Caffery on the 28th and the three of them stayed at a lodging house run by Brian Darby, also at Boughton. And he persisted in his claim that the coat and breeches he had with him at the Greyhound were his; he maintained he had been carrying them under his arm, tied up in a handkerchief, when he and his companions left Darby's to catch the boat to Dublin. He said he had bought them off a hawker in London for '15s and a shilling's worth of beer'. And, of the murder, Johnson said he 'neither committed it nor knows who did'.

In his statement to the magistrate, Caffery (Delaney's deposition, if he made one, is no longer among the court papers) gave a similar account of their journey to Shotwick and also supported Johnson's claim that he carried a bundle under his arm from Darby's — though Caffery said he did not know what was in it. He said he himself carried a cloth bag and that 'he never had anything in it but his own clothes, except one shirt belonging to Delaney'. The statement added, 'He says he is innocent of the said murder.'

Of all the witnesses, Caffery seems to have had the greatest awareness of time. Where others were unhelpfully vague in their estimates, he was more assured when he said the three Irish friends left Chester at 'about half-an-hour after noon' on the day of the murder. From this and a statement made by another witness, Margaret Kendrick of Great Saughall — who said she had seen Bryan Molloy with Delaney, Johnson and Caffery walking along the Parkgate road between 1pm and 2pm — it is probably safe to say that the murder was committed around 1.30.

In a statement she made before Coroner Baker on the 31st, Mrs Kendrick explained that she was on her way home from Chester and overtook the four men (she was presumably on horseback) between Crabhall Bridge and 'the finger post in Mollington'; the latter place, she said, was 'about a-mile-and-a-half from the murder spot'. That would fix the scene of the crime close to the Long Lane junction with Parkgate Road (19th century maps show a milestone a little further along the road, close to Coalpit Lane, where the distance to Chester is given as four miles). This coincides with a second statement made by John Caffery a few days later, which finally laid bare the full shocking truth about the Great Saughall murder . . . but more of that presently.

Remarkably, in an age in which neither travel nor communication was a particularly speedy process, the killers of Bryan Molloy were apprehended within little more than three hours of the murder.

The most likely explanation is that it was all down to farm hand John Morgan. After watching the suspicious goings-on from behind the field hedge, he would sensibly have remained in hiding until the three strangers were out of sight, particularly as he had children with him. He would not have had long to wait. Though it was not mentioned

It was near this spot on the Parkgate road (A540) that Irishman Brian Molloy was robbed and brutally slain in 1750. His attackers probably made their escape via Long Lane (on the right), the nearest route into Shotwick. Photograph by the author.

in his deposition, to get to Great Saughall village the retreating trio would logically have taken the nearest side-road and disappeared from view down what is Long Lane, which was only a short distance away. Handed that key piece of information, the pursuing law officers would have checked first at the local pub only to be told their three suspects had just left heading in the direction of Shotwick.

Delaney, Johnson and Caffery were locked in a barn in the village overnight before being taken to Chester to be lodged in the more secure confines of the Castle Gaol. Two days later, at the inquest into the death of Bryan Molloy, the two main witnesses seem to have been David Molloy and Margaret Kendrick. The former signed a deposition in which he stated that his uncle had left Chester to walk to Parkgate at about 10am on the 29th and he followed around 1pm.

'At Saughall,' his deposition read, 'he saw two men standing by a dead corpse [*sic*] that he thought had been lately murdered.' He recognised it immediately as the body of his uncle. He had seen the three suspects after they had been 'taken up' and he said Johnson had in his possession a coat, a pair of breeches, a snuffbox and an old handkerchief, which had been in Bryan Molloy's shoulder bag when he set out for Parkgate. He said his uncle had also had on him at that time a purse containing 'two fresh guineas, as if new from the mint, and five shillings in silver.'

In her inquest deposition Margaret Kendrick confirmed seeing the four men on the road to Parkgate. Bryan Molloy, 'an elderly man with a bundle of a whitish colour over his shoulder', was among them. She, too, had seen the suspects after their capture. She identified one of them, who was 'wearing a lightish coloured coat', as Delaney. Johnson, she said, was the one who 'wore a blue coat and carried a stick and a sickle in his hand'. She was also certain that the fourth man was John Caffery.

The jury's verdict was that all three were guilty of the murder of Bryan Molloy and the Coroner signed the warrant committing them for trial at the next county assizes. But two days later, from his cell in Chester Castle Gaol, Caffery sent a message to magistrate Thomas Salusbury offering a deal: withdraw the charges against him and he would turn King's evidence and spill the beans on the others.

And that was how, at Chester Assizes on Monday 3 September 1750, Garrett Delaney and Edward Johnson (whose real name, John Caffery claimed, was Murray) found themselves in the dock on charges of robbery and murder and their erstwhile companion Caffery appeared as the chief witness against them. Earlier, the Grand Jury had returned a 'true bill' — the verdict that announced they believed there was a *prima facie* case for prosecuting the other two men — and the indictments listed the charges in meticulous detail.

The first was that the defendants stole Molloy's coat ('worth 5s'), his breeches (3s), stockings (6d), linen handkerchief (1d), coarse linen bag (6d), leather belt (1d), snuffbox (1d), leather purse (1d) and 'two guineas and 6s 6d in money'. Indictment No. 2 charged that they both 'assaulted Bryan Molloy and with a certain knife . . . gave him a certain mortal wound three inches long and three inches deep'; and that they 'did kill and murder Bryan Molloy'. There is nothing in the official paperwork, however, to help determine where in Ireland any of the harvesters — including the Molloys — had come from originally.

In his new statement, dated 2 September, John Caffery was careful to distance himself from the murder, though having Molloy's two guinea-pieces in his possession at the Greyhound he had obviously been a willing party to the robbery. This second deposition, which formed part of the prosecution's brief at the trial, explained how he and his companions had arrived at Brian Darby's lodging house at Boughton at six o'clock in the evening of 28 August, after travelling together from London. On the road to Parkgate the next day, about half-a-mile from Chester, they overtook a man carrying a bundle over his shoulder. After accompanying him for about three miles — confirmation that they had not reached the four-mile marker when Molloy was attacked — he said Delaney, on the pretext of waiting for two friends who were supposed to be following behind, suggested they should stop until their friends caught up with them.

Caffery said that while the others rested he went over to the field hedge alongside the road 'to pick blackberries'. His deposition went on, 'After about a quarter-of-an-hour Molloy got up to leave, but as he did so Delaney gave him a blow upon his head with his stick'. Johnson also gave him several blows with his stick and Molloy fell to the ground.

The *Adams's Weekly Courant* of Tuesday 4 September (the paper changed its name to the *Chester Courant* in 1793), was printed too early to bring its readers news of the opening of the trial. 'Our Assizes began yesterday,' the *Courant* reported, 'so that these inhuman Miscreants will, in all Probability, be soon brought to Justice.' But it did carry an earlier report of the crime, in which the newspaper stated that Molloy's assailants 'beat him most unmercifully with their sticks and, when he was almost dead, despatch'd him by striking a Reaping Hook into his Neck, under his Ear, and cutting him to the Wind-pipe'.

It is one of several myths and misconceptions surrounding the case that have been perpetuated by subsequent writers. John Caffery's trial statement put the record straight. 'Delaney called him over,' it read, 'and as he did so Delaney took a white-handled knife out of his pocket and cut Molloy's throat.' With due attention to detail, the murder indictment valued the murder weapon at 'two pence'.

Caffery admitted that Delaney, after rifling Molloy's pockets, had handed him a purse containing 'two new bright guineas, two half-crowns, one shilling, one sixpence and some half-pence'. Then, his statement went on, 'With Delaney holding one leg and this examinant the other, they dragged the body into a ditch'. Delaney also gave Caffery Molloy's 'wallet' — meaning a bag or knapsack — containing the dead man's coat, breeches 'and a pair of old stockings'. He said that in 'passing near a farm', he had thrown away the wallet, the stockings and Molloy's purse and the leather belt to which it was attached.

Caffery's deposition ended, 'They then all went to an alehouse where they drank only one pot of beer. They then went to another house where they were apprehended.'

The second pub is easily identified as the 16th century Greyhound Inn at Shotwick, which has in its time been the manor courthouse and a farmhouse and which is now a private residence. It occupies a prominent position in the centre of the village, close to the entrance to the 12th century Parish Church of St. Michael. As to the 'other house', local tradition has it that it was the Swinging Gate at Great Saughall, an alehouse since the 15th century but which closed in 1964, since when it, too, has been a private residence.

At the end of the trial Delaney and Johnson were found guilty and the Judge, Chief Justice William Noel, sentenced them to death. So it was that John Caffery saved his own neck by ratting on his 'Comrades', as the *Weekly Courant* described them in its edition of 11 September. The report also revealed the full implications of the sentence for 'the Irish ruffians' . . . and hinted at the problems being caused locally by the migrant harvesters.

After their executions, the paper stated, the two men were to be 'hanged in Chains in the great Road leading to Parkgate which, it is hoped, will be a Terror [that word again] and a Warning to their Countrymen who have of late committed many Villainies in that Part of the County'. The situation was so serious, in fact, that the Cheshire Quarter Sessions had in March of that year decided to open a House of Correction about a mile south of Parkgate on Neston Quay.

Both hangings were carried out on Saturday 22 September. It was reported that from the place of execution at Boughton — which the two men would probably have had to pass by on their journey out of the city four weeks earlier — their bodies were taken in a cart to Two Mills Heath, Great Saughall, where a double gibbet was awaiting them.

Its supposed site is occupied today by a windmill, which stands beside the A540 some 400 yards north of its junction with the A5117 (T). It ceased grinding corn in 1926 and has since been imaginatively adapted for residential use. The Grade II listed building was originally the Great Saughall Mill, but has long been known locally as 'Gibbet Mill' or 'Gibbet Windmill'. It doesn't, however, appear on any maps until later in the 18th century. And there are several fields fronting on to the road whose names suggest they are also worthy of consideration as the scene of the gibbeting.

On an 1848 tithe map, in fact, no fewer than five field names bear the word 'gibbet' in one form or another. There were two 'Gibbett Fields' and two 'Gibbitt Fields' within a hundred yards of the mill; while the only one correctly spelled 'Gibbet Field' was about 700 yards further north on the opposite side of the road.

A story still being quoted in local histories, that could be said to give credence to the mill site being where Delaney and Johnson were hung in chains, tells that the gibbet was erected on the footpath that still runs from Parkgate Road along the edge of the field immediately to the north of the windmill. However, while this would have been the highest part of the surrounding countryside, and therefore a good place visually to have a gibbet, the theory is marred by the claim that it was fashioned from an ash tree which grew beside the path. Gibbets were specially made and were free-standing structures; this was a double gibbet, too, so it would hardly have been knocked up on some convenient tree.

There are many aspects of the Molloy murder case that have, over the years years, been distorted by myth and legend, of which the most common is that the four Irishmen on the road to Parkgate (sometimes it is three) had all been pals together but quarrelled about their harvest earnings and the one with the most money was killed by the others. Another version of the story has it that three

The old windmill, now a private dwelling, beside the Parkgate road that is the reputed site of the gibbet on which the bodies of convicted murderers Garrett Delaney and Edward Johnson were 'hung in chains'.

Photograph by the author.

harvesters murdered a woman at the Swinging Gate and were captured near the windmill; while a third records how they were caught red-handed attempting to rob the landlady at the Greyhound.

That their bid for freedom did end at the Greyhound is beyond dispute; what is not so apparent from the surviving evidence, official or otherwise, is what they were doing there in the first place. Could it be they realised that, once the law was on their trail, the Parkgate packet-station was the first place for which their pursuers would also head? And that they now needed a safer escape route?

They obviously decided the first thing to do was to get off the main road; and the quickest way was down Long Lane, which ran westwards from the Parkgate road quite close to where they must have ditched Bryan Molloy's blood-soaked body. Having slaked their thirst at Great Saughall, they then pushed on to the next village. Shotwick had been a major point of embarkation for Ireland in the 15th century, but now the smaller vessels that could still berth there at high tide operated on purely local routes. The fleeing felons might have thought, however, that by following the 'sand roads' they could get to one of the other Wirral-side outports such as Burton, Denhall or Neston and book passage home from there.

Or, alternatively, they may just have considered making their way to the other side of the estuary and disappearing into the wilds of North Wales until the heat had died down.

To do that would have involved a journey largely by ford but also by ferry, the two modes of transport that had helped shape Shotwick's fortunes since time immemorial. There had always been a Dee ferry between Shotwick and Flint, though the river's massive silting meant that the Lower Ferry now only operated over the narrow river channel of the New Cut. The ford was in Roman times used to transport Cheshire salt into North Wales, and by the Middle Ages had become part of an established trade route, the 'Saltesway', for the salt producers of Northwich, Nantwich and Middlewich. It had also served as a military crossing point for the armies sent to do battle with the rebellious Welsh, first by Henry II in 1156 and 1165, then Henry III in 1245 and Edward I in 1278 and 1284.

The ford, a continuation of Shotwick Lane, one of the two main routes into the village, was still negotiable in 1750 and remained in use until the last decade of the century — though traversing the treacherous sands remained a hazardous business. Traveller and writer Celia Fiennes (1662-1741) made the crossing from the Welsh side around 1700 and in her book, *Through England On A Side Saddle*, not published until 1888, she noted how the effects of the tides constantly changed the safest route across the estuary.

She wrote, 'The sands here are so loose that the tides do move them from one place to another at every flood, that the same place one used to af-ford [*sic*] a month or two before is not to be passed now, for as it brings the sands in heaps to one place so it leaves others in deep holes . . . that would swallow up a horse or carriages.'

Chester's inquest files also contain numerous reports of people coming to grief on the sands. Between nine and ten o'clock on the night of 26 June 1745, a yeoman by the name of Richard Cooper of Capenhurst, having disembarked from the Lower Ferry, was making for Burton 'and the tyde comeing in very briskly, he . . . attempted to go over Shotwick Ford, but with the force and strength of the tyde . . . was suffocated and drowned'. The jury decided that he had died 'by misfortune'. A similar verdict was recorded following a doubly tragic accident around noon on 8 January 1753, in which husband and wife, Thomas and Anne Harrison, perished together when they were also swept to their deaths by a rapidly incoming tide as they walked from Shotwick to Hawarden.

The relentless march of the Dee silt eventually sank the 'port' of Shotwick; on a plan published in 1772, showing the land holdings and premises of the River Dee Company, where once the waters of the estuary lapped against the wall of the Parish Churchyard, there is a huge sweep of white sand and an area of reclaimed riverbed. Today, the view from the churchyard is one of green fields and industrial units, with the river itself two miles away marking an invisible line somewhere in the far distance beneath the dramatic backdrop of the Welsh Hills. Over time Shotwick has settled comfortably into its modern image as sleepy backwater, though it still attracts a steady flow of visitors, who go there nowadays to admire its picturesque rural setting and soak up its atmosphere of peaceful seclusion. It has rightly been described as one of the best preserved villages in the country, virtually frozen in time for more than 200 years.

Shotwick's fate also befell the port of Parkgate. Early in the 18th century, as the Dee silting progressed northwards along the Wirral side of the estuary, Parkgate's still accessible waterfront — combined with the unsuitability of the alternative mountainous journey overland to Holyhead — had enabled it to become the North West's premier port (second only to Bristol) for trade with Ireland as well as for passengers travelling to and from Dublin. During its peak period in the final decade of the century, the packet boats sailed across the 120-mile stretch of the Irish Sea at least four times a week. The crossing, it was reputed, could take as little as 10 hours, but in unfavourable

Parkgate in the mid-19th century: still a magnet for visitors, though no longer famous for its Irish ferry service but as a fashionable resort noted for its healthy climate and the quality of its sea bathing. *Illustration courtesy of The Parkgate Society.*

Below: The Parade at Parkgate as it is today. Apart from times of exceptionally high tide, there is now little to be seen of the waters of the estuary that once lapped against its sea wall. *Photograph by the author.*

weather three days and more. Parkgate was only ever an anchorage, though; it never actually had a quay and, before 1810, had no sea wall or permanent landing stage either. Vessels anchored in the estuary, sometimes a long way out, and goods and passengers were trans-shipped and rowed ashore, to be landed in front of the old Customs House — a tall, narrow building that stood at the water's edge on the site of what is known locally today as the 'Donkey Stand'.

A sea wall and promenade called The Parade were eventually constructed — the central section was completed in 1810 and the rest in the 1830s and 1840s — but they were not built to improve docking facilities for shipping but for the benefit of those members of fashionable society who were drawn to this pretty spot on the Wirral coastline for the quality of its sea-bathing. It was an attraction that, combined with the salubrious sea-air, had made Parkgate a popular holiday resort since around 1760. The Irish ferry service ceased in 1815, transferred to the fast-developing port of Liverpool; but by then Parkgate had acquired another claim to fame and a reputation — as one writer described it — as 'the most fashionable watering-hole in the North of England'. It was a position it maintained for the next 40 years.

In the end, though, it was powerless to hold back the inexorable forces of nature, as the river retreated further and the spreading sands turned to salt-marsh and then became colonised by grass. Parkgate is still a popular and attractive location, with tourists seeking out its regionally famous homemade ice-cream and its locally-caught shrimps. The marshes are a haven for a wide variety of birds, which also makes the village a magnet for 'twitchers', who arrive in their hundreds particularly during periods of high tide.

And when the spring tides are exceptionally high there is another deluge of visitors, this time to witness the rare sight of the waters of the Dee estuary once again reaching the Parkgate shoreline; the place to where in 1750 three Irishmen travelled hopefully in search of a few months' labour at the harvest . . . and never arrived back in their homeland again.

CHAPTER TWO

Nightmare At Rake Farm

F armer's daughter Margaret Porter was alone in the kitchen when the back door suddenly swung open. In the yard outside she was confronted by half-a-dozen strange-looking men, some with their faces blackened others painted red. Though it was well after dark, the teenaged girl felt no immediate sense of alarm. She assumed from their oddly theatrical appearances that the unexpected arrivals were one of the motley groups of agricultural workers who — in the tradition of soul-cakers or mummers — toured local farms at that time of the year performing folk plays in exchange for food and drink and the chance to earn a few coppers to augment their menial wages.

So when they asked to see the master of the house, Margaret had no qualms about showing them into the candle-lit parlour, where her father, wealthy yeoman farmer John Porter, and her elder sister Eleanor, aged 22, were preparing to sit down to supper. As the men filed past her, however, she could make out in the half-light that some of them carried pistols and cutlasses. Too late she realised the weapons were no mere stage props and that this was no friendly social visit.

Over the next hour or so, isolated Rake Farm in the Cheshire village of Eccleston, two-and-a-half miles south of Chester, would be the scene of a violent robbery, a fatal shooting and the same kind of epic fight — symbolising the eternal struggle between good and evil — portrayed in the age-old morality stories enacted, with less harmful intent, by the authentic travelling folk troupes.

And, like all true tales of derring-do, it had its heroes. And a heroine. For on that winter's night in 1752, before three gallant young men rode to the rescue of the beleaguered occupants of Rake Farm, it was a remarkable show of

A now enlarged Rake Farm, Eccleston, scene of the robbery. Most of the terrifying events were acted out in the kitchen, which was situated on the ground floor in the centre of this picture.

Photograph by the author.

34

defiance by 16-year-old Margaret Porter that proved the decisive moment in the terrifying affair.

It was Saturday 1 February. The robbers had targeted the farmstead in the belief that John Porter had that day been to Chester Market to collect a considerable sum of money from a business deal. But, unbeknown to them, the other party in the transaction had failed to turn up. And it was as the six-strong gang assaulted her father and sister, in a futile attempt to find out where the money was, that Margaret dived under a table and, in the confusion, made her escape.

Displaying resourcefulness beyond her years, she slipped through the back door — having the presence of mind to lock it after her — and ran to the stables. Her plan was to summon the help of her older brother, also called John, who was enjoying an evening out with his friends at an inn in the nearby village of Pulford. In her haste, however, she had forgotten to pick up the key to the saddle-room; so, with no other choice, she mounted one of her father's horses and rode there bareback, a distance of about three miles. In pitch darkness she risked life and limb in coaxing her skittish colt across the fields, and over the numerous hedges and ditches along the way. Reaching the inn, she breathlessly related what was happening at the family farm. Immediately, John and two of his pals, farm labourer John Craven and tailor John Barrow, both of Pulford, leapt on their horses and took off at full speed for Eccleston.

Their subsequent bravery in overcoming the heavily armed robbers, and the courage and enterprise shown earlier by the dashing Miss Porter — which undoubtedly saved her father and sister from more severe injury — were the vital factors in ending the siege of Rake Farm and ensuring that at least some of the villains were brought to justice.

The jury at Chester Assizes heard the full story of the Porter family's ordeal, and their eventual deliverance, on 6 April 1752, when four Irish labourers appeared before them charged with breaking and entering the farmhouse and stealing £80 in gold and silver coins and various items of silverware to the value of £9 12s 0d — a total sum which, it has been calculated, would have the purchasing power today of about £12,000.

The accused were Richard Stanley (alias Handal, alias Tullough Owen), Edward M'Cannelly (alias M'Nolling), Patrick Boyd (alias Boden) and Henry Morgan. A fifth suspect, Fergy Neale, one of Mr Porter's farm servants, had been discharged after the Grand Jury found there was insufficient evidence against him. Another Irishman, he seems to have been 'the inside man' who helped set up the robbery.

There is no record of the trial extant; but the surviving court files contain the depositions of the witnesses who appeared for the prosecution. Sworn before local magistrates in the days immediately following the robbery, they reveal how the Porters' supper preparations were startlingly interrupted at around nine o'clock when Richard Stanley, the leader of the gang — a small but broad-set man of about 60 with a shock of reddish-brown beard — burst into their parlour. With a pistol in his right hand and a 'swipple' (the free-swinging, 'business' end of a threshing flail) in the other, he bore down on an unsuspecting John Porter.

Widower Mr Porter, whose wife (also called Eleanor) had died in August 1750, deposed, 'Pointing the pistol at him the robber said, "Deliver your money or I will blow your brains out" and "God damn your soul, if you do not deliver your money I will kill you and all that are in the house."' As well as the Porters there were three of the family's servants working that evening, including Neale. The rest of the staff had been given the evening off and were spending it at a house in Eccleston village; Neale, apparently, had been asked to join them but declined the invitation. He had a more compelling reason for staying in that night.

Then, said Mr Porter, four more robbers rushed into the room, including 24-year-old M'Cannelly and Boyd (the latter's age is unknown, being referred to throughout only as 'a youth'). Each of the quartet carried an improvised club; three of them were armed with pistols. Stanley also had a short sword hanging from his belt. They easily overpowered the middle-aged farmer and tied him up.

His statement continued, 'His daughter Margaret scrambled under a table, whereupon Stanley said to his companions "Damn her, shoot her."' This may have been more bluster from the swaggering Stanley, but in any event the other members of the gang were preoccupied with pinioning Eleanor Porter and the command went unanswered. It was the stroke of luck that gave Margaret Porter the chance to make her daring break for freedom.

Stanley ordered M'Cannelly to 'stand fast' and, if Porter made a move, he must 'blow his brains out, or I will blow yours out'. Stanley searched the farmer's pockets and took from him about £14 in gold and silver (about £1,800 in today's money), then pulled his breeches down around his ankles, swearing 'By God I will burn you'. The terrified farmer was then dragged into the kitchen and flung down by the fireside.

Fearing what was about to happen to her father, Eleanor Porter 'fell down on her knees and begged them to spare his life', at which Stanley 'damned her for [being] a fat bitch and said he would burn her afterwards'. A short while later, Eleanor was somehow able to loosen the rope binding her father and he made a dash for the door. 'But', said Mr Porter, 'Stanley caught him a blow with the swipple and M'Cannelly struck him with a cutlass and wounded his hand and face.'

Just before his son and his friends arrived at the farmstead, Porter added, 'three pistols were fired by some of the robbers by which one of the gang was killed' — an unfortunate accident amid the heat and smoke of battle, seemingly. However, in her later years, daughter Margaret would cast the shooting in a much more heroic light . . . as we shall see shortly.

Eleanor Porter, in her deposition, also dated 2 February, stated that when the gang burst into the parlour Stanley 'put a pistol to her breast and bid her deliver or she was a dying woman'. Like her father, she was tied up with a rope and Stanley, handing his pistol to M'Cannelly, 'struck her a violent blow with a stick', then bound the servants, the man Neale and an unnamed young boy and girl. Eleanor was dragged upstairs by Stanley and two other members of the gang and ordered to open all the doors and boxes to which she had the keys. Stanley broke open two other boxes with a chisel and took out of one of them the two purses containing the gold and silver. From a 'buffet' (cupboard) he also removed a silver tankard and another silver drinking cup.

Sister Margaret, who was absent during most of this time, of course, limited her statement to commenting on two incidents involving Fergy Neale. She said that when the robbers first entered the house she was 'very certain that she did see one of the persons look earnestly at Fergy Neale . . . and wink at him and that Neale winked back'. Later, when the violence started, and her sister Eleanor urged Neale to make a break for it and go and fetch her brother, Neale 'refused so to do and said he could not get out of the house'.

It is entirely due to her, however, that the real story of the Rake Farm robbery — of its deadly, dramatic ending and its thrilling aftermath — can be told.

Some years later, as Mrs James Butler (she married her cutler husband at Eccleston Parish Church in February 1757 at the age of 21), she sat down and wrote a comprehensive account of the crime, the subsequent arrests and the trial of four of the robbers. Her narrative — there is at least one indication in it that it was written towards the end of her life — was later transcribed in immaculate italic script in an old exercise book by an unknown writer, who added more information about the case. In the late 1960s this expanded version was known to have been in the possession of local historian Mr Heber Fearnall, a former occupier of Rake Farm.

In more recent times several Xerox copies were made of the transcript.

One of them is held by the Cheshire Record Office at Chester and another is in the archives of the Duke of Westminster's Grosvenor Estate, which acquired Rake Farm in 1758. It is obvious that these were not copies of Margaret Porter's original as her 'signature' is inscribed in the same hand as the rest of the manuscript and differs significantly from that on her marriage certificate. However, there seems little doubt that the work is based on her experiences and, as she acknowledged in the text, on the memories of the other members of the Porter family who lived through the nightmare.

Much of it coincides with the few surviving newspaper reports of the crime, though, it has to be said, there are occasions when it veers uncomfortably close to historical romance and it contains a number of instances where she obviously embellished the facts to reflect more favourably on her family, her brother in particular. At least one claim has to be regarded as highly questionable; while her memory seems to have let her down a couple of times. Nonetheless, it is a fascinating read and, as it constitutes the most complete record of

On the faded cover of the Margaret Porter memoir, it is just possible to make out the image of the heroine of Rake Farm riding off to raise the alarm.

Illustration by permission of Cheshire Archives and Local Studies (CALS).

the events, it is reproduced here at some length.

In it Margaret recalled how she had gone into the kitchen that night to fetch some 'table aprons' (napkins), when the door was thrown open and she was surrounded by a gang of men, 'some with their faces red, others black and others coloured with clay water [mud?] or something of that sort'. When they asked to see her father she had let them in 'thinking them some of the farmers' servants who usually came about at that time from farmhouse to farmhouse to perform small pieces, and after[wards] were entertained with meat and drink and a little money given to them'.

The men were 'all dressed in a curious manner', said Margaret, who learned later that they had met up on nearby Eccleston Hill, where they changed out of their regular work clothes and left them 'beyond a stone seat, which stood under some trees on a bank at the four lane ends'. And John Porter formed the same impression as his younger daughter, welcoming the uninvited guests cordially, declaring, 'Gentlemen, you had better have some meat and drink before you begin your performance.' But Richard Stanley quickly made his intentions clear. He shouted contemptuously, 'Damn your eyes, we do not want meat and drink. It is your lives and money that we want, and by God if you make any resistance I will shoot you.' To emphasise the point he raised his pistol and clubbed Porter to the ground with it.

After explaining how she was able to steal unnoticed out of the parlour, she wrote, 'I, being much affrighted, ran into the kitchen where a thought struck me that I would have a trial [*sic*] to fetch my brother . . . at Pulford . . . I took the key of the stables going out of the back door and [went] through the kitchen garden to the stables [where] . . . I found that my brother had taken the mare which . . . I always rode. There being one [old] horse and a colt in the stable, I, in preference, took the colt.'

In her fright, she said, she had forgotten that the colt had not been 'backed', meaning that it had never been ridden before. There was no saddle or bridle available to her, either. The colt did, however, have a halter on so she grabbed a second one and 'put it on the horse the other way' round and tied the ends together to form makeshift reins to give herself more control over the inexperienced animal. Margaret considered going to Pulford via Rake Lane, in which the farm was situated, but decided she might be stopped by other members of the gang. So she opened a paddock gate at the back of the farm, mounted the colt and set off on her perilous journey on what was, according to one newspaper report, 'a very dark night'. She said that on her way across the fields horse and rider 'took many leaps both of hedges and ditches'. But she said a story circulating afterwards, that they had also

jumped a five-barred gate, was untrue. She pointed out, 'I ran the colt at the gate three or four times, but I could not get [him] to take the leap. I dismounted and opened

Eccleston Hill, where the robber gang met up — 'under some trees on a bank' — to change into their costumes/disguises before making for Rake Farm, nearly a mile away.   *Photograph by the author.*

the gate and led the colt through, then mounted again and made the best of my way to Pulford.'

At the village inn, the Talbot, later the Grosvenor Arms — humble forerunner of today's plush Grosvenor Pulford Hotel & Spa — she told her brother what was happening at Rake Farm (the original farmhouse, now modernised and enlarged, was built some time after 1720). John Craven was the first of young John's drinking mates to volunteer to go back with him. 'Craven', said Margaret, 'was much [the] worse for liquor, but he was determined to go with him.' Before leaving her at the inn, where she stayed overnight, brother John told Margaret he would call at the home of a farmer friend of his, named Trevor, and 'borrow a gun'.

From this point in her story, Margaret cautioned her readers that she was relying on what she had been told by her father, brother and sister. First, she said, the three Johns stopped off at Mr Trevor's house, which was situated in the delightfully-named Cuckoo's Nest, half-way between Pulford and Eccleston, and 'asked for a gun and for it to be loaded with a double charge'. Trevor wanted to know what they wanted the weapon for, but, said Margaret, 'my brother would not tell'.

Meanwhile, back at Rake Farm, after her father was tied up, Stanley and other gang members began 'abusing and kicking him violently'. They then 'dragged him into the kitchen and pulled down his small clothes [close-fitting knee breeches fashionable in the 18th century] to examine him for money, not having found a sufficient quantity upstairs'. Porter had protested from the start that he had not received the money he was expecting that day — the gang had been tipped off about his promised payment by the double-dealing Fergy Neale — but the robbers refused to believe him. Instead they decided to apply a little torture to try to force him into revealing its whereabouts.

'They attempted to burn my father, having had him on the kitchen fire three or four times,' Margaret related. Each time, however, Patrick Boyd persuaded his fellow thieves not to go through with their threats. Said Margaret, 'Boyd . . . begged hard of the other villains not to take my father's life.' Gang members had also abused sister Eleanor by 'striking and kicking her . . . and being disappointed in finding no more money than about eighty pounds, they were determined to take my father's and [my] sister's lives'.

It was about this time that young Porter and his two friends entered the fray. They had travelled to Eccleston along the Wrexham road and, a short distance up Rake Lane, they passed a man apparently stationed in the hedgerow as a look-out. It transpired that another look-out had been posted at the opposite end of the lane on Eccleston Hill and two more were left guarding the main entrance to the Porters' farm. They lay in hiding under an old cart in the paddock through which the driveway ran. With the six we know were in the house that night (including Fergy Neale), this brought the total number of gang members to ten, though various numbers up to a dozen have been cited by previous writers. The 'sentries', who were never caught, had orders to ignore people going to the house but to stop anyone leaving it — which underlined the wisdom of Margaret Porter's decision to stick to the fields in her bare-back ride to Pulford.

As the three young men clattered into the cobbled farmyard, they spotted two figures under the cart and Craven shouted at Porter to open fire; but, said Margaret, 'my brother . . . being eager to go to the house, replied that they were some young cattle sheltering for the night'. Reaching the back door they dismounted and entered the house unchallenged. They had arrived not a moment too soon.

In her graphic account, Margaret Porter revealed that brother John's first sight on pushing open the kitchen door was of one of the robbers, later identified only by his surname of M'Sherry, 'with one arm round my father's neck and in the other hand a knife or coot [coulter: the vertical cutting blade positioned in front of a ploughshare] . . . red-hot and [which] he was going to plunge into the body of my father'.

Her brother, said Margaret, 'instantly fired his gun' and shot and killed M'Sherry. As well as her father's account of the shooting, the *Derby Mercury* also carried a similarly contradictory version of the incident. On 7 February it had reported that during the pandemonium in the farmhouse, 'one of the Rogues levell'd a Pistol' at Eleanor Porter 'and as he pulled the Trigger, one of his Comrades was, in the Fray, instantaneously jostled' into the line of fire and 'received the shot in his Breast [and] fell down dead'.

Her memoir continued, 'Then he [her brother] dashed into the kitchen and when the smoke had dispersed, he saw Stanley kneeling on the body of my sister by the dresser [sideboard] in the act of cutting her throat. He seized the kitchen poker and struck Stanley on the head, which knocked him senseless. My sister got up as soon as she was able and unbound my father.'

As the mayhem raged on, young John together with his two friends and his newly freed father were engaged in a ferocious struggle with the robbers; Margaret, with some understatement this time, described it as 'a very sharp fight'. Further shots were fired and the Porters' maid and servant boy were wounded, one of them seriously. In 'a severe fight' with one of the robbers, John Craven was 'very much wounded about the head with a cutlass and thrown to the ground', his assailant shouting out to Stanley, 'Captain, Captain, I have him!' The robber's sense of triumph was short-lived, however, as Craven was eventually able to wrest the weapon from him and use it to give the Irishman a taste of his own medicine. Judging by the injuries he was later seen to be sporting, this must have been Henry Morgan.

Amid the uproar John Barrow, seeing Stanley lying flat out on the floor as a result of the blow from the poker, made sure that at least one of the thieves would not escape by snatching up a cord and tying the gang's leader to the bow of the Porters' massive cast-iron kitchen grate.

And suddenly it was all over. With one of their number dead and their 'Captain' out of action, the rest of the ragtag band fled, some of them hurling themselves through a window in their desperate attempt to escape — or, in Margaret Porter's rather more poetic words, they 'flew to the window and, darting through lead and glass, made off'.

In their flight from the farm, the robbers left behind many items of plunder; the silver tankard was abandoned by Boyd during his getaway attempt; while the two purses containing the £80 in gold and silver and some stolen silver spoons, were also recovered. It meant the robbers' total haul for their night's work was about £15 (£2,000 today).

In describing what happened next, Margaret in her memoir, recollected that it was early the following morning, Sunday 2 February, when her brother and Craven went in pursuit of the fleeing robbers. But she had to be mistaken. For she wrote that after they spotted three of them at Handbridge and managed to capture two, the third robber, Henry Morgan, got away.

But the 30-year-old Morgan was confirmed later as the man who had turned up 'in a very bloody condition' at a public house in Flookersbrook, in the village of Hoole, at around midnight *on the day of the robbery*. After having his wounds tended to he left, telling the landlord and his wife that he was on his way to Eastham to catch the ferry to Liverpool. So Porter and Craven must have ridden the two miles or so to Handbridge soon after the robbers had fled Rake Farm — which would have been a much more sensible response than leaving it until morning — and got ahead of them while they were making their way across the fields.

Margaret wrote that, on reaching Handbridge, the pair called at 'a public house' by the old Dee Bridge. This was the Ship Inn, which had been there since at least 1741 (after some years lying empty it was re-opened in 2009). They ordered drinks and Porter 'stood in the doorway to observe if he could see any of the villains coming down Handbridge [also the name of the village's main street] towards Chester.' It seems

Porter had 'persuaded' Richard Stanley — with the aid of the red-hot coulter, apparently — to reveal that the gang had arranged to meet up in the city after the robbery. According to Margaret, Stanley had also told him that, had her brother been at home on the night of the robbery, 'their intention was to have instantly murdered everyone in the house then to set fire to [it] so that the murders and the robbery might be concealed'.

Almost immediately three men hurried past the pub. Recognising them as three of the robbers, John Porter abandoned his pint of ale and gave chase. Just before the bridge he caught up with one of them (M'Cannelly) and knocked him down. As he was dragging the Irishman back towards the inn, three men who knew him came out and asked if they could help. He replied, 'Take care of this man. Don't let him go. I want the other two.' He then ran after the others and managed to capture one of them (it turned out to be Patrick Boyd) before he reached the other side of the bridge. But Morgan escaped.

With the assistance of the three men from the pub, Porter and Craven marched the two collared criminals across the Dee Bridge to Chester Castle. Stanley was later brought from Rake Farm to join his accomplices in the cells there; and on the Sunday all three were taken before local magistrates Ralph Leycester and William Farrell. When charged with the farm robbery, Stanley promptly confessed (having been detained on the premises, he could hardly have done otherwise). Boyd, who was said to have ditched John Porter's silver tankard in his struggle to evade capture on the bridge, denied being involved, claiming

The Ship Inn at Handbridge (on the left) and, in the foreground, the parapet of the old Dee Bridge, where young John Porter captured two of the gang who robbed his father's farm. *Photograph by the author.*

he had been in Chester the previous evening; that he had 'supped alone', describing his meal as consisting of 'a roll and small beer'. M'Cannelly, however, rather undermined his alibi by claiming that he had dined with Boyd that evening at 'the sign of the Hen and Chickens', a timber-built tavern formerly situated on the east side of Northgate Street, next

43

to the Northgate. He said he had had bread and cheese and Boyd bread and butter. They had left at about 7pm and gone to the Market Place.

Fergy Neale, who in the general melee at the end of the robbery, had also run off, was arrested on the following Monday and, after a lengthy interrogation, was also committed to the Castle and clapped in irons. In an obvious attempt to deflect any suspicion that he was in some way involved in the robbery, he had been tied up along with the other two servants when the thieves first forced their way into the farmhouse, but was freed soon afterwards. If the gang thought he might lend them a hand when young Porter and his pals came galloping to the rescue, however, they were mistaken. As Margaret Porter observed, 'This man, when they had unbound him, stood an unconcerned spectator not rendering the least assistance.'

With Stanley, M'Cannelly, Boyd and Neale now in custody charged with house-breaking and robbery, the hunt began for the escapee Morgan. In Margaret Porter's colourful story it was once again largely through the boldness and determination of brother John that the fifth suspect was eventually behind bars.

From the information wrung from Stanley, he went first to the Hen and Chickens, the inn where the gang had planned to rendezvous after the robbery — a somewhat curious choice since it stood in the very shadow of Chester's fearsome Northgate Gaol. He was told that a man answering Morgan's description had been there earlier 'very much wounded in the forehead [and] the side of his head and [with] the fingers much cut on his left hand'.

From what he learned at the city inn, Porter was able to trace Morgan to the public house of William and Ruth Starkie in Flookersbrook, a tiny hamlet off Hoole Road on the outskirts of the city. The road was, and remains, one of the two main northern routes in and out of Chester (now part of the A56). Historically, the Flookersbrook was where cattle were rested and watered before being driven to market in the city. The couple told him of the man with the injured head and hand who had arrived at the house around midnight on Saturday. Mrs Starkie had dressed his wounds, which were identical to those suffered by Morgan, and sent him on his way. She said he told her he had received them earlier in the evening after being attacked on the road by two men, who had 'very ill used' him.

An advertisement offering a reward for his capture detailed Morgan's tell-tale injuries and expressed the hope that 'these marks . . . will be sufficient to bring about his apprehension'. The way he was dressed on leaving Chester might also have been a bit of a giveaway had he maintained his appearance. Referring to the notice in an item in that 7 February edition, the *Derby Mercury* reported that he was 'a middle-sized Man, and when he escaped, had on fine black Shag Breeches and a check Shirt, but having lost his Hat and Wig, a Pair of Sailor's Trowsers [*sic*] were wrapped round his Head'. He was one of the men who had 'blacked up' for the raid on Rake Farm, but it would seem that since then he had at least taken the precaution of washing his face.

When, or how, Morgan reached Liverpool is uncertain; but on Tuesday 4 February he embarked as a passenger on board the *Parkside,* bound for Jamaica, on which his brother, apparently, was a cook. The merchantman set sail later that day but only got as far as Great Orme Head off Llandudno, North Wales, where strong winds forced her to turn back. Retreating to the shelter of the Mersey Estuary, she dropped anchor in the Liverpool channel near Black Rock, the hazardous reef off the north-eastern corner of the Wirral peninsular, on which, in the 1820s, the Fort Perch Rock coastal defence battery and lighthouse would be built to protect the entrance to the port of Liverpool. They are now among the visitor attractions of the seaside resort of New Brighton, which was developed in that part of Wirral in the second half of the 19th century.

In the meantime, John Porter and his good friend John Craven had also travelled to Liverpool. The following day, Wednesday, after learning that the *Parkside* was still in the estuary awaiting more favourable weather, they hired a boat to take them out to the West Indiaman. After they had explained their mission to the ship's master, Captain Fowley, Morgan was brought out on deck and, as he clearly answered the description of the wanted man, he was handed over to them. Back on shore Morgan was questioned by the Mayor of Liverpool, Henry Winstanley, who placed him in custody and also ordered the arrest of his brother, who lived in the city, 'upon strong suspicion of being an accomplice'. He was later released without charge.

In the contemporary press reports of Morgan's capture there were no references at all to the involvement of Porter and Craven; the *Derby Mercury* of 14 February, for instance, stated that the Liverpool magistrates, having been acquainted with the particulars of the robbery and the escapee, ordered a search to be made of all the ships berthed in the harbour, and when the fugitive was not found, they 'sent out the King's Boat' (probably a Royal Navy cutter) to search the *Parkside*. The paper reported, 'The Man was soon discovered by his Wounds and other Marks . . . and he is to be conveyed to his Companions in Chester Castle.'

The New Brighton Battery on Fort Perch Rock, the anchorage in the Mersey where escapee Henry Morgan was recaptured. He was aboard a vessel bound for the West Indies, which had set sail from the port of Liverpool before being forced back to the river estuary by bad weather. From the author's collection.

According to Margaret Porter, Morgan was landed in Cheshire at Eastham, where a ferry service to and from Liverpool had operated since medieval times. She said that her brother was there to collect the prisoner and then made the bizarre claim that John had him 'tied fast beyond him on his horse' to convey him the 10 miles to Chester.

Did she really mean that Morgan was trussed up in front of Porter on the same horse, slung across the animal's neck, in the manner of a US marshall bringing in a wanted outlaw in a Wild West movie? Or were there two horses tethered together and Morgan was lashed to the leading mount? Either way it would have been a highly unconventional, not to say unsafe, way for a suspect in a capital crime to be taken into custody, even if, for example, Porter had been sworn in as a deputy constable for just that purpose. It is also at odds with the one surviving Cheshire newspaper report of Morgan's capture.

The Chester-based *Adams's Weekly Courant* informed its readers on Tuesday 18 February, 'This Afternoon [the 17th] between two and three o'clock, Henry Morgan, one of the Persons who broke into and robbed the House of Mr John Porter in the Night of the 1st instant was brought hither from Liverpool *under a strong Guard* [author's italics]. He had been apprehended on the 5th Instant on board the *Parkside*, a Vessel then in the Liverpool Channel. Immediately upon his Arrival here, he was examined before two of His Majesty's Justices of the Peace, when Mr Porter Senior swore fully that he was one of the Principal Actors in the Burglary and Robbery . . . and that he was very positive as to his Person, notwithstanding that his Face was blacked at the Time.'

In her memoir, Margaret Porter also wrote that 'it was supposed that there were six or seven thousand people on the road' to see Morgan brought back to the city. Again there was no mention of this patently newsworthy statistic in the *Courant* or any other newspaper.

And, of equal significance one might think, is that in its monthly miscellany of historical notes and queries, the respected *Cheshire Sheaf* chose not to repeat either of these particular assertions when, in January 1922, it printed a series of articles about the case, which drew heavily on Margaret Porter's written reminiscences. The *Cheshire Sheaf*, regarded as an essential work of reference for any Cheshire historian, ran intermittently from 1878 to 1990. It was originally published as a column in the *Courant* and each year the columns were reprinted in volume form.

The official case file reveals that when he was interviewed by the magistrates Morgan admitted he had been in Hoole late in the evening of 1 February, but denied that he was one of the gang who raided Rake Farm. This time he claimed he had received his injuries 'in a mob [affray] some time ago at Liverpool'.

John Porter Junior told the magistrates, however, that he was certain that the prisoner was a member of the gang and that he was the same man who had eluded him on the Dee Bridge. William Starkie was also convinced that Morgan was the wounded traveller who called at his Flookersbrook pub on the night of the robbery. In a third variant on the cause of his injuries, Starkie said Morgan told him he had got them 'fighting near the bridge in Chester'.

The late 14th century Dee Bridge, a seven-arched structure built of local red sandstone and now a scheduled ancient monument, also figured in a darkly humorous sidelight to the story of the Rake Farm robbery, about which Margaret Porter's memoir is again the sole source of information. It followed her brief reference to the inquest into the death of the mystery man M'Sherry, killed in the fight at the farm. It appears to have been held on the day after the robbery, somewhere south of the river. And, said Margaret, the jury's verdict was one of 'justifiable homicide' — apparently supporting her contention that her brother John *had* fired the fatal shot after all.

That night, Margaret recounted, a man known by the unlikely nickname of 'King Pippin' (the original King Pippin, or Pepin, was head of the Carolingian Empire that ruled large parts of western Europe in the 8th century, and the father of Charlemagne) was hired by a Mr Crewe, a Chester surgeon, to fetch M'Sherry's body across the river to his surgery in Northgate Street. The body, evidently, had not been claimed by family or friends and, though M'Sherry had not been tried let alone convicted of any felony, the coroner — almost certainly with the approval of the trial judge — had apparently allowed it to be released for anatomical study.

In 1752 the Dee Bridge had, on the Handbridge side, a large gatehouse, with a draw-bridge and portcullis (later converted into a final arch) and a toll-house. It is perhaps best illustrated in an engraving published by Samuel Hooper in 1784 and reproduced in Francis Grose's *Antiquities of England and Wales*, the first volume of which was printed the same year. Tolls were levied on all cart-loads coming into the city via the bridge, then Chester's only River Dee crossing. It was as Pippin approached the toll-house, with the body concealed in a sack in his handcart, that the odd incident occurred.

Margaret's text explained, 'The toll-man insisted [on] a toll, when King Pippin . . . told him to put his hand into the sack and take the toll. The man accordingly put his hand into the sack and drew it out immediately in a great fright, having felt the face of a dead man. King Pippin tossed the sack and the body down, saying, "Here, take all for your toll. I shall go and inform my employer, who will soon make you bring the sack and its contents to him." King Pippin went to the surgeon and told him what had taken place, when Mr Crewe sent him with a note to the toll-man informing him [that] if he did not instantly bring the body to his surgery he would bring an action against him without delay.'

M'Sherry's corpse was soon on its way to Northgate Street. There was no charge.

At the trial of the Rake Farm robbers, which was held on the opening

The 1784 engraving of the old Dee Bridge showing the large gatehouse and the toll-house on the Handbridge side of the river, where the curious incident of the farm robber's corpse was said to have taken place.   *From the author's collection.*

day of the assizes, Margaret Porter revealed that she had had two close encounters with the gang's leader about five weeks before the raid on Rake Farm. In her written account, she said that in the witness box she had told the court the first time was on Christmas Day 1751. While the rest of the family were attending morning service at Eccleston Parish Church, she answered a knock at the kitchen door and two men were outside begging for alms. Though understandably nervous, she gave them some money and food and they went away.

At dusk that evening she was riding home from an errand in Cuckoo's Nest, when, in Rake Lane, she made out the figures of two men standing one either side of the road. As she approached them they made a move towards her. At that moment, her horse stumbled and, on being whipped up, the animal 'took off very quick'. As she galloped towards the safety of her home, she said, she heard one of the men shout to his companion, 'Damn her; why didn't you stop her.' Margaret recognised him as one of the men who had called at the farm earlier in the day. She subsequently identified him as the red-bearded Richard Stanley.

Considering the extent of the circumstantial evidence against him, it came as a surprise to most observers that Fergy Neale was not in the dock with his four countrymen. Stanley, McCannelly, Morgan and Boyd were not so lucky, and at the end of the trial they were each found guilty. Following the system then in place, in which convicted felons had to wait until the end of the sessions before being sentenced, they were brought back to court three days later, on Thursday 9 April, and each received the death penalty.

In the *Cheshire Sheaf*'s 1922 'serialisation' of the case, it was noted that, on hearing the Judge's pronouncement, Patrick Boyd 'threw into the well of the court a paper, which was handed up to the Judge'. It was a personal plea for mercy but its contrived, highfaluting language betrayed the fact that the supposed 'author' — who was unlikely to have had much, if any, schooling — had had considerable help compiling it.

It began, 'I humbly beg leave . . . to throw myself at your Lordship's feet, earnestly imploring your passionate regard towards an unhappy youth, whose want of consideration and due reflection, together with the miseries of extreme poverty, have caused him to be so far drawn aside by others to become consenting unto thieves and . . . a partaker with the malefactor.'

It continued in similarly elaborate vein, 'After I had been enticed into this iniquitous combination, I was, by a sort of compulsion, detained in it, being continually watched by my suspicious companions, lest I should escape from them before the perpetration of those facts for which we now stand before the judgment seat. But, O, my lord! Let me represent to you that even in the height of our violence, when I saw outrages going to be done to Mr Porter, which might have been fatal to him, I, with great earnestness, interceded for him and, with repeated entreaties, begged of my companions not to add to our guilt by doing any injury to his person; and for the truth of this I appeal to the prosecutors.

'Commiserate then [with] an unfortunate young man, a stranger, friendless and forlorn; one who is to have no advocate but your lordship's own innate goodness, and if there be any room for it, for His sake, who delighted to be merciful, admit me to mercy.' And the letter was signed, 'the very wretched, but seriously repentant, Patrick Boyd'. It's hard to tell how much influence Boyd's extraordinary appeal had on Judge William Noel's subsequent decision; one suspects he had already made up his mind on the basis of the evidence presented to the court. But, after reading it, he seemed determined to respond in similarly ornate style.

Chester's Chief Justice, addressing the four men in the dock, spoke of the 'heinousness' of their offences and, drawing on his personal religious convictions, remarked that there had been 'an extraordinary interposition of Heaven in their detection and punishment'. In the *Cheshire Sheaf* article, the Judge explained, 'Providence had endued [furnished] one, even of tender years and of the tender sex, with an uncommon sagacity and resolution and had ordained her to be a means of bringing seasonal relief to a spoiled and oppressed family, and thereby preventing a further aggravation of their [the prisoners'] guilt, the spilling of innocent blood.'

As well as this reference to Margaret Porter's selfless heroism, he also applied his 'heavenly interposition' belief to Henry Morgan's eventual capture. The escapee, he said, had been trying to flee to another part of the world — 'Yet the Almighty, who makes the storms and seas subservient to His will, had caused the winds and waves to bring back the fugitive, that he might be yielded up into the hands of justice.'

On account of his youth and 'his endeavours to prevail upon the others not to murder Mr Porter', His Lordship commuted Boyd's sentence to one of transportation for 14 years. It was a decision that would have found favour with the head of the Porter family. As his daughter Margaret explained in her account, John Porter Senior, who would die three years later, had 'interested himself very much in regard to Boyd' who, she wrote, had 'prevented her father, sister and brother from being murdered and had taken father off the fire two or three times'. On 5 March 1753 Patrick Boyd left Chester Castle, where he had been incarcerated since the trial, bound for Liverpool and the long and arduous trans-Atlantic voyage to his temporary exile in the American colonies.

The three other convicts were taken down in shackles to the Castle's underground cells to await their executions. This was more than 30 years before architect Thomas Harrison completely re-modelled the Castle complex (the work began in 1788) and the prison was still in the huge medieval main gatehouse, which consisted of two half-drum towers flanking a drawbridge over a moat said to be 26 feet deep. The total lack of hygiene in the damp, foul-smelling, almost airless dungeons often led to infections that were communicated to the local population.

Alfred Ingham, in his book *Cheshire: Its Traditions and History* (1920), described the impression a visitor had on approaching this formidable-looking edifice: 'At the main entrance there was a high wall with a heavy oak and iron door bristling with nails, and of immense thickness, the whole having a forbidding and desolate appearance.' It was, he suggested, paraphrasing Dante, the sort of place that condemned felons would have entered and abandoned all hope.

Gang-leader Richard Stanley was an altogether stronger-willed fellow, however. And on Thursday 23 April — two days before he was due to hang — he fashioned a means of escaping from the gaol . . . by dressing as a woman. Once more Margaret Porter supplied the most detailed version of the break-out. It began with two men and a woman going to the gaol late in the evening to visit the prisoners who were by then locked up for the night. Here she commented that this was nothing unusual 'in the old gaol'. Given that the new gaol at the Castle was not completed until 1798, and Margaret died in 1803 (at the age of 67), it suggests that she penned her journal during her final years.

'The descent to the cells,' Margaret wrote, 'was down about twelve steps. Halfway down the steps there was a door which was generally bolted on the outside by the Gaoler or one of the debtors when visitors went into the cellar area, where there were five cells. On this evening the turnkey [warder] went down first, the other three following him.'

From Margaret's account it seems that Stanley had already managed to cast off his irons and had hidden himself on the floor above, possibly in the felons' day-room. Then, as the turnkey entered the cellar area, he rushed down the steps and closed and locked the door behind the surprised prison officer. The three visitors, obviously friends of Stanley, had remained on the steps outside and the woman had on a second dress beneath her outer clothing. The ankle-length garment Stanley quickly put on over his own clothes and, possibly donning a wig or some other form of head covering, he strode brazenly back up the steps with the other three and up to the Castle gate. In the dimly lit entrance lodge, the disguise was enough to fool the Castle gate-keeper (there was talk that the prison guards were all a little the worse for drink that night) and he let them through.

The old gaol at Chester Castle, as captured in this watercolour by Moses Griffiths (1749-1819), was in the medieval gatehouse and it was from this formidable edifice in 1753 that Richard Stanley made his daring escape dressed as a woman.

Image courtesy of the Grosvenor Museum, Chester.

While Stanley was thought to be lying low in a house in St. Werburgh Street, near the Cathedral, wanted notices, offering a £10 reward for information leading to his capture, were posted. They described him as wearing a blue coat, which was said to be too long for him, and leather breeches. The distinguishing marks on his head and face, the injuries he sustained in the fight at the farm, were still visible; what was not noticeable was the sore on his left ankle which had helped him walk out of the gaol . . . and, ultimately, escape the shackles of the law. For, as a result of his blistered limb, he had been allowed a less close-fitting pair of fetters in gaol and he was able to slip out of them in time for the arrival of his friends.

'Captain' Richard Stanley, self-elected commander of the Rake Farm raiding party, a rough-and-ready labouring man and sometime worker on the land, eventually got clear of the city and may have reached Liverpool, where he had previously lived and worked under the alias of Tullough Owen. It is possible he even made it back to his native Ireland and simply disappeared. All we know for certain is that he never kept his appointment with the hangman.

For Edward M'Cannelly and Henry Morgan, however, there was no escape. Just before noon on Saturday 25 April, market day, they were taken from the Castle Gaol to the place of execution at Boughton, a little over a mile away, in a cart the City Sheriffs had commandeered from the local coal market. In contrast to the fate of M'Sherry, it was reported that, after the double hanging, the bodies of the two men were handed over to friends for burial.

From the expanded version of the 'Margaret Memoir' and the *Cheshire Sheaf* series of articles, it is certain that the Rake Farm robbery was by no means a one-off; but that it was part of a series of crimes committed by the Stanley gang, operating latterly in the Liverpool area. In the addendum to the Margaret Porter manuscript, Morgan was said to have 'acknowledged himself to have been concerned in committing many enormous crimes in company with the gang, besides the robbery for which they suffered'; though M'Cannelly had 'not been so particular in his Confession of the many crimes he has committed, as a person in his dismal circumstances might be expected to'.

M'Cannelly did, however, reveal how the robbery was conceived. Margaret's manuscript explained, 'When the fund was exhausted from the [previous] robbery, they [the gang] consulted how they should supply themselves with more. At that juncture they met with a countryman of theirs [obviously Neale], one whom had formerly . . . belonged to the gang who, apprehending what they might be about, encouraged them to make an attempt on his Master's House, promising them all the assistance he could give therein.'

The *Cheshire Sheaf* confirmed that it had been Stanley and Neale who had set up the robbery; that Neale was to have had an equal share of the booty, and that Stanley, 'who was afterwards the most cruel actor in the robbery', was the person who had 'proposed the affair'. There had been six in the gang (including Neale) and that 'all had been solemnly sworn to secrecy by Owen [Stanley] and to stand faithfully by one another'.

There is, however, no reliable evidence of the previous activities of M'Cannelly, Morgan and the rest of the Stanley gang before they burst into John Porter's farmstead on that frantic, frightening night in 1752 — not even the parts of Ireland from where they originated. And with most of them having at least one alias, the task of tracking them down brings to mind that not inappropriate old saw about needles and haystacks. The problem here, though, is that from this distance in time it is impossible to find the haystacks, never mind the needles.

Even whether Stanley and Co. were itinerant harvesters, like their fellow countrymen featured in Chapter One, is by no means certain. In her original account of the robbery, Margaret Porter made no such claim; the only two references to it were in the title of the expanded version ('An Account of the robbery of Mr Porter of Raike [*sic*] Farmhouse, near Chester, by Irish Haymakers') and in its preface, which, together with its rather romanticised front-cover illustration, was also the work of the anonymous writer who later updated the Margaret memoir. The *Cheshire Sheaf*, which drew heavily on the more recent compilation, stated categorically that the gang members were 'all Irish haymakers', who it stated, were generally 'a wild, ferocious and knavish lot, and mix among the industrious and [the] honest for the purposes of plundering their employers'.

However, the robbery occurred at the beginning of February, well before the start of the harvesting season, indicating strongly that the Stanley gang were not strictly of the same breed as the murderers of Bryan Molloy. They may have started out as casual harvestmen when first coming to England; but at some point, when gathering-time was over, like many of their countrymen, they seem to have stayed on at farms in the area or gone into other labouring jobs and taken up longer-term residence here.

In fact, from the evidence of at least two contemporary publications, it could be that the gang were settled in the Liverpool area. The *Derby Mercury* (1 May) and the *Scots Magazine* (1 June), in reporting the executions of M'Cannelly and Morgan, revealed that both men not only claimed the Rake Farm raid was planned by Stanley and Neale but that Neale (the *Mercury*'s wording) 'came to them [the gang] in Liverpool to let them know when was the most convenient Time for them to come over to rob his Master's House'.

The main attraction for the Irish labourers was that the wages were significantly higher in England than in their own country. As far as the 'wild, ferocious and knavish' members of the Rake Farm gang were concerned, they were obviously not high enough and, once here, they worked hard at making extra money in the field of crime. But, more often than not, that kind of 'overtime' came at a price. For Edward M'Cannelly, Henry Morgan and the mysterious Mr M'Sherry it was the highest price of all.

CHAPTER THREE

The Guilty And The innocents

She was young, friendless, alone. And scared. The secret she had struggled to conceal from her family and employer these past few months was about to become common knowledge. After weeks of agonising, she had finally decided that there was only one way out of her terrible dilemma. Now, as she picked her way cautiously towards the crude little outbuilding known in polite circles as a 'house of office', she told herself once more that if she was to avoid the shame of unmarried motherhood, she would have to get rid of the baby that was already straining to break free of her womb.

Moments later, in the dark and foetid surroundings of her master's outside privy, Sarah Dean sank to the floor and gave birth to a baby girl. She used a penknife to cut the umbilical cord . . . and the baby's throat. She then pushed the tiny lifeless infant into a hole at the back of the closet. The body was discovered two days later in the brook that ran at the rear of the baker's shop where she worked as a live-in servant.

On 15 April 1755 the *Chester Courant* reported the bald facts, 'Last Thursday our Assizes ended, at which one Person was capitally convicted, viz Sarah Dean, late of Congleton, for the Murder of her Bastard Child. She was executed the Friday following. Her Behaviour was very penitent and to the last [she] denied committing the Murder for which she suffer'd'.

Now fast forward nearly 130 years — and 16 miles — to 1881 and the hamlet of Buerton, in the deep south of Cheshire, and the case of Ann Smith, also convicted at the county assizes of the murder of her illegitimate child. She had dropped her one-year-old daughter into a local mill stream and left her there to drown. She, too, was sentenced to death.

The stories of these two Cheshire women, though separated by more than a century-and-a-quarter, are remarkably similar. Both were immature, illiterate and vulnerable; husbandless, poor and working 'in service' miles from home without moral or financial support. In the 18th and 19th centuries, in fact, a large proportion of single mothers charged with child murder in England and Wales were domestic servants. And of all the murders committed by women, in almost half of them the victims were their illegitimate children.

The one big difference between Sarah Dean and Ann Smith is that, while the former was hanged for her actions without any apparent outpouring of public sympathy, Ann Smith was eventually reprieved following a major campaign led by no less a figure than the judge who signed her death warrant. In looking at the two crimes in detail it is possible to see how changing social attitudes towards single motherhood — and greater understanding of the medical, psychological and emotional factors involved in cases of child murder — helped Ann Smith escape the rope . . . but came too late to save Sarah Dean's neck.

Sarah was born at a time when most of respectable society looked upon illegitimacy as reprehensible and shameful and regarded unmarried mothers with a degree of contempt that is difficult to appreciate today. The social stigma and ostracism they endured cannot be overstated. Since the early 17th century the law had considered all single mothers to be promiscuous, immoral women, no better than whores, and that — turning legal convention on its head — should they conceal the deaths of their newborn babies they were presumed guilty of murder *unless they could prove they were innocent.*

An Act of Parliament passed in 1624, during the reign of James I ('King of England, Scotland and the American Colonies'), had set out the strict judicial, and ethical, position. Entitled *An Acte to Prevent the Destroying and Murthering of Bastard Children*, it began, 'Whereas many lewd Women that have been delivered of Bastard Children, to avoid their Shame, and to escape Punishment, doe secretlie bury, or conceale the Death of their Children, and after, if the Childe be found dead, the said Women doe alledge that the said Childe was borne dead . . .'

And it went on, 'For the preventing therefore of this great Mischief, be it enacted . . . [that] if any Woman . . . be delivered of any Issue of her Body, Male or Female, which . . . should by the Lawes of this Realme be a Bastard, and that she endeavor privatelie either by drowning or secrett burying thereof . . . whether it were borne alive or not . . . in every such Case the Mother soe offending shall suffer Death as in the case of Murther, except [unless] such Mother can make proffe [proof] by one Witness at the least, that the Childe . . . was borne dead.'

For the first time a separate category of murder had been established that related solely to the killing by a mother of her 'Bastard Childe'. Thus, the indictment against Sarah Dean — phrased in similarly archaic language bordering on the Gothic — stated that on Thursday 16 January 1755, 'being Big with a Female child [she] did bring forth the said child [out] of her body . . . alone and in secrett . . . and the said Sarah Dean, not having the Fear of God before her Eyes, but being moved and seduced by the instigation of the Devil . . . as soon as the child was born did make an assault and with a certain knife to the value of 6d [six old pence] cut the child's throat, giving it one mortal wound . . . from which the child instantly died.'

Her trial took place at Cheshire's Spring Assizes on Monday 7 April before the county's Chief Justice William Noel. Her age was not stated on the indictment, nor is it to be found anywhere in the assize papers; but from a search of local parish registers it would appear she was about 20 years old. Six witnesses — John Bason, Elizabeth Cooke, John Vaudrey, Elizabeth Vaudrey, James Barrett and James Forde — had been bound over to give evidence. No record of their court testimonies has survived; so to get some flavour of the proceedings we have to rely on the depositions taken down at the inquest into the death of the murdered baby, presided over by County Coroner John Hollins on Thursday 23 January. The documents, which would have been part of the prosecution's case file at the trial, include the important, though unsatisfyingly short, statement of the accused herself.

Sarah Dean worked as a servant at the home of Mr John Vaudrey, 'breadmaker'. As well as his house and bakery (and that outdoor privy), the site appears to have contained a cowshed and a pigsty that accommodated the small collection of livestock he kept on his adjoining land. Their location was most likely to have been the east side of Mill Street, Congleton (then one of the town's four main thoroughfares), somewhere between Bridge Street and what would become Antrobus Street (not built until 1844). The house and the bakery — which, along with several other properties in the vicinity, Vaudrey seems to have inherited on the death of his widowed mother Mary in 1748 — stood on high ground above the little valley through which ran the Howty Brook.

Rising on Congleton Moss to the south of the town, Howty Brook once flowed gently northwards through Priesty Fields and the town centre before discharging into the River Dane via a small 'fleet', or creek, a little way upstream from Dane Bridge (formerly Mill Bridge, it was rebuilt and widened in 1888). In times of heavy rainfall, however, it has always been susceptible to flooding, occasionally with serious consequences. Today most of the town centre section is culverted; its only visible presence being the short length that runs parallel with lower Mill Street between the old Brook Mill (now converted into apartments) and the modern Mountbatten Way inner relief road.

Howty Brook's main historic significance is that, along with the River Dane, it helped drive Congleton's development as Cheshire's premier silk manufacturing town during the second half of the 18th century and the first half of the 19th. Originally its water powered the Brook Mill, which was built in 1785 little more than a hundred yards 'downstream' from the probable site of John Vaudrey's bakery and less than 200 yards from the Old Mill, the factory built by John Clayton and Nathaniel Pattison — in what had been the garden of the old workhouse beside the Dane — that had sparked the silk town revolution just two years before the events described here occurred.

The only town centre section of Howty Brook now visible. It was near here, probably higher up the valley at the rear of Mill Street, that the body of Sarah Dean's murdered child was discovered. On the left is the former Brook Mill, now an apartment block.
Photograph by the author.

In 1755 the Howty also ran on the surface behind and below upper Mill Street. And on the bank, between the Vaudreys' bakery and the brook, was the little privy (a not unusual scene of this type of crime, by all accounts) that throughout the inquest depositions was referred to by the curious euphemism 'house of office'.

It was to there, shortly after 5pm, with darkness settling around her, that Sarah, after slipping unseen from her master's house, made her halting way on that chilly winter's evening. And it was there, almost immediately, that she was delivered of her baby. The privy, she said in her inquest deposition, was 'on the bankside' of the bakery and she confirmed that she was 'alone and without company' at the time. As to the crucial question of the child's condition at birth, however, her deposition recorded, 'She does not know whether it was alive or dead.'

Asked what arrangements she had made for the baby's arrival, she said she had 'not made or provided any cloaths [*sic*] or other things for the child, nor acquainted any person with her condition during the time she was with child'. Having done her utmost to keep her pregnancy a secret for so long, it must have been fairly obvious that she had decided that she was not going to keep the baby.

After the birth, Sarah said, 'She laid or put the said child . . . under the floor of the house of office and that she saw the child lying there the next day. But what became of it afterwards she knows not.' She 'signed' the bottom of the statement with a spidery cross, her usual mark.

Sarah told the same story to Congleton midwife Katharine

Greenwood. On Wednesday 22 January, six days after she had given birth, the accused was ordered by a local magistrate to submit to a physical examination, carried out by Mrs Greenwood. In her statement to the Coroner, the midwife said, 'She examined the girl and found she had recently been delivered of a child, which she acknowledged, and declared that on Thursday the 16th she had been delivered of a bastard child in the house of office . . . belonging to Mr John Vaudrey and that . . . she put the child in a hole in the corner of the house floor and had seen it lying there the next day, but did not know what had become of it since then.'

What had become of the little innocent surfaced on Saturday 18 January, when labourer John Bason went 'down the garden' to make his regular early morning visit to his own 'house of office', which was also on the bank overlooking Howty Brook and only a short distance from that of the Vaudreys. During his previous morning's call of nature, between seven and eight o'clock, he had noticed something in the brook, which ran between the bottom of his garden and the meadow belonging to wealthy local landowner Mr Philip Antrobus. He took it for a dead pig and, with more pressing needs to attend to, forgot about it. Now, seeing the same object still lying there, he went to take a closer look.

His deposition stated, 'He took a rake and pulled it out and found it was a dead female child.' At that moment he spotted Mr Antrobus — a dyer and descendant of an ancient Cheshire family with considerable property interests in Congleton, including most of the land between Bridge Street and the Dane — who was walking in his meadow, on the other side of the brook, with John Vaudrey; so he called them over to witness what he had discovered. He went on, 'He examined the child and saw a wound in her throat which appeared . . . to be cut with some kind of instrument.' He said he took the child to the home of Humphrey Newton, one of the Congleton constables.

James Barrett, surgeon and apothecary, deposed that on the afternoon of Wednesday 22 January, at around five o'clock, he went to Newton's house to view the child who, he had been informed by some people, 'had been found with its throat cut ' and, by others, that it had been 'destroyed by the ratts'. The wound, he noted, was a clean cut as though 'some instrument had caused it', and 'the muscles were torn from the mouth of this wound'. Also, one side of the lower jawbone was broken.

The inquest heard from several witnesses about Sarah Dean's behaviour both before and after the murder, including Mrs Greenwood. She told the Coroner that on the previous Saturday (18th) she had had a conversation with Sarah's mistress, John Vaudrey's wife Elizabeth, at the baker's shop. After inviting her in, Mrs Vaudrey remarked that she had not seen her friend for some time and wondered why she hadn't been to visit her. Mrs Greenwood replied that there had been rumours that Sarah Dean was pregnant and that she hadn't called in case Mrs Vaudrey thought she was there to see her servant in a professional capacity

Mrs Vaudrey admitted that Sarah had been 'much talked of' around the town. But when she had tackled her about it, Sarah had responded by saying 'she had been a good servant to her and that she was no more with child than she was'.

As they were chatting Sarah passed by the shop and the midwife observed that the rumours must have been untrue as the girl 'looked very thin'. By then, of course, she was no longer carrying the child that had proved more than just a physical burden to her. It would be only a short time later that the two women heard the news of that morning's grim discovery in Howty Brook and learned the truth.

In her own deposition, Mrs Vaudrey explained that Sarah had worked for her for two years and nine months. She recalled, 'About half-a-year ago, it was commonly reported and talked of amongst the neighbours that she was with child. She several times charged her with it and said that if it was true she should discover [disclose] it and make it known.'

Under the Poor Laws of the day, if a woman 'named and shamed' the father of her illegitimate baby he could expect an official visit from the parish Overseer and, if he admitted paternity, he would be encouraged to provide financial support for the child so the cost would not fall on the local rate. However, when challenged, said Mrs Vaudrey, 'Sarah always denied it'.

In fact, if the surviving evidence is to be believed, Sarah died without revealing the name of the father of her dead child and, if the Vaudreys or any of the other witnesses had their suspicions, they were not telling. Officially, at least, his identity was never made public.

Around 2pm on 16 January, only a few hours before she did away with the baby she was expecting, Sarah had complained to her mistress that she had 'got the gripes'. Mrs Vaudrey boiled her some milk and 'sweetened it and made it

Mill Street: On the right-hand side of this narrowest part of the street was the likely location of John Vaudrey's bakery . . . and that outdoor privy.

Photograph by the author.

good'. After drinking it, she added, Sarah said that 'it had made her feel much better'. Her deposition ended, 'She never suspected that Sarah was pregnant.'

In his evidence at the inquest, John Vaudrey — whose breadmaker father William had owned the family bakery business up to his death in 1734 — described Sarah as having been 'well behaved in the family' throughout her employment. His statement continued, 'About three months ago [*sic*] it was reported in the neighbourhood that she was with child and he asked her if it was true.' She insisted it was not.

Of events on the 16th, he said he was baking bread during the afternoon and Sarah was going about her work as usual. He was not feeling too well and went to bed about five o'clock. He left Sarah sitting by the fire in the parlour complaining she was 'bad of the gripes'.

Vaudrey said he was still awake at about 9pm when he heard Sarah 'cross the chamber floor to her bed'. At seven o'clock the next morning he called his servant up to make a fire. This she did and then attended to the Vaudreys' livestock: she 'milked the cow, suckled the calf, served the swine and [did] anything else that was necessary to be done in and about the house'. He said she continued to do her work as normal 'until she was taken up by the constable'.

For the Vaudreys the death of the baby girl would have brought back particularly distressing memories of their own daughter, Jane, who had died prematurely in 1752 at the age of three. The couple had three other children at this time, William (16), Elizabeth (14) and Mary (13).

Of the depositions of the six inquest witnesses who signed recognizances to appear at the trial, only four have survived. So we have no way of knowing how Elizabeth Cooke and James Forde were involved in the case or what bearing their testimonies had on the eventual outcome. The inquest jury's verdict was that Sarah was guilty of murder and it was on the Coroner's warrant that she was committed for trial. The warrant contained the chilling detail that she had 'cut the child's throat from one ear to the other'. She would have been held first in the lock-ups in the basement of the old timber-framed Town Hall in Congleton (sometimes referred to as 'the dungeons') before being taken under guard to Chester Castle Gaol by one of the passenger coaches that departed daily from the Bulls Head and the Coach and Horses, two of what at this time were Mill Street's seven pubs.

At the end of her trial at the Castle, the jury also wasted no time in finding her guilty, though Sarah would have to wait three days before she learned her fate. Finally, on Thursday 10 April, she was brought from the cells below and placed in the dock to hear the judgment, Chief Justice Noel pronouncing the obligatory sentence of death.

Admittedly, much of what the jury heard is missing from the official files; but on the basis of the evidence given here, it is perhaps remarkable that Sarah Dean pleaded 'not guilty' and, according to contemporary press reports, maintained she was innocent until her dying breath. As we have seen, many of the women who found themselves in a similar situation claimed they had miscarried or that their babies were stillborn. But, having taken a knife to her little girl's throat, neither was a defence Sarah Dean could have relied upon. In any case, in 1755 the law decreed that, when a mother concealed the death of her newborn baby, she was guilty of murder unless she had a witness who could swear the child was born dead. In what was almost always a private and solitary act, that was hardly likely to happen. It has been calculated that between 1735 and 1799 a total of 80 females were hanged for this crime in England and Wales.

Of the many missing links in the chain of events that led Sarah Dean to the gallows, however, perhaps the most tantalising is how the baby's body she said she had hidden in a hole in the floor of her master's outside lavatory ended up in the local brook.

In the middle of the 18th century sanitation methods were fairly primitive and there is evidence that some properties close to the Howty discharged their effluent directly into the brook. Even as late as 1874 the local medical officer of health was complaining that water quality in the streams in the town, and particularly the Howty, was little better than diluted sewage. Perhaps the hole in the privy was part of John Vaudrey's private drainage system. Or simply a means of escape for the water that would undoubtedly have flowed down the bank behind his premises in periods of heavy rainfall and which would otherwise have flooded the building. It was possible that the tiny body was somehow 'flushed' out of the privy and into the brook 30 or 40 yards below; though, it has to be said, there is nothing to show that it rained on the night of the murder. The most logical explanation, of course, is that Sarah, after recovering a little from the shock of the birth, became fearful of the consequences of what she had done and returned later that evening, or in the darkness of the following morning, and transferred the body to the brook in the hope that it would be washed downstream and into the river.

Under the terms of the 1751 Murder Act, which ordained that condemned murderers had to be executed within two days of being sentenced (three if the second day was a Sunday), she was hanged at Boughton, Cheshire's centuries-old place of execution on the outskirts of Chester, on Friday 11 April 1755. Afterwards her body was handed over to local surgeons for dissection.

The harsh 1624 Act was still in force up to 1803 when it was repealed by the Ellenborough Act (named after the then Lord Chief Justice Lord Ellenborough, who introduced it), which ruled that the burden of proof demanded in other murder cases should also apply to mothers charged with killing their babies. It also gave juries the option of convicting on the lesser charge of 'concealing the birth', the penalty for which was up to two years in gaol or a house of correction.

But it wasn't until the Infanticide Act of 1922 that the murder of a newborn baby by the mother ceased to carry an automatic death sentence, establishing a partial defence that took account of such factors as the disturbed mental state of the accused. This provision was extended further by the 1938 Infanticide Act which abolished the death penalty altogether in such cases.

*　　　*　　　*

A DEATHLY hush descended on the crowded courtroom as the chaplain placed the 'black cap' — in reality a nine-inch square of silk — on the Judge's bewigged head. The hubbub created by the jury's verdict was replaced by a respectful silence. The awful, inevitable sentence was about to be pronounced.

In a voice that echoed sombrely around the cavernous, colonnaded surroundings of Cheshire's classical Greek-style Shire Hall at Chester Castle, His Lordship addressed the ominous words to the convicted murderess.

'Ann Smith,' he intoned, 'you will be taken hence to the prison in which you were last confined and from there to a place of execution, where you will be hanged by the neck until you are dead, and thereafter your body will be buried within the precincts of the prison. And may the Lord have mercy on your soul.'

It was a gloomy recital, expressed in language that affirmed the omnipotence of the law and society's reprobation of those who committed the ultimate crime. Across the court, however, the short — she was an inch under five feet tall — plump and oval-faced figure in the dock, who had occasionally failed to stifle a laugh during her trial, stared vacantly ahead, seemingly unconcerned about the solemn ritual taking place before her.

It was generally agreed that 18-year-old Ann Smith, latterly employed as a domestic servant at a farm in north-west Shropshire, was somewhat slow-witted; 'dull' was the characteristic most commonly ascribed to her. But her demeanour on that day in February 1881 was rooted, not in any lack of understanding, quite the opposite: it was the knowledge that she was not going to die for murdering her baby daughter.

The Judge, Mr Commissioner Joseph Brown, had himself assured her he would use all his not inconsiderable influence to persuade Her Majesty Queen Victoria, to exercise the royal prerogative of mercy and grant her a reprieve. There was no guarantee his efforts would succeed, of course. But Ann Smith's legal advisers would also have made it known to her that no woman had been hanged in England for what we generally understand today as infanticide for more than 30 years.

The ostensibly doom-laden climax of her appearance at Cheshire's Winter Assizes was something of a charade: the jury had found the accused guilty of murder, the law said the mandatory penalty was death by hanging, so the Judge had to stand on age-old ceremony and formally impose the prescribed punishment . . . even though he knew that not since 1849 had it been carried out in cases such as this. Sir George Grey, the then Home Secretary, had confirmed the fact in 1865 when giving evidence to the Royal Commission on Capital Punishment. Between 1849 and the end of 1864, he reported, 39 mothers had been convicted of child murder, 34 of them for killing their illegitimate children. But not one of them was hanged. A staunch advocate of the total abolition of capital punishment, he stated, 'The practice has been established that no woman is executed for the murder of an infant.' And a leading cleric, the Reverend Lord Sydney Godolphin Osborne, Rector of Durweston in Dorset, another prominent abolitionist who also gave evidence to the Commission, declared that in nine cases out of ten, trying women for their lives for infanticide was 'a cruel farce'.

As previously written, the spectre of death was not officially exorcised from the law relating to child murder until as late as 1938; but public opinion on the use of capital punishment in general had softened considerably since Sarah Dean's day. And, in the case of infanticide, the courts were now taking a more humane approach to dealing with the mostly young, helpless — and usually hopeless — women who felt compelled to kill their newborn babies. There was greater understanding of the mental issues that could have a critical effect on the mother's actions and a determination to expose the medical evidence to greater scrutiny; in short, a realisation that the whole subject of child murder was far more complex than had previously been recognised.

This more liberal attitude had begun in response to what has been described as 'an epidemic' of child-murder that occurred in Victorian England. In the early 1840s, it is recorded, Thomas Wakley, coroner, surgeon, MP and social reformer, shocked Parliament by claiming that infanticide was 'going on to a frightful, to an enormous, a perfectly incredible extent'. Twenty years later the situation was considered to have reached crisis proportions, becoming one of the great social evils of the day, alongside prostitution, drunkenness and gambling.

In London the sight of a dead baby abandoned in the street was commonplace; police officers reported that it was no more unusual than finding a dead cat or dog. Police records revealed that in 1870 the bodies of no fewer than 276 infants were dumped on the streets of the capital.

Much of this outbreak of child murder was blamed on 'puerperal insanity', which accounted for a rising number of female admissions to asylums. Known today as puerperal (or postpartum) psychosis, it is now a much better understood mental illness that affects many women after giving birth. Symptoms include mania, depression, confusion, hallucinations and delusions. In the most extreme cases, sufferers try to harm themselves or their babies. As the 19th century progressed, judges became increasingly disposed to accepting this kind of temporary mental disorder as a defence to infant murder. And the younger the mother, the more leniently she was likely to be treated.

That she was only 18, and probably suffering from a recurrent nervous affliction, did not prevent Ann Smith from being found guilty of murder and sentenced to death, however. Nor was it a factor that evidently impressed the then Home Secretary, Sir William Harcourt, a leading Liberal and close political aide of Prime Minister William Gladstone. As expected, in response to the various appeals for clemency, he granted the convicted woman a reprieve; but he was not about to let her off scot-free. Despite Judge Brown's further intervention and pressure for a lesser punishment, the Minister decided to commute her sentence to 'penal servitude' (prison with some form of labour) for life. How long she would actually serve is another matter, and one to which we shall return presently.

Ann Smith was born, illegitimately, on 25 April 1862 into an unconventional family unit in which bastardy was the norm. Her mother Jane, who never married, was also illegitimate, as were her three other daughters, Martha (born 1847), Mary (1855) and Elizabeth (1866) and her son Thomas (1859). The baptism registers show they all shared the surname Smith, though Martha, the eldest of the five siblings, looks to have had a different father from the others, as she was consistently described in court documents and newspaper reports as Ann's half-sister.

From census records it appears that for more than 20 years Jane Smith lived in Buerton, near Audlem, with a widower whose name was variously given as John Hodskiss (1851), John Hodkiss (1861) and John Hodskinson (1871). In each of those years she was described as 'housekeeper', but the head of the household, an agricultural labourer, was also listed as the father of four of her children: Mary, Elizabeth, Ann and Thomas. In 1851, when Martha made her first appearance, however, the three-year-old was identified only as the daughter of his servant Jane Smith. The couple seem to have begun their un-married life together in Longhill Lane, Buerton, but by 1871 the family, now including an eight-year-old Ann, had moved to nearby Chapel Lane.

In the troubled life of Ann Smith, her relationship with her father — who she herself named as 'Mr J. Hodskiss' in what was her only personal reference to him throughout the extensive official documentation — seems to have been the cause of her difficult childhood, which set the pattern for the misfortunes that were to follow.

A report from John Manning, Governor of Chester Castle Gaol, to where Ann was returned after her trial, was obtained by Judge Brown as part of the dossier he presented to the Home Office in the campaign to win Ann a reprieve. In it the prison chief said Ann had 'no friends . . . and a father who has deserted her since she was ten years old'.

And the Reverend Arthur Atkinson, Vicar of Audlem, in another appeal to the Home Secretary, wrote, 'Ann Smith is an illegitimate child who had no advantages whatever, having been harshly used and refused any education . . . she has always been considered dull and sometimes rather eccentric, which may probably [*sic*] be owing to the harsh treatment which she received as a child.'

John Hodskiss, as we must now call him, was also alluded to in several of the many reports Ann accumulated at Millbank Prison in Pimlico, London, to where she was sent to begin her 'life' sentence on 22 March 1881. Among the file's periodic assessments of her 'character, habits and family background', was a reference to her father being 'a convicted thief' — though another noted that he was 'convicted years ago [and] has since redeemed his character'.

But the greatest emotional upheaval in Ann Smith's unhappy childhood was the death of her mother at the age of 47. Jane Smith was laid to rest on 7 April 1872 in the graveyard of Audlem Parish Church, where at least three of her children had been baptised. Ann claimed later that she was then eight years old when, in fact, she had her tenth birthday less than three weeks later; but, more significantly, her estrangement from her father had by then become irrevocable. As she would tell prison officers at Millbank, this was the time when she 'lost the only parent she had'.

Afterwards her half-sister Martha 'took charge as mother', said Ann. This, despite the fact that Martha was only 24 herself and newly married. She had wed husband Charles Clewes, also 24 and a labourer in an iron works, in July 1871. The Clewes family had been the Smiths' next-door neighbours in Chapel Lane, but Charles and Martha made their marital home in the nearby Moblake area of Buerton and the 'mother' comment suggests that Ann went to live with them there.

If so, it was a short-term arrangement, for when Ann turned ten her father set her to work in-service at Rookery Farm, the home of Robert Boffey, 48, his wife Elizabeth (38) and their eight children, five miles away at Burleydam in Dodcott-cum-Wilkesley, Cheshire's southernmost parish. This was the moment, presumably, when Ann felt her father had 'deserted her'.

It was while living-in with the Boffeys on their 265-acre farm that the second tragic event in Ann Smith's young life occurred. Around Christmas 1878 she was given some extra time off work by her mistress and she took a holiday. What happened on the journey back to the farm — situated on what is now the A525 Whitchurch Road close to the Shropshire border — she would reveal publicly for the first time in a petition to the Home Office dated 10 July 1882.

The petition was written on her behalf by a member of the prison staff at Millbank — by then her ability to read and write was still being assessed as 'imperfect' — in an unsuccessful bid to have her sentence reduced. It stated in part, 'When she was returning home she had to walk two miles across the country [and] she was accosted and assaulted by a stranger.' Translation: she was raped. She was 16 years of age.

The appeal letter went on, 'She was too much afraid to tell anyone what had happened, but it was found out by her mistress, who was very fond of her.'

And it was no doubt Mrs Boffey who helped make the arrangements for Ann's confinement with, one suspects, a little help from her married daughter, Mrs Sarah Mottram. For Ann was accepted for admission to the Whitchurch Workhouse. Ordinarily, through her place of work she would have achieved the official 'settlement' qualification she would have needed to gain admission to her local

When Ann was ten her father found her a job as a live-in servant at Rookery Farm at Burleydam (above). Shortly afterwards tragedy struck for the second time in her young life.

Photograph by the author.

workhouse, situated in Nantwich, in whose Poor Law Union area she lived. Now it was understandable that she might wish to have her baby as far away as possible from the locality in which she was known, but the Poor Laws did not usually allow unmarried women to pick and choose where they went to have their illegitimate children. Mrs Mottram, however, lived in the area of the Whitchurch Poor Law Union, and she had agreed with her mother to provide Ann with a new position in her household once the child was born. These were well respected, influential people and undoubtedly possessed the clout to persuade Union officials to bend the rules on this occasion and award Ann advanced settlement, particularly as her child was not going to be a burden on the parish.

However it was engineered, it was at the Whitchurch Workhouse in Claypit Street where Ann's little girl, who she named Mary Jane, was born on 23 September 1879. Her Millbank Prison file stated that Ann and her baby remained 'in the Union', as more sensitive folk preferred to call it, for eight months after she gave birth (though in the accepted chronology of events it could not have been more than six months). This suggests she suffered some post-natal complication and spent at least some of the time in the infirmary. So it was not until May 1880 that she finally started her new job as an 'inside servant' to Mrs Mottram (24) and her husband William (25) at their farm in the village of Whittington, near Oswestry.

During the previous March, by which time Ann seems to have returned to live and work at Rookery Farm, her half-sister Martha had sent for her, telling her she could find her employment and a nurse for the baby nearer home. However, as it turned out, she was unable to get a job locally and so Martha offered to look after little Mary Jane. Ann agreed to pay her three shillings a week as 'keep money', which Mrs Boffey was to deduct from her wages and give to Martha in quarterly instalments. 'To this,' her prison file recorded, 'Ann gladly

Whitchurch Workhouse. Ann Smith's baby girl was born here in Sepember, 1879; afterwards she spent some months in the infirrmary, apparently suffering from a post-natal complication.

Photo by kind permission of Peter Higginbotham/ workhouses.org.uk.

acceded, wishing once more to work for her living'. And she went back to Rookery Farm.

While working there Ann visited her daughter three times. But from the Mottrams' home in Shropshire it was a long, and costly, near 60-mile round trip (including train travel, presumably), and from the following May she managed only two further visits. It was during the second one that the most catastrophic episode in Ann Smith's miserable life story occurred.

Each time she returned to Moblake, Ann had let Martha know she was coming. But on Saturday 4 December 1880 she turned up out of the blue with no luggage and the intention of spending the weekend with the Cleweses and her little girl. What followed created enough of a sensation to attract wide coverage in the local and national press. But the account rendered here is based substantially on the personal review of Ann Smith's trial written by the Judge, Mr Commissioner Brown, from the notes he made at the time. Compiled in support of his mission to see the young woman reprieved, it was submitted for the private attention of Home Secretary Harcourt. It has never been published before.

The Assizes opened on Monday 31 January 1881 and her trial took place on the following Thursday, 3 February, when, according to both Press reports and the court records, Ann Smith was aged 19. In fact, as her birth certificate showed, she would not be 19 for another three months. When the prisoner was arraigned she pleaded not guilty. In doing so she apparently muttered some injudicious remarks which were overheard by the two opposing counsel. Her comments, spoken in a barely audible voice, were relayed later to representatives of the press and in the *Cheshire Observer* of Saturday 5 February they were reported as being to the effect that she was 'very sorry' and that 'I am very funny sometimes and don't know what I am doing'.

Martha Clewes was the prosecution's first witness. Judge Brown recalled that she had told the court that her half-sister's child was 14 months old, and 'in very good health', when her mother last came to see her. On the Saturday night, Martha and Ann had a conversation in which it became clear that the 'stranger' who had raped Ann had since become somewhat better acquainted with her and had recently been in contact. Ann said the man had promised her a new dress and a jacket, whereupon Martha became angry and, the Judge's dossier revealed, she replied that what he would get her was 'into another scrape' and she would 'have to do as she had done before', i.e. she would find herself pregnant and having to go into the workhouse again.

At first Martha thought Ann may already be in the family way (she would discover later that she was not) and rebuked her, saying, 'You can't keep two.' Ann ignored her. Judge Brown noted that Martha then told Ann that 'she shouldn't like to part with [Mary Jane] as she had had the child so long', but that 'she couldn't keep it as she had a family of her own'. At this time Martha and her husband, by then a labourer at Crewe Railway Works, had three children, two boys aged five and three, and a daughter of about six months. They went on to have two more sons. Another boy had died at the age of two in 1874.

During Sunday, said Martha, Ann 'seemed kindly disposed' to her child and was 'kind and affectionate to her up to the moment she left'. She described her half-sister as a 'healthy and sober woman, if rather dull and [with] rather a sulky temper'.

Mid-morning on the Monday Ann announced she was taking the child 'a ta-ta' (or going 'ta-tas', a northern expression meaning going out somewhere). But, said the *Cheshire Observer*, because she had seen little of her daughter since she was born she (Ann) was 'strange to her' and the child 'did not care to go'. Nonetheless, about 10am, Ann tucked the little one under her arm and the two of them set off, heading across the fields in the direction of Bunsley Bank. Ann said they 'wouldn't be many minutes away'. Neither of them would return.

Taking up the story again, the Judge noted that about 20 minutes later, Ann passed by the home of Lucy Ann Prince on Bunsley Bank. She was walking on the footpath that led down across a meadow to a bridge over the brook that meandered through the little valley beyond. Mrs Prince, 31, was quoted by the Judge as saying in her evidence, 'She had a baby in her arms and I thought she carried it rather carelessly, rather low down. I would not carry mine so. She was going very fast towards . . . the brook. The child's legs were dangling down and this, and her going so fast, made me notice her.'

About ten o'clock the next morning, Tuesday 7 December, an 11-year-old boy called Alfred Dale was on the same path — it was used regularly by children going to and from school in Audlem and by other local people — when he discovered the body of a small child lying largely submerged in what he referred to as 'the brook'. In fact, at this time, as police sergeant Thomas Fowler would later have to explain to the jury, there were two water courses running side by side in the valley: the brook itself and an artificial stream constructed only a matter of yards away to power the nearby Audlem Mill. And, to add to the confusion, there was a bridge over each of them. The 1,100 yard long cut, or 'mill race', seems to have been created by tapping into the old brook higher up the valley, the water decanting into one of the two large pools that served the flour mill. It was from this stream, at a spot

The footpath on Bunsley Bank on which Ann Smith was last seen with her 14-month old child heading towards the footbridges in the bottom of the valley.

Photograph by the author.

about 600 yards from the mill, that the body of Mary Jane Smith was recovered. At first young Alfred thought it was a man's arm. When he realised the truth, he ran home and told his step-father, Joseph Sant, what he had seen. 'He came back with me and took the child out of the water,' he said.

Mr Sant, a 40-year-old farmer, testified that the body was snagged on a small bank of sand in the middle of the stream and, though only one arm was visible above the water, 'it could be clearly seen' from the footbridge about 15 yards away. The water, particularly shallow at this point, was less than a foot deep.

Dr William Robert Tough, described in Judge Brown's memorandum as 'a medical man practising at Audlem', examined the body at the

A little wooden single-railed footbridge still crosses the brook that once ran alongside the mill stream in which Ann Smith's baby drowned. The mill stream, now long since filled-in, was situated just a few yards to the right in this picture.

Photograph by the author.

scene and testified that the child had been dead 'for many hours . . . maybe even 24.' The body was conveyed to the Combermere Arms, a 16th century pub in Burleydam, where the inquest was to be held. In his postmortem examination, Dr Tough, 28, found no marks of violence on the body, which was well nourished and healthy. He confirmed that the little girl had died from drowning.

The whole of his trial testimony is taken from Judge Brown's case notes. Cross-examined by defence counsel Mr Ignatius Williams, the doctor said in a child of this age falling into a stream and being suddenly immersed in cold water (it was winter time), 'might produce nearly instantaneous numbness'; the child would be 'insensible in a very few seconds' and, if its head was under water, would be 'very soon asphyxiated'.

Pressed by Mr Williams, Dr Tough recalled attending the prisoner's committal hearing before the magistrates and described how Ann had twice experienced 'a sort of fainting attack'. He said, 'The girl got quite pale, lay back with her head on the chair back and kept fanning herself with her handkerchief in a half fainting condition. She wasn't thoroughly recovered [from the first attack] when the second one affected her'.

The doctor agreed that if such an attack had come on while she was carrying anything of any weight, it would have 'tumbled out of her arms'. She would not, he asserted, have been able to carry it.

Explaining to the jury that there was a condition called *epilepsia petit mal*, he commented, 'The nature and cause of fits is little understood and sometimes very obscure. Very often sudden and complete unconsciousness ensues [or] it might be a feeling of vertigo followed by mental confusion lasting a few seconds.' And he added, 'While under the influence of such an attack, it is possible the patient might do and say things [he or she] might afterwards forget and deny. A patient could not think while she had a fit of that nature.'

In response to questioning by prosecuting counsel Mr Edward Julyan Dunn, in which he referred to the fact that, after the drowning, Ann Smith had run off and made her way back to her mistress's home in Shropshire, Dr Tough stated, 'If she got up and ran away, that would not be consistent with a fit. If she knew the next day exactly what she had done, that also would not be consistent with a fit.'

It was his opinion that this less severe form of epilepsy might have been the reason for Ann's behaviour, but he thought not. He added, 'From what I have seen of the prisoner and heard of her bodily condition and history, I did not attribute the fainting before the magistrates to anything more than mere anxiety.'

Sergeant Fowler, aged 39 and stationed at Audlem, was the officer in charge of the investigation into baby Mary Jane's death. After transporting the body to the Combermere Arms, he said, he went in search of the child's mother. He found her at the home of Mrs Mottram. According to Judge Brown's notes, when he charged her with the child's murder, 'She did not speak [but] threw herself backwards on a chair and went into a fit. She was insensible for a few seconds.'

It was a cold night with a chill wind blowing and the officer suggested Ann might want to put on some warmer clothing. But she replied that 'she only had the clothes she had on her back [as] it took all her money to maintain the child'.

Then she told him that 'she didn't think of drowning the child until she came to the brook and some funny thoughts came into her head.' She dropped the baby into the water and ran up the meadow towards Audlem. 'Some funny thoughts', Sgt Fowler believed, were her exact words; though he admitted under cross-examination that she might have said '*when* I came to the brook' rather than '*until* I came to the brook'. On the train journey from Oswestry to Chester, he said he noticed she was sleepy; when he mentioned it to her she explained that 'she had had no sleep the night before as she was afraid someone would be after her'.

Of the murder scene, the sergeant explained that the footbridge over the mill stream consisted of just three wooden planks with a handrail on one side only.

In his closing speech for the prosecution, as reported in the *Cheshire Observer* of 5 February, Mr Dunn pointed out that, if this was an accident, 'the most natural thing would have been for the prisoner to have gone back to her half-sister's house and told her what had happened, instead of going away without saying a word to anybody'. The defence, he said, had suggested that the accused woman was 'attacked by illness at the time the affair took place'. But, he argued, 'Other circumstances lead to a contrary impression.'

Mr Williams, in his closing speech, spoke of the prisoner's 'fall [from grace], such as it was'; he thought the jury would 'probably find there was very little moral guilt about it'. It 'must have taken place when she was 17 years of age' (wrong: her birth registration indicated she was still only 16). The *Observer* report went on, 'That her character must have been good, was proved by the fact that in her short life she had for six years [sic] been employed in the same family, and continued in service up till the time of her apprehension, thus showing that her mistress took a tender interest in the unfortunate girl.'

Defence counsel said he was 'ashamed to hear it suggested that the prisoner went [to visit her daughter] with the intention of murdering her child'. In a fuller account of his speech, which appeared in the *Chester Chronicle* of 5 February, Mr Williams presented the jury with his interpretation of the events of that fateful Monday morning. He was quoted as saying, 'When the prisoner came to the bridge, only protected by a handrail on one side, the child fell from her weak grasp and into the cold water and was at once benumbed and drowned. The poor girl then seeing her child motionless in the water, [she was] in such a state of mind that, overcome by the calamity, she ran off in a state of terror and went to [her mistress's] . . . where she passed a sleepless night from her terror at what had happened.'

At the conclusion of his summing up, Mr Commissioner Brown told the jury that he 'trusted that even in the event of the prisoner being found guilty of murder the extreme sentence of the law would not be carried out', for, he remarked, there were 'circumstances in the case which rendered it peculiar'.

The jury took just under an hour to reach their verdict, the foreman announcing that they had found the accused had drowned her infant child but 'without premeditation'. The Judge ruled that it was not an acceptable verdict. If the defendant knew what she was doing, and she had done it on a momentary impulse, it was murder; he therefore told the jury they must retire and reconsider. They returned 20 minutes later with a guilty verdict, 'with the strongest recommendation to mercy'.

Judge Brown turned to the prisoner in the dock and commented, 'I am sorry it becomes my very painful duty to pass upon you the sentence of the law.' After imposing the death penalty, he continued to speak to the convicted woman. He told her, 'I shall do what is in my power to recommend you to the mercy of the Crown.' He was true to his word.

With his memorandum to the Home Office, he enclosed a personal letter to Sir William Harcourt in which he wrote, 'I was obliged by law to sentence her to death and also to sign a warrant for her execution, but I wish to recommend her to her Majesty's mercy. Had the law allowed me I should certainly not have sentenced her to death.'

The letter went on, 'The prisoner is a girl of 19 years [even the Judge got her age wrong] , of a very low order of intellect and of simplicity bordering upon childishness, as appeared by the manner in which she drowned her child, which was done in broad day[light] in a stream beside a public footpath where people were constantly passing, where it would not remain many hours without being seen.'

Referring to Ann's comments to Sgt Fowler about the 'funny thoughts' she sometimes had, the judge said, 'Her conduct and demeanour at the trial impressed me with the idea that she is a person of very limited intellect and responsibility.' And with the jury's eventual murder verdict and recommendation to mercy, he said he 'strongly concurred'.

With the execution date set for 21 February, Home Secretary Harcourt replied on the 9th announcing a reprieve. At the same time the Minister asked the Judge what sentence he would consider appropriate to the circumstances of the case. On 10 February Mr Commissioner Brown wrote to say he thought 'a sentence of seven, or even five, years penal servitude would meet the requirements of justice'.

However, after receiving his departmental officials' advice that Ann Smith's offence should be judged in comparison with three other similar cases — in which two of the offenders had been sentenced to life and the other to 20 years — Harcourt, a robust defender of law and order, opted for a tougher line. His view, communicated to Judge Brown on 12 February, was that, 'The mental condition of this wretched girl makes it only too possible that her early release would be followed by a repetition of her offence.' No doubt to the surprise of the Judge, and Ann, too, she was given a life term, though with the proviso that it should be reviewed after five years.

Just over a month later, she was moved from Chester Castle to Millbank, where, as Prisoner No. H24, her work included repairing stockings and laundering. On her arrival she had given her next-of-kin as her sister Elizabeth (or 'Lizzie', as she called her), rather than her father or her half-sister Martha. Lizzie was then aged 17 and living as a kitchen maid and domestic servant at the home of Mrs Sarah Dutton at Gorsecroft Farm in Longhill Lane, Bunsley Bank. During Ann's time in prison, Lizzie wrote to her on a regular basis; she was the only

Millbank Prison in Pimlico, where Ann Smith, Prisoner No. H24, began her 'life' sentence in March 1881. She spent 14 months there before being transferred to HM Convict Prison, Fullham.

member of the family who seems to have bothered to keep in touch, in fact. And out of this close bond would eventually come the chance of a new life for the hapless Ann.

From as early as the middle of 1882, with the help of Millbank officials, Ann had been pressing for a reduction in her sentence. In her 10 July petition to the Home Office, referred to earlier, she claimed that, when she went to see her daughter that December, Martha had got angry with her, telling her the money she was paid to look after Mary Jane was not enough. The appeal letter then went on, 'Not knowing scarcely what she was doing, she took the child and went out. She has no recollection but thinks she must have thrown [the baby] into the water, and then gone back to her situation. She told her mistress what she must have done.'

Begging for mercy, she said she knew full well that '[her] sin is great', but that she had 'always suffered very much with her head'. Having words with Martha 'must have caused her to be quite unconscious of what she was committing'. If the Home Secretary would grant her wish, she promised 'henceforth in all ways to make amends to God and Man for [her] one false action'.

Sir William Harcourt would not be moved, however; in his reply of 28 July he pointed out that he had agreed to review her situation after five years and she had only served 18 months. A subsequent report from William Sale, Medical Officer at Fullham Prison, to where Ann had been transferred on 12 July, contained his opinion that, apart from suffering occasionally from vertigo, Ann was 'in reasonably good health'. Sir William informed her he was sticking to his deadline.

She was finally released on licence (No. 7388) in 1886, the order, dated 4 March, noting that she was to be liberated through the Royal Society for the Assistance of Discharged Prisoners 'for emigration'. She had been told that, under the terms of the licence, she would have

to find someone who was prepared to offer her a home. Sister Lizzie came up with the solution.

As well as writing to Ann in prison, Lizzie had also been in contact with their other sister Mary, who had recently emigrated to America. With her husband William Harding, she had settled in the city of East Palestine in the Midwestern state of Ohio. After exchanging letters with Ann — and with the Discharged Prisoners' Society, which promised to help her find work — Mary, 31, agreed to take her in.

Sir William Harcourt: unmoved by appeal.

Prison records indicated that her time inside had

certainly made her better prepared physically for working life. On her arrival at Millbank she was described as 'stout' — the official photograph in her Home Office file shows her as having a pudgy, rather child-like visage and dark, straight hair worn in a severe, swept-back style with a centre parting — but on her release from Fullham her build was termed more kindly as 'small'.

Whether she managed to obtain some meaningful employment, and so make a new start in the New World, however, is unknown. What is certain is that some of the personal remarks about her in her prison file would not have provided the most helpful of job references. Although she was variously described as 'hard-working', 'industrious', 'steady and quiet' and 'of sober habits', every one of the 'respectable persons' who were asked to provide 'trustworthy information' about Prisoner H24 raised doubts about her honesty, even her long-time master William Boffey, for whose family Ann had worked for the best part of eight years. When he was invited to give his assessment of her character, he could not resist adding that he had always found the poor girl 'rarther [sic] peculiar'.

Sill only 23, Ann Smith did, at least, have the opportunity to atone for her 'one false action'. In a more unforgiving age, as Sarah Dean discovered to her cost, there were no second chances.

CHAPTER FOUR

Last Of A Dying Breed

From the moment the trial judge sentenced him to death, Thomas Mate harboured a deep-seated hatred of those he felt had been his undoing. Now, as he stood beneath the gallows, the noose already around his neck, he poured out his rage towards the neighbours who had testified against him and the lawyers who had prosecuted him. But, bitter and unrepentant to the end, he reserved his most vitriolic attack for his wife who, he swore, was the cause of the marital rows that had driven him to violence and, eventually, to murder.

In a loud voice he declared arrogantly to the large crowd assembled for the hanging that he would never forgive her for being unfaithful to him, blaming their frequent quarrels on her infidelity. A not unusual source of domestic friction, maybe; the difference here, though, was that he was 64 and she was nearly 70. And it was reported that, while their relationship might have been volatile, they had had 'at least twenty-one' children together.

In the grim roll-call of long-forgotten criminals executed at Chester, the case of Thomas Mate is memorable for a more historically-significant reason, however. For he and Abraham Stones, about whom we shall hear later, share the doubtful distinction of being the last two people to be condemned to death under Chester's own courts system at a time when, uniquely, the city's sheriffs had the unpalatable task of carrying out all capital sentences imposed at the county assizes as well.

Elsewhere in England it was the county's High Sheriff who was responsible for arranging the executions of persons capitally convicted at the assizes. But, due to an obscure medieval agreement, Chester's sheriffs were, from Norman times until the second half of the 19th century, bound to execute criminals from all over Cheshire (see *Cheshire's Execution Files* by this author). And their doubly deadly role meant they performed their onerous duty almost entirely on criminals from outside their own jurisdiction. Between 1750-1866, for instance, of around one hundred hangings in Chester, only eight resulted from sentences handed down by the city courts, four of them at one session.

Thomas Mate was convicted by Chester's ancient Crownmote Court, the highest criminal court in the city, whose origins are similarly unclear. Along with the Pentice and Portmote Courts, the Crownmote (pronounced 'Crown*moot*') is known to have been in existence since at least the 13th century and was the city court that dealt with the more serious cases of felony. The Chester Corporation archives, as we shall see in the second part of this chapter, indicate that it was still operating as late as 1826 and probably survived until the passing of the 1835 Municipal Corporations Act, which fundamentally reformed local government in the incorporated boroughs of England and Wales.

Like all the city courts at this time, the Crownmote sat in the old Exchange Building which, until it was destroyed by fire in 1862, stood in Northgate Street in what is now the Town Hall Square. So it was just a short walk from the infamous Northgate Gaol, in which Mate had been incarcerated since his arrest, to the courtroom to where, on Monday 12 January 1789, he was escorted in irons to face a charge of murder. It was not, however, his wife who was the victim but one of the city's 'ward constables' (or 'Officer of the Peace', as the newspapers described him) by the name of John Parry, who was shot while trying to intervene in Mate's latest bust-up with the long-suffering woman with whom he lived in Handbridge, the Chester suburb on the south bank of the River Dee.

Historically, Handbridge had seen its fair share of hostilities since the Roman invaders established a settlement there following the construction of the fortress of Deva on the opposite bank of the river between AD 70-80. After their departure the area was the target of Viking raiders; and later it was regularly pillaged and torched by the

Like all Chester's local courts, the Crownmote, where Thomas Mate was tried, was located in the Exchange building, which stood on the north side of what is now the Town Hall Square.

From the author's collection.

marauding Welsh, who named it *Treboeth*, meaning 'burnt town'. It was burned down again during the Civil War to hamper the progress of Cromwell's forces besieging the Royalist stronghold of Chester. Now the warring Mates were the scourge of the neighbourhood.

The court heard that trouble flared between the couple on the morning of Friday 5 December 1788 and Mate, a labourer who seems to have worked on farms at one time or another, began knocking his wife about. It was becoming an almost daily occurrence, but on this occasion the disturbance was such as to convince his neighbours — a group of whom had been drawn into the street outside the Mates' house alarmed at the screams coming from inside — that Mrs Mate's life was in danger. So two of them hurried to the Mayor's office, where they 'laid an information' (made a statement on oath) to a local magistrate about the incident.

Adams's Weekly Courant, forerunner of the *Chester Courant*, reported on Tuesday 9 December, 'The neighbours deposed that Thomas Mate was then beating and cruelly treating his Wife, who frequently cried out "Murder" and appeared at the Window with her face very bloody, and repeatedly told the Bye-standers, whom her cries had collected together, that she was afraid her Husband would murder her, intreating them to apply immediately to the Magistrates for their Assistance to save her life.'

The newspaper stated that the two informants had cited 'many instances . . . of the Husband's brutish Treatment of his Wife, and [expressed] their opinion that, if he was not immediately taken into Custody, he would be the Death of her'.

The *Chester Chronicle*, in its edition of 12 December, also told of the 'many similar acts of violence . . . committed by this man not many months ago' (he was arrested but released after obtaining sureties for his good behaviour) which, the paper claimed, 'had since rendered him particularly an object of dread'.

Based on the neighbours' fears, a warrant was issued for his arrest on a charge of 'ill usage of his wife'. John Parry, aged 50, a blacksmith by trade — like all law officers at this time he was part-time and unpaid — was handed the signed order and he and three fellow constables went to Mate's house to serve it. When they arrived they found the front door locked and barred. This, 'added to the dangerous disposition of his mind,' said the *Chronicle*, justified the constables' decision to call for reinforcements. Two further officers were dispatched to the scene and the six of them eventually forced their way into the house.

Parry led the way and he was immediately confronted by Mate, standing defiantly at the top of the stairs armed with a sickle, or reaping-hook, 'threatening, with the most horrid imprecations', the *Chronicle* stated, 'that he would kill or be killed, as he was determined not to be taken'. For several minutes Parry tried to reason with him, pointing out 'the folly and hazard attending such rashness'; but Mate was implacable.

The constable retreated into the kitchen where he spotted the wooden shaft of a scythe. He grabbed hold of it, as much for his own protection as with any aggressive intent, and went again to tackle Mate. The serial wife-beater, his fury increasing at what he obviously felt was an unjustified invasion of his privacy, was still on the landing; but this time he held a musket in his hands. Parry had only got one foot on the stairs when a shot rang out and the constable staggered backwards out of the front door and into the street, where, with a cry of 'He has done for me', he collapsed and died.

At the inquest into his death, held by city coroners Peter Brooks and John Wright, sitting with a 13-man jury the following day, it would be revealed that the three-quarters-of-an-inch diameter lead musket ball had struck Parry first in his right arm, shattering a bone, and thence continued on an upward trajectory into his breast, puncturing his right lung. The musket — a muzzle-loading shoulder gun traditionally used by infantry soldiers between the 16th and 19th centuries, with a barrel length of between 42-46 ins — was a particularly accurate weapon when fired at close range, and its large but soft projectiles were capable of inflicting major damage on impact.

With the accompanying officers rushing to the aid of their fallen comrade, Mate seized his opportunity to bolt and bar the door once more. And, after recharging the

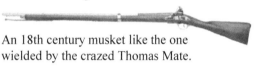

An 18th century musket like the one wielded by the crazed Thomas Mate.

musket, he continued his angry tirade from the window of the marital bedroom upstairs, his demeanour a mixture of menace and triumph at his temporary victory over his perceived persecutors. With his battered and bloody wife cowering in fear nearby, he 'threatened Destruction to any Person that should attempt to take him,' reported the *Courant*.

It was a stand-off that demonstrated just how short-handed and inadequately trained were Chester's 'peace officers' who, together with the nightly watch patrols, were the city's only form of law enforcement at this time. Not until 1835 did Chester have a paid police force. It was now obvious that some rather more heavyweight help was needed. This had become a potentially serious civil disorder; and, as was the usual practice in such situations, it was time to call out the militia.

Application was made to the military chiefs at Chester Castle (where there had been a garrison since William the Conqueror fortified the place in 1070) and in double-quick time a detachment of men of the 40th Regiment, under the command of a Major Adlam, was on its way across the river to Handbridge to, as the *Courant* put it, 'assist the Civil Power in apprehending this daring offender'.

With a peace officer at their head, the troops advanced on the Mate house, which was probably situated in one of the steep, narrow streets of terrace properties that were then crowded between the main Handbridge/Overleigh Road through route and the River Dee. The houses, wrote historian George Ormerod (1785-1873), in his *History of the County Palatine and City of Chester*, were 'almost exclusively inhabited by the lower orders'. The wanted man again refused to come out, and so the soldiers loaded their weapons in readiness to attack the house. It was only when the order was given to

A row of old cottages in Handbridge, typical of the kind of 18th century properties in which Thomas Mate lived with his much-abused wife.

Illustration by permission of CALS.

charge that Mate opted for discretion over his misguided valour and finally surrendered.

He was hauled off to the Northgate, Chester's common gaol since medieval times and an institution whose reputation for cruelty and terror matched that of its newest inmate. By this time, it was in a ruinous and neglected state and nearing the end of its life (it was pulled down in 1808 and replaced by the new City Gaol in City Walls Road, which had been completed the previous year). The terrible conditions inside are well documented.

The main prison occupied apartments above and on each side of the arched gateway; but its most inhuman feature was a range of dungeons, hewn out of the sandstone rock on which the gate and gaol were built, some 30 feet below ground. Here, beneath the Roman foundations of the city wall, was to be found a torture chamber, one of whose most fiendish devices was the so-called 'Little Ease'. A variation on similarly-named 'accommodation' in the Tower of London, this was an alcove 4ft 6ins high by 17ins wide and no more than nine-and-a-half inches deep from the back of the 'cell' to the inside of its solid wooden door. In earlier times, a prisoner would be forced to stand in an agonising crouched position and, by the operation of adjustable draw boards at the top, the height of the recess could be gradually reduced to about three feet. The antithesis of the rack, it was designed to literally crush the resistance of any poor wretch unwilling to co-operate with his interrogators.

Then there was the 'Dead Men's Room', the condemned cell, where prisoners awaiting execution spent their last miserable hours. George Ashdown Audsley, in his book *The Stranger's Handbook to Chester*, published in 1908, described it as 'a dark stinking place in which snakes and other venomous reptiles gambolled at [their] discretion'. Its only means of access was by a trapdoor in the ceiling. These diabolical dungeons, where no light of day entered, perpetually ran with water and the only fresh air to reach them came from pipes that exited through holes set at street level in the outer wall of the gaol.

Knutsford-born prison reformer James Neild (1744-1814) visited Chester several times between 1801-1805, and his report published in *The State of Prisons in England, Scotland and Wales* (1812) indicated that conditions at this 'horrid gaol . . . which so long disgraced this very ancient and respectable city' would have been no better when Thomas Mate entered its grey, forbidding walls. And, although he seems to have had at least one previous spell in Northgate Gaol (all the records tell us is that he was held there on 30 October 1758 'on suspicion of felony'), it would probably not have prepared him for that subterranean hellhole in which he would eventually find himself.

The inquest on the shot law officer, on Saturday 6 December, was a formality. After hearing the circumstances of his arrest and the medical report on the victim's fatal injury, the jury returned a verdict that 'Thomas Mate . . . with malice aforethought did kill and murder John Parry'. He was committed for trial on the Coroner's warrant and returned to the Northgate.

The following day (Sunday) John Parry was buried in the old graveyard of St. Giles, near his home in Boughton. At that time in the care of the Church of St. John the Baptist in the city (whose parish burial register mistakenly names him as James), the cemetery was originally attached to the hospital of St. Giles, built in the early 12th century to accommodate lepers and cripples. The hospital, which gave the area its original medieval name of Spital Boughton, was destroyed in 1643 as part of the 'scorched earth' strategy of the Royalist soldiers defending Chester during that famous Civil War siege. Many of the Royalists killed in the action

The notorious Northgate Gaol, depicted here in another watercolour by Moses Griffiths, was Chester's common gaol since medieval times, until it was finally torn down in 1808.

Image courtesy of the Grosvenor Museum, Chester.

were buried there, as were the ashes of the Protestant martyr George Marsh, who was burned at the stake on nearby Gallows Hill on 24 April 1555. The last burial took place in 1854. Now only an elevated section of the graveyard and a sandstone commemorative plaque remain as reminders of the cemetery's historic past.

Ironically, Parry's killer would forfeit his life for his mindless crime less than 200 yards from the murdered officer's final resting place. Gallows Hill, Cheshire's centuries-old place of execution, is traditionally identified with modern Barrel Well Hill, at the top of which stands the obelisk whose inscription records that George Marsh perished 'near this spot'. The 1789 map by local engraver James Hunter actually places the gallows some 60-70 yards further west, closer to the junction of Boughton and what is now Hoole Lane (identified on the map only as 'the road to Guilden Sutton').

Parry, said the *Courant* (9 December), had been of 'an unexceptionable good Character', while the *Chronicle* (12 December) lamented that he had 'left an almost helpless widow and six children'.

The final resting place of murdered constable John Parry. The old disused graveyard of St. Giles at Boughton also contains the remains of Royalist soldiers killed in the Civil War Seige of Chester.   *Photograph by the author.*

Detail from James Hunter's 1789 map showing the site of the Boughton gallows, Chester's place of execution from time immemorial.

Image by permission of CALS.

Thomas Mate's court appearance, five weeks later, also produced the expected verdict, though, as reported in the *Chronicle* of 16 January 1789, the hearing lasted almost five hours, during which 'every possible investigation of the evidence . . . took place'. He was sentenced to death and, under the terms of the 1751 Murder Act, his body was ordered to be handed over afterwards to local surgeons for dissection.

For the story of the Parry murder we have to rely largely on the diligence of the local press, for there are no surviving records of cases heard in the Crownmote Court for this period. The most comprehensive report of Thomas Mate's trial was carried in that *Chester Chronicle* edition of 16 January. From it we learn that the presiding judge, barrister-at-law Mr Foster Bower Esquire — more correctly styled Recorder — conducted himself 'in a manner that did the highest credit to his humanity as a man, and his ability as a lawyer'. After passing sentence, he said that, while on the one hand it was 'essentially important that peace officers were protected in the exercise of their duty', it was also 'not less important that the rights of private individuals should be protected'. It seems he had some misgivings about the validity of the warrant by which Mate was arrested and imprisoned.

He went on, 'If, unfortunately, an act of homicide should be committed on the person of a constable who may rashly or ignorantly force an entrance into a house, arm'd with an illegal warrant, the offence could amount to no more than manslaughter. But, on the contrary, where the legality of a warrant is admitted, and it is fully proved that the nature of an officer's errand was made known to the person charged, to take the life of a constable under such circumstances is, clearly and unquestionably, murder.'

And, no doubt having in mind Mate's belief that his house was his castle and what he got up to in it was his business, and his alone, Bower pointed out that a man's home 'afforded him security only in civil processes, or actions for debt' but that 'in all criminal charges it ceased to become a sanctuary'.

The Recorder announced that he would be referring the case for the consideration of the 'Twelve Judges', the senior common law judges in Westminster with whom trial judges consulted on particularly problematical matters of law and procedure. There was no formal appeal system at this time and Bower was concerned to see that the correct legal process had been followed. So he granted the condemned man a respite of three weeks while he sought the judges' opinion.

The *Chronicle* reporter, obviously believing that the man in the dock hardly deserved such judicial consideration, wrote, 'During the whole of the . . . solemn trial, we are sorry to say, the prisoner did not shew the smallest emotion of sensibility; but, on the contrary, even at the moment of receiving the dreadful sentence (which Mr Bower prefaced by an address as pathetic as ever was delivered from a bench), he betrayed a heart lost to every sense of feeling, and seemed sunk to a degree of ferocious and savage obduracy, incapable of receiving the least impression.'

It took less than a week for Recorder Bower to sound out the Twelve Judges, despite some severe weather conditions on his journey from London. On Saturday 18 January he wrote to William Hall, 'Clerk of the Peace for the City and County of the City of Chester' (more commonly known as the Town Clerk), in the following terms, 'After being two or three times dug out of the Snow, and being detained upon the Road two days, till the Passages were opened, I reached home last night. I have this Morning waited upon two of the Judges upon whose Opinion I can rely, and they being of [the] Opinion the Conviction of Mate was proper, I shall send no further Respite.'

His letter, retrieved from the Chester Mayoral Files at the County Record Office, instructed Hall to let the 'unhappy Man' know immediately that the Death Warrant was signed and that Mate should 'make the best use of the short time he will be allowed before his Execution'.

Bower commented, 'It was suggested to me that it might be proper to execute him near the place where the fact was committed. If it is thought right, the Sheriffs may execute the Sentence where it is thought best within the City Liberties.' And, as the body was to be released for anatomical research, he told the Corporation's Clerk, 'You will let it be given to any Surgeon who may wish to have a Subject for dissection, and if nobody desires it, you must apply to some Surgeon to dissect it, and let it be exposed at the Gaol, Infirmary or some fit place for the Inspection of such as may be curious enough to see the Spectacle, as is practised at Surgeons' Hall in London.'

In the event, the usual place of execution, on the city side of the river at Boughton — about a mile, as the crow flies, from the Handbridge murder scene - was deemed a suitable enough spot for the hanging. Thomas Mate was executed on Wednesday 4 February 1789, the last man to die for a crime tried by Chester's Crownmote Court. By then he had spent some 60 days in the abomination that was the Northgate Gaol, terminating in that ultimate chamber of horrors, the Dead Men's Room. After being paraded through the streets in the back of a horse-drawn cart, he arrived at Gallows Hill amid the clamour of the usual collection of thrill-seekers and the morbidly-curious.

Chester's two rival newspapers carried almost identical execution reports. 'Seldom have the awful solemnities of public justice exhibited a more shocking instance of an impenitent and unrelenting mind than was shewn in this man,' wrote the *Chronicle*'s gallows-side reporter on 6 February. 'From the moment of his condemnation to that of his dissolution, be betray'd a rooted, fixed and almost savage obduracy; which the most solicitous and arduous endeavours of a reverend divine, and other well-disposed persons, could not possibly shake, or in any degree soften.'

Pulling no punches, the report continued, 'Whilst on the tremendous brink of a dread eternity, and when the soul was about to launch into the presence of an offended God, whose chief attribute is [*sic*] mercy and forgiveness, to hear the inexorable spirit of this poor creature loudly declare, *he would not forgive his prosecutors*, and particularly his *wife* (who, tho' near 70 years old, he charged with infidelity), impress'd the heart of every spectator with a mixture of horror and astonishment. In short, he fell, at the age of 64, a lamentable instance of human depravity, unenlightened by those rays of religion and morality, which fortify against the fear of death and support the soul under every circumstance, however painful, of affliction and adversity.'

There was no explanation as to whether the alleged infidelity was of recent origin, though, given their respective ages, it would seem more likely that it was a longer-standing issue that had festered inside Mate's 'unrepentant and unrelenting mind' and which periodically erupted into violence, no doubt when he'd been drinking.

How the execution was performed was not stated, either; but by this time it seems that the old method, in which the culprit was 'turned off' a ladder propped up against the crossbeam of the scaffold, had fallen out of favour. Under the new method, the convict, having had the rope tightened around his neck, was made to stand at the back of the cart and, at a given signal, the vehicle was swiftly driven off, leaving him twitching obscenely in mid-air until dying from slow strangulation.

There is, however, a more intriguing omission from the various press reports both before and after Mate's final dance of death. For it is a singular fact — and an indication, possibly, of the subservient position of women in society at this time — that neither of the two local papers felt it of sufficient significance to record the Christian name of the murderer's much-abused wife. An absence of any reference in the local parish registers to Thomas Mate, labourer, of Handbridge — a man who was said to have fathered at least 21 children, remember — has left the husband as something of a mystery figure, too. Tracing their family history, therefore, was always going to be a challenge.

However, when closer examination of the registers threw up a Thomas *Meat*, a labourer with a similar propensity for procreation, who was living in Handbridge at the same time, a possible explanation suggested itself. And when this man's first three children turned up in the baptismal records of the church of St. Mary-on-the-Hill, the parish in which Thomas Mate was known to have resided, it looked a fair assumption that they were one and the same person.

In the jumbled-vowel speech of the old Cheshire dialect, in which 'night' came out sounding like 'neat', 'week' like 'wake' and 'out' like 'ite', the hard 'a' was pronounced as if it were an 'e', as in 'dee' and 'leet' for 'day' and 'late'. Hence the name 'Mate', when spoken, could easily have been mistaken for 'Meat' by the parish scribe and registered as such (it was also entered several times as 'Meate'). This was a period in which there was no national system of compulsory education. There was an assortment of schools, some of them offering free, charity-funded learning; but the majority of the poor were illiterate and the degree of literacy among the rest of the population varied widely. And in church documents the same family's name, even their place of residence, was often spelled in several different ways. And Thomas Mate couldn't write his given name, so would have been unable to recognise whether it was being spelled correctly or not.

If this hypothesis is right, his wife was called Ann, the former Ann Moores, who married Thomas 'Meat' at St. Mary's on 17 March 1755. However, while the number of children the couple had may have been as high as 11, it was nowhere near the reputed figure the *Chester Chronicle* quoted when first reporting the shooting of John Parry on 12 December. Referring to Mate's stormy marriage, the *Chronicle* stated at that time, 'What is very extraordinary, the cause of all his quarrels with his wife was *jealousy*; altho' he has had not less than twenty-one children by the woman, whose age exceeds his own.'

Also, if her age was 'near 70' in 1789, as the paper stated in its execution report of 6 February — only the *Chronicle* made that claim also — she would have been in her late 30s in 1755. Which meant it would have been physically impossible for her to have given birth to 21 babies during her remaining child-bearing years. Even allowing for pre-marital offspring, multiple births and stillborns, such a 'production rate' would have been a rare, not to say life-threatening, achievement for any mother, however young she was when she had her first child. It would surely have gained the woman a certain local celebrity/notoriety and her personal history a more prominent place in the Chester papers' running story of alleged adultery, domestic violence and murder that would have caused quite a stir even in those morally-incontinent times.

No, the *Chronicle*'s information has to be considered unreliable. That being so, could this Ann really have been the wife of the murdering Thomas Mate? With no other official sources available to provide a definitive answer to the question we must conclude that, in a case involving evidence as clear-cut as any ever heard in a Chester court, the jury is still out on that one.

*   *   *

IN HIS distinctive white hat, Jonathan Marsden cut quite a figure as he walked, albeit a little unsteadily, through the city centre streets. He'd had a couple of drinks and was feeling pleasantly mellow. It was a few minutes past ten o'clock and he was on his way to another local tavern to share a late night jug or two with one of his pals. When he was accosted by a female stranger he assumed she was a 'woman of the town' soliciting for business. In his 70s, and in a hurry, he had neither the time nor the inclination to dally, so he gave her some small change to get rid of her.

If he thought he had extricated himself from a potentially tricky situation, however, he was about to be confronted by a far worse threat to his body and his purse.

No sooner had the mystery woman disappeared into the darkness, than he was set upon by three men. One of them was armed with a wooden bludgeon and before he knew what was happening the old man was struck by several heavy blows to his head and neck, which left him barely conscious on the ground. When he had fully regained his senses, he discovered all his pockets had been turned inside out and his wallet stolen. It had contained promissory notes and banknotes amounting to £129 (a cash equivalent of well over £9,000 today). His treasured silver snuff-box and several other personal items were also missing.

Marsden, 73, a mining agent working for the Llanfair lead and silver mines in Llanfair Clydogau, then in Cardiganshire (now Ceredigion), was on a brief visit to Chester with one of his sons, staying at the Golden Lion Hotel in Foregate Street. The robbery, on Tuesday 11 October 1825, occurred just around the corner in Frodsham Street. Moments later he was found sprawled in the roadway bleeding badly and groaning loudly by a hatter named Thomas Dakin. Dakin had been standing in the doorway of his shop in Frodsham Street, some 200 yards away, when he heard scuffling and a man's cry of 'Murder!'

With a certain amount of trepidation he went to the spot, close to the Cow Lane canal bridge, from where the sounds had appeared to come, and saw the elderly man stretched out on the ground and a young man apparently trying to help him to his feet. But when another resident arrived at the scene carrying a lantern, Marsden accused the young man of being one of his assailants. The man denied it. After hanging around for a few minutes, however, he began to walk away down Frodsham Street, slowly at first but then he quickened his step until he was running fast in the direction of the city centre. Dakin

A rare photograph of the old Golden Lion Hotel in Foregate Street, Chester, where Jonathan Marsden was staying when he had his violent encounter with the highway robbers.

Image courtesy of Steve Howe at www.chesterwalls.info.

watched him until he was out sight, the young man's sudden flight enough to convince the hatter that he must have been involved in the robbery. It was Dakin, significantly, who also stumbled on the blood-stained bludgeon lying in the shadows nearby. It turned out to be the broken-off leg of a wooden bench, which would prove an important piece of evidence in the ensuing court case. But of the two other men apparently involved in the incident, Dakin had seen nothing.

Earlier that evening, between five and six o'clock, four other visitors to Chester, two men and two women, had left their lodgings in Boughton, also seemingly intent on sampling the city's night-life. They were William Rice and Mary Johnson, who he claimed was his wife, and their new-found friends Abraham Stones and his paramour Maria Robinson. On the way Stones met a man in the street and stopped to talk to him. The two women walked on together, while Rice went ahead on his own.

Their movements over the course of the next few hours are largely unknown. At some time between 7.00pm and 8.00pm, Stones and Johnson met up in the street but, after exchanging a few words, they went their separate ways. About 10pm Johnson and Robinson were together. According to Johnson, Maria Robinson then left her and began following 'a gentleman in a white hat' along Frodsham Street. She went after her and overtook the pair of them, apparently in conversation. She continued on over Cow Lane Bridge, which carries Frodsham Street over what was then the Chester Canal; but, curiosity getting the better of her, she turned back. As she retraced her steps she heard moaning and saw the old man on the ground, with his white hat lying beside him. He was surrounded by three men. The only one she recognised, Johnson would state later, was Stones.

One of the others approached her and, pushing his face into hers, snarled, 'Damn your eyes, what do you want whore? What business have you here?' And he threatened to throw her in the canal to prevent her from 'snitching' on them. When it was suggested that she should swear an oath that she would not tell anyone what she had seen, she readily agreed. She was immediately dragged along the nearby canal towpath, where on her knees she was made to recite: 'So help me God, may I never enter into the kingdom of Heaven if I mention it.'

It was a promise, however, that she would never keep. For on Saturday 1 April 1826, at the Chester Quarter Sessions, Mary Johnson was the key prosecution witness when 20-year-old Abraham Stones went on trial on the capital charge of aggravated highway robbery.

It looked at first as if Johnson, aged 30, Maria Robinson (24) and Rice, a 20-year-old Irish labourer, would also be standing in the dock with him, for the city constables clearly believed they, too, were involved in the crime. The 'police officers' — press reports of Stones's trial show the title was in use long before it became more generally associated with the first properly organised police forces that appeared in England in the middle of the century — had wasted no time in tracking them down. They were arrested the following day at their lodgings in Boughton. Stones, however, had already settled his bill and left.

Cow Lane Bridge, pictured in the 1880s, showing the section of towpath along which the robbers marched Mary Johnson and swore her to an oath of silence. It was also close to here where they are thought to have temporarily hidden some of the items stolen from Jonathan Marsden.   *Image courtesy of Steve Howe at www.chesterwalls.info.*

After being questioned by magistrates the three others were committed to the new City Gaol on suspicion of being accomplices in the assault and robbery. On 26 November, however, magistrate Alderman William Massey, on the advice of the gaol's surgeon, determined that Rice was unfit to stand trial on account of his health and he was released.

Stones was apprehended two weeks after the robbery when he unwisely returned to Chester. He was no doubt curious to discover what had happened to his former companions, particularly Maria Robinson; but his motive may also have been to check the canalside hiding place in which the three robbers had apparently stashed some of the items plundered from Jonathan Marsden. He was recognised and, following a tip-off, he was arrested by the city's police chief George Dawson — or 'Intendant of Police', as the *Chester Chronicle* described him — and was reunited with his fellow suspects in the City Gaol.

For some reason, they missed the next sitting of the Quarter Sessions in January and had been imprisoned for almost six months by the time they appeared at the Easter Sessions. After making their preliminary assessment of the evidence, the Grand Jury decided there was no case to answer against either of the two women and they were discharged — leaving Stones the sole defendant and Mary Johnson, who had volunteered to turn King's Evidence early in her lengthy period of detention, free to testify against him.

His trial was held in the Common Hall of Pleas in Chester's Exchange building. The relevant Order Book preserved in the Chester Corporation archives at the Cheshire Record Office reveals that the case was heard 'at the General Quarter Sessions of the Peace *and Court of Crownmote*' (author's italics), for by 1826 the two courts were held at the same time on three occasions each year. The Quarter Sessions were presided over by the Mayor, Alderman John Fletcher (long-time proprietor of the *Chester Chronicle*), assisted by the Recorder, Richard Tyrwhitt — though he was a judge in his own right he was the 'junior' prosecuting counsel in this case — and six aldermen justices. Mr John Hill, the Attorney General for the Chester Circuit, prosecuted and Stones was represented by Mr Deacon.

The defendant, who pleaded not guilty, was said to be a silk weaver originally from Liverpool, where he was born on 17 November 1805. It also seems likely to have been the place where he sought refuge after the robbery. Prison records described him as being 5ft 6½ins tall, with black hair and a dark complexion. He had two tattoos on his left arm — the letters 'RM' and 'the figures of two pugilists' — and the letters 'MS' and 'WS' and four diamonds on his right arm.

The official indictment charged him with 'feloniously assaulting Jonathan Marsden on the King's Highway in the Parish of St. John, in the city of Chester, on the 11th day of October last' and — 'putting him in bodily fear and danger of his life' — stealing from him a red morocco leather pocket-book containing promissory notes for £105 and £20 and three £1 local notes, plus a silver snuff box, a silver pencil case and a gold seal, to a total value of about £129.

In outlining the facts of the case, Mr Hill revealed that the witnesses Mary Johnson and Maria Robinson had originally been charged with the same offence but that the Grand Jury had thrown out the bills of indictment against them. According to the *Chronicle*'s trial report of 7 April, he told the jurors that the women's characters were 'of such a loose nature as to require the strictest exercise of their judgments', and he cautioned them to believe only those parts of the women's evidence that were supported by the testimony of other witnesses.

Jonathan Marsden told the court he had been walking along Frodsham Street on his way to meet a friend when a young woman approached him. 'Not wishing her company,' he said discreetly, 'I gave her some silver to get rid of her. After proceeding a few steps further the woman stepped suddenly [to] one side, and half-a-minute had not elapsed before three men came up and attacked me.'

'One of them struck him with a club', the *Chronicle* report went on, 'first on the arm and then on the side of the head. The second blow felled and stupefied him.' When he 'came to himself' there were several people standing around him. He said he did not think that he accused any of them of robbing him; nor could he swear that the prisoner at the bar was one of the attackers. 'I had had liquor but I knew what I was about as well as I do now,' he was quoted as saying.

Cross-examined by Mr Deacon, Marsden — who was revealed as the father of 14 children — said that when the woman had accosted him he had 'given her some silver', telling her, 'Be a good girl and go about your business. I don't want to have anything to do with girls of your sort.' In reply to a question from Mr Tyrwhitt, he said the woman had walked with him for between 50 and 100 yards and 'went away a minute or so after I gave her the money'.

Of his injuries, Mr Marsden said the blows he received were 'very heavy ones'; his arm was badly bruised and it was some time before he could raise it beyond shoulder height. The head wound had 'bled profusely', even after he returned to his hotel (the Golden Lion was on the south side of Foregate Street, where the Marks and Spencer store now stands). 'There were marks and scratches all over my face where the depredators had fixed their hands,' Marsden added.

It was just before he suffered the blow to the head that he noticed that there were three men involved in the attack, but he could not make out their faces. It was a moonless night and the only form of street lighting was provided by oil lamps (gas lighting would not arrive in Chester city centre until the end of the decade). The windows of the ten pubs then located in Frodsham Street would also have cast a faint glow from the oil lamps burning inside; but none of these meagre sources of light was obviously close enough to illuminate the crime scene. The robbers had picked their spot well.

From the *Chronicle*'s account, the prosecution's case was that the young man seemingly offering a helping hand to the robbed mining agent was Stones. Thomas Dakin had also been close to him but he, too, said in court that he could not positively identify him — though he was able to say that 'the prisoner at the bar in his dress, complexion and size answers to his general appearance'.

Dakin testified that when he came upon Marsden lying on the ground, he thought he heard the young man who was leaning over him say, 'Get up my friend. Don't lay there in the street.' But Marsden became abusive and, despite his subsequent denial, Dakin maintained that he had accused the man of being one of the robbers. He thought Marsden 'had the appearance of being very much in liquor'. Because the young stranger had waited for five minutes before leaving, Dakin said he thought at first that he must be innocent. It was only after watching his hasty departure that he realised he might be mistaken.

When she took the stand, however, Mary Johnson had no doubts about what she had seen that night. The first of the witnesses the Recorder had declared to be unreliable, she stated that when she returned to the place near the canal bridge where she had seen Maria Robinson talking to the white-hatted gentleman, he was moaning and groaning on the ground with three men standing around him. One of them, she stated unequivocally, was Abraham Stones. It was he, she said, who intervened when one of the other men threatened to 'chuck her in the canal'. She said Stones told the other man, 'Don't touch her. She lodges in the same house as I do.' And it was Stones, she said, who had suggested making her swear an oath not to 'snitch' on them.

Cross-examined by defence counsel, Johnson said she did not see her boyfriend Rice there nor did she know if he had 'anything to do with the stolen property'. She denied that Rice had bribed her to say he was not involved in the hold-up, whereas she said that, while they were in prison together, Stones had offered her money to change her story in order to clear him. He had told her forebodingly that he would 'have his liberty but for me, but if I snitched he should surely hang'. A week before the trial Johnson had been moved from the City Gaol to the adjoining House of Correction, presumably to protect the star witness from any further contact with Stones.

Earlier, the Irish-born drifter told how she and William Rice had been at the lodging house of William Davies and his wife Mary in Boughton since 9 October, the Sunday before the robbery. They had travelled from Frodsham where, she said, she had first met Rice. Though they had only known each other a short time, for the next three nights they shared a bed at the Davieses' house. Johnson said she had told the landlady he was not her husband. Stones and Maria Robinson, neither of whom did she know before, arrived at the house on the 10th and also slept together. They were both married, but not to each other.

After relating the events of 11 October that culminated in her canalside oath of secrecy, Johnson said she was threatened a second time with a ducking in the canal. However, she ran off and made her way back to Boughton, where she later met up with Rice in the Cross Foxes pub. All four companions returned to their lodgings around the same time, about 11 o'clock, and went to bed.

The *Chronicle* (7 April) reported Mary Johnson as saying that the following morning (Wednesday), she saw Stones hand a silver watch, a pencil case and a silver snuff-box to William Davies, who placed them in a box. Stones then went out, but returned moments later in an agitated state, saying he was 'afraid of the constables'. He was particularly concerned about the snuff-box, which was a personal gift to its owner and bore the inscription 'J. Marsden, Llanfair Mines' (possibly made from silver extracted from his company's mines). Davies, a shoemaker by trade, replied, 'There's no danger; but it will be better to take it to Liverpool as it will fetch more money there.'

When Stones was still not pacified, Davies told him, 'You be off out of the way, and I'll put the things by.' Shortly afterwards, said Johnson, Davies went out to the back yard, taking with him the box of stolen articles and a fire-poker; when he returned his hands were 'all mucky'.

After eating his breakfast Stones took the landlord's advice and left the lodging house for good. Not, however, before he was questioned by Maria Robinson about the stolen 'bills' (promissory notes). Johnson said Stones told Robinson they were 'planted [buried] by the waterside'. Whether, in his haste to be away, Stones failed to recover the hidden money orders, and whether they were one of the reasons he returned to the city a fortnight later, was never made clear. Robinson also asked him what he had done with 'the stick'. Stones, said Mary Johnson, replied, 'I have lost the club. I left it behind.'

According to the *Courant* (4 April) Johnson had testified that Stones handed some of the booty — 'a silver box, a pencil case and a chain' — to *Mrs* Davies. And it was she who had put them in the box, which her husband then apparently hid in the back-yard coal house.

Mary Davies herself testified that when the four of them returned to the lodging house on the night of the robbery, they sat around the kitchen fire talking. She overheard one of them mention something about 'planting by the waterside'. The next morning, she said, Stones and William Rice went out together saying they were going to 'wash themselves by the water's side'.

They returned half-and-hour later and offered her a pencil case and a silver snuff-box with the name 'Marsden' on it — presumably some of the items the robbers had 'planted' near the canal. Mrs Davies, who revealed that this had been the first time she and her husband had taken in lodgers, refused to accept it. 'I am afraid you have not come by it honestly', the *Chronicle* had her as saying. She gave it back to Stones, who replied, 'You need not be afraid, for we got it very honestly.' He then gave the box to Rice. Mrs Davies said she did not know whether her husband 'shared any of the plunder'. He was now living in Manchester; in the *Courant* report she explained, 'My husband has left me [for] some time.'

Mrs Davies also revealed the significance of the wooden leg used in the attack on Mr Marsden. It had come from 'an old bench or form' that she had thrown out because it only had one leg. It was placed on the roof of the privy in the back yard. She knew the leg had been on the bench on the Monday; but by Wednesday it was missing. When the bench was brought into the court it was seen that the leg, which Dakin had handed to Officer Dawson the day after the robbery, fitted it perfectly.

When Stones was asked whether he had anything to say in his defence, he replied, 'I have nothing to say other than I am innocent.' He called three character witnesses to speak on his behalf.

Maria Robinson, the other witness described as being unreliable by the Attorney General, said that while they were in gaol together, she heard Mary Johnson say that she was sorry for incriminating Stones and vowed to contradict her original statement to the magistrates when she got to court. The *Chronicle*, 'Witness heard Johnson say she had taken a false oath and could not sleep night nor day for thinking about it.' Robinson also heard Johnson say that Rice had urged her to 'lay all the blame upon the prisoner' so that he (Rice) would be freed.

Originally from Pontefract, the diminutive Robinson — her prison file recorded her as being just 4ft 10½ins tall — also claimed that Rice had told Johnson that she would be acquitted at the Quarter Sessions and that, in the meantime, he would 'supply her with plenty of money'. Later, said Robinson, she heard Johnson say that if she had known Rice would not send her any money, 'the bloody rogue should not have escaped any more than the prisoner'.

Cross-examined by Mr Hill, she denied being with, or seeing, a man in a white hat on the night of 11 October. She declared, 'I do not know anything about the robbery, nor did I partake of any of the plunder.'

Two other prisoners who had been in the City Gaol with Johnson also swore that they had heard the same conversation.

At this juncture Stones shouted from the dock that Johnson was 'a vile wretch and would do anything to hang him' and that she had been 'in two gaols before'. Recalled, Mary Johnson stated, 'I never was in gaol before in my life. Between God and me, I never said what these witnesses have sworn. What I have said [today] is the same . . . as what I told the magistrates.' She did admit, however, that she had been 'ill-used by Rice' and that 'by his treatment of her she became ill'.

The jury consulted together for a few minutes only before giving their 'guilty' verdict. This was the decade in which the so-called 'Bloody Code', the harsh statutory catch-all that since the middle of the 18th century had accumulated no fewer than 220 capital offences, was beginning to be dismantled; the process would continue into the 1830s so that by the end of that decade the death penalty was effectively reserved for murder. But in 1826 anyone convicted of highway robbery was still liable to be executed, especially if it involved violence.

Two days later, at the end of the Sessions, Stones was returned to court to hear the Recorder pronounce the death sentence. His Honour Mr Tyrwhitt told him, 'You have been indicted for highway robbery, attended with circumstances of great aggravation . . . the evidence upon which you have been convicted entirely shuts out all hopes of mercy being extended to you in this world. You have shown so little value for the life of a fellow creature, as to attempt to deprive him of it, for the accomplishment of your object of plunder. With a club, with which you had armed yourself, you attacked your victim in a part that was most likely to be fatal, and repeated those attacks with the most determined malignity and unrelenting cruelty.'

'Here,' wrote the *Chronicle*'s court reporter, 'the prisoner wept aloud and betrayed strong feelings of agitation.' At the conclusion of the Recorder's address, the paper added, 'Stones fell down in a state of entire insensibility, in which condition he remained for ten minutes or a quarter-of-an-hour, being with difficulty held by several of the officers around him'.

There would be no speedy end to his agony, either, for, as with Thomas Mate before him, a legal complication delayed the execution.

Traditionally, death warrants were addressed formally to the *Sheriffs* of Chester (the City Assembly had had the right to appoint two such officers each year since the early 13th century); but, following the recent death of William Bevin, there was at that time only one sheriff in post. The latter, William Grace, and Recorder Tyrwhitt were both uncertain as to whether it would be correct in law for an execution to be conducted in the presence of a single sheriff. While the Mayor and Aldermen made haste to arrange an election to find a successor, Grace set off on Thursday 20 April by mail coach for London and a meeting with the Home Secretary (Robert Peel) to obtain a definitive ruling in case the election was contested and dragged on for several days.

He returned on the Saturday with a respite for Stones and the answer that it would be in order for only one sheriff to be present at the execution (the *Macclesfield Courier* of 29 April wondered what all the fuss was about, claiming that numerous executions had taken place at Chester attended by only one sheriff). In any event the Assembly election had been held the previous day and Mr Simeon Leet, a chemist and druggist with business premises in Foregate Street, had been nominated for office unopposed. Sheriff Leet was sworn in on Tuesday 25 April, which meant his first civic duty was officiating at Abraham Stones's hanging the following day. As the *Chester Courant* reflected on 2 May, 'The most unpleasant part of the sheriffs' duties was the very first official act of the new Sheriff.'

It took place at the 'new' City Gaol. Erected on the site now occupied by the Chester Girls' Grammar School, this purpose-built prison and house of correction was the successor to the crumbling old Northgate Gaol and had opened in 1807. For a time afterwards it was still occasionally referred to in the local press as 'the Northgate Gaol'; but it had little else in common with its pestilential predecessor. It had one important feature that did hark back to the bad old days, however: its gallows. For, with the ancient site at Boughton finally abandoned, the new gaol was now the official place of execution for both Chester and the whole of Cheshire, thus maintaining the city's unique role in the history of capital punishment. All hangings would be carried out there (not at the County Gaol at the Castle, as some writers have asserted) up until 1866, two years before the Act of Parliament that ended forever the degrading spectacle of public execution.

In 1826, though, there were still plenty of people who enjoyed a good hanging; to them such events were part human drama, part carnival and visitors from all over the county swelled the large number of locals ever keen to witness a fellow creature's ignominious death swinging from the end of a rope. Possibly with this macabre 'customer demand' in mind, the gallows had been resited at the west end of the gaol, on the railed balcony atop the porticoed front entrance, where it would remain, perched almost at roof level, for the remainder of its working life. It was more accessible than at its previous location, a temporary platform over the entrance to the adjoining House of Correction; and the move also meant there was more space for the spectators who turned up in their thousands on these occasions, while the city wall, which ran past the front of the gaol a short distance away, afforded a convenient viewing area.

Detail from what may be the only surviving print depicting Chester's City Gaol and the adjoining House of Correction. It was the place of execution for the city and the county of Cheshire for 60 years and where, in 1826, Mary Johnson, the star witness in the Stones trial, was segregated to prevent her from being intimidated.

Image by permission of CALS.

And there was the added attraction of a double hanging to whet the appetites of the crowd — 'an immense concourse', according to the *Courant's* execution report of 2 May — which assembled below the scaffold on Wednesday 26 April. For as well as Stones, Phillip McGowan, another convicted highway robber who had attacked a fellow traveller on the old Buxton road at Disley and stole from him a silver watch and other articles, was also for the 'drop' after being convicted at the recent Spring Assizes.

The pair were to be 'launched into eternity', as the popular newspaper cliché went, by the raffish Samuel Burrows. This sometime butcher, rat-catcher and confirmed alcoholic was Chester's longest-serving common hangman, though his occasional alcohol-fuelled antics provoked disgust among his City Corporation paymasters and the more sensitive souls in the community (see *Cheshire's Execution Files*).

On the morning of his execution, reported the *Courant*, Stones had sought permission to be allowed one last visit from Maria Robinson, 'the wretched woman with whom he cohabited'. But, said the paper, the prison chaplain, Rev. William Clarke, 'very properly refused'. Only prison officials and clergymen were normally permitted to see condemned prisoners immediately prior to execution so as not to interrupt the religious preliminaries and personal devotions they were expected to attend to in preparation for their impending demise.

Stones was brought from his cell shortly after noon and on his way to the fatal platform, had to be supported by the Chaplain and the Gaoler. At 12.30pm he mounted the scaffold where, with remarkable composure, he stood with the noose around his neck and addressed the crowd below. He admitted he had taken part in the robbery of Mr Marsden but 'denied that his was the hand that struck the blow which nearly deprived him of his life or that he had participated in the booty'. And, added the *Courant*, 'he freely forgave the woman upon whose evidence he was convicted'.

For once Burrows had turned up that day completely sober, though his preparations were not entirely faultless. When, at 12.40pm, the drop fell, the two men 'struggled violently, Stones in particular, and several minutes elapsed before the convulsive struggles were over', the *Courant* noted. 'There was a general opinion among those present that the ropes were too short to admit a sufficient fall to break the neck effectualy [*sic*] . . . [and] owing probably to Stones having turned round to address those behind him, the loop of the noose got from under his ear to the nape of the neck, which no doubt protracted his sufferings.'

This silhouette portrait is the only known likeness of notorious Chester hangman Samuel Burrows.

Image by permission of CALS.

The *Courant* made no reference, however, to the claim made in the *Chronicle*'s execution report, published four days earlier (28 April), that during his speech on the gallows Stones had named William Rice as the man who 'beat Mr Marsden with a club'. And rather than 'freely forgiving' Mary Johnson, Stones, said the *Chronicle*, had insisted that her evidence 'should not have been taken, as she was a bad character and (as we understood) was likewise concerned in the depredation'.

Keen to put a new slant on the story, the *Courant* dug into the condemned man's background and on 2 May was able to report, 'Stones bore but a very indifferent [i.e. very bad] character previous to the commission of the crime for which he suffered; and his cruelty to his wife [note: no name again] is said to have been of the most savage description. On one occasion, while she was far advanced in pregnancy, he rolled her out of bed and leaped upon her body, in consequence of which the child was stillborn and she herself nearly killed.'

Not unexpectedly, after this, she left her abusive husband; she subsequently went to live with a man named Thomas Robinson, whose own wife, it turned out, was the same Maria Robinson who had by then taken up with Abraham Stones. And, as the *Courant* put it, Stones was 'living in this state of double adultery' when he committed the highway robbery.

Robinson was among the 'immense concourse of spectators' at Stones's execution and, said the *Courant*, she 'walked wildly about, crying and wringing her hands'.

The *Macclesfield Courier* had also delved into Stones's past and, on 29 April, reported that he had been apprenticed as a silk stocking weaver. The paper then made the extraordinary claim that, following some kind of spiritual experience, he had for the past three years hawked religious tracts around the country for sale.

So if Stones (definitely) and Rice (arguably) were two of the participants in the robbery, who was the third? Was it (possibly) the unidentified man Stones met in the street on the way into Chester city centre in the early evening of 11 October? Or was Jonathan Marsden so badly traumatised by his Frodsham Street ordeal that, in the darkness and confusion, he failed to recognise that the third shadowy figure was that of a woman — a returning Maria Robinson, maybe, or, as the *Chronicle* believed, Rice's mistress Mary Johnson?

Whoever it was escaped the hands of the law, for nobody else was ever brought to trial charged with the crime . . . leaving Abraham Stones with the dubious celebrity of being not only the last person to be hanged on the orders of Chester Quarter Sessions but of any city court.

CHAPTER FIVE

Sailing Into Perilous Waters

During 16 years' service aboard various Royal Navy warships and other armed vessels, seaman Peter Martin risked his life many times 'for King and country'. Between 1779-1781, with Britain embroiled in the American War of Independence, he saw extensive action in the Caribbean, including such places as Hispaniola, Puerto Rico, Guadeloupe and the coast of Cuba. Most memorably, though, he was present at the 'Glorious First of June', the first and largest sea battle of the French Revolutionary Wars.

Martin was among the crew of HMS *Royal Sovereign* on that celebrated day in 1794, when the British Channel Fleet, under the command of Admiral Lord Howe, inflicted serious damage on the fleet of the First French Republic. The epic battle, which came a year after France had declared war on Britain, took place in the North Atlantic, some 400 nautical miles west of the French island of Ushant.

HMS *Royal Sovereign*, the ship on which Peter Martin served during the 'Glorious First of June' battle.

From the author's collection.

Afterwards both countries claimed victory: France because Admiral Howe had failed to achieve his main objective, which was to prevent a convoy of grain ships from America reaching starvation-threatened France. And Britain because six French ships of the line were captured and another was sunk (Howe lost none), and the thus depleted French fleet was in a much weaker position to forestall British blockading campaigns later in the war.

The 'Glorious First' was generally considered as a *tactical* triumph for the Royal Navy, demonstrating the bravery of its sailors and confirming the supremacy of British sea power. The press here reflected the mood of patriotism that swept the country; and, like his comrades-in-arms, Peter Martin returned home to a hero's welcome.

He no doubt considered himself lucky to have survived; nearly 300 British sailors died in the battle, 14 of them his shipmates on the *Royal Sovereign*, one of three First Rate, 100-gun ships of the line in the British fleet. Yet less than four years later, having moved into the comparatively calmer waters of the mercantile marine, he was to throw away his life over a minor skirmish with . . . the Royal Navy.

This particular 'engagement' took place in the rather less exotic location of the River Mersey estuary on Monday 7 May 1798. Two days earlier, Martin's latest berth, a 212-ton, three-masted square-rigger called the *Henry* (Samuel Every, Master), was anchored close to the Wirral shore when she was approached by a cutter from *HMS Actaeon*, a 'retired' man-o'-war on permanent station in the mouth of the estuary. In 1795 the *Actaeon*, a Roebuck Class two-decker former fighting vessel of 887 tons, had been re-commissioned and re-classified as an 'Unrated Receiving Ship' and assigned to harbour duties at the fast-developing port of Liverpool. These included accommodating newly-recruited sailors before they were posted to their ships and also men forced into naval service by the dreaded press gangs. She was operating under an impressment warrant when the cutter's boarding party swooped on the *Henry* during the night of Saturday 5 May.

Two crew members, by the names of Smith and Kirby, were consequently taken off the merchant vessel, which was then being made ready to sail on one of her regular trading runs between her home port of Liverpool and

HMS Argo, also a Roebuck Class vessel and identical to the *Actaeon*. The ships were built specifically for service in the American Revolutionary War.

the West Indies. In the Royal Navy's desperate attempts to solve its interminable recruitment problems, especially during times of war, merchant seamen were particularly prized by the press gangs, as they already had seagoing experience and required less training — though any able-bodied man between the ages of 18 and 55 was likely to find himself a target for pressing (also known as 'shanghai-ing' or 'crimping').

According to the naval officer in charge of the *Actaeon*'s impressment operation, Smith had been brought aboard 'without his clothes'; so on the Monday, in order to retrieve them, the single-masted cutter was rowed out again to the *Henry*. It was as it hove to alongside the merchantman that the shooting began.

Believing more of their shipmates were about to be seized, some of the *Henry*'s crew decided that this time they would resist the unwelcome visitors. Among them was William Kirby, one of the two men recently snatched by the *Actaeon*, who had in the meantime been released as being unfit for the Royal Navy and returned to his ship. He and the others armed themselves with pistols and a number of shots were fired at the cutter. Most prominent in this ragged insurrection was Peter Martin who at one point, it was claimed, was seen leaning over the *Henry*'s quarter-deck rail with a pistol in each hand, both of which he discharged at the unarmed sailors below. In the mêlée that followed, one of them, boatswain's mate Edward Murphy, was shot and wounded.

The cutter wisely backed off and returned to the *Actaeon*, where orders were given for another boat — with a fully armed crew — to carry out a more determined raid on the *Henry*. Martin and the four other accused were eventually captured as they attempted to make their escape in a jolly-boat. They were taken on board the *Actaeon*, put in irons and secured in the hold. As the *Henry* lay closer to the Cheshire side of the Mersey than the Lancashire side — the traditional boundary between the two counties was down the middle of the river — they were later ferried ashore at Bebbington, Wirral, and transported to Chester Castle Gaol to await trial. Which is how a case with strong Liverpool connections came to be heard in a Cheshire court.

On Monday 27 August 1798 the five members of the *Henry*'s crew found themselves in a less familiar 'dock' at the county's Summer Assizes, charged under the draconian Black Act: Martin, aged 33, with 'shooting at His Majesty's Ship *Actaeon*' and wounding Murphy, and the others — William Corrigall, William Shuttleworth, John Macay and Kirby — with 'aiding, abetting, helping, comforting, assisting and

An engraving of the Mersey and port of Liverpool from the Wirral shore by S. Davenport (1840). Martin's ship lay half-a-mile from the Cheshire side of the estuary when the press-gang struck.   *Image courtesy of Welland Antique Prints and Maps.*

maintaining the said Peter Martin to do and commit the said felony'. They all pleaded not guilty.

The 1773 Waltham Black Act, of which it has been said that no other single statute passed in the 18th century equalled it in severity, introduced the death penalty for more than 50 new offences. It was actually framed in response to a spate of organised poaching in the Windsor and Waltham areas of the Home Counties, carried out by so-called 'Blacks', gangs of poachers who disguised themselves by blackening their faces. But, as well as toughening up the game laws and turning lesser acts of rural vandalism, like cutting down trees and rick-burning, into felonies, it was further expanded to make it punishable by death to 'wilfully and maliciously shoot at any person in any dwelling-house or other place' — even if that person was uninjured.

The Martin shooting case was one of the most controversial cause célèbres *of the Black Act years, which lasted until 1823, when the legislation was repealed.*

It was heard by His Honour Judge William Grant, in what was his first trial after being appointed Cheshire's new Chief Justice at the beginning of the month. And it is from his trial notes, preserved in Home Office files in the National Archives, that most of the following events are detailed.

Judge Grant recorded that Lieutenant Robert Aichison had explained to the court that on the night of 5 May, acting on the press warrant granted to the *Actaeon*, he was the officer in charge of the original boarding party. They pressed two men, Smith and Kirby. After it was realised that they would have to make a second journey to the *Henry* to fetch Smith's clothes, it was he who gave orders for the cutter to return. The crew members were unarmed, he said.

Judge Grant: full record of the trial.

Kirby, added the lieutenant, had been discharged 'on the Sunday or Monday as being unfit for the service'.

Central to the prosecution's case was the testimony of Warrant Officer John Saunders, a gunner who, Judge Grant's review revealed, led the 10-man crew of the Royal Navy cutter on its second visit to the *Henry*. He estimated that the merchantman 'lay about half-a-mile from the low water mark on the Cheshire shore and about two miles from the Lancashire shore'.

Saunders stated, 'When we got within half a pistol shot [in naval terminology a pistol shot was calculated to be between 25 and 30 yards], the people on board the *Henry* desired us to keep off and, before any answer was given, they fired at the boat. I could not then distinguish who it was that fired. What was fired seemed by the report to be a pistol. I called out and told them not to be alarmed, [that] I was not coming on the impress service. They could not but hear me. They made no answer, but kept on firing and abusing us.

'I saw the prisoner Martin discharge a pistol. It seemed pointed towards our boat. He was supplied with two more pistols, by some person on the quarter-deck. Then, holding one in each hand, and speaking to me he said, "You rogue, I'll shoot you." He then fired the two pistols, one after the other. They were apparently pointed at me. He looked me steadfastly in the face.'

At that point, however, the naval cutter's stern bumped against the side of the merchant ship and, as it started to swing away, one of the pistol rounds tore a hole in the sail and the other struck Able Seaman Murphy in the thigh. There were 'not less than seven or eight pistols fired in all,' Saunders claimed.

Cross-examined, he said he could see the *Henry* crew members clearly as they were leaning over the deck rails and he was stood higher in the cutter than the others. Martin had on a white jacket. Saunders added, 'I took particular notice of Martin's dress and features. I have no doubt that Martin is the man [he saw firing at the cutter]. I saw him two hours afterwards on board the *Actaeon* and likewise when I was examined by the magistrates at Liverpool. I knew him by his dress and complexion.'

Christopher Emmett, 23, from 'Cowen' (possibly Colne) in Lancashire, was also among the *Actaeon*'s boarding party. From the Judge's notes, we read that Emmett said that when the cutter approached the *Henry* 'some people got on the gangway and began firing.' He heard Saunders explaining why they were there and he heard Martin shout two or three times to 'keep off'. The bowman tried to push off from the ship as they were firing, and one shot struck his oar. Other shots went through the sail.

Emmett continued, 'Martin was before the main shrouds [rigging] standing up on something. He bent over the netting [below the quarter-deck rails]. I am certain the prisoner is the person I saw on board. I saw Martin the next day and knew him.' Martin, said Emmett, 'seemed much agitated'.

A third member of the cutter's crew, Able Seaman Benjamin Haselton, 22, from the village of Eggleston in County Durham, said he did not know who fired at the boat but he had seen Martin with a pistol in his hand. He agreed that the prisoner seemed 'greatly alarmed'.

Murphy, a 28-year-old able seaman from Kinsale, County Cork, confirmed that he was shot in the thigh 'with a musquet [*sic*] or pistol ball'. Navy records show that one month after the incident he was 'discharged at Liverpool sick quarters'.

Lieutenant John Brown told the court that, after the shooting, he was detailed to round up a second crew to go aboard the *Henry*; but before they got there they 'fell in with a small boat that was coming away from her'. Lt. Brown's men stopped the boat and took off the eight occupants. They included Martin, Corrigall, Kirby, Shuttleworth and Macay, who were later handed over to the civil authorities. In the boat, too, were several cutlasses and pistols.

Captained by Commander Azaria Uzuld, the *Actaeon* (Daniel Ross, Master), had left for her Mersey posting, on 21 May 1795 after a re-fit at Plymouth Dockyard. Her ship's company of 125 included a crew of 82 and 21 marines. Launched at Rotherhithe in January 1778, she was classified by the Royal Navy as a 'Roebuck' type Fifth Rate ship of 44-guns, one of 22 similar vessels built mostly for service during the American Revolutionary War (1775-1783), though, with five others, she was still on the active list in 1793. With an overall length of 140 feet, she had two complete decks of guns, though whether that was the case in May 1798, is uncertain; for her previous role as a troopship (between 1787-1791) it would have been the usual practice for the lower battery to be removed.

Named after the fabled huntsmen of Greek mythology, who was turned into a stag by the goddess Artemis and killed by his own hounds (legend has it that his fatal mistake was seeing her naked, bathing in a forest pool), the *Actaeon* was originally commissioned for duties in the North Sea and later had two spells of service in the West Indies. She was not, however, one of Britain's illustrious fighting ships of the age of sail; her one real claim to 'battle honours' was taking part in 1779 in the recapture of the island of Gorée. This tiny speck in the Atlantic Ocean, a land-form with a surface area of just 45 acres a little over a mile from the harbour of Dakar, capital of Senegal, was a minor transhipment port in the slave trade. Britain had claimed ownership in 1664, but it was retaken by France three years later. It was occupied by the British again from 1758-1763, but in 1763 it was ceded to France, America's ally in the war with Britain, under the Treaty of Paris, which formally ended the hostilities. The *Actaeon*'s naval service ended in 1802 when she was sold at Liverpool and broken up.

Peter Martin does not appear to have been long aboard the *Henry*, a relatively small ocean-going merchantman some 85 feet long built at Chester in 1784. In fact, from Samuel Every's muster rolls in the Board of Trade archives, it would appear that he had been a crew member for less than two months when he and a handful of his crew-mates decided, rather rashly, to take up arms against the Royal Navy. For he does not appear on the list of seamen on the ship between 20 September 1797 and 17 March 1798; and the next muster roll doesn't begin until 21 May, two weeks after he and the other four alleged rebels had jumped ship. These logs, which were completed by the shipmaster at the end of each voyage, also included details of any events involving individual crew members, such as discharges, deaths, injuries and desertions. The time-gap in this case was the period when the *Henry* was not at sea.

The voyage Martin was forced to miss, beginning on 21 May, seems to have been a particularly eventful one: Every recorded that between then and 25 January 1799, when she returned to Liverpool, the *Henry* had gone to Jamaica, been captured by the French, then re-taken by the British and 'carried' (towed?) into Plymouth harbour; she sailed a second time for Jamaica, lost 14 of her crew to the impress service, had two men wounded and one killed, two more died from unrecorded causes and no fewer than 26 deserted.

There may have been another reason why the name Peter Martin was missing from the muster rolls, however: for it was disclosed later that he had assumed various aliases during his time at sea. It was one of several aspects of his past that would lead to a serious re-evaluation of his character after the initial wave of sympathy.

His Assize Court hearing lasted six hours, at the end of which he was found guilty and sentenced to death. The date for his execution was fixed for Saturday 22 September. The four other members of the *Henry*'s crew were acquitted (one of them, William Corrigall, would in 1799 take over from Samuel Every as the ship's master). Martin called no witnesses to testify to his character (defendants had no inherent right to legal representation in those days); instead he passed the Judge a hand-written sheet of paper — headed 'A List of Engagements I have been in on Board English Ships of War & English armed Vessels' — to speak for him.

As well as the *Royal Sovereign*, the world's largest warship of its day, which went on to become Vice Admiral Lord Collingwood's flagship at the Battle of Trafalgar (21 October 1805), he also mentioned the *Stag*, which seems to have been a British 'privateer' (a merchant ship hired and legally authorised by the Government to attack and plunder any vessel flying the flag of an enemy nation) on which he was involved in various actions in and around the Caribbean in 1780 during the American War. In total he listed 13 different engagements, identifying the ships and the number of guns they carried, the names of their captains and the theatres of war in which they operated.

It was an impressive record, and the *Chester Chronicle* was moved to comment, 'In all such actions he behaved as a gallant sailor and an honest man.' It showed that, like many sailors in the 18th century, he had gone to sea as a boy and that, at the age of about 14, he joined his first ship, an armed sloop by the name of *Rover*. He claimed to have been on board the *Rover*, another possible privateer, when she was in action in 1779 off Hispaniola in the war with America.

Martin also wrote his personal account of the River Mersey incident in a statement he prepared while he was in Chester Castle Gaol, leaving instructions for it to be published by a local printer as his 'dying declaration'.

Quoted in several contemporary newspapers, it read, 'On the 7th day of May 1798, I was on board the ship *Henry* at Liverpool, and in a short time the man-of-war's boat came and we thought they were coming to press some of us, for two nights before they had pressed two men from our ship; so we thought to stand in our own defence. We therefore told them to keep off, but they continued to come towards us. I then fired a pistol right over the boat's masthead, without the least intention of hurting any man. The boat then came alongside of the ship and I fired another pistol into the water, which I am certain did not hurt any man.

'Saunders, the gunner of the *Actaeon*, swore he saw me fire three pistols and that I fired two at him, which I am innocent of; and he swore that he saw a man give me two pistols, which he did not, for no man gave me one, and his mind was to do me some injury, but I would have him to look back into the 109th Psalm.'

[This Psalm of David sets out as an appeal to God to help a poor man whose soul has been damned by wrongful accusations. It begins, 'Hold not thy peace, O God of my praise; for the mouth of the wicked and the mouth of the deceitful are opened against me: they have spoken against me with a lying tongue.' But it also contains some unusually unpleasant curses in its plea for divine vengeance, one of the less graphic being 'When he shall be judged, let him be condemned: and let his prayer become sin'.]

Martin said that he 'freely forgave' Saunders — 'as I hope God will forgive me' — but he alleged that he and Benjamin Haselton had conspired together to 'speak with a lying tongue'. His declaration went on, '[Haselton] swore that he saw another man give me two pistols, which he did not; [but] if he had sworn the truth, he would have contradicted the gunner; so they both swore false against me.' And he bewailed, 'This is the reward they have given me for venturing my life so often for the honour of this country.'

His final words were a personal thank-you to 'the good people of Chester for being so kind to me'. It was a message that would have resonated far beyond the bounds of the city. For Martin's conviction loosed a flood of public support and a far-reaching campaign to save him from the gallows, which attracted the backing of some good people in very high places.

While various newspapers had stated that Martin was born 'near Whitehaven' (then a substantial commercial port specialising in the export of local coal), it was widely reported after his trial that he claimed to be an American citizen, though no other details were forthcoming or have been since. It is a fact, however, that the claim encouraged the

Rufus King, the US Founding Father who tried to save Martin from the gallows.

American Consul in Liverpool and, subsequently, no less a figure than Rufus King (1755-1827) — one of the Founding Fathers of the fledgling United States of America and the then American Minister to Great Britain — to intervene in the fight to obtain Martin a reprieve.

The Consul, James Maury (1746-1840), was the first to take up the cudgels on Martin's behalf. On 8 September, writing 'as a matter of urgency' to the Secretary of State at the Home Department, the Duke of Portland, he noted that the condemned man was 'a citizen of the United States of America'. After a brief resumé of the incident in the Mersey and the resulting trial — at which, he said, it had 'appeared that Martin fired the shot by which the Seaman of the *Actaeon* was wounded' — he wrote, 'Conceiving my Lord [that] there are circumstances which may recommend the Convict to Royal mercy, I intreat your Grace's humane interference, either by recommending him to his Majesty's mercy or granting him a respite until the circumstances of his case can be more fully known.'

Maury, the USA's first ever Consul, who had been appointed to the post in June 1796 by the nation's inaugural President George Washington, pointed out, 'The wounded man is in a fair way of recovering and I can only add that it appears that the crime was not committed by any premeditated malice, but merely from sudden impulse.'

Then, on 10 September, on behalf of his Minister (the equivalent of an Ambassador today), he sent a diplomatically-worded (some might say sycophantic) letter to Lord Portland. It read as follows:

Mr King presents his Compliments to the Duke of Portland; and, actuated by motives of humanity, perhaps influenced by a sense of duty, takes the liberty of soliciting his Grace's kind and immediate interposition [on] behalf of Peter Martin, an American Citizen and Seaman who has been Capitally convicted at the late assizes at Chester and ordered to be executed there on the fifteenth instant [the original date was the 22nd]. The particular nature of his case and the offence for which this unhappy person is doomed to suffer, are truly stated in a letter that Mr Maury, the American Consul at Liverpool, appears to have addressed to the Duke of Portland.

Mr King, far from wishing to extenuate, much less to justify Martin's crime (even had it been committed in the more excusable resistance to an actual attempt of impressing him), only begs leave to submit to his Grace's charitable mercy whether there are not in the situation of this poor man, such alleviating circumstances as would, if properly represented to the King [George III], induce His Majesty to extend towards him the Royal Mercy, either by granting a total pardon, by respiting the sentence, or by mitigating, at least, the punishment of the Delinquent.

Unwilling as he is to urge public or national considerations, Mr King, on this occasion, rests satisfied with appealing to the Duke, in whom power and inclination to do good actions are united, for the benevolent exercise of those moral and compassionate feelings which, sympathising with the miseries, misfortunes and errors of mankind, dispose a severer virtue to look indulgently on human frailty, and to make allowances for the violence of human passions where, in the present instance, the guilt is neither premeditated nor heinously deep, and where too the consequences, tho' injurious indeed, have not proved fatal to the Wounded Sailor, who is pronounced out of all danger.

Under these circumstances, therefore, Mr King permits himself to ask if it be impossible to reconcile the justice and the Laws of the Country with something short of the rigorous penalty of death, when confessedly no life has been lost, and the wrong does not seem to be wholly irreparable?

Members of Parliament on both sides of the Mersey also threw their weight behind the mercy campaign. John Blackburne, Tory MP for Lancashire, endorsing the Americans' top-level intervention, urged the Secretary of State on 11 September, 'There is no time to be lost as the poor Fellow is to be executed next Saturday [he was also a week out], unless a reprieve arrives before that time.' In a second letter later the same day, in which he again called on Lord Portland to give the matter his 'immediate attention', he said of Peter Martin, 'The poor Criminal, before this miserable business, I am told, bore an excellent character.'

The following day the Home Secretary (William Henry Cavendish Cavendish-Bentinck, 3rd Duke of Portland, to give him his full title) received a letter from the Admiralty Office, informing him that the Lords Commissioners of the Board of Admiralty — in whose hands

Martin's life was ultimately expected to rest — would be preparing a report on the incident and had ordered their solicitor to 'state the case of the said Person'. The Minister was told the Commission's findings would be communicated to him as soon as the report was available.

On September 13th Lord Portland (who would become Prime Minister for the second time in 1807) announced that the King had granted Martin a respite of 10 days while Home Office officials studied the opinion of the trial judge and obtained the Admiralty Commissioners' findings. The respite was set to expire on 2 October.

Judge Grant, who was knighted the following year, had prepared his report on the case at the request of Portland, and sent it to the Duke on 12 September. In it he gave a detailed account of the evidence against Martin, which, he said, 'seems to fully establish his guilt'. He repeated Martin's claim to be an American citizen and enclosed the naval service record he had placed before the court. But, having apparently been asked what he thought should be done with the convicted sailor, he declined to offer an opinion, stating, 'How far, upon other considerations, it may be thought proper to relax the rigour of the law, it is not for me to judge.' His Honour's only personal observations about Martin, were that he was 'a good looking man aged about 34' (*sic*) and that he had 'behaved with great decorum during the trial and seemed much affected when sentence was passed'.

Any hopes Martin had that he would cheat the hangman seem to have been dashed, however, on 18 September. In a brief, guarded note sent to the Home Secretary, Mr (later Sir) Evan Nepean, Secretary to the Board of Admiralty, wrote, 'I have it in my command to acquaint you . . . that their Lordships [the Admiralty Board Commissioners], upon a consideration of the case of Peter Martin, cannot see any ground for recommending him . . . as an object deserving His Majesty's Mercy.'

The message was forwarded by Portland's Under-Secretary William Baldwin to Rufus King and to Robert Grosvenor, Viscount Belgrave, the Chester MP who had also interested himself in Martin's plight. Lord Belgrave had said in a personal petition to the Home Office minister that 'from the information I can collect, his case seems so particularly unfortunate'. Two days later he received another communication from Baldwin, which was similarly lacking in detail. Discovered among the Chester Sheriffs' files at the Cheshire Record Office, the letter merely stated that the Admiralty Commissioners' report had been 'very unfavourable'.

Those two devastating words —which were effectively a sentence of death for Peter Martin — were all that was ever officially disclosed to explain the Commissioners' conclusions.

Efforts to rescue the condemned seaman continued, however. On 27 September James Maury, in a third letter to the Home Secretary, called for a further respite while a more detailed report of the Admiralty Commissioners' inquiry was sought. And the same day the Mayor of Liverpool, Thomas Staniforth, a banker and one of the city's most prominent slave traders, also urged a stay of execution in the light of a petition 'intended to be procured from the crew of the *Actaeon*'. He forwarded the petition to Admiralty Secretary Nepean that evening.

Meanwhile, Lord Portland's respite announcement had posed some difficulties for Chester's sheriffs, who had the task of arranging the execution. And on 27 September Town Clerk George Whitley wrote to the Secretary of State saying that, while they had been informed by MP Lord Belgrave that the Commissioners report was unfavourable, the sheriffs had not themselves been notified and until they heard officially from the minister they were not prepared to carry out the execution — 'and time is running out to make the arrangements'. Whitley's letter ended, 'It seems to be the Wish of every Person here that the poor Fellow may be pardoned.'

Three days later Whitley received further correspondence from the Home Office . . . and a stern rebuke from Lord Portland. Under-Secretary Baldwin wrote, 'I am directed by His Grace to inform you that he is highly displeased at their [the sheriffs'] conduct on this occasion, His Majesty's respite being expressly for the Time stated therein; and unless the King signifies his further Pleasure, the sentence passed upon Peter Martin must take the due course of law.'

And take its due course it did. Martin was hanged on Wednesday 3 October 1798 at Boughton 'amidst the sighs and lamentations of the commiserating spectators who,' said the *Chester Chronicle* two days later, 'were grieved to see a man cut off in the prime of life, who had been, and might still have been, an ornament to his country'.

By the following week, however, a resourceful journalist had obtained a closer look at the convicted man's naval records. What he discovered — first revealed in the *Chester Courant* of 9 October — was to take much of the gloss off Martin's image as the 'gallant and honest sailor' . . . and go some way towards explaining why the Admiralty Commissioners, in the face of overwhelming public sympathy, had issued their 'very unfavourable' report.

Lord Portland: no reprieve for Martin . . . and a rebuke for the Chester Sheriffs.

The paper recorded, 'We are sorry to be

obliged to state that, on reference to the books in the Navy-office, it appeared that the . . . unfortunate man had assumed different names and deserted many times from several ships into which he had entered into his Majesty's service, and there is no doubt but that the great interest which was humanely exerted in his favour would have prevailed to have saved his life, had he not forfeited all claims to mercy by his repeated desertions and previous misconduct.' The story was repeated virtually word-for-word by the *Chester Chronicle* three days later.

Martin's most recent alias, which was noted on the court documents, was Joseph Lowther (though that name was not to be found in the *Henry* muster rolls either). Now, it was not unusual for men pressed into the navy to give false names; it made deserters — a major problem for the Royal Navy in the 18th century — more difficult to track down. But there is no evidence that Martin had been coerced into service. On the contrary, his talk of 'venturing his life' for the honour of Great Britain would suggest that he was a volunteer and that he had been proud to serve this country.

Many of his countrymen were not so fortunate. Officially foreigners were exempt from impressment; but Royal Navy warships were always short of men and to ensure Britannia continued to rule the waves the Admiralty was prepared to waive the rules. In fact, the large number of American merchant seamen pressed by the British (some sources put the figure as high as 10,000) was one of the areas of conflict that led to the Anglo-American War of 1812.

The press gangs did not always get their own way, however. Though it was regarded by the Royal Navy as a necessary evil, the impressment service was a crude and ruthless business — tantamount to legalised kidnapping — and the amount of hostility it fomented in ports like Liverpool and Chester meant the gangsmen would inevitably meet with fierce resistance from the townsfolk as well as their intended targets. In Liverpool, if a gang was spotted, the cry would go up 'hawks abroad!' and mobs would gather to help men avoid being snatched by jostling and intimidating the gangsmen. And street riots, often involving hundreds of people, would ensue. Occasionally, the headquarters of a press gang, known as a 'rendezvous', was attacked and set ablaze.

Merchant ship captains also devised ways to try to prevent their most valued crew members from being pressed. Some had special hiding places built into the hulls of their ships, like the priest-holes of old. Merchantmen bound for Liverpool (the gangs were prohibited from intercepting outward bound vessels) would drop anchor briefly to the west of the Wirral peninsula, to allow seamen to row ashore, leaving just enough crew to get the ship into port. The disembarking sailors would then seek temporary refuge in places like 'Highlake' (Hoylake) and Parkgate until their ships were ready to sail again.

Tradition has it that others were landed on the Mersey side of the peninsula at Egremont, Wallasey, and made for a little old stone inn close to the shoreline that became known locally as 'Mother Redcap's'. Built in 1595, it acquired its nickname in the 1770s, when it was taken over by one Polly ('Poll') Jones, who always wore a distinctive red hood or cap. Under her shrewd proprietorship, the inn — whose coastal location was cut off from the rest of Wirral by the treacherous Bidston Moss — became a notorious haunt of smugglers who, it was said, so trusted the buxom Poll that they would happily leave contraband with her for safe-keeping. She would also look after sailors' wages while they were at sea. And any seaman fleeing the press gang was sure of a warm welcome, and a place to hide, at Mother Redcap's, which was reputed to have several secret tunnels. After it closed as an inn, it became a fisherman's cottage; in 1888 it was rebuilt and enlarged in rather more ostentatious style complete with turreted attic and, following periods as a café and a night-club, it lay empty and derelict until its demolition in 1974. In more recent times a private nursing home (retaining the name 'Mother Redcaps') was built on the site between Lincoln Drive and Caithness Drive on Egremont Promenade.

Parkgate was the place to where Chester sailors would also decamp to outfox the press gangs, the Deeside ferry terminal eventually acquiring a reputation as a 'resort for sea-faring men without parallel in the kingdom', according to John R. Hutchinson in his book *The Press Gang Afloat and Ashore* (2004). An attempt was made to establish a press gang rendezvous there in 1804 but, Hutchinson related, 'The seamen fled, no "business" could be done, and the gang were soon withdrawn.'

Chester's rendezvous was located

Two views of 'Mother Redcap's'. Top: an artist's impression of the original old stone-built inn where Cheshire sailors seeking to escape the clutches of the press gangs were given refuge. Below: the much later building that stood on the same site on Egrement Promenade, now also demolished.

Images from the Hidden Myths and Legends *website. With permission.*

at the former Blue Bell Inn in Northgate Street. The building, which dates back to at least 1494, is said to be the city's only surviving example of a genuinely medieval inn. This was where men pressed locally were secured, in a backroom with iron-stanchioned windows and treble-locked doors, before being transported in handcuffs to a Royal Navy receiving ship like the *Actaeon* lying in the Mersey.

In the remarkable story that would elevate sailor and native Cestrian Daniel Jackson to the rank of local folk hero, however, the decisive action was centred on the old common gaol less than 30 yards away in the Northgate. It was the most notable incident in Chester's long-running history of opposition to the Liverpool press gangs, though some of the details have probably gained a little in translation over the years. In 1803 the port of Chester was no longer the scene of the great commercial activity it had once enjoyed (see Chapter One); but it still boasted a substantial shipbuilding industry. Daniel Jackson had served his apprenticeship in the shipyards before going to sea. After a short absence he returned home to visit friends and on Friday 28 December

A painting by an unknown artist of the ancient Blue Bell Inn in Northgate Street which, early in the 19th century, was used as the Chester 'rendezvous', where local men press-ganged into the Royal Navy were held while waiting to be assigned to their ships. *Image courtesy of www.chestertourist.com.*

he had been back in the city for some months. It was a time when the French, under Napoleon Bonaparte, were making preparations to invade England; consequently, in a burst of loyalty and patriotism, thousands of men flocked to the recruiting centres ready to defend their homeland. Following a meeting on 27 July, one of these 'Volunteer Associations' — a kind of 19th century Home Guard — had been formed in Chester; in a few days its effective strength had reached more than 1,200.

Jackson and some of his former workmates in the shipyard, carpenters mostly, were among those who signed on. They and other members of the infantry corps had been on parade in the city that day when the press gang learned of Jackson's sea-going background. In 1900, writing under the pseudonym 'An Old Citizen', an anonymous contributor to *Cheshire Notes & Queries* — a quarterly miscellany of historical topics relating to the county founded in 1886 and published by the *Stockport Advertiser* group of newspapers — described Jackson as being 'of good character, a fine handsome man' and explained that with the press gang about, he had to be kept in hiding. 'He was, however, ferreted out by these vipers.'

Despite his newly-acquired military status, the press gang seized him and attempted to take him to the rendezvous. A fight broke out, as his comrades tried to set him free, but eventually the gangsmen managed to have him locked up in the infamous Northgate Gaol. The move was the signal for further disorder, which eventually developed into a full-scale riot. The *Cheshire Notes & Queries*' article went on,

> *Towards seven at night the ship-carpenters, some volunteers and a few other daring fellows assembled at The Cross [the junction of Chester's four ancient city streets] and, after a short consultation, a company hied to the ship-yard and presently were seen approaching with a heavy mast, shouldered. St. Peter's Church corner was turned and soon the battering ram was laid at a convenient distance from the gaol door. The release of the prisoner was then demanded, and no answer obtained. A second summons and then a third were made with like effect. The Governor, however, from one of the windows, viewed the dense crowd beneath (for by that time half the city was up) as well as the door smasher lying in the street. He then presented a blunderbuss and threatened to fire, which he did once or twice — in the air! This was treated lightly; and soon to the shoulders of the sturdy carpenters was raised the immense mast and they were now waiting for the word from their Captain to run it at the door and so make a way to the inner court. The Governor, by this time, had become disposed to parley and*

soon Daniel was in the street, mounted on the shoulders of four men and carried in triumph before the mast to The Cross.

At least one contemporary source indicated that the gaol door had actually been broken down before the Governor was persuaded to let Jackson go. And according to a report on the rescue mission that appeared in *The Times* newspaper of 17 January 1804, the destruction continued even after he was released. It stated, 'The naval rendezvous house was the next object of attack, the doors and windows of which [were] destroyed. At their approach the press gang retired; but, leaving their colours, the Volunteers tore them from their staff and dragged them in the kennel [gutter].'

To take the heat out of the situation the Mayor, mercer Edmund Bushell, and the city magistrates called on the officer in charge of the press gang to withdraw his men until army reinforcements arrived. At the same time an urgent dispatch was sent to Prince William, the soon-to-become 2nd Duke of Gloucester and Edinburgh, the district's commanding officer who, during a visit to Chester three months earlier, had received the freedom of the city and inspected the Volunteers on the Roodee (the former water meadow in the crook of the River Dee, on which the present racecourse stands, has been the scene of numerous military, civic and social events over the centuries). The following day four companies of the Shropshire Supplementary Militia were marched in from Liverpool which, in terms of affrays and anti-impressment riots, was said to be one of the most violent ports in the country at the time. However, according to the *Courant*, calm had returned to the streets of the city as early as ten o'clock the previous evening.

It was estimated that, at its height, the riot involved a mob of at least 400 men, though it included considerably more than a *few* daring fellows unconnected with the Volunteer Corps. Afterwards it was claimed that the scale of the disorder had been exaggerated by certain elements of the press; however, the local magistrates made no attempt to play down the seriousness of the day's events. In a public notice advertised in the *Chronicle* of 27 January, offering a £50 reward for information leading to the arrest of any of the 'instigators, promoters and actors', they condemned the incident as 'a disgraceful outrage'.

At the subsequent court of inquiry set up to investigate the riot, the Volunteers, as a body, were cleared of blame, much to the delight of both Chester papers, neither of which had carried a single line in its news columns about the unprecedented civil disorder at the time. They both claimed later that they had refrained from running the story until the results of the inquiry were made public. In fact, it wasn't until nearly a month later, on 24 January, that the *Courant* first made mention of it — and then only to rebut what it described as 'a most scandalous and unfounded statement of the disturbance' that had appeared ten days previously in *Cobbett's Weekly Political Register*.

The *Courant* branded the *Register* — founded in 1802 by the radical journalist and campaigner for Parliamentary reform William Cobbett (1763-1835) — as an 'abusive and illiberal publication' and set about demolishing the *Register*'s story almost sentence-by-sentence. The paper refuted the latter's allegations that the Volunteers had marched to the gaol in their 'regimentals' (uniforms) and wearing side-arms; that their commanding officer, an ex-regular soldier by the name of Major Wilmot, had threatened to shoot the first man who attempted to force the gaol door, and that his men had then turned on him and threatened to 'break his sword over his head'.

Understandably, in the face of France's invasion threat and the patriotic fervour it had engendered in England, the *Courant* explained that its only wish was to 'vindicate the general character of the corps', a duty it was 'determined to discharge'. The *Chronicle* of 27 January was also anxious to be seen as standing up for the 'honour of the regiment'. The Royal Chester Volunteers, as the paper was now calling them, 'instead of being treated with that candour and tenderness [*sic*], which ought to be shown to men voluntarily stepping forward in defence of their King and Country, have laboured under considerable prejudices and have been exposed to unwarrantable calumny'.

At the court of inquiry it was claimed that, out of a total strength of more than 1,200 men, only about a dozen Volunteers had been involved in the riot. Of that number three were charged in connection with the 'springing' of Daniel Jackson and only one, Daniel Humphreys, was convicted. Appearing at the Court of King's Bench on 27-28 November 1804, he was said to have been 'at first active in the riot, but he soon repented and took the Lieutenant [in charge of the press gang] under his protection and escorted him to a Magistrate'. Afterwards he visited other magistrates in the city and 'did all he could to stop the mischief he had been at first instrumental in exciting'. It was during his absence that the rioters forced the gaoler into freeing the pressed man Jackson. Humphreys was spared a custodial sentence on the grounds of his 'bad state of health' and walked free after agreeing to be bound over in the sum of £100 to be of good behaviour, with two others standing surety of £50 each.

Finally, one man who *wasn't* there when the riot broke out also found himself in trouble. William Dennis was the Mayor's Porter and also a city constable; he was suspended from both offices when his

Chester Corporation employers discovered he had been 'in a state of extreme intoxication which rendered him incapable in a great degree of discharging his Duty as a Peace Officer' on the night in question. When the rioting began he had been at home sleeping it off. However, in a report of a meeting of the City Assembly on 10 May, in the Corporation archives at the Cheshire Record Office, it was revealed that, when he learned of the disturbance, Dennis, like Daniel Humphreys, 'used his best exertions to suppress it'. He helped detain one of the rioters and 'was also instrumental in protecting the Press Gang from the fury of the Mob, remaining with them for their protection until midnight'.

The Assembly agreed to reinstate him after he had begged forgiveness and promised that he would 'in future conduct himself according to his Duty'.

*   *   *

IF, AT the end, Peter Martin seemed resigned to his fate, fellow seaman John Chapman, sentenced to death for robbery at the county assizes in 1771, had determined he was not going down without a fight. It was evident he was in belligerent mood as soon as he stepped through the gatehouse of Chester Castle Gaol to be led to the cart waiting to carry him to his execution.

After being bundled aboard, he was offered a prayer book by the hangman. He snatched it from him and threw it into the body of sailors who had turned out to accompany him to the gallows. They reacted in similarly aggressive fashion by promptly ripping it to shreds. When a priest climbed into the cart and exhorted him to behave with more decency and to prepare himself for the 'sudden change' that he was about to undergo, he went berserk.

It had been feared that there could be a rescue attempt by his sailor friends, so an unusually large body of constables was on duty that day; and whether enraged by the size of their presence, or emboldened by the show of support from his 'brother shipmates', as he termed them, he attacked the unsuspecting cleric. With his arms already pinioned, he head-butted him in the stomach, spilling him out of the cart. Chapman followed him overboard and, plunging into the midst of the sea-faring fraternity, attempted to disappear into the crowd. But, being hampered by his shackles, he was soon recaptured, bound with a rope and replaced in the cart. He wasn't finished yet, however.

At the place of execution, he verbally abused the poor clergyman and continued to ignore his earnest ministrations; then, to the astonishment of the assembled crowd, as the rope was being secured around his neck, he sank his teeth into one of the hangman's thumbs and all but bit it off. It was only with the help of two bailiffs that the executioner, bloodied but unbowed, was finally able to subdue the crazed convict and send him tumbling to his death from the back of the cart . . .

At least that was how the proceedings were reported in several London-based newspapers, as well as a number of provincial weeklies. Later the extraordinary story of John Chapman's Last Stand was picked up by *The Annual Register*, a yearly record of British and world events first published in 1758 (under the editorship of Edmund Burke, the Irish-born statesman, author, orator, political theorist, philosopher and MP) and still going strong today. It was from this apparent eye-witness account, in an article headed 'Extract of a Letter from Chester, Sept. 7', printed in the *Register*'s 1771 edition, that the above details are taken.

It was not, however, the way the *Chester Courant* saw it. The *Courant*, the only paper circulating in the city until the *Chester Chronicle* hit the streets on 22 May 1775, made only a brief reference to the actual execution in its edition of 10 September. It merely stated that Chapman was 'very penitent' and 'acknowledged the crime for which he suffer'd' — along with the condemned person being 'launched into eternity', such stock expressions were common to most execution reports of the day — and that 'he made no declaration [as to] who he was or where he came from'.

All local newspapers at this time contained a large amount of contributed material, and it was likely that the *Courant* didn't have its own reporter at the hanging and wanted to assure its readers that it had not missed a cracking good story; but in the following week's issue there was a disclaimer, which protested in no uncertain terms that all the other papers had been duped into printing a pack of lies by some mischief-making correspondent.

In the same superior tone it would adopt 33 years later when railing against the *Political Register* (as we saw earlier), it declared disdainfully, 'The paragraph in most of the London papers, concerning John Chapman, who was executed here on Saturday se'nnight [short for sevennight, i.e. a week ago] is entirely false and groundless in every Particular, and calculated by some *Wiseacre* to impose on [deceive] the Public in general.' And the paper added, somewhat harshly, that 'if he does not employ his Talents better, [he] may in all probability come to share the same fate'.

With no other Cheshire newspapers with which to compare the *Courant*'s coverage, however, it's difficult to know which version of the hanging to believe. But the undisputed facts of the case, borne out by the assize court files in the National Archives, are that on Thursday 1 August 1771 John Chapman and his partner-in-crime George McCartney, after attending the final day of Knutsford Races, had taken a high-risk gamble and lifted money and various fashion items off the person of one of the refreshment stall-holders . . . as he slept unawares. And later that night they were alleged to have been up to their sleight-of-hand tricks again when the sleeping landlady of the Knutsford inn at which they had been staying, had her pockets picked and a chest of drawers was broken into and more cash stolen.

At their trial at Chester's Autumn Assizes on Wednesday 21 August, William Woolley, an Altrincham inn-keeper, testified that on Monday 29 July he had taken 'a cartload of ale and spiritous liquors and cyder[*sic*]' to Knutsford in readiness for the start of the three-day race meeting on Knutsford Heath the following day.

There had been horse racing on Higher Knutsford Heath since at least 1679. In the 18th century meetings were usually held around the end of July/beginning of August. During the 19th century, when the course extended southwards across what is now Northwich Road, it became a popular and fashionable event among the county's landed gentry, and a suitably elegant grandstand was added in 1865. The last races were run in 1873 and there is now nothing to be seen of the course, though the road called Ladies Mile was laid out along the line of what had been the straight on the western side of the circuit. And remnants of the iron-work that once graced the front of the grandstand were incorporated into the building (until recently home to the Knutsford Conservative Club and Association) later erected on the site at the junction of Northwich Road and Manchester Road.

The race meetings were not everyone's favourites, however. In 1832 the *Macclesfield Courier* struck a note of disapproval when it reported that 'the number of gamblers, swindlers and pick-pockets at the late Knutsford Races amounted, it is said, to about 1,000'. There were some light-fingered rogues at work at the races in 1771 . . . as William Woolley was about to discover.

Woolley had a booth on the course; it seems to have been a more substantial version of what today would be called a beer tent, and it was his routine during meetings to sleep in it overnight. In his court deposition, made before magistrate Ralph Leycester of Toft, the obviously fashion-conscious Mr Woolley stated, 'On Thursday night, 1st August, when the races were over, about 10 or 11 o'clock, growing drowsy and sleepy, he lay down in his booth to rest, but did not undress.' When he awoke around four o'clock the next morning he realised that the silver-plated buckles had been removed from his shoes,

The popularity of Knutsford Races is captured in this rare aqua-tint published by C. Richards of London in 1815 and entitled *The Adventures of Knutsford Race Course.* The annual meeting was also reported to be a favoured haunt of 'gamblers, swindlers and pick-pockets' . . . and, in 1771, by thieves like John Chapman and George McCartney.   *Illustration by kind permission of Frank Marshall LLP.*

along with the steel buckles that had adorned the cuffs of his knee breeches and a black silk band with a silver-plated buckle attached, which had been around his black beaver fur hat. He admitted he might have been wearing the hat, too; he couldn't remember whether it was 'on his head or nearby' when he dozed off. A French dollar and three shillings in silver were also missing from his breeches pockets.

Woolley's statement went on, 'He went to the next booth to inquire whether any bad company had been seen that night about his booth.' He was informed that two men had been observed coming from his booth shortly before midnight. 'One was a big broad fellow and the other was more slightly built,' he was told, 'and they *each wore sailors' trousers* [author's italics], which were striped.'

Until the middle of the 19th century ordinary seamen in the Royal Navy and the Merchant Navy had no official uniform; but they all wore the distinctive bell-bottomed trousers, which were designed so they could be easily rolled up when swabbing decks or wading ashore from the ship's boat.

In those press articles dismissed by the *Chester Courant* as 'entirely false and groundless', following a reference to the presence at Chapman's execution of a 'vast concourse of sailors', there was the claim that Chapman was 'one of that profession'. Now here, in the official court papers, William Woolley's informant was also pointing to a sea-going connection. If the other newspapers got that right, perhaps there was more to their reports than the *Courant* was prepared to admit.

Woolley also learned that two men had been arrested and were to be brought before local squire Leycester, 71, descendant of one of the oldest gentry families in North Cheshire whose lineage dates back at least as far as the 12th century. He went immediately to Toft Hall, the magistrate's 17th century mansion in Toft Road, Knutsford, where he found Chapman and McCartney being questioned. Before he arrived the men had been searched and items of his stolen property were found on each of them.

The two suspects had been collared early that morning (Friday 2 August) following a second robbery, in which the victim was Martha Hewitt, wife of Thomas Hewitt, brick-maker, ale-seller and landlord of an unnamed public house at Nether Knutsford, close to the racecourse. Late the previous evening Mrs Hewitt, in her 60s, was in the kitchen, where several men, including Chapman and McCartney, had been drinking earlier.

In her deposition, she recalled that around midnight, 'being drowsy', she fell asleep in a chair by the kitchen fire. 'Awaking about daybreak', her statement continued, 'she perceived that one of her pockets, in which she kept her silver, had been picked and that all the silver that she had in it was gone, except for two sixpences. Realising what had happened she hastened to check that the drawer, in which she kept her money and which was locked, was safe. She found that it had been broken open and that all the money that had been inside (amounting to, as she thinketh, about £7) had been taken, save for two sixpences left in one bag and about three or four shillings-worth of copper in another.'

She said that, 'when she fell asleep, several people were drinking in the kitchen; among them was the man calling himself George McCartney and that Chapman was either

Local squire and magistrate Ralph Leycester began his inquiries into the two robberies after suspects John Chapman and George McCartney had been brought to his Toft Hall home (above), where later the same day he also examined the witnesses.

From the author's collection.

in the house at the same time or not far from it'. Her 26-year-old joiner son John Hewitt, who had been roused by a neighbour, deposed that he had gone to his mother's house about 4am and found a crowd in the street outside the pub. A tearful Mrs Hewitt told him what had happened. Knowing that McCartney and Chapman had been 'in and about the house during the time of the Races, he suspected them of having taken the money', which in total amounted to almost £8 (its purchasing power today would be more than £1,200).

John spotted McCartney among the group of neighbours apparently commiserating with Mrs Hewitt, and he instructed his elder brother, Thomas Junior, a 28-year-old flax-dresser, to take him into the house and stand guard over him while he went in search of Chapman. On his way he met local constable William Whittaker, who told him he had just seen Chapman 'at the end of Knutsford Common'. So John and a friend, wheelwright Richard Allen of Lostock Gralam, near Northwich, set off after him and managed to detain him before he could make his getaway. When challenged, Chapman admitted he had stolen money from the public house and Hewitt said to him, 'if you give back the money you have taken, we will do you no harm'. Whereupon Chapman 'directly threw into his [Hewitt's] hat' £5 6s in silver and a silver dollar.

Whittaker deposed that he searched McCartney and found on him a pistol, which was 'loaded and primed', and a knife. He was 'very loth' (loath) to give up the weapons, the constable said. Thomas Hewitt, who was present at the time, confirmed, 'McCartney struggled much before he would be searched, and it was with some difficulty that we managed to do it'. Chapman was also in possession of a loaded pistol, 'primed with some balls', powder and a bullet mould, Whittaker testified.

In the second search at Toft Hall, when the two men's pockets were emptied, McCartney's turned up William Woolley's stolen hatband with its silver-plated buckle and his shoe buckles. And Chapman's contained Woolley's knee buckles. He claimed they were his and — another possible pointer to a maritime past — he said he had brought the pistol, the pistol balls, the powder and the bullet mould with him *'from a ship* [on which] *he had come in from America'*. Also recovered from the two men's pockets were a pair of earrings, some finger rings and other trinkets.

At the Assizes Chapman, thought to have been aged about 40, was convicted of robbing both William Woolley and Martha Hewitt and received the death penalty. McCartney was tried on the former count only. The jury found him guilty and the Judge, Cheshire's Chief Justice

John Morton, ordered him to be transported to the American colonies for seven years.

Approaching mid-day on Saturday 7 September 1771 the condemned man was marched less than a hundred yards from Chester Castle to Gloverstone, a tiny, long-disappeared parish adjoining the east side of the Castle precincts, where, following age-old tradition, he was handed over to the city sheriffs to be carted off to Boughton to be hanged at the place overlooking the River Dee that, after centuries of legalised killing, had come to be known as Gallows Hill. There (if certain press reports are to be believed), with his 'brother shipmates' looking on, the still infuriated Chapman launched a last, futile attempt to save his neck . . . and left one unfortunate hangman with the bite-marks to prove it.

CHAPTER SIX

Memoirs Of A Posthumous Assassin

A bullet fired at close range from a flintlock pistol killed Stockport police constable William Birch . . . 15 years after he was shot. The attempt on his life, in the summer of 1819, came during a particularly turbulent period in the town's history: a period in which strikes, riots and radical rabble-rousers brought chaos and anarchy to the streets there and in other parts of this rapidly expanding textile-manufacturing region. Revolution was in the air as the objectives of mill hands protesting against low wages and high food prices were exploited by political activists agitating for parliamentary reform. Now, to the disquiet of the authorities, an armed assault on a police officer seemed like a disturbing new development in an already combustible situation.

In Stockport, as elsewhere, the maintenance of law and order was in those days in the hands of the local magistrates, whose front-line troops were the town's small body of unpaid constables, reinforced when necessary by the recruitment of special constables and — in major emergencies — mobilisation of the local militia.

Encouraged by a national government fearful of the kind of popular uprising that had led to the violent overthrow of France's *Ancien Régime* a score of years before, they adopted a hard line in clamping down on any signs of public unrest. The determined and dependable William Birch was in the vanguard of the battle to preserve the peace and bring the law-breakers to justice, which made him a much-valued ally to his magisterial masters but a bitter enemy to the more subversive elements in the working-class revolt.

Men like Irishman Jacob M'Ghinness. A disaffected cotton weaver beset by poverty and ill health, he had only lived in the town for about three years. But in that time he had become increasingly embittered by what he saw as the harsh treatment of his fellow operatives by their autocratic bosses; and (though he would later claim that he was not part of the radical reform movement that was gaining ground throughout the country) at strikers' rallies, at public meetings and in private conversations he could be heard urging his fellow workers to rise up and 'assert their rights'. When his calls for the use of force fell on deaf ears, however, the dangerous malcontent decided it was time to take a more drastic form of direct action to draw attention to the workers' plight, while simultaneously aiming a symbolic blow at a repressive ruling class.

His plan: no less than the assassination of a prominent authority figure.

His first-choice target was Stockport solicitor John Lloyd who, behind the rather unassuming title of Magistrates' Clerk, exercised immense power, provoking a corresponding amount of animosity in the process. In the second decade of the 19th century the radical reformers' cause — they were demanding improved parliamentary representation, an annually elected government and the extension of voting rights to all men — found increasing support in Stockport and the other textile towns of north-east Cheshire and south Lancashire, and the lawyer acted as an agent for the Government, hiring spies and sending reports of the militants' activities in Cheshire and neighbouring counties to the Home Office. He was also responsible for swearing-in special constables and calling out the full-time militia and the Stockport Troop of the Cheshire Yeomanry volunteer cavalry, in both of which he was a serving captain.

In the latter role, he rode on horseback at the head of his men on several occasions to break up marches and riots; most notably he and his Stockport Yeomanry (of which William Birch was also a member) were among the 1,500-strong cavalry contingent at what has gone down in history as the 'Peterloo Massacre' of 16 August 1819, in which 12 people were killed and more than 600 were injured when the 15th Hussars, backed up by Lloyd's troop, waded in to disperse the

Powerful: John Lloyd, lawyer, cavalry officer and Government agent, was M'Ghinness's first-choice target.
Image by permission of CALS.

crowd at a mass meeting of reformers in St. Peter's Fields in Manchester. He later described it as 'the glorious day in Manchester'. Also, following the Luddite attacks of 1812, he had been instrumental in securing the conviction of some of the ring-leaders and obtained evidence leading to the arrest of a number of members of 'combinations' (illegal forerunners of the trade unions).

Birch, who seems to have been Lloyd's chief 'enforcer', was second on his hit-list when, in the evening of Friday 23 July 1819 — with murder in his mind and the small pistol he had recently acquired for the purpose in his coat pocket — M'Ghinness left his lodgings in the neighbouring hamlet of Edgeley to walk the mile or so into the centre of Stockport to hunt down his quarry. As fate would have it, John Lloyd was not at his home in the aptly-named Loyalty Place, off

Churchgate; but, when he spotted Birch leaving his own house further up the street, the would-be assassin decided it was too good an opportunity to miss.

Learning that the constable had in his custody the Reverend Joseph Harrison, a dissenting minister and leading radical — who he had just arrested in London on a charge of making a seditious speech at a rally in Stockport the

The spot, close to the steps leading up to the former Rectory, where Constable Birch was shot. On the left: the entrance into what was Loyalty Place and the home of John Lloyd, both now long demolished.

Photograph by the author.

previous month — a mob had descended on the house. Shielded by some of the men who were milling about in the street, M'Ghinness closed in on the 27-year-old constable and fired a single shot into his chest. The crowd scattered in all directions and, by the time the gun smoke cleared, M'Ghinness had also made his escape. He was to remain at liberty for five weeks before being (quite literally) caught napping at a relative's home in his native County Down.

Birch survived the shooting because the pistol ball had struck the edge of his breastbone and been deflected downwards, narrowly missing vital organs. Due to its position, it was considered to be too risky an operation to try to remove it and for some days afterwards there were concerns that his wound might yet prove fatal. Gradually, however, he recovered and, though the bullet remained inside his body, he was able to return to his policing duties. So much so, in fact, that in 1829 he was appointed a Special High Constable and put in command of the Stockport Division, a promotion made possible by the ground-breaking Cheshire Constabulary Act, which authorised the establishment of the first divisional forces of paid police officers in the country, pre-dating the creation of Robert Peel's Metropolitan Police by 18 days. His was the first such appointment under the new legislation.

However, towards the end of 1833 he began to experience severe breathing difficulties and while attending Cheshire's Spring Assizes the following year he was taken ill and forced to return home early from Chester. He died at his Churchgate home on 19 May 1834 at the age of 41. The surgeons who carried out the post mortem reported that the pistol ball had been lying against the lining of his chest and over time had caused serious damage to his left lung, to the point where, for a considerable period, it had ceased to function altogether.

The medical men noted the bullet's location and speculated that, 'had there been twenty more grains of powder in the charge', Birch would probably have died instantly. They were quite certain about the cause of his premature death, however: the pistol ball that was meant to have ended the peace officer's life a decade-and-a-half earlier had finally done its deadly work.

Its discovery came as a surprise to Birch's more cynical opponents, who had refused to accept he had been shot, claiming it was all an invention by the authorities to arouse sympathy for the police and turn the public against the radical movement. Curiously, the section of breastbone containing the bullet is today one of the more unusual exhibits in Stockport Museum.

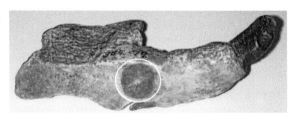

'Exhibit A': the breastbone of the shot police officer with (circled) the fatal pistol ball still lodged in it.

Photo © Stockport Museum. With permission.

It was particularly ironic that Birch's final duty as Special High Constable of Stockport was attending the county assizes in April 1834 where, among several serious cases that had occurred on his patch recently, the calendar included the trial of a Stalybridge stone-mason and trade unionist sentenced to death for attempting to kill a local mill-owner. . . by shooting at him with a pistol (see *Cheshire's Execution Files*).

Although public outbreaks of violence against people and property were a regular occurrence in the area during these tumultuous times, the shooting of Constable Birch caused considerable alarm, bordering on panic, among the upper ranks of society, not only in Stockport and throughout the county but all the way to the highest levels of Government. The *Chester Chronicle* observed on 30 July, 'An indescribable state of uneasiness pervades Stockport and the environs: a letter from a most respectable gentleman in that town, to a friend in this city, says [alluding to the attempted assassination of Birch], "God only knows whose turn may come next; I am fearful the matter will not end here."'

Four days earlier the Home Secretary, Henry Addington, 1st Viscount Sidmouth, had revealed that the police were looking for three men, their names 'at present unknown', in connection with the shooting. And in an advertisement placed in both the national and provincial papers, he announced that His Royal Highness the Prince Regent would grant a pardon to either of the accomplices whose evidence helped convict the person who fired the actual shot, also a reward of £300 for anyone else providing information leading to the apprehension of the gunman and £50 for each of his two alleged accomplices.

The majority of the newspapers, remaining fiercely loyal to both the Government and the Monarchy, were unequivocal in condemning the assassination attempt and the rising tide of lawlessness of which this was the most shocking outcome to date. A leader in that 30 July edition of the *Chester Chronicle*, summed up the press reaction, 'We almost shudder at the execution of a duty we are this week called upon to perform in announcing the [attempted] assassination of Mr William Birch, the active Police Officer of Stockport — the individual who apprehended the incendiary Harrison in London and to whose activity the peaceable inhabitants of this populous county have been several times highly indebted.'

And the writer (presumably the paper's Editor, John Hanshall) added, 'It is high time now to crush at once the vile and infamous associations of Revolutionary anarchists, which pollute this once-flourishing district of the Kingdom. There must be no parleying with them — their object is defined, and the manner by which it is to be accomplished is practically enforced.'

The *Chester Courant*, on 10 August, described it as a crime 'abhorrent to the nature of Englishmen' and, on a more practical level, called upon the public to support a subscription to reward Birch (or his widow, should he not survive) for 'discharging with faithfulness and zeal a public duty of the highest import'. It went on, 'By so doing he stood forward and made himself a marked man . . . if "England expects every man to do his duty", England must be ready to reward and to honour those who discharge perilous duties with zeal and intrepidity.'

Following a petition by 'numerous respectable inhabitants' of Stockport, the *Chester Chronicle* reported that at a public meeting on 18 August, called by the town's three leading magistrates, a subscription was opened by everyone present donating one guinea. It was agreed that up to 200 guineas be awarded to Constable Birch and, should that figure be exceeded, the remainder would go towards setting up a fund for local police officers similarly injured in the line of duty.

A week earlier, in a letter date-lined 'Whitehall, Aug 12, 1819', and sent by the Home Secretary to Stockport's principal magistrate, the Rev. Charles Prescot, Rector of the Parish of St. Mary's, it was announced that the Prince Regent had also agreed to grant Birch an annual pension of £130 for life and that, 'in case [his] wound should (contrary to the hope which may now be reasonably indulged) unhappily prove fatal', the allowance would pass to his wife Sarah for the maintenance of herself and her family. At this time she had produced four children and was pregnant with a fifth.

Lord Sidmouth had good reason to 'indulge the hope' that Birch's wound would not be the death of him (at least for the time being), for the patient was beginning to show signs of recovery. A medical bulletin given on 31 July in one North West newspaper, had expressed the solemn view that Birch was still alive but that 'the result anticipated is far from being favourable'. However, by 10 August the *Chester Courant* was able to inform its readers that 'Birch is rapidly recovering from the effects of his wound', though the pistol ball had not yet been extracted.

The Prince Regent, later King George IV, who granted Birch an annual pension of £130, equivalent to about £9,000 today.

From a lithograph by George Atkinson, printed by C. Hullmandel, 1821.

By then four men had been named as suspects in the assassination bid: James George Bruce, 22, a teacher at the Stockport school run by the Rev. Harrison; William Pearson, also 22, a weaver from Edgeley — both of whom were in custody — and brothers Jacob and James M'Ghinness, who were still at large. Jacob M'Ghinness was eventually arrested on 27 August, two months short of his 25th birthday, near his family home in the picturesque village of Dundrum on the south-east coast of County Down. After being held for a few days in the old Downpatrick Gaol the fugitive was transferred to Dublin and thence taken by boat to Liverpool. He was finally committed to Chester Castle on 8 September. James M'Ghinness seems to have evaded the law entirely.

The three men were due to appear at the county assizes in September but, while Birch was making satisfactory progress, his doctors advised that he was not yet well enough to travel to Chester. When John Lloyd, acting now as attorney for the prosecution, pointed out that, as he was such a crucial witness, the Crown's case could not proceed without him, his application for a postponement was granted.

The trial was re-scheduled for the following Spring sessions, which began on Wednesday 5 April 1820, and which were presided over by

The old Downpatrick Gaol in County Down (now the county museum). M'Ghinness spent a short time there before being taken to Dublin to be shipped back to Cheshire to face trial.

Image by kind permission of Mr Eamonn Andrews.

Cheshire's Chief Justice Charles Warren, sitting with His Honour Samuel Marshall, the county's 'Puisne' or Second Justice. The expectation was that it would not get under way until at least the following Tuesday; so when, on the Saturday morning (8 April), the Clerk of Arraigns called up the prisoners immediately after the Judges had taken their seats, there was only a handful of spectators present. However, as the *Chronicle* reported, 'in the course of the day, as the inquiry became known in the city, the Court was much crowded and excessively thronged at its conclusion'.

At the outset, as well as the absconded James M'Ghinness, there was another noticeable absentee in the dock. For, during his extended stay in Chester Castle Gaol, William Pearson had been persuaded to turn King's Evidence on the understanding that all charges against him would be dropped. He also provided county magistrates with information on the activities of the Stockport radicals and identified some of their more active supporters. Jacob M'Ghinness stood charged with shooting at the police officer with intent to kill and Bruce with aiding and abetting. They both pleaded not guilty (M'Ghinness doing so 'in a loud tone of voice', the *Chronicle* noted). Pearson had also been accused of aiding and abetting and was still a prisoner in the adjoining county gaol when he made his court appearance. His testimony would have a particularly important bearing on the outcome of the trial.

In the introduction to its account of the court proceedings published on 10 April, the London-based *Morning Chronicle* — the newspaper on which, in 1834, Charles Dickens would begin working as a political journalist — sketched word portraits of the two defendants. M'Ghinness (several variants of the name have appeared in print over the years, but this is the spelling he himself attached to the personal memoir he is said to have written while in prison, and which will be set out in more detail later) was described as 'a young and athletic man with hair inclined to be red, of fair complexion, and altogether what is usually termed a smart made man'. His dress, said the paper, was 'decent' and his behaviour 'modest'.

Bruce, on the other hand, was a rather less prepossessing figure, the *Morning Chronicle*'s reporter observing that he was 'hunchbacked and somewhat below the middle size' — *The Times* of 2 August would describe him as being 'about five feet high' — and that 'his silver-rimmed spectacles were a complete contrast to his threadbare grey frock-coat'. He was, however, '[an] intelligent-looking young man' and his general demeanour 'evidently exhibited a consciousness of innocence'. Several London papers were represented on the press benches, testament to the far-reaching interest the case had excited; but, unless stated otherwise, it is the *Chester Chronicle*'s extensive record of the trial, published on 14 April, that is the source of the quoted passages that follow.

In his opening remarks, Attorney General Samuel Yate Benyon told the jury that the crime was 'one of the deepest dye' and that 'had there not been an almost miraculous interposition of Providence', M'Ghinness would now be facing a charge of wilful murder. However, due to its 'foul nature' — it was, he said, 'abhorrent to the proud and noble feelings of Englishmen' — the law, in the guise of Lord Ellenborough's Act of 1803 (see Chapter Four), also deemed it a capital offence to shoot at someone with intent to kill; also that anyone found guilty of aiding and abetting the felony should likewise suffer death.

Outlining the evidence, Mr Benyon (who in 1820 would be appointed Recorder of Chester) recalled that at the Cheshire Quarter Sessions in July 1819 the Rev. Joseph Harrison and the Staffordshire baronet Sir Charles Wolseley, another prominent figure in the radical movement, had been indicted on a charge of sedition. It followed a mass meeting at Sandy Brow, Stockport, in June, at which it was alleged that both men had urged those present — estimates of the attendance ranged from 4,000 to 20,000 — to 'rise up *en masse* to suppress a tyrannical Government'. They were committed for trial at the county assizes and their case was also heard at the Spring sessions (more of which later).

Wolseley was granted bail but Rev. Harrison — better known in Stockport as 'Parson Harrison' — had left the county to attend another radical meeting in London. A bench warrant was issued and William Birch (No. 2 to John Stapeley Barratt, who was also the keeper of Stockport Gaol) and another constable, 31-year-old Nathaniel Pass of Altrincham, were sent by John Lloyd to the capital. Birch arrested the cleric on the platform at the rally in Smithfield. The officers arrived back in Stockport between seven and eight o'clock on the evening of 23 July and Harrison was locked up in a secure room in Birch's house in Churchgate.

Said Mr Benyon, 'It was soon known in the town that Harrison had arrived, and great numbers of people began to assemble in the streets, and particularly opposite to the house of Birch, in a noisy manner.' When it got to ten o'clock, and the mob had not dispersed, Birch, having become increasingly alarmed, left his house with the intention of seeking further advice from chief magistrate Prescot, who lived at the Rectory a short distance away lower down the steeply-inclined Churchgate (John Lloyd was at that moment attending a magistrates' meeting, at the Warren Bulkeley Arms on the corner of Bridge Street and Warren Street, to settle the terms of Harrison's bail).

Birch made his way unmolested through the main body of the jeering, jostling crowd but as he neared the steps at the bottom of the path leading up to the Rectory, he was accosted by a group of three or four men coming in the opposite direction. They were, said the Attorney General, 'undoubtedly in company with each other'. When one of them, who Birch knew as James George Bruce, engaged him in conversation — initially inquiring as to whether he had Rev. Harrison in custody — Birch found himself surrounded and a second man, who he did not know, came forward and, placing a pistol over Bruce's shoulder, opened fire. When M'Ghinness was captured and locked up in Chester Castle, the constable visited the gaol and immediately identified the prisoner as the man who had shot him, said Mr Benyon.

In what was the most eagerly-anticipated moment in the trial, Birch took the stand to give his account of what happened as dusk fell on that summer's evening in Churchgate. The first witness to be called, he told the court that, although it was late, it was still light enough for him to recognise Bruce as the one who stopped him in the street, as he had known him for 'many months' (he had latterly been employed as a 'writing master' at the Sunday School the Rev. Harrison had established in the Windmill Rooms in Edward Street, Stockport, two years earlier).

After confirming that Harrison was under lock and key at his home, said Birch, 'I observed a man turning towards my left hand. Bruce was in front of me; the man came to the left of me and walked to the rear. I kept my eye on him as he was turning round. I had a reason for observing him, for I had left a great crowd and I expected they were going to trip up my heels. When the man was fully behind Bruce, I saw a movement of his hand or arm. He had something in it. I was not more than a minute or a minute-and-a-half with them before I was shot . . . the shot entered right in the centre of my breast.'

The black cloth waistcoat the officer was wearing at the time was then shown to the jury. 'The shot entered about the fifth button from the collar,' the *Chronicle* noted.

Birch said he had no doubt whatsoever that it was M'Ghinness who shot him. When, about six weeks ago, he had been well enough to travel to Chester Castle Gaol to try to identify his assailant, he said, he had seen M'Ghinness with several other men in one of the felons' yards. He insisted, 'I could have picked the man out of a thousand.' He explained, 'For many nights after I was shot, I almost thought I saw him before me, so strong were his features in my memory.'

Cross-examined by Mr David Francis Jones, Recorder of Chester, who was defending M'Ghinness, Birch denied he had originally described the gunman as being 'a low, dark-complexioned man'. The description he had given to John Lloyd, he said, was of a young man of similar height to himself, with high cheekbones and 'sandy whiskers'. In his entry in the Chester Castle Gaol Criminals Book for 1818-1823, preserved at the County Record Office in Chester, M'Ghinness's personal statistics were listed as: 'Age, 25; Height, 5ft 8½ins; Make [*sic*], Stoutish; Visage, Long; Complexion, Fair; Eyes, Grey; Hair, Sandy.'

Birch, being a muscular man apparently possessed of strong bones, was not felled by the pistol ball and, fearing there might be further gunshots aimed his way, he ran for his life into Loyalty Place. After jumping over the back fence of John Lloyd's house, he clambered over a brick wall beyond and fell more than 12 feet into the garden of a house in Millgate occupied by a cotton spinner by the name of Lane. It was only then that the wounded man cried out for help before collapsing to the ground clutching his chest.

During further cross-examination by Mr Jones, Constable Birch agreed that a succession of men had been brought to his bedside to see if he could identify any of them as having been among the group who stopped him in Churchgate. Defence counsel invited him to consider the names of five men; but Birch said that, while they may have been among those arrested on suspicion, he only picked out William Pearson as being 'very near me when I was shot and in company with them [the three other main suspects]'. Bruce had been in custody since he was arrested in the early hours of the day after the assassination attempt.

When he eventually received medical attention, Birch was examined first by the unfortunately-named surgeon 'Mr Killer' — this was John Egerton Killer, who also lived in Millgate — then by another Stockport surgeon, Robert Flint. By that time the patient, at his own request, had been moved to his father's home in Lower Hillgate, where he remained during the early days of his confinement.

Mr Flint, also of Lower Hillgate, told the court he had visited the injured man a little after ten o'clock that night and found him 'labouring under a considerable degree of mental agitation, arising from the apprehension of imminent danger'. He said the wound was on the left side of his breastbone; he was able to trace its path to a depth of two-and-a-half inches but could not locate the bullet.

He added, 'I discovered that the edge of the breastbone was evidently fractured. There was little or no bleeding.' And in answer to a question from Judge Warren, he commented, 'The ball went in a slanting direction, downwards and backwards; and I attributed the reason . . . to the ball having struck the edge of the breastbone, which reflected it (*sic*) in an opposite direction'.

Cross-examined by Mr Jones, the surgeon agreed the wound had produced fever — but, he asserted, it was 'nothing like lightness of head or delirium'. The mind was not at all affected, 'except what arose from mental apprehension'. Despite widespread press reports about Birch's critical condition, the surgeon stated that, on leaving the constable's bedside, he did not consider him to be in 'imminent danger', though the bullet remained inside him.

After Birch, the most anxiously awaited witness was always going to be William Pearson, the alleged accomplice-turned-informer; and an expectant murmur ran around the Shire Hall as he entered the box. The prosecution's other major hope did not fail them, either.

Pearson testified that he had been employed by a Mr Stanley Hamilton in Edgeley (now a suburb of Stockport but then a hamlet in the adjoining parish of Cheadle to the west of the town). He had known Jacob M'Ghinness about a year, ever since the Irishman had also gone to work there. They were both handloom weavers plying their trade in Hamilton's basement workshop. They also lived on the premises and, latterly, had not only shared a room but also a bed. Pearson admitted he had been present when William Birch was shot; he, together with the M'Ghinness brothers, James Bruce and another man, were 'in company together when Birch came up' — though, he said, 'I was more by myself than the others'.

Pearson stated, 'Jacob M'Ghinness fired the pistol. Birch put his hand to his stomach [*sic*] and ran off. Bruce drew a little back and ran off with the two M'Ghinnesses . . . up Churchgate and Birch [ran] down. I soon lost sight of them.' An hour later he returned to his lodgings in Edgeley — they seem to have been in the Castle Street area — to find Jacob M'Ghinness already there; the latter's brother turned up some 20 minutes later. James M'Ghinness, said Pearson, first called his brother out of the house; then they both called him out. They wanted to speak with him, but not there. They took him instead to a place they called 'Gee's Field' because, as Jacob M'Ghinness explained, 'hedges have ears'.

At this time brothers James and Robert Gee were the proprietors of Edgeley Mills, a pair of adjacent cotton mills on a site immediately west of the junction between modern Arnold Street and Hardcastle Road, Edgeley — almost opposite the Stockport County football ground — having inherited the business from their father, Robert Gee Senior, in 1818. They also owned several plots of land in the vicinity, but the most likely location for the clandestine meeting was one of their four large fields that flanked what is now Grenville Street, just north of Castle Street.

Pearson continued, 'Jacob asked me if I knew what had been done in Churchgate. I said, "Am I a witch, that I should know everything that has been done in Churchgate?" He then said, "Birch has been shot, and you saw me do it." He then drew the pistol out and said, "This is the pistol, and anyone who gives information to Mr Lloyd, or any Magistrate, shall have the contents of it." He further said he'd come from [as far away as] North America to do it. I said I knew nothing of the matter, nor did I want to know, from the fear I was in.' Witness said Jacob M'Ghinness returned to Mr Hamilton's that night but did not sleep there again.

During his lengthy spell in the witness box, Pearson said he had not seen M'Ghinness with a pistol in his hand before the shooting, though he claimed to have 'seen the resemblance [outline?] of one in his trowsers pocket'. And, when questioned by Mr Jones, he was adamant that it was Jacob M'Ghinness who shot Birch. 'I saw him fire and saw the smoke from the barrel with my own eyes,' he testified. He denied he had ever said on oath that at the time he was between 100 and 150 yards away from Birch. 'I was about as far away from him as I am from you', he told counsel (which the *Chronicle* adjudged to be about four or five yards).

He admitted he might have said 'something to that purpose' when he was first taken up; but, said Pearson, 'I should have been in danger if I had not said so, for they would as soon have shot me as a sparrow'. He said he had told the magistrates in Stockport that before he would make any statement on oath they must commit him to Chester Castle Gaol. He said, 'I durst [dared] not for they would come and murder me. I was frightened for my life.' He also denied that he had ever been a member of a reform society; and when Mr Jones suggested he had turned King's Evidence in order to avoid prosecution, Pearson replied, 'I don't expect I shall get off by doing so; God forbid I should. I am a weaver. When I was apprehended I was in good employ, and had just enough money to pay my way and keep me decent.'

When he was offered the chance to question the witness, James Bruce also set out to discredit Pearson's motives for giving evidence against him. But, in an extraordinary exchange across the court, he ended up on the receiving end of more damaging testimony and, unwittingly, giving the prosecution's case against his co-defendant a helping hand as well.

Bruce first asked whether he knew anything about him, to which Pearson replied, 'What I know about you is not a bit better than of the other prisoner, for your actions on the ground were every bit as bad, aye as bad as the man that fired.' Possibly thrown by the witness's unexpected counter-attack, Bruce, without thinking, turned and pointed at M'Ghinness and inquired, 'What, as [bad as] his?' Pearson, 'Yes, for you drew up before Birch to cover him, and as Birch sided on the edge of the footpath, you sided in the same way to keep opposite to him and in front of M'Ghinness.'

Without realising what effect his slip of the tongue might have had on the jury, Bruce pressed on, 'Don't you expect a reward for your evidence against me?' Pearson replied, 'No, I do not expect to get a reward.' Bruce asked him whether he knew anything about him before the shooting. And, taking a further swipe at the prisoner, Pearson said, 'I know you once kept a speaking school for the radicals'.

This actually referred to the Rev. Harrison's school in the Windmill Rooms, of which Bruce briefly took charge. The premises were also the headquarters of the Union for the Promotion of Human Happiness, established in October 1818 for the advancement of the radicals' agenda, and of which Harrison was the treasurer and leading activist.

John Ross, a Special Constable for the Barony (former administrative district) of Leckhale in County Down, told the court how, working on information received from Stockport and forwarded to him from Dublin, he tracked Jacob M'Ghinness down during the night of 27 August at his aunt's house in Dundrum.

'He was in bed with another man,' said the law officer, adding bizarrely, 'He was dressed in a woman's cap.' Ross went on, 'I had a candle in my hand when I went to where he slept and, looking at his face, I saw his red whiskers.' When Ross ordered him to get dressed, he said, M'Ghinness remarked, 'I suppose I am the man they are looking for.' The constable took his prisoner to his own house in Dundrum where, he claimed, M'Ghinness told him, 'You'll be well rewarded for this night's work . . . for I am sworn against in England.' Ross said the captive explained that 'a man who had wrought [worked] with him in a cellar in Stockport' had implicated him in the shooting of Constable Birch. He declared he was innocent and that it was 'a man who was arm-in-arm with him' who had fired the pistol.

At the close of the prosecution's case, M'Ghinness was asked if he had anything to say in his defence. Speaking with a strong Irish accent, he replied, 'I have nothing to say to this jury. I will leave it to my counsel.' Bruce, on the other hand, had plenty to say for himself. He stated, 'I did certainly speak to Birch, but with no evil intention. I wished to see [Rev.] Harrison to render him what assistance I could.' While in conversation with the constable, he said, 'the pistol was discharged in the direction of my left cheek.' He went on, 'I am no stranger to the feelings of humanity, and I am sorry that I should be charged with so atrocious an act as this.'

Bruce said he had only been in Stockport three months, after landing a job at Joseph Harrison's school. He was hired initially as a writing master, but when he took up the post, Harrison — an Essex man who, around 1817, had apparently left his job as Minister of an Independent Chapel in Glossop under a cloud — had remarked that he had arrived just at the right time, as he was expecting to be 'fully employed at Chester during the Assizes'.

This seems to have been a reference to his involvement in the defence of three men charged with sedition at a radical rally in Stockport on 1 September 1818, of which he was the chairman. They were expected to appear at the county assizes later the same month, but the trial did not get under way, in fact, until a full year later. So Bruce took over the running of the school whenever Pastor Harrison was absent — a position in which, he said, he had 'acquitted himself with honesty'. He had since purchased the goodwill of another school in Stockport from the book-keeper of local magistrate Mr Peter Marsland for £8, by which he was supporting himself at the time of his arrest.

Bruce insisted he was not acquainted with M'Ghinness, nor had he seen him on the night of the shooting; at which point Pearson shouted across the courtroom, 'What! Never see the prisoner?' The interruption earned him a ticking-off from Judge Warren. Bruce said he saw him for the first time on 9 March 1820 in Chester Castle Gaol; during their time in prison, it later emerged, they had been confined in separate yards. Nor had he known Pearson before they were in prison. And, turning towards the jury, he commented, 'I assure you, Gentlemen, I know no more of Birch being shot than you do.'

Pearson was recalled and, examined by Mr Jones, he said he did not know whether Bruce and M'Ghinness were particularly acquainted, but he had seen them talking together in Rev. Harrison's school-rooms. On the night in question he had seen the two of them, in company with James M'Ghinness, walk out of the Market Place and up Churchgate and 'they were in conversation together all the way to the place [where Birch was shot]'. He followed, between four and eight yards behind. 'I could see them talking together, but could not hear their conversation.'

Foremost among the seven defence witnesses was a woman named Mary McDonald of Stockport. She had also been among the crowd in Churchgate on the night of 23 July. 'The street was very full,' she said. 'We could have walked on their heads.' She claimed that when the pistol was fired she was standing with M'Ghinness 'about a hundred yards from the place where Birch was shot'.

'We were talking about one foolish nonsense or another like other people,' she testified. 'The prisoner was tickling and toying with the girls as they passed him. As soon as the pistol was fired the people began to run. M'Ghinness ran up Churchgate and I saw no more of him that night.' Cross-examined by Attorney General Benyon, Mrs McDonald said she was a widow and a weaver who had known M'Ghinness for two years. She was not a member of a reform society.

Her evidence as to where she and M'Ghinness were when Birch was shot was corroborated by two brothers, Richard and Thomas Morris, also weavers, who had been walking down Churchgate at the time. Richard Morris, from Edgeley, said he knew M'Ghinness well through seeing him 'at Edgeley at the house I worked at', though he only discovered his name a day or two before the shooting. M'Ghinness, he said, 'had a white waistcoat or something white on' and was 'about 100 yards from where the pistol was fired'.

Chief character witness on Bruce's behalf was Joseph Harrison himself — though he almost didn't arrive in court in time. Having failed to answer to his name when called at the start of his defence, he turned up as Judge Warren was about to complete his closing remarks to the jury. Permitted to interrupt the Judge's recapitulation of the evidence, Harrison said of his young assistant, 'So far as I know of him, he is a faithful, honest, industrious man. He was employed by me in my school, and executed his trust with great credit to himself and, further, I believe he is respected by all who know him.'

When the Judge finally asked the members of the jury to consider their verdicts, they didn't even bother to retire. After only a few moments' consultation with his colleagues, the foreman announced they found both men guilty. No sooner had the jury's decision been announced, than M'Ghinness stood up on the bench in the dock and exclaimed loudly, 'My Lord, Bruce knows nothing of this business. He is innocent. I only am the man who shot Birch. I had my reasons for doing so. No one knows anything of the matter but me.'

It was a sentiment he expressed in almost identical terms when the pair were brought back into court for sentencing on the following Monday (10 April), adding, 'I never spoke to him [Bruce] before I came here.' He also alleged that Pearson and Birch had 'sworn falsely' against him. Bruce declared, 'My Lord, I am perfectly innocent of the crime laid to my charge; and am ready and able at any moment to meet my God.'

Addressing M'Ghinness, Judge Warren declared that — 'on the clearest and most satisfactory evidence' — he had been found guilty of a crime that was 'looked upon with detestation and abhorrence' and which was 'contrary to the high and open conduct which is characteristic of the people of Great Britain'. The prisoner had charged prosecution witnesses with perjury; but, said His Honour, 'those who swore falsely were those whom you produced to perjure themselves in swearing you were 100 yards from the place where the pistol was fired and that they were with you . . . in defiance of the confession you have just now made'. The Judge added, 'You do not affect any contrition for this offence, but rather [you] justify it and boast of it.'

He noted the value of the evidence of William Pearson and, most importantly, his account of his conversation with M'Ghinness in Gee's Field. And turning to M'Ghinness, he said, 'You told him you had shot Birch and that [any] man should have the contents of the same pistol who should betray the frightful secret. A more aggravated case than yours was never before a jury.'

He added, 'The Judges of this Court, therefore, feel it is their duty to mark the enormity of your crime, aggravated as it is by threats and perjury. The punishment with which the law visits your crime is death, and the firm determination of the Court is that it be carried into execution on Saturday next.'

Turning to Bruce, Judge Warren was echoing the fears and the vilification which the reform movement had provoked among the Establishment of the day, when he told him, 'You have stated . . . that you possess a moral character . . . you have been represented as the instructor of youth, that you had employment in a school. But it would appear from the evidence that in your school assassination is the leading doctrine inculcated, and that your scholars are educated in principles contrary to the peace of the King's subjects and the well-being of mankind.'

Reciting the dread words of the death sentence, the Chief Justice ordered both men to be hanged, whereupon M'Ghinness called out sarcastically, 'Thank you, My Lord, [that's] a good cure for a pain in the head!' Earlier, when he was not eating oranges — apparently biting into them as if they were apples — he had sat in the dock, wearing a black coat and red silk neckerchief and an expression of 'bold confidence'.

In the case of Bruce, the Judge did not set an execution date, an omission the press interpreted as a sign that the convicted man might get off with a lesser sentence. And, indeed, on 5 May Viscount Sidmouth — who was known for the ruthless and efficient way he cracked down on dissent during his record ten years as Home Secretary (1812-1822) — sent a letter to him at Chester Castle, granting him a pardon on condition that he was 'transported to the coast of New South Wales or some one or other of the Islands adjacent . . . for and during the term of his Natural Life'.

Initially, both men were returned to the Castle Gaol, where M'Ghinness was moved to cell No. 11 (then said to be the condemned cell) to await his execution. And there the one-time regular church-goer, who in adulthood became an fervent believer in atheism, seems to have found his faith again. His amazing conversion he chronicled in his life story, written in prison in between visits from the man who was to bring about his near-miraculous transformation, Thomas Keeling.

Described in the *Chester Courant* (18 April) as 'a pious gentleman' — though not a clergyman — Keeling was M'Ghinness's religious guide and confidant from the day he was condemned up to the moment of his execution and, said the *Courant*, 'had constant access to him in his cell'. To start with M'Ghinness was hostile to his patronage but, as the days went by, he became more and more responsive to Keeling's inspirational words. His gradual change from reformist firebrand to religious zealot he explained in the farewell letter he wrote to a Mary Jones of 5, Union Street, Stockport — who, despite some press suggestions of a more romantic relationship, turned out to be an aunt of his — in which the following passage appeared (spelling as original),

> *After I was sentence to Death I Come out of the Court laughing, Thinking that Both Soul and Body would be soon dead. All that greeved me was to think a innosent Man Should Suffer for my transgreations* [more advocacy on James Bruce's behalf]. *My dear frends I Come into my Sell and in a little after a man come in to me and begun to spake to me about my Soul. I laughed at him. He asked to pray by me, but I told him I wanted no Priest Craft about me. He reasoned very fairly and said he*

was no priest and got me to consent to Neel down. He prayed and pointed out Christ to me, Home [whom] I have oftimes denied, in such a manner that I begun to have a doubt about my own princapals. After he went out of my sell I neeled down at my bed side and asked god for pardon if I was rong and Begged for the truth. My dear frends I said No More for I was Speechless. I fell down on my fase to the ground and if ever Christ was reveailed to Man He was reveailed to Me. I seen the future rewards and punishments. I seen as it were Hell gaping [before] me. And all this time I did not Spake a word. I was sased [seized] in such a Horror to think I had so far been deluded that I lay on the ground for I dar say a Hour in such a state of Madness that it was most Shocking to see tears run down my Hardned Cheek. I sied [sighed] and groned and seen all my Sins before me. So my dear frends rejoice that God has been so kind to me to revail Himself to such a ratch [wretch] at the last hours. My dear frends trifle no longer, look to me, look to yourselves, disblieve no more, pray to God sincarely for the truth, pray for me and think it a blessing that I am gowing to everlasting Hapines.

M'Ghinness ended by sending his love to all his friends, begging forgiveness from 'those I have led astray by my false doctrine'.

The letter was included in what was claimed to be his 'official' life story, which he was said to have completed on the morning of his execution and which he authorised Thomas Keeling to publish after his death. His 11 sheets of foolscap were afterwards transcribed into a 50-page pamphlet, whose 'short' title said it all: *Jacob M'Ghinness; or A Memoir of The Extraordinary Life and Wonderful Conversion of an Infidel, Atheistical Reformer, Written by Himself*. It was edited, mostly for spelling and (lack of) punctuation, by the Reverend John Hollist, Minister of St. James's Church, formerly of George Street, Manchester, and also featured some observations by Keeling.

Though much of it was devoted to his 'Wonderful Conversion', the pamphlet provided the only known detailed account of his early life in Ireland, the circumstances of his arrest and, most revealingly, 'his reasons' for attempting to murder William Birch (to which he had made cryptic reference in his end-of-trial comments to Judge Warren).

Jacob M'Ghinness, his memoir began, was born in County Down on 28 October 1794 of 'poor but honest parents' who, he said, 'gave me the best education their humble station could afford'. At age 13 he was apprenticed in the linen trade. His master, he said, was 'a very religious man' who also instructed him in the teachings of the Bible; he became a good Christian, a Protestant who was 'never known to curse or swear or tell lies as the poor peasants do in general'.

But when he fell in love with the boss's 'beautiful and virtuous' only daughter, a girl about his own age, M'Ghinness was 'forced to go away to prevent her character from being injured'. While working for himself in another part of the country, he 'got acquainted with men of a more gay disposition' (by the early 19th century, as well as its original meaning of 'joyful' or 'carefree', the word 'gay' had also become a euphemism for loose or immoral behaviour by heterosexual males and prostitutes) and he was persuaded to 'broaden his choice of reading'. He put aside his religious books and after reading what he referred to as 'Legerdemain' (full title: *The Whole Art of Legerdemain, or Hocus Pocus in Perfection* by Henry Dean, first published in London in 1722), he became a professional conjurer and fortune-teller

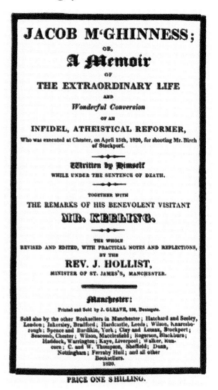

Having decided religion was a 'mere delusion', he moved again and began to mock all things religious, at one point leading a class dedicated to what he described as 'my new trade', spreading a doctrine based on the notion that there was 'no sin in anything' and that 'Man was no more than any other animal'. Among his listeners was a young woman to whom he was attracted; and, though she was 'a full cousin', he set about seducing her.

Facsimile copy of the front cover of the pamphlet in which M'Ghinness gave an account of his 'extraordinary' life story.

M'Ghinness wrote, 'I deluded her by every stratagem, till at last she gave way to my wanton desires.' The girl fell pregnant and, he added matter-of-factly, 'This was the reason I came to England.' He explained, 'Though I loved her dearer than my life, I could not be persuaded to marry her for . . . I had more to go through, yes, more wickedness. My sins were then found out . . . and I was forced to fly, for her friends sought my life.'

Arriving in England some time in 1816, he got a job as a cotton weaver in Stockport and settled in the town, at first living with an uncle (husband of the aunt who in 1820 was living in Union Street, perhaps?). He then lodged with a man who shared his free-thinking principles. 'I endeavoured to make as many converts as I could,' he said. 'All the journeymen that came to my employer's house were made infidels by us.'

Shortly afterwards, when the cotton trade was going through one of its periodic slumps and wages plummeted, he began championing the cause of workers' rights. At private meetings with other similarly disgruntled men, he urged them to embrace the belief that 'all of mankind were equal' and that it was 'beneath the principles of any man to humble himself to such poverty as they were oppressed with'. He said he soon 'began to speak more freely and openly' on such matters. However, as he became more and more hardened, the response from his fellow operatives was too restrained for his liking.

'It grieved me to think that the people were so quiet. I told them that if they did not assert their rights, and quit talking, I should have nothing more to do with them. I told them I was ready to lead them, I was ready to die with them and would freely and willingly sacrifice every interest to be revenged on my oppressors.' But they only came up with excuses, and he ended up reviling them for their cowardice. So he 'swore . . . in my heart to be revenged upon someone'.

His poverty got worse so that, he said, he could 'scarcely furnish myself with daily food'. Then he was struck down with a form of pleurisy, which left him with a pain in his side so severe he was unable to work. He was on the point of committing suicide when, 'meditating on my hard fortune, it came into my head what I must do'. He would pawn his watch and 'with the money I will buy a pistol and shoot one of these villains that oppress the poor'. And for many weeks afterwards, every time he went into the town, he always carried with him the loaded pistol he purchased for 12s.6d. at a hardware shop in Stockport in case he met John Lloyd or William Birch — he did not care which one of them as, he declared, they were 'the worst men I know'.

His moment came on the evening of Friday 23 July 1819. Aware that passions were running high over the impending arrival in Stockport of the radicals' hero William Harrison, M'Ghinness recollected saying to himself, 'This will be the time to raise a stir among the people. Perhaps I can now get them to do something. This night I will break it off [get it started] for them, and they may please themselves whether they do anything or not.'

At his lodgings he charged his pistol and, putting it into his pocket, he vowed 'Lloyd will have the contents of this before two hours'. In Stockport's Market Place he met William Pearson. After having a drink together at the Warren Bulkeley Arms (where John Lloyd's bail meeting with local magistrates was being held in an upstairs room), they retraced their steps and headed for Churchgate 'to see the crowd that was at Mr Birch's house'. He did not tell Pearson what he intended doing.

He continued, 'I saw Bruce and another man going slowly before us. We had almost overtaken them when they met William Birch. Bruce and Birch stopped to speak, and Pearson stopped too. I

The Warren Bulkeley Arms. In the pub, as M'Ghinness plotted to seek out and kill his enemy John Lloyd, unbeknown to him the Stockport lawyer was at a magistrates' meeting in an upstairs room.

Photo by permission of Stockport Local Heritage Library.

said to myself, "Now is the time." I stood behind both Pearson and Bruce. Pearson looked Birch in the face very earnestly and said nothing, which made Birch say to him in my hearing "Do you know who I am?" Pearson said nothing still. Birch added, "I am Birch of Stockport." Pearson walked off then and I stepped up to Birch, pulled my pistol out and said to myself, "I will let you know I am M'Ghinness of Edgeley." So I put the pistol to his breast and shot him.'

When they learned what had happened, his friends advised M'Ghinness to flee the country, and so he made his way to Liverpool where he booked passage on the Newry ferry under the name of 'John Elliot'. Landing at Warrenpoint, County Down, he had to travel another 30 miles overland to reach his father's house near Dundrum, 35 miles south of Belfast. While he was there, though he knew it would be risky, he planned to visit the mother of his illegitimate child, the son he had never seen. However, on the day before he was due to go, his father, who had re-married following the death of M'Ghinness's mother, received word from Stockport that William Pearson had informed on him for shooting Birch.

On the move again, he took refuge in the home of another aunt, a sister of his mother, some 20-odd miles away. Travelling on unfamiliar roads overnight, on foot and in a thunderstorm, he arrived at the remote cottage around breakfast time. When he was finally arrested there by John Ross a few nights later, he was convinced his stepmother had betrayed him — 'for there was none that knew about my being there but my father and she'.

During the winter of 1819, while incarcerated in Chester Castle Gaol,

M'Ghinness made a daring escape attempt. In his memoir, he recalled that, having acquired a rope and a sack, he eluded a routine check by one of the turnkeys and secreted himself in the prison yard privy (he claimed his friends kept him supplied with money while he was inside, so a well-placed bribe or two may have brought on some temporary blindness in certain warders). There had been a recent fall of snow and it was freezing hard when, between two and three o'clock in the morning, he ventured out of his hiding-place.

'I came out of the privy, scarcely able to walk with cold,' he said. Yet, with the aid of the rope and the sack filled with snow to act as a weight, he managed to get on the top of the prison wall. But as he attempted the descent the rope broke and he went crashing to the frozen ground 20 or 30 feet below. Sustaining a badly injured foot, he was forced to abandon his bid for freedom. Prison officials, without apparent irony, said he was lucky he wasn't killed.

Back in his cell, brooding over his misfortune, M'Ghinness reflected on the 'several wicked designs' he had meant to carry out when he escaped. He declared he would have shot Birch again (with more deadly accuracy this time, one assumes) and taken similar revenge on all the other people who he blamed for his current situation, including John Lloyd, his stepmother, Constable Ross and, most of all, the treacherous William Pearson.

All that, of course, was before he met Thomas Keeling. By the time of his execution, after almost daily sessions with his saintly visitor, he was a changed man — to such an extent that, as he wrote in his memoir, 'The sins I had taken a delight in before appeared now of the blackest hue. The people who I had sworn in my heart to injure a few days before, I now forgave, and was ashamed of myself, and found a desire to ask their pardon.'

The *Chester Courant* in its report of the execution on Saturday 15 April referred to the 'striking evidences' of M'Ghinness's conversion and stated, 'We dare not deny to it the genuine marks of a divine interposition.' As a sign of his regained faith the condemned man carried a Bible with him in the cart taking him to Chester City Gaol and his meeting with the hangman and was observed to be reading passages from it throughout the ride, seemingly oblivious to the huge crowd following what the *Courant* described as 'the awful procession'.

The cart was also accompanied from the Castle by a guard of the 71st Regiment and, according to the *Courant*, as a further precaution against a possible attempt to liberate the prisoner, a file of troops was also stationed en route at The Cross at the top of Bridge Street and 'arrangements were made for the immediate assembling of a further military force' if it proved necessary. However, 'there was not the slightest appearance of any disposition among the people to impede the execution of the law', the paper reported.

The night before, M'Ghinness had slept well, so that when Mr Keeling went to his cell at seven o'clock the following morning, he found him 'placid and collected' and finishing off his life story. As he arrived at the gallows, constructed over the entrance to the gaol's adjoining House of Correction, he told his mentor he was 'quite comfortable'. When he reached the platform, still limping slightly from his foot injury, there was every expectation of a final address to the spectators; but he had obviously reserved all his most pious sentiments for his 'Memoir'. Just a curt 'Gentlemen, farewell' and the opening drop slammed the door on the 'Extraordinary Life' of Jacob M'Ghinness.

Previously the *Courant* had printed extracts from an interview with Thomas Keeling. He was asked what, in their discussions together, M'Ghinness had said about a possible radical connection to the attempt on Birch's life. Scotching early rumours that the assassination attempt was part of a conspiracy involving as many as a dozen reformists, M'Ghinness continued to insist that he had acted alone. Mr Keeling revealed, 'He said that he never connected himself with the Radicals [because] he thought too meanly of their spirit; but that he had deeply drank of the essence of disaffection, and was prepared to go [to] any lengths in resistance to Government.'

In its execution coverage the *Chester Chronicle* (21 April) reported Keeling as stating that M'Ghinness had not communicated his intention to shoot Birch to the reformers as he 'dispised them' and 'thought them too contemptible to entrust with the secret'.

M'Ghinness's remains were interred in unconsecrated ground in the Churchyard of St. Mary-on-the-Hill. Chester, adjacent to the Castle, early on Monday 17 April . . . much to the chagrin of Stockport's radicals who, reported the *Manchester Mercury* on 25 April, were expecting the body to be brought there for burial and were 'making great preparations to meet it, in grand procession'. The news was greeted with relief locally. The possibility of another large, and potentially disorderly, demonstration in the town, said the *Mercury*, had excited 'no little alarm . . . in the minds of the peaceable inhabitants'.

The trial of Parson Harrison and Sir Charles Wolseley was held on Monday 10 April, when they were both found guilty of making seditious speeches — designed to 'excite the people of this realm to hatred and contempt for the Government and Constitution' — at a rally at Sandy Brow, Stockport, on 28 June. During this period Sandy Brow became synonymous with the radical reform movement (the site of this popular meeting place was in the area of what became Duke Street, now Piccadilly), and Wolseley, who chaired the meeting, is said to have hoped that the name would become 'more famed in history than the field of Waterloo'. He claimed to have taken part in the storming of the Bastille (14 July 1789) during the French Revolution and said he would be happy to take similar action to put an end to the Government's 'tyranny and corruption'. He was sentenced to 18 months imprisonment. Harrison received the same sentence and, following a separate trial, he was given an extra two years for preaching seditious sermons on two subsequent occasions.

● After serving several months on the prison hulk *Justicia*, moored at Woolwich, James Bruce was finally transferred to the transport ship *Elizabeth* and, along with 171 other convicts, left England on 18 August 1820. The vessel, under the command of William Ostler, arrived at Port Jackson (modern-day Sydney) on 31 December, after being at sea for 135 days. From there Convict No. 4766 disembarked in chains to begin his new life in the Sydney Cove penal colony — just one of an estimated 160,000 British men, women and children exiled to Australia between 1788 and 1867.

● John Lloyd continued to be a thorn in the radicals' side until the summer of 1822, when he became the last person to be appointed to the ancient office of Prothonotary, or Clerk of the Crown, for the counties of Chester (Cheshire) and Flintshire, which included the Chester Palatinate Court of Great Sessions. When the court was abolished in 1830, he became Clerk of Assize for the newly-formed Chester and North Wales Circuit. He resigned the position on health grounds in January 1842 and died aged 73 on 14 November 1844 at his home at The Mount in Spital Boughton, Chester. He is buried in Chester Cathedral, where a memorial tablet records that his son, Edward Watson Lloyd, and grandson, Horatio Lloyd, also held high office in the administration of justice in the county.

CHAPTER SEVEN

A Jilted Suitor's Bloody Revenge

In more than 30 years' experience, John Dunstan had never known anything like it. The Governor of Chester Castle Gaol was all too familiar with inmates trying to break *out* of prison. But here was someone pleading to be let *in*.

One of his turnkeys had alerted him to the wild-eyed stranger who had just arrived at the lodge door in an agitated state to announce that he wanted to 'surrender'. Thinking him to be a debtor responding to a court summons, the Governor took him to his office, where he inquired, 'Is it about a debt?' He was totally unprepared for the answer. 'No,' replied the respectably-dressed young man standing before him, 'it's about a murder. And I did it.'

Then he listened in astonishment as Samuel Thorley blurted out the story of how, after being spurned by his former sweetheart, he had, late the previous evening, made one last attempt at reconciliation. When she again rejected him, in a fit of blind rage he had cut her throat with a razor. It was something of an understatement. In fact, he had almost decapitated the poor woman in his fury.

When he had finished he went slowly through it all again as Dunstan took down his statement. In an age when the speediest means of communication still relied on horse-power (of the four-legged variety), the prison Governor was unaware of so recent a murder in the township of Leftwich in the parish of Davenham, near Northwich. But when he had inquiries made he discovered that, sure enough, such a crime had been committed and that Samuel Thorley, the suspected murderer, had gone missing.

After brooding over his horrific act, Thorley, it appeared, had been so overcome with remorse and self-recrimination that, in the early hours of the following morning, he made up his mind to turn himself in. So he set off to walk the 20 miles to Chester and the county gaol. And when he arrived at the Castle, he begged the Governor to place him in solitary confinement so that he could prepare himself for his inevitable death at the hands of the hangman.

First Dunstan summoned a local magistrate — who, in formally committing Thorley to gaol, finally granted him his wish to be locked up in the Castle — and in the JP's presence Thorley signed the statement in which he had related the full shocking details of the bloody slaying of 21-year-old farmer's daughter Mary Pemberton at her Leftwich home on a cold winter's night in December 1833.

There is now no trace of his sensational confession anywhere in the official records; but from a study of the few surviving court files, and the many column inches devoted to the case in the newspapers, it is evident that for 31-year-old Thorley — gardener, nurseryman and seed merchant — the roots of his destruction took hold the moment he set his cap at the attractive young woman from solid Cheshire farming stock.

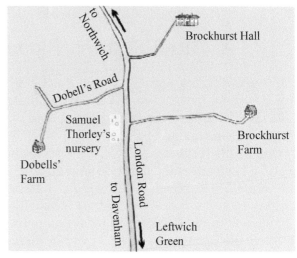

Sketch map of Leftwich in 1833, showing the Pembertons' farm, Samuel Thorley's nursery and the farm of the Dobell family.

The doomed affair seems to have begun towards the end of 1832 or early in 1833. At this time Samuel Thorley was a well-regarded and successful businessman who seems to have employed several workers. Land tax records show that he had the tenancy of a shop and house owned by John Weston in High Street, Northwich — situated between William Pickering's brewhouse and stables and the bank and warehouse of Thomas Firth — and lived on the premises, which backed on to the Market Place. It is likely that he also had a stand at the weekly market. His nursery was situated to the west of London Road, Leftwich, three-quarters-of-a mile away. Its entrance was just across the road from the lane that led to Brockhurst Farm, family home of the Pembertons; so he and Mary would have had plenty of opportunities to strike up an acquaintance. Her father Joseph may well have been one of his customers.

Before long Thorley, more than 10 years older than Mary, was head over heels in love. She responded equally affectionately to the attentions of her tall,

London Road today. The opening on the right once led to Brockhurst Farm. *Photograph by the author.*

152

handsome suitor who could have passed for a man in his mid-20s; and after a courtship lasting the best part of a year, there appeared every likelihood that they would marry. After the murder it was widely reported that Thorley had furnished a house in which he and Mary planned to live after the nuptials, had bought his wedding clothes and was on the point of buying Mary a ring, though the claims were strongly denied by her family.

Around the beginning of November 1833, however, an incident occurred that would bring an end to the relationship . . . and the lives of both partners in this outwardly fine romance.

For the three people sat around the parlour at Brockhurst Farm that Sunday afternoon, it had started out civilly enough, Thorley having been invited to the traditional, rather genteel English ritual of 'taking tea' with Mary and her 59-year-old widowed mother Sarah. But somewhere between the stiffly polite conversation and the home-made pastries, Mrs Pemberton dropped her bombshell. She would dismiss it vaguely at Thorley's trial as 'something I said at that time', and does not appear to have been pressed for an explanation; but a week after the murder a report in the *Chester Chronicle* told of 'secret whispers or anonymous slanders . . . respecting Thorley's circumstances' that had been brought to her attention.

Mrs Pemberton's displeasure had been aroused, apparently, by an anonymous letter she had received — its author was thought to have been a member of her own family — in which Thorley's intentions towards Mary were stated to be less than honourable. On 17 December the *Chester Courant* carried an interview with an unnamed informant, described only as 'a relative of the murdered female', who claimed that Thorley was not as financially sound as he had made out and that his primary motive was 'probably to obtain possession of the young lady's property', meaning the share of the estate willed to her by her recently deceased father. The paper's informant, possibly the same person who wrote the letter, also alleged that Thorley had fathered 'several illegitimate children'.

The *Courant* printed the story in response to the mystery relative's insistence that the account of the murder in the previous week's edition of the paper was 'incorrect in several particulars'. According to the Pemberton family, Thorley had *not* furnished a marital home; nor had he bought wedding clothes or made any preparations for the ceremony.

But the *Courant* countered, 'Whether our statement [about the extent to which the couple's relationship had progressed] be true, may be answered by the fact that the deceased had given him a ring [which she habitually wore] in order to buy a wedding ring of the same size.'

After being lodged in the county gaol, the paper revealed, Thorley gave the ring to one of his brothers along with a written statement in which he accused a relation of Miss Pemberton, who he named, of 'using certain means, which if true, were anything but creditable, to frustrate their marriage, and to this circumstance he traces the lamentable occurrence'. The *Courant*, which declined to disclose the family member's identity, also claimed that, when Thorley turned up at the Castle, he was wearing the clothes he had purchased for the wedding, and that a subsequent check on his account books 'showed clearly that his circumstances were not embarrassed'. No evidence was ever produced to validate the 'illegitimate children' allegation, either.

In any event, the outcome of the tea-time contretemps was that Mrs Pemberton announced that the family was now totally opposed to Thorley marrying her daughter and that he was no longer welcome at the farm, home also to Mrs Pemberton's three grown-up sons.

'In consequence,' the *Chronicle* reported on 13 December, 'his whole conduct and appearance underwent a complete change, which was fully perceptible to all his friends; deep sorrow and a settled gloom took possession of his hitherto cheerful countenance and he appeared as if he had given himself up a prey to despair.' The version of events provided by Mary's 'relation', as reproduced in the *Courant*, was (unsurprisingly) less generous. It stated that Samuel Thorley then 'took to drinking' and that for two or three weeks before the murder he was 'constantly in a state of intoxication'.

On Friday 6 December Mary Pemberton visited Northwich Market and, some time between 6pm and 7pm, she ran into Thorley and, when she told him she was on her way to Cooper's shop — this looks to have been Cooper's confectioners in nearby Apple Market Street — he followed her. He does not appear to have been at his stall in the market that day and, as she came out of the shop, he took hold of her basket and said he would walk her home. Despite the recent storm among the tea-cups, Mary was happy to take his arm as they headed for London Road. He only left her when they caught up with Mary's married sister, 24-year-old Mrs Ann Dobell, and the two women continued on together. As will be revealed later, Thorley had particular reason to shun the wife of farmer Richard Dobell.

Later that evening Samuel Thorley was observed drinking brandy in the Angel Hotel in Northwich's Bull Ring (the grand old coaching inn, built in 1790, was demolished due to structural damage caused by the severe flooding that hit the town in 1920). It was not his usual tipple and it was afterwards surmised that it had been to stiffen his nerve for what he was planning to do.

Around ten o'clock he turned up at Brockhurst Farm, which is shown on 19th century maps to the south-east of Brockhurst Hall (the latter converted in recent years into luxury apartments) on a site that coincides approximately with the junction of modern Langley Road and Whittington Close. During the 1980s, by which time its name had been changed to Danebank Farm, the buildings and much of the surrounding agricultural land were swallowed up by private housing.

The Angel Hotel: The old Northwich coaching inn, where Thorley drank brandy before confronting his former sweetheart, stood on the site, in the town's Bullring, now occupied by the NatWest Bank.

Photo courtesy of Mr Colin Lynch.

Some press accounts suggested that Mary was expecting him: the *Chronicle* of 13 December, for example, reported that 'from nine to ten o'clock she repeatedly went out to the door and, on returning each time, seemed as if disappointed' — though, as only Mary and her mother were in the house at the time, it is hard to fathom how the paper came by that particular item of intelligence. From Mrs Pemberton's understandable reluctance to talk about the murder afterwards, it seems unlikely that she was the source.

At any rate, with her mother upstairs in bed, Mary let her lovelorn former sweetheart into the house. At 10.15pm her brother John, at 32 the eldest of the Pemberton siblings, returned from a night out and Mary opened the back door for him. He noticed a light in the downstairs front parlour — in country homes this was a 'best room' reserved for entertaining guests and other special occasions — and assumed his sister had company and, tactfully, decided he would go straight to his bed at the rear of the house.

At about 11.30pm he was awakened by his mother's screams and he jumped out of bed and dashed down the front stairs into 'the lobby', a passageway that ran the length of the building. There he found his mother, who shared a bedroom with Mary, collapsed on the floor and his sister lying beside her in a pool of blood. It seems Mrs Pemberton had gone downstairs to investigate when she heard the front door being slammed shut, and had fainted after stumbling over the body of her heavily-bleeding daughter in the darkness. John carried his sister into the kitchen and, sitting down with her across his lap, he examined the young woman more closely.

The *Chronicle* stated, 'On looking at her, to his horror he discovered by the faint glimmering light which the few dying embers remaining in the fire emitted, her throat was cut and that to all appearances she was quite dead. Terrified and almost in a state of frenzy, he laid his sister, who was literally bathed in her own blood, on the floor and hastened to carry into another apartment his afflicted mother.'

After contacting his two brothers — Roger, aged 29, and Joseph Junior (27), both of whom also lived at the farm — and his other sister Ann to inform them of the night's terrible events, John had a message delivered to the Witton home of Northwich surgeon William Hunt. In a report Dr Hunt presented to the subsequent inquest, he stated that the wound in Mary's neck was 5ins long by 1½ins deep. It had cut through the windpipe, gullet and the root of her tongue, and the front part of the vertebrae of the neck; the left side of the carotid artery and the jugular vein were also lacerated. The *Chronicle* report added that 'a frothy, bloody fluid issued out of the divided windpipe from [her] lungs in great quantities . . . and an immense quantity of blood was on the lobby floor and on the wall, and the stairs to a considerable extent were covered with it'. It would have come as little comfort to Mary's family to be told that such a devastating injury would have caused instantaneous death.

The murder weapon was found three days later in a bed of carrots at the farm. It was an old-fashioned straight razor with a single round-ended blade, sharply honed on one edge, that folded into the handle. As well as blood, also identifiable on the handle was the roughly-carved inscription 'Thorley'. The only practical way for a man to shave until the turn of the century, this type of razor was traditionally known in Britain as a 'cut throat', because of its inherent risk to a less-than-careful user. As in this case, however, it occasionally lived up to its nickname in an act of more deliberate blood-letting . . .

Having disposed of the razor in the vegetable patch, Thorley returned to Northwich and his High Street home. There he awoke his young shop-assistant, a boy named Peter Banks, who also lived on the premises, and told him what he had done. After asking the lad to fetch him a bowl of water, he washed the blood off his hands and face and removed some of his bloodstained clothes and threw them on the fire to burn. After changing, he went out, returning in about an hour (his absence would be explained at the inquest into Mary Pemberton's death). He lay down on a sofa in front of the fire for some time, then went to bed. At around 4am he got up and, after Banks had made him a cup of tea, he told his young servant he was going to Chester.

Banks, who seems to have been about 14 or 15, volunteered to go to

Northwich High Street circa 1910. Thorley rented a shop here in the early 1830s, close to the town market.

Photo courtesy of Mr Colin Lynch.

Betchton, near Sandbach, where Thorley's much-respected father tenanted a farm, to let him know what had happened; and, as they would be going in the same direction for part of the way, they walked up London Road together. At the entrance gate to his nursery, however, Thorley asked Banks to go across the road to Brockhurst Farm to try to ascertain whether Mary was still alive or not. Banks went, reluctantly; but, finding he was too scared to go all the way to the house, he turned around a short distance down the 300-yard track that led to the farm. When he got back to where he had left his master, Thorley had disappeared.

Undaunted, young Banks, as he had promised, walked the 16 miles to Betchton Farm, close to Cheshire's border with Staffordshire, where lived Samuel Thorley's father, 74-year-old widower John Thorley, with his two other sons — John Junior, aged 45, and Jonathan (36) — and daughters Mary (43) and Hannah (33). The property, since renamed Thurlwood Farm, still stands today on what is the A533 Sandbach Road directly opposite the Betchton and Rode Heath/Thurlwood boundary sign.

Banks returned later that Saturday morning when, said the *Chronicle*, 'the utmost consternation and dismay spread through Northwich and the neighbourhood'; but, locally at least, Thorley's disappearance remained a mystery. The paper went on, 'As Thorley had the key of his premises in his possession, it was conjectured that he had returned to his house and destroyed himself.' So, at around 10.30am several individuals decided to break into his home. In the living quarters they found a black coat and a pair of trousers, both bearing 'numerous spots of blood'. Also, in a drawer, was a cloth bag 'on which it was supposed he must have wiped his hands &c., as it was very bloody'.

By this time Samuel Thorley, after walking for almost six hours, had arrived in Chester. On his way to the Castle he stopped at the Old

Queen's Head in Foregate Street — a 16th century inn at this time called the Old Queen's Head Vaults and which was re-built in 1939 — and ordered a glass of porter (a strong stout), but left before finishing it. He reached the gaol around 10am and went to the prison lodge. The *Chronicle* again, 'He was respectably-dressed and had nothing singular about his appearance besides a little wildness of the eyes.' However, after hearing Thorley's garbled explanation, the gate-keeper, 'incredulous or conceiving him to be mad', sent for the Governor.

When he was safely locked in a prison cell, Thorley quickly lost his wild-eyed look. The *Chronicle* report went on, 'His calmness and composure since his committal is [*sic*] most astonishing.' On the following Wednesday (11 December) he had a meeting at the gaol with 'a professional gentleman' (his solicitor or accountant, presumably) to put his business affairs in order 'with as much coolness as if he was about to go on a journey'. He was. And it was a journey from which he knew there would be no coming back.

The Old Queen's Head Vaults in Foregate Street, Chester. Thorley was in so much of a hurry to hand himself in that he left the pub without finishing his drink. *Image courtesy of Steve Howe at www.chesterwalls.info.*

The paper added, 'He says his mind is now more tranquil than it was before he committed the offence, for he was so greatly moved by the frustration of his hopes that he believes he could not have lived [without her]. He speaks of her in the highest terms, and says she was the most amiable and virtuous of her sex.'

The inquest 'on the body of Mary Pemberton' — as well as the Coroner, jurors at this time also inspected the corpse before deliberating on the cause of death — was held on Monday 9 December at the Bowling Green in London Road, Leftwich. Formerly the Bowling Alley House, the pub, which dates back to at least 1650, is reputedly the longest trading licensed house in Northwich, and is less than half-a-mile from the site of the murder. The hearing was conducted by veteran Cheshire Coroner John Hollins, 79, who filled the office for more than 50 years until his death in 1841. Only four witnesses were heard and their hand-written depositions are all that remain in the Chester Assize case file in the National Archives.

Of most interest to a public desperate for some insight into the cause of this rare and seemingly motiveless murder in their midst was the evidence of teenager Peter Banks. In his deposition Samuel Thorley's 'shop-boy' revealed that on the night of the murder his master had gone out around 8.30, returning between 11 and 12 o'clock. Banks, who had worked for Thorley for about 18 months, was in bed and, as the house door was locked from the inside, he got up to let his master in. He fetched a candle and when he lit it, the boy immediately noticed blood on his employer's right hand and forehead. His shirt collar and neckerchief were also blood-stained.

'The first thing he said to me,' Banks stated, 'was "I have cut her throat. They will be after me directly."' He went on, 'He then washed himself and then took his handkerchief [*sic*] and shirt collar off, being bloody, and threw them upon the fire. He pulled his coat and waistcoat off and then his shirt, which he [also] threw on the fire.'

Drawing a sofa up to the hearth, Thorley lay down for about an hour, then announced he was going out. He came back an hour later. Where had he been? He had returned to the scene of the crime, no less. 'He said he had been at the same place where he had been before [i.e. Brockhurst Farm],' said Banks. 'But he could hear nothing and see nothing but a light. He then went to bed.'

Thorley was obviously trying to establish definitely that he had, in fact, killed Mary — though his decision to give himself up to prison officials in Chester indicated he must have realised that he had. Nevertheless, he made one final attempt to learn the truth before making his way to the county gaol.

Banks deposed, 'He got up at four o'clock in the morning and said he would have a cup of tea, and whilst drinking it he said he would go to Chester, but did not say for what. He presently left the house and asked this witness to go with him up towards the nursery, and he went with him to Pembertons' gate.' Having set off down the drive, he went only part way to the farm before turning back, as he was 'afraid of going to the house'. Thorley had said he would wait for him at the gate to his nursery but when Banks got there he was nowhere to be seen.

After his trip to Betchton, Banks returned to Northwich and the High Street home he shared with his horticulturalist boss and, in the drawer in which Thorley kept his two razors, he found only one. He confirmed to the Coroner that the black razor shown to him was the missing one. He knew it by the name 'Thorley', which he himself had scratched on the handle.

Of Thorley's relationship with Mary Pemberton, Banks said he 'believed a courtship had been going on between the deceased and his master, because she several times drank tea at his house'. However, she had not been there for 'a few weeks'.

John Pemberton recalled how his pleasant evening out ended in unimaginable horror after arriving back at the family farm on that never-to-be-forgotten Friday.

The jury at the inquest at the Bowling Green pub in Leftwich (above), heard Samuel Thorley's shop boy confirm the razor used to kill Mary Pemberton belonged to his master.
Photograph by the author.

He found the back door 'fast' (locked), but his sister responded to his knock and opened the door to let him in. Mary then went through the kitchen and into the parlour, which was faintly illuminated by the light from the dying fire. As she did so Pemberton heard Thorley distinctly say to Mary, 'You know I always told you so', without hazarding a guess as to what it might have meant. As he went upstairs to bed he could hear the couple talking but could not tell what was being said. He did not actually see who was with his sister, but he was confident it was Thorley as, he explained, 'He frequently conversed with him . . . and his voice was a particular one.'

His statement went on, 'In about an hour afterwards his mother awoke him by screaming, on which he hastened downstairs and found the deceased sunk down against the staircase, quite dead. Mary slept with her mother and he believes his mother was awoke by the shutting of the door or some other cause and not finding the deceased come to bed was the reason she got up.' He observed that 'the neck of the deceased was cut and a great quantity of blood was discharged from it, which lay upon the floor'. Of his sister's courtship with Thorley, John said, 'For two or three months together he was in the habit of coming to visit the deceased, several times a week. But for the last month he had not seen him at the house.'

Constable Joseph Munday, stationed at Middlewich, deposed that he had gone to Chester Castle with an arrest warrant after being informed that Thorley had surrendered himself. During the interview Thorley told him that the razor with which he had committed the murder he had 'thrown over a hedge near to the house'. With several others the officer carried out a search of the farm and, he said, he 'found it lying open and bloody upon a bed of carrots' about 12 yards from the front door.

After surgeon William Hunt had given his evidence about the dead woman's injuries, the inquest closed with the jury returning the predictable verdict of 'wilful murder against Samuel Thorley'.

The following day, Tuesday 10 December, Mary Pemberton was laid to rest in the graveyard of St. Wilfrid's Parish Church in Davenham. The funeral, said the *Chronicle*, was 'attended by a vast crowd of spectators, and sorrow seemed to sit on every countenance'.

Mary had been born at Brockhurst Farm on 11 April 1812. Her parents and their four other children appear to have moved there about two years earlier from Stanthorne Hall Farm, Stanthorne, near Winsford, which had been farmed previously by Joseph Pemberton's father John (died 1801) and then by his uncle Roger. At Roger's death in 1803, the farm passed to his brother Joseph (Mary's father). It was formerly part of the Cheshire estates of Sir John Fleming Leicester of Tabley House, near Knutsford, 5th Baronet and later the 1st Baron de Tabley and a former High Sheriff of Cheshire. Stanthorne Hall itself was rebuilt between 1804-1807, after the property had been acquired by a member of the Dutton family. The new hall, now a listed building, can be seen from the A54 Winsford-Middlewich road, set imposingly among a stand of trees.

After he had made his written confession and been placed in the cells, Samuel Thorley refused to talk any more about the murder. When Cons. Munday visited him at Chester Castle on the following Sunday and began questioning him, the *Chester Courant* (17 December) reported, the prisoner cut him short saying, 'There is enough said on this subject. I have acknowledged to it [*sic*].'

After a few days' incarceration, however, he seems to have given up his vow of silence. For in that same edition of the

The 'new' Stanthorne Hall (above) was built on the site of the farm Joseph Pemberton tenanted prior to moving to Brockhurst Farm, Leftwich, where daughter Mary was born in 1812.

Photograph by the author.

161

Courant there appeared what purported to be his personal account of Mary's final moments. The report quoted the prisoner as saying that he 'stood at the door with the deceased at least ten minutes, with one arm round her neck and the other under his coat, with the razor open in his hand'. It went on, 'He used as much persuasion as he was master of to induce her to consent to their marriage, or at least to give him some hope, but his persuasion and his tears were of no avail and, on being told not to repeat his visits, he cut her throat . . .'

Thorley had made it clear from the outset that he intended to plead guilty at his trial, his stated view being that 'he did not trouble anyone to apprehend him and would not trouble anyone to try him'. That was still his position when he finally appeared in the dock at Chester Assizes on Friday 4 April 1834. It was exactly one week away from what would have been Mary Pemberton's 22nd birthday. When the Clerk of Assize (the John Lloyd featured in Chapter Six) read out the indictment, the prisoner, seemingly anxious to get matters over with as quickly as possible, responded impatiently 'Guilty, Guilty' even before being asked how he pleaded. However, his counsel, Mr Cottingham, informed the Judge that Thorley's friends had instructed him to say that he was not in a fit condition mentally to plead (*Chester Chronicle*, 11 April).

The Judge, Sir John Gurney, Baron of the Exchequer, said he knew nothing of the prisoner's state of mind, that the indictment must proceed in the usual manner and that the defendant had to plead. At this point, Thorley, in a firm voice, interjected, 'I am guilty.'

Before proceeding further Sir John called John Dunstan, Governor of the county gaol, to the stand. He testified that during the whole time Thorley was in prison he had 'not manifested any signs of insanity'.

Mr Baron Gurney then told Mr Cottingham that if he had any evidence to demonstrate that the prisoner was of unsound mind, he was ready to hear it. Counsel replied that he had no such evidence, but he had evidence that the prisoner had been 'labouring under a delusion before he committed the act and that it still possessed his mind'. His Lordship agreed to a 'Not Guilty' plea being entered on the prisoner's behalf. From Thorley's agitated manner it was clear that he was not pleased; but the decision stood.

The trial got under way in a Shire Hall bursting at the seams. Setting the scene, the *Chester Courant* (8 April) recorded, 'Multitudes of persons, some of them [having come] from a great distance, anxious to obtain a sight of the unfortunate individual, crowded round the court long before the hour appointed for its opening, and the pressure to obtain admission was in consequence very great. Hundreds, however, were greatly disappointed, for the Hall, notwithstanding its vast extent, was unable to hold more than a fractional part of the crowds that wished to be present.'

When the court came to order, the first case called was that of a 22-year-old Marple man, James Mason, accused of carrying out a sickening assault on his pregnant girlfriend with the intention of causing her to miscarry. Mason was hanged and the woman later died as a result of her injuries (see *Cheshire's Execution Files*). The details of the crime, said the *Courant*, 'were of a very indelicate description'; consequently, to add to the chaos in the courtroom, 'the great number of females that crowded the porticoes, Grand Jury room and the avenues [aisles] were excluded.' At 2pm they were allowed back in for the Thorley trial and 'the rush then became alarming, many females screamed in great afright and a number lost articles of wearing apparel in the struggle'.

The commotion didn't appear to unsettle the man in the dock. He was accompanied throughout the hearing by the Rev. John Hoskins (Chaplain of the County Gaol) and Rev. Thomas Harrison, described as 'lecturer' at the Church of St. Mary's-on-the-Hill, right next door to the Castle. However, when the first witness, Mrs Sarah Pemberton, began giving her evidence, the *Courant's* court reporter observed that the prisoner 'covered his eyes with his fingers and exhibited some uneasiness'. And when his young shop assistant later took the stand 'the wretched man's soul appeared to be harrowed up [*sic*]; he writhed about in apparent agony, his head sank to the front of the dock and, ultimately, he sank upon a chair and covered his face with his hands, which he supported on his knees'. However, 'a flood of tears . . . tended to greatly relieve him and he then recovered his self-possession'.

The *Courant's* piece went on, 'The appearance of the prisoner was exceedingly neat and respectable, and the duties of his toilet appeared to have been performed with more than ordinary care and precision. He wore a claret coloured coat, a light striped waistcoat, light pink neckerchief and a beautifully white and tastefully plaited [pleated?] shirt.' Physically, however, things did not look so fine and dandy. Obviously showing the effects of his self-inflicted misery, the once handsome and healthy-looking farmer's son was now said to be 'a man of very sallow complexion, with sunken eyes and overhanging forehead . . . and of rather slender frame'.

Unless stated otherwise, what follows is taken from the *Chronicle's* report of the trial.

Mrs Pemberton, who described her daughter as 'an amiable and affectionate girl', told the court, 'I had perceived there was an acquaintance between my daughter and the prisoner, Samuel Thorley. He drank tea at my house about five weeks before my daughter's death and, in consequence of something I said at that time, there was a cessation of their acquaintance.'

She related how, on the night of Friday 6 December, she went to bed at nine o'clock. She had been asleep for some time when she was awoken by the sound of voices downstairs. She went to the head of the stairs and heard her daughter talking to a man she took to be Samuel Thorley. She went back to bed. Then at about 11 o'clock she was aroused once again (probably by the noise of the front door being shut). She went downstairs. The house, she said, was in darkness and she could not see a thing. Then she made the extraordinary claim that 'she fancied she heard blood gushing from the body of her daughter'. It was then that she stumbled upon Mary, blood indeed gushing from her body, lying on the floor of the lobby.

Cross-examined by Mr Cottingham, Mrs Pemberton said she did not know how long Mary and Thorley had 'kept company together'. Defence Counsel then questioned her about the contents of the anonymous letter she had received — including its allegation about Thorley and her daughter's inheritance money — and the possible identity of the person who wrote it.

She admitted she had a son-in-law named Dobell. This was Richard Dobell, 30, who had married her daughter Ann in 1828. They lived at Leftwich Farm, also known as Dobell's Farm, close to Samuel Thorley's nursery in what became Dobell's Lane, Leftwich. But Mrs Pemberton said she did not know that 'he was the cause of breaking up the acquaintance between my daughter and the prisoner' (in other words, that he was the author of the malicious letter). As to her daughter's inheritance, she revealed that in her late husband's will — Joseph Pemberton had died on 26 April 1833 at the age of 69 — Mary had been left £2,000, a sum that would have the purchasing power today of more than £165,000.

John Pemberton spoke of the moment he came downstairs and found the mutilated body of his sister. She was on the lobby floor close to the door to the parlour. Her throat, he said, was 'dreadfully cut . . . her head was nearly severed from her body'.

In cross-examination, Pemberton said he had known Thorley about four years and that he thought he and his sister had 'kept company for about eight months' (in his evidence to the inquest he had said it was 12 months). He added, 'From what I observed, I believe they were attached to each other.' He had on one occasion the previous summer accompanied Mary to Thorley's home in Northwich, and taken tea with them. He confirmed that the anonymous letter had been the reason his mother had taken against Thorley. Asked if Thorley had always appeared to him as being 'in his right mind', John Pemberton replied, 'I never saw anything to the contrary'.

Next on the witness stand was Thorley's shop-boy, Peter Banks. After giving details of his conversations with his master on the night of 6 December, and his subsequent trip to Betchton, Banks was asked by Mr Cottingham about Thorley's behaviour in the period prior to the murder. He said that a few weeks before, he had seen him 'take brown medicine out of a bottle several times'. Asked if it might have been laudanum, he said he did not know.

In Victorian times the sale of drugs was largely unregulated: they could be bought like any other commodity. Laudanum, a mixture of alcohol and opium, was a strong pain-killer used to treat a wide variety of ailments, from the common cold to heart disease. Victorian nursemaids administered it to pacify crotchety children. As it was cheaper than gin it was also a popular recreational drink among the working-class as well as writers and artists.

His master, said Banks, 'appeared to be depressed and unhappy in his mind'. He continued, 'His manner was altered lately. I used to sleep with him and have known him to get up in the middle of the night. He neglected his business and used to cry and sit with his hands between his knees for hours.' On the night of the murder, speaking of Mary, Thorley had said to him that she was 'the sweetest creature who ever lived'.

On the Sunday before Mary's murder (1 December), Thorley was drinking in a Davenham pub — possibly the White Lion (formerly the White Hart), now disappeared but which was then situated on the north side of Church Street — when Joseph Pemberton, the youngest of Mary's three brothers, came in. He told the court that Thorley saw him and asked him to come outside, where they could speak more privately. The accused wanted to know why he was no longer allowed to visit Mary. Pemberton said he did not know, whereupon Thorley declared that he wished to see her once more, commenting, 'I don't care if I go to the devil afterwards'. He proposed going home with the witness to see Mary there and then; but he was advised that this was not a good idea. Joseph Pemberton stated that when he left the pub the prisoner said, 'Probably we shall not meet again.'

Joseph seems to have had a degree of sympathy for the jilted Thorley, whom he had also known for about four years. After his split with Mary, Thorley returned for a short time to his family home in Betchton, where he had been born around September, 1801, the youngest of the four surviving children of John and Hannah Thorley. According to the *Chester Courant*'s trial report (8 April), Joseph Pemberton said that his sister was 'very uneasy' at this time. 'She cried much', he said. 'I suppose it was about Thorley's absence.' So he had gone to visit him at his father's farm. He 'had no intention of bringing him back'; he had called to see him, he said, 'in consequence of there having come an anonymous letter'.

We can only presume he challenged Thorley about the allegations contained in the letter. It would have been an interesting conversation; but, inexplicably, there was no reference to it in any of the newspapers. Of the ill-fated match, Pemberton was quoted in the *Courant* report as saying that Thorley 'appeared very fond of my sister and I understood she returned his affection'. After the break-up, however, he said Thorley 'did not appear in such good spirits as formerly'.

In the same report we learn from Thorley's friend John Whitlow that, 'around December 1st', the defendant came to his house; 'house' was then common shorthand for 'public house' and in 1833 a John Whitlow, then aged 72, was the licensee of the White Lion in Davenham. He was still the landlord when he was 80. Was this the friend in question? There is another possibility: John Whitlow's son, a brick-setter also called John, lived at the pub with him and, at 40, he was closer to Thorley's age.

Either way, the witness John Whitlow testified that Thorley had asked him to write to a friend of his in London who might be interested in leasing his nursery. Thorley mentioned the letter that had been received by the Pembertons 'about his character', as a result of which 'he had decided to give up the business'. Whitlow cautioned him not to be too hasty, as the family could change their minds about him.

It was at this point that Thorley said something that seemed to suggest that it was not only his lease that he was thinking of terminating. He was alleged to have told his friend, 'I don't know, Whitlow, but if I have not her, nobody else shall.' Whitlow again urged him not to talk of such things, adding prophetically, 'People might say you have murdered the girl.'

Witness also recounted seeing Thorley on the day of the murder. It was market day but the nurseryman was 'not about his business when I saw him'. Whitlow went to Thorley's shop, where he found Peter Banks serving behind the counter. Thorley was in his private quarters 'lying on a sofa with a top coat on and a handkerchief on his head'. Whitlow said to him, 'Thorley, you appear like a lunatic; why don't you pull those things off and clean yourself [up].'

Thorley did eventually stir himself and the pair of them went to the Angel Hotel and 'took a glass of whiskey punch together'. The *Chronicle* report stated that afterwards Thorley went to the bank and, on his return, paid Whitlow 'a few shillings' he owed him. Another sign, perhaps, that he was not expecting to be around after the day was out.

John Dunstan, 37, who also held the ancient title of Constable of Chester Castle, told the court of the day he came face to face with the man with a murder to get off his chest. The prison governor detailed Thorley's confession and the subsequent written statement he made. Then, cross-examined by defence counsel Cottingham, Dunstan said he had been 'concerned with gaols upwards of 20 years and it is the first case which I ever heard of a prisoner surrendering himself'. In fact the true figure was well over 30 years as Dunstan had been born 'inside' — or, more precisely, at the Governor's House at the New Bailey Prison in Salford, Manchester, in February 1797. His father William Dunstan was Governor there until his death in 1817.

In 1819 John was appointed the first Governor of the House of Correction at Knutsford, Cheshire, and was promoted to his latest post in 1822. He retired as Governor of Chester Castle Gaol in 1865, after 43 years in the job. In court he was asked about Thorley's mental state. He replied, 'I am of opinion that the prisoner is perfectly sane.'

In the *Courant*'s trial report Thorley was said to have revealed in his prison statement that he had tried to persuade Mary to take him back on the previous Tuesday night but 'she refused to have him'.

Constable Joseph Munday gave evidence as to the discovery of the murder weapon. When the razor was shown to the jury, the *Chronicle* reporter noted, 'there were marks of blood [still] on it.'

At the close of the prosecution's case, Thorley was asked if he had anything to say. He moved to the front of the dock and replied, 'No. I am guilty, my Lord.'

His brother Jonathan — it seems likely that it was he to whom Thorley gave Mary's ring while in gaol with the request that it be buried with him — was the first of two witnesses called by the defence. He recollected Samuel returning to the family farm at Betchton on Sunday, November 10th, shortly after the break-up with Mary: 'He was in a very distressed state of mind [*Courant*]. I thought him deranged. He was quite wild and gazely in his eyes [staring absently]. I have never seen him in that state before. He did not stay in bed all night, but got up and wandered in the fields and garden. He often held his head in his hands and at other times heaved the heaviest sighs I have ever heard. It was distressing to see him.'

Jonathan also remembered Joseph Pemberton coming to the farm on 13 November and a visit he paid to his brother's home in Northwich on 5 December, the day before the murder. He arrived at noon to find Samuel still in bed. Jonathan chastised him for 'not looking after his

After his break-up with Mary, Samuel Thorley returned briefly to his family home at Betchton Farm, near Sandbach (left). Brother Jonathan recalled the distressing scenes he witnessed as Samuel wrestled with his conscience.

Photograph by the author.

business and his men'; but he could not persuade him to go to work at the nursery. 'I slept with him that night,' Jonathan said. 'Sometimes he cried and sat by the bedside and went on in such a manner as I never saw in my life. I wanted to take him home to his father's house because of the state he was in, but he refused, saying "I must go to Leftwich."' His brother had also told him that 'he had never deceived her [Mary] and never would as long as he had breath in his body'.

Mr Cottingham's other witness was described in both Chester papers as simply 'Mr Twemlow, Surgeon, of Northwich'. This was probably William Twemlow of Witton Cottage. He said he had known Thorley for four years and 'had always considered him a very humane and kind-hearted man'. Of what may have driven the defendant to commit such a ferocious attack on the woman he professed to love, Twemlow ventured, 'I have known instances wherein persons have been quite of sound mind on all subjects but one.' However, he added, 'There are no facts that have been stated on his trial which, in my opinion, are evidence of insanity.'

It was a view shared by the Judge. In his summing up, Sir John Gurney said he thought the prisoner had 'displayed more selfishness and self-love than insanity, in saying [that] if he did not have the deceased, nobody else should'. He added, 'He might be distressed, he might cry, but that might not deprive him of reason.'

The jury may well have reflected, too, on the fact that three days after Thorley's Tuesday night rebuff, he had gone to see Mary with a razor in his pocket seemingly prepared to carry out the implied threat in his comment to his friend John Whitlow should she reject him again. It was obvious that any plea for a lesser verdict, on the grounds of the defendant's mental state, was going to fail; and, considering Thorley's persistent admissions, the jury had little choice but to find him guilty. After a trial lasting two-and-a-half hours, they consulted only a few moments before the foreman announced their decision.

When the Clerk of the Court asked Thorley if there was any reason why sentence of death should not be passed upon him, he replied 'None', once more repeating, 'I am guilty.'

With the black 'coif' on his head, Baron Gurney began his grim oration. He told the prisoner at the bar, 'You are indeed a melancholy instance of a man, who had previously been esteemed by those who knew you as a good and humane individual, coming to an untimely end. Being disappointed in your expectations, you wreaked your vengeance on the person . . . whom you appeared to regard as the object of your affection. The remorse of conscience which prompted you to a confession of your heinous crime and to surrender yourself into the hands of justice, I trust, still continues and deeply afflicts your soul. Your days are numbered . . .'

In a speech delivered with undisguised emotion, it looked at this point as if the Judge might break down altogether. 'His Lordship's feelings so overcame him that he could scarcely proceed', the *Chronicle* reporter noted. In a faltering voice the Judge continued, 'You must soon appear before the bar of the Almighty, for mercy on earth cannot be extended to you. The laws of God and man demand that he who sheds innocent blood shall die. I have only now to perform a duty which to me is most painful.' He then passed sentence in the usual form.

The *Courant*'s report had this rather extravagant coda: ''The keenest feeling was also manifested in court, and scalding tears trickled down the cheeks of the females present, who thus evinced the strong interest they felt for this ill-fated man.' Thorley, by contrast, 'left the bar with calm, undisturbed resignation to his fate'.

On 11 April, referring to Samuel Thorley, the Editor of the *Chronicle*, wrote, 'Although a murderer and, as such, a man who justly deserved to die, it is impossible to suppress a certain degree of sympathy in his fate, from the peculiar circumstances under which the crime was committed. It was indeed a melancholy sight to see a man who moved in a respectable station in society as a tradesman, and who enjoyed the reputation of being a humane, and even kind-hearted man, die at the hands of the common hangman.'

Judge Sir John Gurney: almost broke down in sentencing Thorley to death.

Illustration from Some Particulars of the Lives of William Brodie Gurney and his Immediate Ancesters *by W. B. Gurney (C.1850), courtesy of Colin Salter.*

It has to be remembered that the England of the 1830s was still a male-dominated society; that women — disenfranchised and debarred from the educational, employment and social opportunities they rightly enjoy today — were considered 'the weaker sex', both physically and intellectually inferior to men. However, one might have expected that, among all these instinctive expressions of sympathy for the guilty man, there might have been a little more consideration given to the suffering of the innocent young woman he cut down in her prime and to the 'life sentence' he imposed on her family.

Returned to gaol, Thorley continued to express his 'astonishment and deep regret' that his friends had succeeded in pressing for a 'not guilty' plea. Had he been left to plead guilty, as he had intended all along, he would, of course, have spared himself the ordeal of a trial; but he just might also have been considering the Pemberton family's feelings, wishing to save them the unpleasant experience of having to appear in court and hear the awful details of this bloody business aired in public.

Samuel Thorley was executed on Monday 7 April 1834 at Chester's City Gaol, where all public executions in the city were carried out between 1809 and 1866. The previous evening he had been locked in his cell at eight o'clock and apparently slept soundly until 4am. At five o'clock he was taken from the county gaol and handed over to the City Sheriffs. Even at that time a large number of people determined to witness the hanging had already begun to gather. 'We believe a greater number of spectators was never observed in this city on any similar occasion,' the *Chronicle* declared. 'They continued to arrive from Northwich and the surrounding places during the whole of the previous night, and at the early hour that he was removed from the Castle, the streets contained a dense mass of people.' All this some seven hours before the dreadful 'show' was due to begin.

By 12.20pm, when the condemned man was led out to the gallows (by now transferred to its new position over the entrance to the gaol proper), 'the crowd was so great that hundreds could not obtain even a sight of the instrument of death, and returned without gratifying the curiosity that induced them to visit this city'.

When 'the fatal bolt was drawn and this world closed upon him for ever', Thorley 'struggled for a few minutes before life was extinct'. After hanging for the customary hour, his body was cut down and, in accordance with the conditions attached to the death sentence for murderers, his remains were interred during the evening of the same day 'within the precincts' of the County Gaol (actually a piece of unconsecrated ground that formed part of what was in earlier times known as the Castle Ditch, which ran between St. Mary's Church and the wall of the prison).

Less than three months later the name of another Thorley appeared in the county's burial records: this was John Thorley, Samuel's father, who died on 5 July 1834 aged 75. He was buried on July 8th in the graveyard of Sandbach Parish Church. After his death the then 70-plus-acre Betchton Farm was run by his son Jonathan and his two daughters Mary and Hannah, none of whom appears to have married. In his will, which he had drawn up in 1832, for reasons unknown he specifically prohibited his elder son John from living there or having any involvement in the business, though he, too, inherited a fourth share of his father's personal estate. The farmland straddled Sandbach Road and, to the south, occupied areas on both sides of the Trent and Mersey Canal. Some time before 1910 the name of the farm was changed to Thurlwood Farm. Samuel Thorley's mother Hannah had died in March 1821 at the age of 60.

At the death of Mary Pemberton's father, Brockhurst Farm passed to his sons John and Roger. A tithe map of 1841 shows that by then the farm also extended to around 70 acres, all lying between London Road and the River Dane. By that time John occupied the farmhouse, while bachelor Roger was living with his mother Sarah in one of the terrace properties he owned in London Road just across from the farm entrance. Mrs Sarah Pemberton died in January, 1857, aged 83.

It is an odd coincidence that Mary Pemberton's murderer was not the only cut-throat called Samuel Thorley to be executed at Chester. In 1777 a man of that name, a feeble-minded odd-job man and latterly a butcher's assistant, was hanged after being found guilty at the county assizes of the barbaric murder of 'tramping ballad-singer' Ann Smith at Congleton. On that occasion Thorley used a knife to kill and then dismember his victim, before dumping the body parts in Howty Brook (see *A Vintage Casebook of Cheshire Crime* by this author).

The *Chester Courant* was one of several newspapers to make the connection with the earlier crime. Moreover, in its edition of 17 December 1833 it had gone so far as to say that the Congleton killer was the 'paternal grand-uncle' of the latter day Samuel Thorley, meaning the brother of his paternal grandfather. But the paper then undermined its claim to accuracy by stating that the 18th century murder happened at a place called 'Westgreen' and that, afterwards, Thorley cooked and ate part of the woman's flesh 'at a public-house'. In fact, Thorley committed his hideous act in Priesty Fields, a secluded valley between Congleton and Astbury, and his body was *gibbeted* at West *Heath*. Yes, Sam-the-butcher's-man did sample a portion of the dead woman's calf, to discover, he said, whether it tasted like pork, as he had been led to believe. But he indulged his cannabalistic curiosity — he had his answer almost immediately when he was violently sick — in a private lodging-house in Astbury.

Initial examination of available sources failed to trace any link between the two Samuel Thorleys; so, while it could be said that the pair were bound up *with* blood, more careful genealogical research is required to establish whether or not 'The Beast of Priesty Fields' (who was said to have come originally from Leek in Staffordshire) and the Leftwich farm killer (whose family roots lay firmly in Cheshire) were also bound *by* blood.

CHAPTER EIGHT

'The Worst Sort Of Murder'

Of the 72 people executed in Cheshire throughout the 1800s, only four were women. Two of them, however, were responsible for crimes that ranked among the most cold and calculating of the 19th century. Mary Gallop and Alice Hewitt each earned her membership of this exclusive sisterhood of shame by committing what one Chester Assize Court judge described as 'the worst sort of murder': the 'insidious' killing of a parent by poison.

Though the pair displayed shocking inhumanity in carrying out their acts of familial homicide, they were not without their sympathisers; and a number of prominent figures were among those who petitioned for a reprieve. But, having shown no mercy to their victims, they received none in return, and died in ignominy: unpardoned and unpardonable.

The deaths of these two heartless young women did, however, have one redeeming effect: they helped change society's attitude towards capital punishment. Not because they were put to death, but because of the way they died. For the distressing scenes at their executions contributed to the growing pressure that eventually led to the ending of the grotesque and desensitising spectacle of public hangings.

Mary Gallop, convicted of the murder of her father at Monks Coppenhall (modern Crewe), was in a state of total collapse when she went to the gallows in 1844, aged just 20 . She had to be carried on to the scaffold in a chair, and she was still seated when the drop opened up beneath her. As a method of execution it was untried; the chair hampered her fall and her death struggles were agonisingly prolonged.

In 1863 — 19 years to the day later — when 27-year-old Alice Hewitt became the latest culprit to suffer at the hands of the notoriously blunder-prone hangman William ('The Strangler') Calcraft, it took him three attempts to release the lever operating the trapdoors. In the end gaol officials had to be summoned to help free the malfunctioning mechanism. Meanwhile, the condemned woman, sentenced for murdering her disabled mother at their home in Stockport, was left wailing piteously on the scaffold for several minutes before being sent plunging into the abyss below.

Contemporary newspapers called it 'one of the most dreadful and sickening spectacles' to ever disgrace a public execution. It was witnessed by the respected Chaplain of Chester Castle Gaol, the Reverend James Kilner, who ministered to Hewitt right up to her final, excruciating moments and had a close-up view of the painful proceedings. Three years later, he recalled 'the terrible anguish caused by Calcraft's bungling', which, he said, 'I shall never forget.'

Afterwards, making his way through the unusually subdued crowd of spectators, Rev. Kilner, a deeply caring and conscientious man, observed that many of them had also been noticeably unsettled by what had happened. The whole experience, he wrote later, had left him 'with the strong feeling that if executions there must be, they certainly ought not to be in public'.

Influenced by the kind of unfortunate incidents that terminated the two controversial Cheshire executions, it was an opinion shared by an ever increasing proportion of the population. The nation's shifting mood had already been reflected in a Parliamentary act of 1861, which effectively reserved the death penalty for murder. And in May 1864 MPs voted to set up a Royal Commission to examine the whole conscience-troubling issue of capital punishment. The Commissioners in their report, published in January 1866, stopped short of calling for the abolition of the death penalty, but almost unanimously recommended that executions should in future be carried out not in the public gaze, but in the privacy of the county gaols. The resulting legislation came into force on 29 May 1868.

The Mary Gallop case had been controversial for another reason: the campaign to have her sentence commuted aroused much hostile criticism in the press — both at home and abroad — most of it directed at the Bishop of Chester, its most eminent supporter. He was afterwards quoted as saying his reasons for signing one of the mercy petitions had been misunderstood. But more of that later.

Mary Gallop murdered her father Richard following a row in which he forbade her to continue seeing a boy to whom she had become attached. She would claim in a statement released after her trial that she got the idea from a conversation she had had with her half-sister, who told her of a woman who poisoned her husband with arsenic she had bought under the pretext of destroying rats.

She hatched her plot in the autumn of 1844 at the house in which she lived with her widowed father, her older half-sister (Mrs Margaret Smetham) and a lodger, a Scotsman named William Frazer. The property was situated in the south Cheshire township of Monks Coppenhall, then well on its way to being transformed into the major railway town — and the country's most important rail junction — of Crewe. Richard Gallop was a joiner employed by the Grand Junction Railway (GJR), originally in the locomotive, coach and wagon department at Edge Hill in Liverpool. In March 1843 the company relocated the department to this largely rural corner of the county, and he and his family, which then included his wife, also called Mary, followed during the summer. Frazer, a neighbour of the Gallops in Liverpool, was a coach body-builder and, a year later, he also transferred to what would become the world famous Crewe Engineering Works, whose rolling stock was exported to all parts of the globe.

The GJR, which eventually connected Birmingham with Liverpool and Manchester, had reached Crewe in 1837, the year in which Crewe station was completed. The new works were sited to the west of the railway line, from where, to accommodate this mass migration of workers, the company's huge house-building programme began to spread gradually northwards towards Earle Street and westwards beyond Market Street. It has proved impossible to identify the address of the Gallop family's company house: the early records of the GJR no longer survive and the archives of the London and North Western Railway Company, with which it merged in 1846, also proved unhelpful. But we know they were among the first wave of transferees, who were given a choice of homes in what would become Moss Square, Prince Albert Street, Liverpool Street, Manchester Street and Crewe Street — all located within easy walking distance of the works.

Covering around 40 acres of former agricultural land, the houses, complete with gardens, were laid out in neat streets and built in styles that corresponded with the rank of the tenants: from the villa-type homes of the bosses to the two-up-two-down terrace cottages of the labourers. By 1844 more than 200 company houses were occupied in this expanding new 'railway colony'.

It was early that year, about 10 months after she and her family arrived in Crewe, that Mary Gallop's life started on its downward spiral. On the morning of 27 April, when her father had left for work, she came downstairs to find her mother lying on the kitchen floor with her throat cut. A razor dripping with blood, with which she had apparently just committed suicide, lay beside her body. Mrs Mary Gallop, it was reported, had not been on particularly good terms with her husband, who was 20 years her junior, and had tried several times before to kill herself 'in fits of insanity'. Her death certificate recorded bluntly, and rather brutally, that she had 'cut her throat, being lunatic'. She was 65.

Following her conviction for murdering her father, rumours began to circulate in Crewe that, perhaps, Mary had had something to do with her mother's death as well. But she denied it vehemently. In fact, according to Margaret Smetham, the loss hit her hard. Margaret was quoted in the press as saying her half-sister was unable to sleep for days and that her father expressed his concern that she would end up

Above: Some of the company houses that were part of the first phase of the 'railway colony' expansion that brought Richard Gallop and his family from Liverpool to Crewe. These were in Forge Street (the Crewe Works site is on the left) and, along with many other similar streets, were demolished in the 1960s.

Image by permission of CALS.

Left: A few of Crewe's old railway houses have been restored and modernised, like these in Tollitt Street.   *Photograph by the author.*

like her mother. As we shall see in due course, the state of young Mary's mind was called into question at her trial and was afterwards one of the arguments cited by those petitioning for her reprieve.

Richard and Mary Gallop appear to have come from the Warrington area originally. They were married at All Saints Church in the nearby village of Daresbury in March 1821, when they were both said to be from that parish. Mary, the former Mary Travers, already had a young daughter (Margaret) from a previous marriage and was 42. Her new husband was 22. Daughter Mary was born on 2 March 1824 and baptised at St. James's Church in Latchford, where her parents were then living.

When Mary was around nine years old, her father, ever ready to uproot the family in search of work, took her and Margaret, then aged about 15, to live with him and his wife in Runcorn; then, probably in 1835, they landed in Liverpool. They lived first in Rosehill then in Mansfield Street, Islington. When Richard got a job 'on the railroad', the family moved to a newly-developed area of Toxteth known as Windsor — part of the massive residential expansion then taking place to the south of the city — and a home in Upper Stanhope Street. For the next seven years, while her father (a strong Methodist) toiled for 12 hours a day at the Edge Hill works of the Grand Junction Railway, Mary was a regular attender at the Wesleyan Chapel, three-quarters-of-a-mile away in Pleasant Street and became a Sunday School teacher.

The first houses in working-class Windsor were built in 1822; Upper Stanhope Street was laid out in 1826. What conditions were like when the Gallops lived there is not known, but by 1867 the area — sixteen acres in extent and eventually accommodating a population of 4,500 — had become noted for its immorality, drunkenness and disease. That was the year Richard Hobson, later Canon Hobson, become minister of the new parish of St. Nathaniel's, Windsor. In his autobiography, he described what he saw when he first arrived:

Its area was socially and morally the lowest in all the south-east portion of Liverpool. The houses were small and badly built, and narrow courts and inhabited cellars abounded, causing the place to be a hotbed of fever and other deadly diseases. One street was unfit, and even unsafe, for the passage of ladies. Another was given over to the social evil [prostitution] and was known as "the little hell". The inhabitants were styled "the roughs of Windsor" and advertisements for labourers constantly bore the ominous warning "Windsor men need not apply". Sixteen public houses and two beer shops pandered to the drinking propensities of the population.

During her time in Mansfield Street, Mary, then about 12 years old, met a boy a couple of years younger than her, a neighbour's son, and they became firm friends. In reporting Mary Gallop's trial, the *London Standard* of 10 December 1844 revealed the boy's name to be 'Duval'. Over the following few days at least a dozen other newspapers, both in London and the provinces, carried an identical story (though it was not picked up by any of the Cheshire papers). It is likely that the lad was the John *Duvall* who was listed in the 1841 census as being aged 14 and living in North's Buildings, Finch Street, Islington (modern Kempston Street), with his mother, Mary Ann Duvall, and his two younger brothers.

He also visited Mary in Windsor and, despite the best efforts of her parents, their friendship blossomed; and when she went to live in Crewe they regularly exchanged letters, though she kept them a secret from her father. Towards the end of 1843 Mary and her mother spent a few days in Liverpool — where, it would be revealed at her trial, Mary had another half-sister — and she saw 'John' (as he shall be known) several times. He was then aged 16 and an apprentice cabinet-maker.

Some time after the death of her mother, Mary went with Margaret for another extended stay in Liverpool, and while there she again saw a lot of the young man. By the time she returned to Crewe in June they had formed a strong attachment, and in the middle of October Mary asked her father whether he would allow her to spend Christmas with him. He was furious; he told his daughter in no uncertain terms that she could not go and ordered her to end the relationship with her Liverpudlian 'sweetheart', as he described him scornfully.

From that moment on, Richard Gallop's fate was sealed. And when Mary heard Margaret mention the woman who had murdered her husband with rat poison, she realised that here was the means of setting herself free from her disciplinarian father. With him out of the way, she reasoned, she would be at liberty to go wherever she pleased and do whatever she wanted.

On Friday 1 November, having purchased two separate quantities of white arsenic at a local chemist's shop, she baked three cakes: one to share with her half-sister, and one each for her father and the lodger Frazer. She mixed some of the poisonous powder in her father's cake. It has been estimated that an amount the size of a pea can be fatal; but, to make sure her murderous intentions were accomplished, she added a further dose in some arrowroot she gave to her father, ostensibly to ease the pain of the bowel complaint from which he had been suffering for several weeks. The next day she bought another quantity of arsenic from the same shop. That night Richard Gallop was violently ill and died the following day, Sunday 3 November.

A doctor who had been called in to attend Mr Gallop realised he was dying but thought the cause was cholera, a disease that had first struck in Britain in 1831 and which resulted in the pandemics of the 1840s, 1850s and 1860s. A disconcerting feature of arsenic poisoning is that it mimics not only the symptoms of cholera, but also of food poisoning and other gastro-intestinal infections that were rife in Victorian Britain. However, Mary's behaviour in the immediate aftermath of her father's death — and the observations of a keen-eyed police officer — led to a suspicion that the 45-year-old railway worker had been murdered.

The speculation was supported by closer medical examination and the postmortem clinched it: Richard Gallop had died from arsenic poisoning.

At the inquest held two days later by Knutsford Division Coroner James Roscoe, the jury returned a verdict of 'Wilful Murder against Mary Gallop'. She was committed on the Coroner's warrant to appear at Chester's Winter Assizes to answer a charge of parricide. The case was heard on Friday 6 December 1844. She pleaded not guilty.

The written depositions taken at the inquest, preserved in the National Archives, constitute the only official record of the trial that now exists; but, as coroners at that time had a more active role in murder investigations than today, these statements are a reliable summary of the evidence the witnesses would have given in court.

Lodger William Frazer, 25, stated that he had lived at the Gallops' home in Crewe since July; from his evidence it appeared that Margaret Smetham's husband had also lodged there at some time. Of Richard Gallop's heated quarrel with his daughter, he deposed, 'I understood . . . that she wished to go to Liverpool to see a young man and the deceased objected to her going. She did not go . . . in consequence of her father's objection.'

About a week later, Richard Gallop 'complained of being very ill in his bowels', though it did not prevent him from going to work. Frazer said he went regularly to his workshop, which was 'not far from his house' (confirmation, perhaps, that it *was* located among the streets of the first-phase residential development of the Crewe railway community mentioned previously).

On Saturday 2 November he became worse, being 'seized with vomiting and sickness' during the evening. 'I asked him if I should fetch a doctor,' Frazer said, 'but he gave me no reply, so I fetched one of my own accord.' This was Crewe surgeon George Stevenson (named in some newspaper accounts as George *Stephenson*, someone with a rather more famous connection with the railways). The local medic, said the lodger, saw the patient three times during the night. Mr Gallop died around 7.15 on the Sunday morning.

The previous day he had had some arrowroot; in Victorian times arrowroot, usually mixed with milk and sugar, was widely used as an easily-digested, nutritional food for people recovering from illness and to treat stomach and intestinal disorders like diarrhoea. Frazer did not know who had prepared it, but he thought it was Mary, who told him she had given her father some before. She also told him that her father had complained to her that 'it did not have the taste of arrowroot at all'. When he saw the remains of it in a basin in the kitchen, Frazer tried it. It was cold by then but, he said, 'it left a burning taste on my tongue and was slightly sweet'. He thought it might have contained cayenne pepper. His attention had been drawn to the arrowroot in the basin 'by observing a yellow froth upon it'.

He went on, 'Mary saw me taste it. About five minutes afterwards I went for the doctor and returned with him in about a quarter-of-an-hour, and saw that the basin was not where I had left it. I asked the deceased's daughter for the arrowroot and she said she had thrown it away.' The basin 'appeared to have been washed'.

At one point, Gallop vomited into a 'mug' beside his bed and on to the floor. Frazer went on, 'I directed his daughter to clean it up, and she did not appear to be much distressed and did not pay much attention to him. She went to bed and I attended to him. She got up about an hour before he died. His step-daughter [Margaret Smetham] had got up earlier and she and I called the deceased's daughter upstairs. She did not then see her father but afterwards I called her from the kitchen to bring a cup of tea and she did so, but she and her father did not speak to each other at that time.'

Frazer stayed up with his sick workmate who, he said, 'had fits of vomiting at intervals during the night', and he was with him when he died. Afterwards, he noted, Mary 'appeared to be a good deal distressed', but said nothing to him. Less than two hours later, however, she was asking him if he might obtain for her a free rail pass — one of the perks of working for the Grand Junction Company — as she 'wished to go down to Liverpool'. Surprised by her apparent callousness, he refused. Frazer arranged for the body to be laid out and also organised the funeral. Mary, he said, 'took no steps about the funeral' (Richard Gallop had been buried on 7 November, reunited with his wife Mary in the graveyard of St. Elphin's Parish Church in Warrington).

At the trial, as press reports indicate, Frazer also revealed that Mr Gallop had had a penchant for self-medicating and prescribing and preparing treatments for other people's ailments. As well as making up plasters for cuts and bruises, he was also in the habit of 'mixing medicines', and had given a friend 'logwood' (another herbal remedy for chronic diarrhoea and dysentery) for a bowel complaint.

Mrs Margaret Smetham, 26, stated in her deposition that her step-father and her half-sister had generally been on good terms, but quarrelled 'frequently' about her friendship with the boy in Liverpool, 'to whose acquaintance he objected'. On Friday 1 November, her deposition went on, Mary had made some bread and from the left-over dough she baked three cakes for tea. Between them, she, Mary and Frazer ate two of the cakes that evening. They were all sick shortly afterwards, Mary and Margaret more so than Frazer. The third cake was left for Mr Gallop, but at that time he felt too poorly to eat it. Whether he did eventually eat some of it was never made clear; but the medical evidence was that there had been more than enough arsenic in both the cake and the arrowroot to have killed him.

Interestingly, when Margaret was about to take the third cake upstairs to Mr Gallop the following day, Mary, she said, told her, 'If I were you I would not take it, for I don't think it is good.' She had a bite anyway and was again sick. She had seen Mary making the bread and the cakes, using the same table (Mary would suggest later that the flour from which she made the cakes may have become accidentally contaminated with the poison in this way).

In the *Chester Chronicle*'s trial report of Friday 13 December Mrs Smetham was quoted as saying that Richard Gallop treated his daughter 'harshly' after he learned of his daughter's friendship with the boy in Liverpool. Once, after Mary had baked potatoes too hard for his liking, Mr Gallop 'threatened to get the strap to beat her'. And Mary told her she would leave home and go into service to get away from her father as 'she had had no comfort [at home] since her mother's death'.

Of Mrs Mary Gallop, the *Chronicle* reported that Margaret said of her, 'My mother was strange in her manner when pregnant with the prisoner. She [once] set the bed on fire on purpose and frequently went out to drown herself.' Around the time of the inquest, she said, Mary was 'much put out of the way' [upset]. She did not sleep for a week and Mr Gallop said he was 'afraid he should have a deal of trouble with her, as she was going like her mother'.

Mrs Smetham, who revealed that Mary had another half-sister living in Liverpool, corroborated Frazer's evidence that Richard Gallop had 'administered medicines to [his] workmates about Crewe.'

In his inquest deposition, Mr Edward George Thomas, a Crewe druggist, recalled that Mary Gallop, who regularly bought groceries from him, visited his shop between six and eight weeks ago carrying a piece of paper on which was an order for one pennyworth of arsenic, though Mary, whose standard of literacy was described in her prison record later as 'imperfect', had written it as 'anser'. When asked what she wanted the poison for, she said it was 'to destroy rats in her kitchen'. Thomas put the arsenic in a white paper wrap and labelled it 'Poison: With Care'.

About a fortnight ago she came to the shop again, for another pennyworth. He asked her, 'Were the rats not destroyed?' She replied, 'No.' Then, on Saturday 2 November, at around 2.15pm, she called a third time and asked for another two-pennyworth of the poison. There was still one last rat that she had been unable to kill, she informed the chemist, who cautioned her that, once she had mixed all that she intended to use, she must throw the remainder away 'for fear of danger'.

The arrowroot that Mary Gallop 'doctored' with arsenic she seems to have purchased on that same Saturday afternoon shopping expedition from Mrs Ann Pickersgill, 29, wife of John Pickersgill, a druggist and grocer, in Russell Street (modern Heath Street). According to the *Chester Chronicle*, she testified that Mary had called at the shop at about 2.30pm. She bought various groceries, and the arrowroot Mrs Pickersgill packed separately in blue 'cap paper' (a coarse wrapping paper). Mary returned to the shop at about eight o'clock in the evening, saying that her father had told her to take the arrowroot back as it tasted odd to him and he thought it had been

Arrowroot powder — or arsenic? Richard Gallop's food contained both these similar-looking ingredients in his final hours.

contaminated with something. However, after testing it, Mrs Pickersgill announced there was 'nothing amiss with it'.

About two weeks before, Mary Gallop had also bought nux vomica. At the Earle Street premises of chemist and druggist Mr Charles Abraham she asked for a pennyworth of the powder, derived from the crushed seeds of *Strychnos nux-vomica* — a tree native to India and south-east Asia — which contain strychnine. She was served by the proprietor's son William, to whom she explained that she wanted it 'to destroy mice'. In Victorian Britain nux vomica was also a popular choice for ridding homes of rodents (and, by all accounts, of unwanted human residents as well).

In his inquest deposition, William Abraham stated, 'He did not like to sell the poison to her and [instead] made her up a little linseed meal.' Placing it in a white paper packet, he said he labelled it 'Nux Vomica: Poison' and she had taken it away believing that was what the packet contained. Linseed meal is not noted for its mice-killing properties, and for humans it is a source of a several beneficial nutrients.

Key witness at Mary Gallop's trial was Assistant (or Petty) Constable Michael Kenty, who led the initial investigation into the crime. When news of Richard Gallop's sudden death — and the suspicion that he might have been poisoned — reached Crewe police station, he was sent to the house, arriving at around 11 o'clock on the Sunday morning. With him were Constables Boydell and Nash. As well as Mary, Margaret Smetham and William Frazer were also present. He first questioned

Mary who, as stated in the *Chester Chronicle*'s 13 December report, said her father had come home from work the previous day at around 4pm and announced that he would have some arrowroot to try to ease his troublesome bowels. She gave him the arrowroot and some milk and he mixed it up himself.

After relating her visit to Mrs Pickersgill with the 'bad-tasting' arrowroot, Mary said her father was aware of 'rats and mice being about the house' and that it was he who had told her to get the nux vomica. She herself had seen a rat only a few days ago; her half-sister also knew of the problem.

At this point, Kenty informed her that he was going to search the house and on approaching a chest of drawers in the parlour he invited Mary to 'take what she wanted' out of it before he started (possibly not wishing to appear indelicate in case it contained items of an intimate nature, such as underwear). When Mary merely extracted a handkerchief from one of the drawers, he was immediately suspicious.

The officer continued, 'I took it from her and she had a small paper packet in her hand . . . it had written upon it "Nux Vomica: Poison". She said she had purchased it from Mr Abraham about a fortnight before to kill rats.' Then, said Kenty, he saw the prisoner go to the chest of drawers again and appear to place something under some clothes. He looked in the drawer and saw it was a piece of blue paper. It had arrowroot in it. Mary, he said, denied she had put it there, claiming she knew nothing about it. But, said the officer, it had not been there when he searched the drawer earlier.

Kenty took the young woman into custody and at the police station, which at that time seems to have been located in Eaton Street, he found in her pocket the piece of paper she had handed to druggist Mr Edward Thomas, on which she had written 'Two pennyworth of anser'.

Before leaving the Gallop home, the police officers removed various items, including the remains of the dough cake, the bread and the arrowroot and some flour, for scientific analysis. An initial examination was carried out by George Stevenson. The Crewe surgeon confirmed the findings he had reported at the inquest into Richard Gallop's death: namely, that he had tested the arrowroot and the flour, both of which were found to contain arsenic, the greater quantity being in the flour.

Samples were also sent to Mr David Waldie, the eminent chemist for the Liverpool Apothecaries Company, at Apothecaries Hall in Colquitt Street, Liverpool. Waldie, 31, testified that he had received 200 grains of the arrowroot, from which he obtained 'a large portion of arsenic'; the arrowroot and arsenic were 'in about equal parts', the *Chronicle*'s report explained. He had also analysed a portion of the dough cake intended for Richard Gallop, some toasted bread and the flour. He said he had found 'a considerable quantity of arsenic' in each of them, especially in the cake.

George Stevenson also carried out the postmortem examination, the details of which were reported by the *Chronicle* as follows: 'The whole internal surface of the stomach was much inflamed . . . the whole viscera [abdomen] was inflamed . . . [as were] the upper part of the gullet and the rectum . . . the appearances would be produced by arsenic or other corrosive substance.' None of the effects, he said, would have been produced by nux vomica. And he concluded, 'The deceased died from inflammation of the bowels produced by some irritant substance. I found no irritant substance except arsenic.'

In his closing speech, Mr Trafford, counsel for the defence, claimed that there was no conclusive proof that a murder had been committed; that it was 'within the range of probability' that Mr Gallop had been taking small doses of arsenic to treat his bowel complaint for several weeks and 'not being thoroughly acquainted with the properties of medicines and drugs, [he] might have been instrumental in producing his [own] death'. His reluctance to have a doctor summoned when his condition worsened on the Saturday, said learned counsel, 'confirmed the inference that he had been doctoring himself'.

Mr Trafford also drew the jury's attention to the mental state of Mary Gallop's mother and pressed upon them 'the great probability that, as insanity was hereditary, there was some ground for inferring that the prisoner was not free from that calamity'.

It was a consideration the jury seemed to be pondering when, though remaining in the box, they 'deliberated for a considerable time' before giving their verdict. For in finding Mary Gallop guilty of murder they recommended her to mercy. The Judge, Sir John Gurney — in a rather different display of emotion to that which overcame him at the end of the trial of Samuel Thorley a decade earlier (see Chapter Seven) — could not disguise his astonishment. The *Chronicle* reported him as declaring, rhetorically, 'On what grounds can you recommend the prisoner to mercy for the murder of her own father!'

And, in sentencing the young woman to death, Baron Gurney told her, 'I wish I could see any symptoms of repentance for your act, or any feelings of remorse for what you have done. It is impossible for me to show you any mercy'. She had killed her father, he said, 'by the most odious and detestable of all means — that of poison — [in] an act of great deliberation . . . carried on with great perseverance, art and contrivance'.

Mary, observed the *Chronicle* reporter, 'was unmoved during the whole of the trial and heard the verdict and sentence with much unconcern'.

Despite his personal feelings, Judge Gurney was obliged to pass on the jury's recommendation to the Home Secretary (Sir James Graham), who in the coming days would also receive three separate petitions echoing the jury's sentiments. For, as the *Chronicle* pointed out on 3 January, 'Public sympathy has been elicited on her behalf to an extent unprecedented in Chester for many years, and the most vigorous efforts have been made to obtain a commutation of the sentence.' The mercy campaign — and one petition in particular — provoked an unholy row in newspapers far and wide, however.

Signed by no less a figure than the Bishop of Chester, the Right Reverend Dr John Bird Sumner — who in 1848 would become Archbishop of Canterbury — the petition presented a six-point appeal to Queen Victoria, urging her to exercise the 'Royal Prerogative of Mercy' and reduce Mary's sentence to one of transportation for life. Arguably, its most specious argument was that 'Mary Gallop, being at that time in great distress of mind from disappointed affection, and the determination of her father not to suffer her to marry the young man to whom she had been long attached *suddenly resolved to overcome the obstacle to the accomplishment of her wishes, by the dreadful crime of taking away the life of her father* and that she was *not influenced to this great crime by any malignant hatred to her father,* but as a means that occurred to her mind of enabling her to marry the person to whom she had engaged herself'.

Bishop Summer: an unholy row over his mercy petition support.

The point was also made that it was 'highly probable that until the time when she committed the crime for which she was condemned to death, her life had been irreproachable and that she had conducted herself as a teacher in a Wesleyan Methodist School with strict propriety'; and that, should she be reprieved, '*she might prove of great use in being employed in teaching young persons* in one of the schools in such place to which she may be transported' (author's italics in both paragraphs).

The petition, organised by one of Cheshire's (Prison) Visiting Magistrates, the Reverend Dr B. Penny, who had got to know Mary while she was in Chester Castle Gaol, ended with a more general view which, ironically, would assume greater significance after the regrettable manner of Mary Gallop's exit. It noted that, if the petition was successful, 'the revolting spectacle of a young female being publicly executed might be avoided and the inhabitants of Chester spared so shocking and painful an exhibition'.

As well as the Bishop, the *Chronicle* noted that the Chancellor of the Chester Diocese, Henry Raikes, and 'a great body of the clergy and gentry' had also signed the petition. The resulting press outcry reached as far away as Australia . . . and Bishop Sumner was the main target.

A somewhat belated report in the *Cornwall Chronicle* of Launceston, Tasmania, was typical in voicing the Antipodean anger. Pointing to the petition's argument that Mary was not motivated by any malignant hatred of her father, the paper raged, 'Observe the horrible morality that runs through all the distinctions here attempted to be drawn between different kinds of murder. To take the life for the sake of gain is treated as a lighter offence than that of taking it under the influence of passions [from] which you can gain nothing by gratifying.'

The paper also described as 'a revolting absurdity', the notion that the murderess should be 'let off with transportation on account of her admirable fitness for the instruction of youth'. It went on, 'This reasoning comes from a Bishop, and a Chancellor, and clergy, and laity, who are . . . scrupulous in requiring that all education should be founded on religion. Would they confide children to an infidel, or a Papist, or even a Dissenter? Not they; but they would entrust them to the hands that mixed the poison for a parent's draught.'

In England, the 'absurdity' of the 'no malignant hatred' argument was perhaps treated with the greatest contempt by the Leeds-based *Northern Star*, which on 4 January commented derisively, 'Now, should some Dean or Canon put arsenic in the Bishop of Chester's turtle soup, in the hope of obtaining his bishopric, would not the prisoner have his excuse — that he had no "malignant hatred" to the Bishop? Certainly not; only too much love for his see!'

Bishop Sumner explained later that he had signed the petition in the belief that Mary Gallop was suffering from some mental disorder. In doing so, he said, he was also registering his objection to capital punishment in general. Locally, both Chester papers sprang to his defence, pointing out that the Bishop's life and writings proved that he was no apologist for murder, and declaring that the criticism of him, and Chancellor Raikes, was totally unwarranted.

While the Home Secretary was considering the petitions submitted on behalf of the condemned woman, a personal statement she issued from her cell in Chester Castle Gaol did nothing to improve her chances of leniency. Reproduced in several newspapers — and here quoted from the *Chester Chronicle* of 20 December — in it she spoke frankly about the disagreement with her father and the casual conversation with her half-sister that had led her down the path to murder. She stated, 'He said he would never give his consent for me to have anything to do with the young man in Liverpool. I then thought of going into a situation as a servant in Liverpool. If I had I should have been very happy now.'

She recalled the day she heard her half-sister talking of the woman who had poisoned her husband, and went on, 'The idea then first entered my mind of poisoning my father, and I thought I should be at liberty to go where I pleased, and do as I pleased. If I could have opened my mind to anybody, and had received a little good advice, I am sure I should not have committed the crime. I did not think I should be detected. I considered his death would be attributed to the bowel complaint, with which he had been afflicted for several weeks.'

Mary's statement — it was witnessed by the Rev. Penny and the Chaplain of the Castle Gaol, William Eaton, one or both of whom no doubt helped her to compile it — continued, 'I bought a pennyworth of arsenic and, not thinking it would be enough, I bought another pennyworth. I made three cakes, one for my father, one for my half-sister and myself and one for the lodger. I put arsenic in the one for my father. I did not put any in the others. If any got mixed with the flour of which they were made, it was by accident. The cakes were for tea on the Friday night. My father did not eat his. It was put away in the cupboard.

'The lodger, my half-sister and myself partook of the others and were taken ill. I did not put any arsenic in them. I bought some more arsenic next day (Saturday) and mixed it with some arrowroot. I left my father to put milk to it and make it himself. He was taken ill soon afterwards, and died next morning.'

On Thursday 26 December the Home Secretary informed the prisoner that there were no grounds for submitting her appeal for mercy to the Queen. The previous day Mary had been visited by her two half-sisters. 'The interview,' said the *Chronicle* (3 January), 'was of the most distressing nature. After the first burst of agony was over, they all remained for a considerable time incapable of uttering a word.'

Mary Gallop was hanged on Saturday 28 December. At midnight the previous day, she was taken from the county gaol to the city gaol, where the execution was to take place. The *Chester Courant* (1 January) explained that the earlier time had been arranged 'for the purpose of preventing the annoyance to which condemned criminals are exposed from the impertinent curiosity of the rabble that always accompanies such processions'. Long before noon the following day, the hour appointed for her execution, she was 'in such a state of exhaustion' that she didn't have the strength to stand up; she had to be placed on a chair to be pinioned and then carried from the prison to the gallows still sitting on it. And on the drop she remained in that position until the trapdoors were released, with the awful consequences already described.

Thomas Haswell, the Governor of the City Gaol, noted in his Gaolor's Journal on 28 December, 'She died after many severe Struggles, which may be accounted for by the Sitting posture when she fell . . . She was

The specially-adapted chair on which Jane Scott was hanged for murdering her parents at Lancaster in 1828.

From the author's collection.

Conveyed to the Castle about 2 o'Clock this day and was interred there at 8 o'Clock at Night.'

Although contemporary newspaper reports made no mention of the fact, it could be that the chair in question was not just any old chair, but that, like the long-legged 'Dickensian clerk's chair' famously used for the execution of murderess Jane Scott at Lancaster Gaol in 1828, it had been modified in some way especially for the purpose. Scott had also been found guilty of parental homicide — she poisoned both her father *and* mother — but at her hanging the chair, which had been fitted with castors, was snatched from under her just as the drop fell.

On her arrival at the City Gaol, the *Courant* had described Mary's appearance as 'short in stature, and of a florid complexion with a somewhat heavy countenance'; she was wearing the 'black stuff dress with a black-and-white plaid shawl' that she had worn at her trial. After the trapdoors had finally swallowed up the condemned woman and her attendant chair, the *Courant* reported, 'Her sufferings were dreadfully protracted for some minutes' and the watching crowd 'uttered a yell of execration against the executioner'. The execution, the paper added, was witnessed by 'an immense multitude . . . who behaved with becoming decency'.

The *Courant* referred to a meeting Mary Gallop had had with the Castle Chaplain just before the end, at which Rev. Kilner asked her whether she was in any way involved in the death of her mother, as had been rumoured. She 'most emphatically denied all participation in that melancholy circumstance'. And the paper declared, 'We firmly believe that she was innocent of that offence, though an industrious malignity has endeavoured to brand her with that crime also.'

A week later the *Courant* lambasted the unnamed hangman for his 'heartless and bungling manner' and urged the city authorities never to employ him again. The paper added, deprecatingly, 'We understand the fellow is not what may be called a professional hangman, but an amateur in this repulsive vocation.'

There was bitter irony in a footnote to the Crewe murder case provided by the young man for whom Mary Gallop gave her life. A few days before her execution she had contacted her half-sister in Liverpool asking her to tell him of her 'strong desire' to see him before she died. 'An answer was returned from him, couched in very cold terms,' the *Courant* reported on 1 January. 'It merely declined the visit and expressed the writer's thankfulness that he was no way implicated in the murder of her father.'

*　　　*　　　*

BEFORE she died Alice Hewitt gave no such reassurances to the man in her life. On the contrary, after being found guilty of murdering her mother, she made doubly sure that George Holt was very much implicated in the crime. And public opinion at the time was that Holt, the father of the child to whom she had given birth while in prison awaiting trial, had good reason to be thankful that he did not end up in the dock with her.

The couple seem to have met during the late summer of 1861, when a 25-year-old Alice went to work at Tattersall's cotton mill in Radcliffe, near Bury, where Holt was her supervisor. Two months later he was sacked for an undisclosed reason and he moved back in with his parents in Bury. When, three or four weeks later, Tattersall's closed, Alice returned to Stockport to live with her widowed mother, Mrs Mary Bailey, at Hough's Buildings on Lark Hill in the Heaton Norris area of the town; this was a steeply-inclined thoroughfare — known locally as 'Jacob's Ladder' and 'Spion Kop' — where the now unemployed Alice occupied a furnished room in the attic.

She was also a widow; it is possible that she was the Alice Bailey who married George Hewitt, a 26-year-old weaver, in March 1852 in the Chapel of St. Thomas's, Heaton Norris. But if so, she lied about her age. Mary Bailey's daughter would have been no more than 16 at the time, not 25, as shown in the marriage register (at 16 she would have been old enough to get married, though she would have needed parental consent). And the Stockport burial records for 1852-1863 do contain one man named George Hewitt. He was from Heaton Norris and died in the second half of 1852 at the age of 27.

Just before Christmas 1861 Alice sent Holt a letter inviting him to come and live with her and her mother. In order to avoid any conflict with Mrs Bailey's strict Methodist upbringing, Alice told her that she and Holt had been married while she was working away and they began living as man and wife. He, however, seems to have had trouble

finding a job and went back, briefly, to Bury. Then, when Alice sent a second letter informing him she had found him work locally, he returned to Lark Hill.

Two months later, however, Hough's Buildings were earmarked for demolition to make way for developments to Stockport's railway network, and Holt and the two women moved the three-quarters-of-a-mile to 43, Great Egerton Street, Heaton Norris, a two-up-two-down terrace house they rented in Holt's name. This was in 1862, by which time he was working as a blacksmith

'Jacob's Ladder', Lark Hill, where Hewitt and Holt lived with Alice's mother Mary after deceiving her into believing they were married.

Photo courtesy of the I Love Stockport, Stockport Memories *and* Memories of Stockport *websites.*

and (steam) engine driver on a farm in Heaton Mersey, earning 16 shillings a week (about £80 today), and Alice was passing herself off as 'Mrs Holt'.

At the beginning of 1863 a married couple, George Bailey (no relation) and his wife Ann, and their two children, aged 10 and seven, became lodgers at No.43; they occupied the two rooms at the back of the house — a sitting room on the ground floor and a bedroom above — while Alice, her 'husband' and her mother had similar living arrangements at the front of the house. The cohabiting couple shared one bed while Alice's mother was said by Holt to sleep 'on a bed on the floor' (just a covered mattress, presumably).

The idea of murdering her mother may well have occurred to Hewitt as early as January, following a chance meeting at a friend's house with Samuel Garlick, a part-time agent for the Wesleyan and General Assurance Society, which specialised in low-premium policies. She had

Great Egerton Street, Heaton Norris, where, in 1862, George Holt rented a home at No. 43 for himself, Alice and her mother. The houses were demolished in the 1960s.

Photo by permission of Stockport Local Heritage Library.

expressed a passing interest in taking out insurance on the life of her mother and on 18 February Garlick paid her a follow-up visit. He told her that sixpence a week would buy life cover of £25 16s, around £3,000 by modern values. Mrs Bailey signed the proposal form and the poverty-stricken Alice, who regularly resorted to pawning her and Holt's clothes to make ends meet, paid the agent two weeks premiums in advance.

However, Garlick, a 57-year-old schoolmaster from Brinnington, explained that before the agreement could be confirmed, Mrs Bailey would have to be interviewed by his district manager, Mr Peter Scarlett, and pass a medical examination. Which presented Alice Hewitt with a problem. For how could her crippled mother, who could only walk with the aid of a stick and who was also suffering from bronchitis at the time, satisfy the assurance company that she was a sound risk? Her solution: she would get somebody to pose as her mother to accompany her to the two appointments.

Alice at first asked Ann Bailey if she would co-operate in the deception. But her lodger refused to have anything to do with it. So, instead, she persuaded her friend Mrs Elizabeth Wells of Didsbury, near Manchester, to impersonate her mother. When she asked if she would be 'doing right', Alice lied, 'Oh, yes, the collector said anyone would do to pass the doctor.' And widow Mrs Wells would say in court later that Alice told her that 'if she would go with her, it would get her the "club money"'.

And so, on 6 March, with Alice fielding most of the questions posed by Stockport surgeon Henry Heginbotham, Medical Officer for the assurance society, and her friend putting her cross to the certificate, the fraud was complete. At one point Hewitt claimed that her mother

191

had 'always had good health.' Earlier that day the two women's little masquerade had also fooled Peter Scarlett. He signed the official papers and Alice collected them on 23 March. Four days later Mary Bailey died in agony. Walter Barker, Assistant House Surgeon at Stockport Infirmary, one of two medical men who had been treating her, diagnosed the cause of death as gastroenteritis.

His death certificate was in due course presented to Scarlett and on 8 April, though he expressed surprise at Mrs Bailey's sudden demise, he paid the grieving daughter the cash lump sum at his home at 57, Lower Hillgate, Stockport. It was not nearly as much as she was expecting, as deductions had to be made to take account of the undertaker's bill and the cost of mourning clothes provided by 30-year-old Scarlett (who was also a draper and shirt-maker) for her and her 'husband'. In the end her eventual payout was just over £10.

Despite the timing of the assurance application, the circumstances of Mrs Bailey's decease had raised no immediate suspicions, and her funeral went ahead on 31 March. She was interred in the graveyard of the former Brunswick Wesleyan Chapel, demolished in 1955 as part of a massive highway improvement scheme. The walled area of its cemetery (complete with burials, apparently) can still be seen today slap bang in the middle of the busy Portwood roundabout at Junction 27 of the M60 motorway. It wasn't until nearly three months later that the real cause of her death was established . . . and Alice Hewitt was charged with matricide.

The old Brunswick Chapel in whose graveyard the body of Mary Bailey was interred, exhumed and re-buried. The Chapel closed in 1955.

The walled graveyard area is all that can now be seen of the Chapel as it stands isolated in middle of the Portwood roundabout close to the M60 motorway (though the graves are thought to lie there still).

Photograph by the author.

Mrs Bailey's neighbour and long-time friend, Maria Hadfield, a 48-year-old mother of six living in King Street, Heaton Norris, provided the crucial evidence that set the murder investigation in train. She it was who tipped off the

Wesleyan and General that the 'mother' who had attended their interviews was an imposter. Further inquiries followed, which resulted in an order being obtained for the exhumation of the dead woman. And when, on 12 June, the grave was re-opened and the coffin lid removed, the remarkably well-preserved corpse displayed the immediately-recognisable signs of arsenic poisoning.

Later that day Dr William Rayner, of Tiviot Dale, Heaton Norris, carried out a postmortem examination. In reporting the start of the inquest the following day, the *Stockport Advertiser* of 19 June quoted him as saying that Mrs Bailey's body was 'saturated' with arsenic.

After hearing evidence of identification from neighbour Mrs Hannah Hodkinson, who had laid out the body), Stockport Division Coroner William Johnson adjourned the inquest for two weeks.

When it resumed on 4 July, again at the Vernon Arms — the pub stood at the junction of Vernon Street and Warren Street, but was pulled down in the 1980s to make way for major retail developments in the north-west corner of the town centre — the pathologist elaborated on his earlier statement. According to the *Chester Chronicle*, he said he

The Vernon Arms: The inquest heard how Mary Bailey's body was 'saturated' in arsenic.

The photograph, taken in 1913, was kindly supplied by James F. Phelan, whose grandfather, James Edward Sheehan, was then the landlord and can be seen standing in the pub doorway.

found arsenic in the deceased's stomach, liver, bowels, kidneys, heart and skin and, not unnaturally, formed the opinion that death had been caused by 'the administration of arsenic, probably in repeated doses so as to impregnate and pervade the whole of the tissues of the body'. A feature of arsenic is that quite small amounts can remain in the body to form a lethal accumulation.

Dr Rayner disclosed that he had obtained more than 180 grains of the poison from his various tests. As few as four or five grains were known to be enough to kill.

From the depositions that survive in the official court papers, it appears that Mrs Bailey's symptoms had begun in February after her daughter bought some penny pork pies, which made her ill. Lodger George Bailey, a 36-year-old stoker, deposed that Mrs Bailey — though she was referred to throughout the whole of the legal proceedings as 'the old woman', she was, in fact, only 51 when she died — had 'several times sicked up the pork pie'. But Alice Hewitt had continued to buy the pies, each time telling her mother, 'Eat this, it will do you good.'

Bailey himself was offered part of one of the pies and, an hour after eating it, he said, he, too, was 'very sick and vomited a great deal throughout that night'. He was so ill he was off work for a fortnight.

Bailey's 33-year-old wife Ann made two formal statements; in the second one, which she provided after the inquest, she recalled Alice Hewitt saying to her that she would 'not buy any more [pies] for her mother, for when I give it to her she throws it back again'. If she had put arsenic in the pies — the suggestion was that she may have introduced it via the holes in the pastry 'lids' through which the baker added the gravy — perhaps she was concerned that the poison was not having the desired effect and that a new strategy was required. If so, her mother's continuing stomach problems, and the medication prescribed by her doctors, were to prove the almost perfect cover for the next phase of her murder plan.

In her inquest deposition, Ann Bailey had revealed how she unwittingly became a part of Alice Hewitt's final solution. She stated that, on Wednesday 25 March, two days before Mrs Bailey died, Alice had asked her to go with her to the nearby chemist's shop of Mr Henry Davenport in Heaton Lane, Heaton Norris. Alice explained that she had been to the shop earlier to buy some arsenic and was told by Davenport that, before he could sell it to her, she would have to produce someone over the age of 21 to sign the poison register as a witness to the transaction.

These registers, in which sellers had to keep detailed records of every sale, including the names and addresses of the customers and their reasons for purchasing the product, were among the provisions of the Sale of Arsenic Regulation Act 1851 and the subsequent Sale of Poisons Act 1857. They were the first attempts to control the supply of the poison and were introduced in response to increasing public alarm over the incidence of arsenic poisonings, which had reached epidemic proportions in Britain in the first half of the century. During the period, white arsenic, or arsenic trioxide, was widely used domestically to kill rats, mice and other vermin; it was an ingredient of a variety of beauty treatments, of tonic mixtures and other medicines and could be found in the dye of such common household items as children's toys, flypaper and wallpaper.

It was so readily obtainable that, with just a couple of pence, a child could walk into almost any corner shop and purchase enough of the deadly powder to wipe out an entire family. And it was so frequently used by potential beneficiaries of wills that it earned the nickname of 'the inheritor's powder'.

As such, arsenic was responsible for untold numbers of deaths, both accidental and deliberate. A harmless-looking substance that, at a glance, could be mistaken for flour or sugar, it is odourless, soluble in water and, when mixed with hot food or drinks, virtually tasteless; and until 1836 there was no reliable means of detecting whether the victim had died from ingesting poison or from any one of a number of potentially fatal stomach disorders whose symptoms were identical. It is easy to see why it became the poison of choice for murderers, particularly women.

In Alice Hewitt's case, she told her puzzled co-tenant — and later Mr Davenport the chemist — that she wanted the poison 'to kill fleas and bugs'. At the shop both women put their marks to the register and Alice was handed a quarter-pound of arsenic (113 grams), costing three (old) pence, the minimum quantity set by the new legislation. It was coloured blue; the law now also required shopkeepers to dye all arsenic sold over the counter with either indigo or soot. Arriving back home Alice demonstrated her purpose by mixing some of the poison with cold water in a jug and 'degging' (a Northern dialect word meaning 'sprinkling') the beds and bedroom floor with it. She afterwards scalded the jug and 'brewed her tea in it'. Next day she persuaded Ann Bailey to go with her again to buy another three-pennyworth of arsenic and repeated the 'disinfecting' process. This time she put the arsenic solution in a mug which, said Ann Bailey, 'was the one in which the deceased's medicine was usually given'. Afterwards, she added, Alice cautioned her 'not [to] say anything at all about this arsenic'.

During the final days of her life, Mary Bailey was so ill she had a bed made up on a couch in the living room. Ann Bailey's statement went on, 'She continued to grow worse and did not leave her bed afterwards without being carried.' About three in the morning of 27 March Alice came into Ann's bedroom and said her mother was dying. Ann tried to assure her that it was not true; but just before 5am Alice returned to announce that her mother was dead. Ann got up and went to Mrs Bailey and noticed that her face and neck were much swollen.

Later, as Hannah Hodkinson was washing the body, Alice said to Ann, 'Well, Ann, I'm very glad my mother's dead. I've all my clothes fast [a reference to the items held by the pawnbroker] and I wanted this money to release me.' And she remarked that had her mother not died, 'it would be "God help us", for if she had not got the money her "husband" would beat her.' Alice had told Ann that she and Holt were not really married.

Catherine Ryan, of Threadneedle Street, Heaton Norris, a friend of Mrs Bailey for 20 years, stated in her inquest deposition that she had visited 'the old woman' several times during her illness. On the first occasion, on Saturday 21 March, Mrs Bailey had sent for her. She found her friend 'very ill in bed downstairs'; she had severe stomach pains, she was vomiting and very thirsty, and 'drank frequently of milk'. Mrs Ryan returned the following day and, at Mrs Bailey's request, stayed until next morning. During the night, as Mrs Bailey continued vomiting, she said to her visitor, 'This is very hard work' and, pointing to the bedroom Holt shared with Alice, added, 'You watch, upstairs says if I'm not either guded [good] or mended, he will tumble us both out this week.'

Mrs Ryan called again the following Tuesday night (24th) and expressed the view that Mrs Bailey would recover. She said Alice replied sharply, 'I thought you had skill, Mrs Ryan, but I see you have not. Anybody might see she is dying.' She claimed the medicine prescribed by Dr Rayner was 'poisoning her mother'. Not to be confused with the pathologist, this was Dr. Thomas Vernon Rayner, of Stockport, who, as well as Dr Barker, was also treating Mrs Bailey. In Mrs Ryan's presence, Hewitt put some of the preparation in a cup and offered it to her mother, but she was too ill to take it. Alice threw it into the fire. Mrs Ryan commented, 'I'd never go for medicine and throw it away.' Alice, she said, retorted, 'Oh, hell to them and their medicine.'

On the evening of Thursday the 26th Mrs Ryan was again at the house. She stated, 'Between 11 and 12 o'clock, Alice Hewitt asked her mother if she would like a sup of brandy. Mrs Bailey said "Yes" and Alice went out to fetch it. She was away about three-quarters-of-an-hour. She brought a cup and placed it on a table but did not offer it to her mother. I said, "Alice, you should not leave that drop of brandy uncovered as it will lose [its] strength." She said she had grated some root [arrowroot?] in it and wanted it to dissolve.'

The 'cup' — this was Mrs Bailey's regular medicine 'mug' referred to by Ann Bailey — stayed on the table half-an-hour before Hewitt finally handed it to her mother. When Mrs Bailey failed to drink it all, said Mrs Ryan, 'Alice began to sauce her [be rude or impudent to her], telling her to drink it all as it had cost her seven pence'. Mrs Ryan was there when, at about 4.45am the next day, Mrs Bailey finally passed away. 'She had a fit and screamed awfully before she died,' she deposed.

And she informed the Coroner, 'After her mother died, Hewitt said [that] I must not strip her naked.' But she did so. 'I found the body much discoloured,' revealed Mrs Ryan. 'I showed Alice the body. She began to cry and said it was the convulsions.' The inquest jury had no hesitation in returning a verdict of wilful murder against Alice Hewitt.

On 1 July she had appeared at the Cheshire Quarter Sessions at Knutsford charged with defrauding the assurance company. With a far more serious charge ahead of her, she was remanded in custody to appear at the next Chester Assizes on 6 August. By then, however, she was pregnant; so the case was postponed. The *Chester Chronicle* (8 August), reporting her brief appearance, observed, 'The prisoner is a middle-sized and somewhat plain-looking woman, and who appeared to be suffering from illness.' She had her baby, a boy, on 15 August in Chester Castle Gaol and her trial eventually took place over the two days, 9-10 December.

Not surprisingly, some considerable time was spent examining the medical evidence. In the *Chester Chronicle*'s trial report of 12 December Dr Barker testified that he had attended Mrs Bailey the first time on 12 March, when she complained of 'great sickness, pain over [her] back and loins and severe headaches'. He gave her 'soothing medicine'; but the following day, when she had shown no sign of improvement, he changed the prescription, believing now that she was suffering from inflammation of the stomach and bowels. Over the course of the next two weeks, however, Mrs Bailey grew weaker and weaker as the pain increased. The doctor was baffled; he had been preparing the medicine for collection at Stockport Infirmary, yet it was having no effect. On one visit, after checking the quantity remaining, he accused Hewitt of not giving the medicine to Mrs Bailey regularly enough. Hewitt had replied that the medicine was making her mother sick.

In a detailed breakdown of his autopsy findings, Dr. William Rayner said Mrs Bailey's body showed virtually no signs of decomposition even after 73 days in the ground. Delaying decomposition, he explained, was a classic effect of arsenic poisoning. Of the substantial amount of the poison he recovered from the cadaver, 160 grains were extracted from the solid contents of the stomach which, he stated, were 'administered shortly before death'. An expert in testing for poison, Dr Rayner applied a number of what were then fairly new methods of arsenic detection, though one of the tests was rather less scientific: he gave two grains to a pigeon, he told the jury, and the bird was dead within 40 minutes.

Dr Rayner also examined Mary Bailey's medicine mug. It had been found in a cupboard at her house by George Bailey, who handed it to the police. He saw there was a crack in it, caused by boiling water, and this, too, tested positive for arsenic.

George Holt told the court he had known that Hewitt had insured Mrs Bailey's life about eight or nine days before she died. Up to that time, he said, the deceased was 'a hearty old woman'. And, no doubt aware of the public animosity towards him, he insisted that throughout her illness he had given Mary Bailey no medicine, food or drink. In fact, according to the *Chronicle*'s trial report of 12 December, he pointed out that he had 'kissed the old woman in her coffin because he was fond of her'. He did not remember saying he would 'tumble' Alice and her mother out of the house if Mrs Bailey did not get well soon; or threatening to beat Alice if she did not get the insurance money.

On day two of the trial, Edmund Swetenham, regarded as one of the most able defence counsel on the circuit, put up a sturdy fight on Hewitt's behalf, arguing that the whole case against her was built on 'circumstantial evidence and nothing more than strong suspicion'. Much of the evidence, he suggested, could apply equally to Ann Bailey or George Holt. Referring to the medicine mug used regularly by Mrs Bailey, he pointed out that it was also the one in which her daughter had dissolved a quantity of arsenic to disinfect the front bedroom. Just before she died, Mrs Bailey had drunk copious amounts of milk to try to slake her thirst (another classic symptom of arsenic poisoning). And he postulated that traces of the arsenic could have remained in the crack in the mug through lack of proper rinsing; in effect that Mary Bailey died 'through carelessness'.

The jury, however, took only half-an-hour to find the accused guilty, though they did 'strongly recommend' her to mercy. The *Chronicle* reported that when the Judge, Sir James Willes, assumed the black cap to pronounce the death sentence, 'the prisoner fell down in the dock, crying out in the most piteous manner,"I am not guilty. I am not guilty. Oh, my poor baby."' When she had recovered some of her composure, the Judge described her crime as 'the worst sort of murder in the knowledge of the law, because no care can protect against such an insidious attack upon life'.

Mr Justic Willes was known in assize court circles as 'The Weeping Judge', for his inclination to shed tears while hearing particularly moving evidence and pronouncing the death sentence. But this was no sob story. He told the convicted woman he would forward the jury's mercy recommendation to Her Majesty's advisors. But he added, 'I warn you to entertain no hope that it will be acceded to.' Up until then, the *Stockport Advertiser* (11 December) noted, 'the prisoner appeared to be the most unconcerned person in the court' and

Judge Willes: not an occasion for weeping.

she 'actually laughed' when Mr John Lawson, Relieving Officer of the Stockport Poor Law Union — from which Mrs Bailey was receiving a small amount of parish relief — testified that she 'used to complain to him of her [Alice's] conduct towards her'.

After being sentenced, Hewitt was 'carried swooning' from the dock, into which she was followed almost immediately by . . . George Holt. Not to face a charge relating to Mary Bailey's murder, as many people felt was his due, but to save his skin. For in an amazing sequel to the trial, a number of spectators made a rush towards him as the court dispersed (this was the last case to be heard that day). As the *Advertiser* put it, 'The public manifested considerable feeling against [him]. They cried "Fetch him out" and looked as though they were prepared to offer violence to him on his appearance outside.'

On the advice of a member of the prosecution team — who, said the paper, had 'noticed this hostile expression' — he 'jumped into the dock and made his way through the gaol; thence, by changing his hat to disguise himself, he managed to escape to the railway station and, without further molestation, he reached Stockport the same night'.

And the *Advertiser*'s 'verdict' on the affair? 'There is little doubt,' the paper declared on 1 January 1864 ['that] despite Holt's assertions to the contrary . . . the murder of the old woman had been spoken of between the prisoner and her paramour, if he did not actually assist in its committal. He certainly behaved very brutally to her while living in the same house and has shown an utter indifference to her fate since her committal [to prison].'

Holt, who all along denied he had received any of the insurance money, did not exactly endear himself to the public when he admitted that, when she was arrested on the murder charge in July, he had effectively abandoned his 'wife', the mother of his child, and scuttled off back to his parents in Bury. Towards the end of the prosecution's case, he had been recalled to the witness stand and, according to the *Chester Chronicle* (12 December), he said he 'never visited the prisoner since she was in gaol, nor assisted her with money'. The next time he saw her was at the trial. And the *Cheshire Observer* (2 January) reported an incident which, it said, made 'the conduct of her paramour appear [even] more shockingly repulsive'. The paper claimed that Holt had at one point visited Chester but that 'while she was lying in gaol [he] spent his time . . . in drinking and going about playing his concertina'.

Alice herself made her feelings clear in two statements she made shortly before she was executed . . . and alleged he was more than an innocent bystander in the murder. Much more.

In the first of the statements, which were widely reported in the press, she said that when she had brought the insurance papers home, 'Holt then proposed that I should get some charcoal and put it alight under mother's bed when she was asleep, for she would never wake [any] more' (unable to move unaided, she would have eventually been overcome by the poisonous fumes). Then, in bed on the Wednesday night before Mary Bailey's death, she claimed Holt had said that it would be 'a great releasement if she was in her grave and he would buy some stretchnine [strychnine] if I would give it to her. I said, "Thou hast brought me to destruction, and now thou want to drag me to the gallows". Then he beat me.'

After her mother had drunk some beer from her mug, Hewitt's statement added, 'I saw in the bottom a quantity of arsenic coloured blue. I said to him, 'Thou has given my mother arsenic." He said if I told ought he would have me taken up for defrauding the insurance. He said, "Nobody will believe but what thou hast done it thyself." This was the only arsenic my mother ever had.'

Her words were recorded by John Kilner, who spent many hours in conversation with the condemned woman in Chester Castle Gaol. The *Observer* reported that she told him that 'she was conscious of having spent a wicked life and was sorry for it; but she made no special allusion to the murder'.

Pressed further by the gaol's Chaplain, Alice made a second statement modifying her previous accusations by explaining that Holt had only 'offered' her mother the beer and that, when she could not drink it, he had placed the mug on the mantle-piece and left the house. She went on, 'I then said, "Mother, cannot ye sup this gill of beer?" She then took it from my hand and supped it. When I looked at the bottom [of the mug] I seed the arsenic.' About an ounce-and-a-half of beer remained in the mug. 'I put it at the top of the cupboard,' she stated, 'and thought of taking it myself.'

Ann Bailey cleaned the cupboard out and washed up the mug, but not before remarking, 'This is arsenic. This is the [mug] thy mother had that beer in.' Alice's new statement concluded, 'I said "Yes", I said I didn't know how it had gotten in.'

Rev. Kilner, urged on by Hewitt's relatives, was among the many petitioners campaigning for a reprieve; but on Saturday 26 December, as the trial judge had warned, Home Secretary Lord John Russell — quoting the standard civil service response on these occasions — informed the condemned woman that he could 'see no grounds to justify him in advising her Majesty to interfere with the due course of the law'. She was hanged shortly after 8am on Monday 28 December

1863 at Chester City Gaol, watched by a crowd estimated by at least one newspaper as numbering between 4,000-5,000 (though the local *Observer* put it at 'not more than one thousand').

The 'DREADFUL SCENE UPON THE SCAFFOLD', as it was headlined in a number of publications, was described in the 29 December edition of the *London Morning Advertiser* thus,

> *As soon as the criminal stepped upon the platform of death, a subdued murmur ran through the crowd, which was followed by a deathlike silence for a few minutes, broken only by the piteous wailings of the culprit. The cap and rope having been adjusted, she fell upon her knees and prayed that her infant child might be spared a similar fate, and that her death might be a warning to others. She then rose, and in the most piteous manner, begged the executioner to make haste with his dreadful work. Calcraft then withdrew to one side, and pulled the bolt, but the drop would not fall. A second time the attempt was made, but with the same result. All the time the doomed woman was heard exclaiming "Make haste!" and each time she heard the bolt withdrawn she gave an agonising shriek. Calcraft went through his work with the coolness of a practised hand, and the third time, with the aid of some of the gaol officials, the drop fell with a dull, heavy thud. The woman fell with a violent jerk about three or four feet, and the prayer upon her lips was left unfinished. She struggled hard, and her sufferings were aggravated by the incomplete adjustment of the rope, as well as from her being a very light and slender woman. Calcraft almost immediately went in front of the dying woman and strapped her legs more rightly. A few groans, and a few more struggles, and all was over.*

The anger aroused by the conduct of the 63-year-old Calcraft at the execution — and by Alice Hewitt's suffering — was afterwards voiced most forcibly by one of the officials present that day. In a letter to the Editor of the *Chester Chronicle* of 2 January, the anonymous correspondent wrote, 'I have to protest against the bungled way in which Calcraft performed his wretched offices. To prevent the poor sufferer from moving her hands and arms when in the agonies of death, Calcraft had provided a terrible apparatus of

A typical headline in the aftermath of Alice Hewitt's execution — this one from the *Leeds Mercury* of 29 December 1863.

straps. It was frightful to look at; the leather was stiff, and the holes made to receive the tongues of the buckles were too small to admit them, so that the culprit was put to much unnecessary suffering by the inefficient efforts made to insert them. Again, the rope was improperly adjusted, hence the protracted struggles of the poor creature during which she released one of her hands and raised it to her throat. Surely Calcraft has had sufficient experience to render him an expert in his wretched craft, and he doubtless is when he attends to its preliminaries, which he never could have done on this occasion. Witness again his fruitless efforts to cause the drop to fall.'

The correspondent added, 'I write these remarks in the interest of humanity, as the sufferings to be borne and witnessed on these terrible occasions are sufficiently horrible without their being thus intensified.'

During his 45-year career, the Essex-born William Calcraft created a reputation that made him Britain's most famous/infamous hangman of the 19th Century. By the time he retired in 1874 he had carried out an estimated 450 executions. The man who was responsible for the occasional botched-up job was by trade . . . a cobbler.

William Calcraft: carried out 450 hangings in 45 years. But his methods earned him the sobriquet of 'The Strangler'.

Like most of the newspapers that covered the execution, the *Cheshire Observer* noted the 'very singular fact' that the last woman to be hanged in Chester (Mary Gallop in 1844) had been put to death on the same date, and for a similar crime, as Hewitt.

Alice Hewitt's child was eventually taken in and raised by one of her relatives, the same relative who funded her defence, apparently. He assured her the child would be well looked after — which, reported the *Chester Chronicle*, 'gave her great satisfaction, as she appeared to have a great dread of the child becoming an inmate of a workhouse'.

● Alice Hewitt was the last woman to be executed in public in Cheshire, *not* in Britain, as some authors have claimed. That distinction belonged to 25-year-old Frances Kidder of Hythe in Kent who, having been found guilty of murdering her 11-year-old step-daughter, was hanged outside Maidstone Prison on 2 April 1868 — eight weeks before the Capital Punishment Within Prisons Act came into force.

CHAPTER NINE

Was He Hanged By Mistake?

As the last person to be hanged in Britain for attempted murder, Martin Doyle, executed at Chester in 1861, occupies a unique place in criminal history. His destiny was made all the more notable by the fact that, although it did not come into force officially until later, an Act of Parliament, making the offence no longer punishable by death, had received the Royal Assent *three weeks before* his execution.

Considerably less well known, but even more remarkable, is that he was almost certainly hanged by mistake . . . the result of a bureaucratic blunder in the Home Office.

Irishman Doyle had inexplicably attacked his girlfriend while tramping the Cheshire countryside in a search for work. As the couple sheltered under a tree from a sudden downpour, he battered her repeatedly about the head with a large stone. She was so badly injured that she was not expected to survive. But she recovered; and, with her extensive wounds shockingly visible to the court, she appeared as a tragically convincing witness against him at his trial that Summer.

From the sustained savagery of his assault, it was obvious that Martin Doyle had meant to kill the woman; and few protested when he received the sentence that was then usually reserved for murderers. The Judge, Sir Charles Crompton, said it was 'one of the grossest crimes that it has ever fallen to my lot to investigate'. He told the defendant that he had considered imposing a lesser penalty, but added, 'I should not be doing my duty to the public were I not to pass upon you the full sentence of the law.'

Within days, however, Sir Charles's sense of duty would leave him in the improbable situation of questioning his own judgment, after hearing that the Government was about to scrap the death penalty for attempted murder. If his information was correct, he was now equally positive that it would be a miscarriage of justice if Doyle was hanged. He set off for London and an immediate audience with the Home Secretary, Sir George Grey. Sir George, however, was out of town, and he was seen by the Permanent Under-Secretary Haratio Waddington who, it was alleged, told him the Government had no such plans and that, unless there were exceptional circumstances, death was still the prescribed punishment for attempted murder.

All too aware that there had not been one single mitigating factor in the case against Doyle, Mr Justice Crompton left Whitehall re-assured that he had made the right decision. And, as the senior Home Office official — a man with over 20 years experience in the job — had explained what he believed was the current situation, it appears the Judge's concerns were not communicated to the minister. Doyle was executed, his name disappeared from the public prints and he seemed destined to become just another one-line entry in the nation's record book of crime.

At the end of Parliament's 1861 Summer recess, Sir Charles met Horatio Waddington again. By then he was aware that he had been misled; the new legislation, part of the Criminal Law Consolidation Acts, 1861, which reserved the death penalty for four crimes — murder, piracy, high treason and arson in a royal dockyard, though in modern times it has only ever been enacted in the case of murder — was set to take effect on 1 November. Not surprisingly, the subject of the law change was revisited. There is no official record of their conversation; indeed, there would be no public acknowledgement that it had even taken place for another 16 years, so we don't know how, or even if, the Under-Secretary managed to explain the misinformation he had given Judge Crompton at their previous meeting. But it was reported later that he had been keen to emphasise that the Queen's formal consent to the abolition of hanging for attempted murder was signed *before Doyle's conviction* (just two days before, in fact); and it was with some relief, apparently, that he exclaimed, 'It was God's mercy that the man was legally executed.'

Four years later, as the Royal Commission on Capital Punishment was conducting the first of several investigations into the continuing validity of the death penalty, the execution of Martin Doyle was cited by the abolitionists in their (unsuccessful) attempt to have it expunged from the statute book. In 1877, when they made another bid to have the law reviewed, the full story of Sir Charles Crompton's efforts to prevent Doyle's controversial death was finally made public. It would not have made comfortable reading in Parliamentary circles.

All that, however, was in the future, and we shall return to it presently. First, though, a look back at the reasons behind the Judge's fatal decision and the story of this seemingly senseless crime and the case that refused to go away . . .

In 1861 Martin Doyle was a 26-year-old native of County Mayo who was described as a 'tramping glazier', a self-employed jobbing tradesman who roamed from place to place to find business. He had lived for the previous 13 years in Ormskirk in Lancashire. His last known address was in Crompton's Yard in the Aughton Street area of the town, where he resided with his 40-year-old wife Mary. There was, however, another woman in his life, with whom he had been carrying on an affair for some time, apparently. She was Jane Brogine, also from Ormskirk and another older woman (her exact age doesn't appear in any newspaper report or court document and a search among census, church and civil records failed to turn up any trace of her). Her husband John had left her in the autumn of 1860 and taken their two children with him. Also Irish, she claimed she had met Doyle about a month later; that afterwards she spent 'three or four days' with him and that early in 1861 they went to Wigan, where they lived together for about three months.

Doyle would say during his final days that his marriage was an unhappy one and that some time after becoming friendly with Mrs Brogine, whose maiden name seems to have been Livingstone, he left his wife. But, according to census records, they were still living together in Crompton's Yard on 7 April 1861. After leaving their Wigan love-nest Doyle had left his mistress to go looking for work, so it is possible that he returned temporarily to the marital home and was there on the day of the count. However, though his job took him away from home regularly, it seems likely that Mary Doyle had at least an inkling of her husband's infidelity by then.

Around this time Jane Brogine also took up a wandering lifestyle. She travelled first to Blackburn and then Burnley, where she paid a brief visit to her brother, 25-year-old Robert Livingstone, at a lodging house in Bamford Square, before being forced to interrupt her walkabout due to what she described as 'a bad leg'. She spent five weeks in Bradford Infirmary receiving treatment for the problem followed by three weeks recuperating at the home of a friend, Maria Curtis, in the St. Peter's district of the town.

She then got a job as a 'maid of all work' at the Star Hotel in King Street, Oldham (latterly known as the Star Inn, though now no longer a licensed house), and she remained there until 24 May. Returning to Ormskirk, she soon hit the road again; Doyle found out where she was heading and overtook her on the outskirts of the town. They decided to strike out for Newcastle-under-Lyme, Staffordshire, where Doyle had a brother and, he assured her, he would have a better chance of finding work. By this time, though, he seems to have given up the idea of continuing in his old trade, as Mrs Brogine was later reported as saying that, at some point during their ramblings, they had been in Macclesfield, where he had sold his 'glazier's diamond' (glass cutter).

Their journey south took them through St. Helens, Prescot and Warrington and on 29 May the pair were 'on the tramp' through Cheshire. After spending the night at a lodging house near the railway

The farm, now demolished, that stood on the site of the Linley tollgate. On the right, the start of the plantation in which Jane Brogine was savagely beaten and left for dead.

station in Holmes Chapel they left the next morning and took the Newcastle road (now the A50). Two o'clock in the afternoon of Thursday 30 May found them passing through the Linley tollgate on what is now the A5011 Linley Road in the township of Church Lawton, some eight miles south-east of Holmes Chapel and less than half-a-mile from the Staffordshire border. It had just come on to rain and, a short distance beyond the toll-bar (until its recent demolition the building known as Tollgate Farm stood on the site) they took shelter under an oak tree in a wooded hollow beside the turnpike. As the rain persisted they moved further down the steeply-sided hollow — a disused stone quarry — and they found an alder tree and sat huddled together beneath its more protective canopy.

In the mythology associated with the alder, it is said that the Irish once believed it was unlucky to pass one on a journey. What occurred in their little shady nook certainly brought ill fortune down on these two Irish travellers, at least.

When the woman complained of a headache, Doyle laid her head on his knee and told her to rest, a seemingly considerate gesture that

The edge of the woodland, alongside the A5011, leading down into the old quarry and the scene of the attack.

Photographs by the author.

could hardly have prepared her for the acts of unbelievable brutality that followed. She fell asleep almost immediately. When she awoke about three-quarters-of-an -hour later, Doyle had his left hand on the left side of her head and was pressing down on it with all his weight. When she told him to stop, he climbed up the bank towards the turnpike, saying he would go and see if it had ceased raining.

He returned in two or three minutes carrying a large, sharp-edged stone and threw it at her, hitting her on the head and knocking her to the ground. He then knelt on her chest and began throttling her. When she begged him to spare her life he picked up the stone again and beat her about the head and face with it. And still he was not finished with her. When he realised she was still breathing, he knelt on her chest once more and hit her again with the stone until she lost consciousness.

Leaving her for dead, Doyle went to the bottom of the hollow and in the little brook that still flows through it, he washed the blood from his hands. Meanwhile, Jane Brogine was stirring from her blackout and, despite having sustained more than 20 head and facial wounds — most of them cutting to the bone — she managed to crawl back up the bank to the roadway. By her own account 'smothered in blood', she hailed a passing carter, who took her to the lodge of nearby Linley Hall and the police were informed of what had taken place.

When Constable William Beckett arrived he found the woman had passed out again by the roadside and was losing blood; so he had her transported to the Caldwell Arms

At the bottom of the ravine ran a little brook (above), where Doyle washed the blood from his hands.

Photograph by the author.

in the Staffordshire coal-mining village of Talke-o'-th'-Hill, about three-quarters-of-a-mile away in Congleton Road (now the A34), where she received medical attention. The *Chester Chronicle* of 8 June described her condition, 'The woman presents a shocking appearance. Her skull is fractured; her head and face are reduced to the appearance of a jelly

BRUTAL ATTEMPT TO MURDER NEAR SANDBACH.

We have to report one of the most brutal attempts to murder which it has been our lot to record for some time past, especially as occurring in this county. It seems that on Thursday last information was given to the county constabulary that a murder had been committed at New Road, Church Lawton, near Sandbach. An officer proceeded to the place where it was said the murder had been committed, and he found a large quantity of blood there, and several sharp-edged stones, covered with blood. The person who was supposed to be murdered was a woman, and had been removed to a public house a short distance from Church Lawton. Thither the officer went, and found that though the woman was not dead she was in a very precarious state, her body being literally covered with cuts and bruises. A man named Martin Doyle was taken in custody, and was charged with committing the offence, by P.C. Dale of the county force. Dale took his prisoner before G. W. Latham Esq., magistrate, who learning the danger[...]

How the Cheshire Observer *reported the crime on June 8.*

Below: an imaginative sketch of the assault in the more sensational style of the Illustrated Police News.

Images © The British Library Board. All rights reserved. With thanks to Findmypast (www.findmypast.co.uk).

and her hands are much injured. The medical men who are attending her hold out few hopes of her being able to recover.'

Because of the prognosis, on Saturday 1 June Mr George William Latham of Bradwall Hall, near Sandbach, a magistrate and barrister, was despatched to the Caldwell Arms to record what he believed would be the 'death-bed' statement of a dying woman. It began, 'My name is Jane Brogine. I am the wife of John Brogine; he left me at Ormskirk about nine months ago. He took my children with him, a boy and a girl. I have not seen him or them since.'

She then proceeded to tell of her journeyings with Doyle, of reaching Church Lawton and sheltering from the rain in the roadside hollow and of the terrifying moment when she realised her travelling companion was bent on killing her. Her ordeal began when Doyle returned from checking on the weather.

She told the JP, 'He came back with a great stone in his hand, and stood at the back of a tree; he threw it at my head and it knocked me down and made me feel quite silly. I then shouted and put up my hands, and said "Don't. What is that?" He then came and placed both his knees upon my breast, and seized me round my throat and forced my tongue out. He then saw he could not finish me with that, and got [the] sharp stone and said he was determined to have my life as he had come there for it.' At this point, in an apparent attempt to explain Doyle's anger, she said, 'I had expressed a wish that morning [that] if he did not get work at Newcastle, [I would] return back.'

Her statement, which appeared in several newspapers, continued, 'He then began to knock me about the head and face with the stone. I asked him to spare my life; he said "No, your life I intend to have." He kept hammering at me until I was covered with blood. He said, "Now, you bugger, aren't you done." I then drew my breath and gave a great sigh; he then gave me four or five more knocks. I could neither speak nor see, and fainted as he went away from me. As he went away he said "Now, devil, you are done."'

After lying there for a short while, Mrs Brogine began to come to. She heard the sound of a cart clattering along the road above her and, though hampered by her massive injuries and only able to see through one eye, she crawled on her hands and knees up and out of the hollow. When the carter stopped and saw her bloodied head, she said he cried, 'Oh, woman, who has been committing murder?' She replied, 'It is the man who has gone down the road in a white jacket that has done this.'

At that time, however, the man in the 'white jacket' — it was actually a light coloured 'slop' or workman's smock — does not appear to have left the cover of the dense woodland that ran for some distance alongside the turnpike. For it was only after accompanying the badly battered woman to the Caldwell Arms (rebuilt in mock-Tudor style 1939 and now unrecognisable after its metamorphosis into the Caldwell Tavern) that Constable Beckett became aware of a man answering Doyle's description loitering behind them. When the officer arrested him, Doyle made no attempt to resist and freely admitted he was responsible for the woman's injuries. He was secured that evening in the lock-ups in Congleton Road in the nearby hamlet of Hall Green, before being taken to Sandbach to await his appearance before the local magistrates who, on 7 June, committed him to the forthcoming Summer Assizes.

The old Caldwell Arms in Talke. It was here that the full extent of Jane Brogine's injuries were laid bare . . . and a police officer got his hands on the self-confessed assailant.   *Image by permission of J.J. Heath-Caldwell*

His trial, at Chester Castle on Thursday 8 August 1861, opened to a courtroom packed to the limits, such was the amount of public interest the case had generated. After being arraigned by the Clerk of the Court on the formal charge of 'cutting and wounding with intent to murder', he pleaded not guilty. Confusingly, press descriptions of the prisoner in the dock ranged from 'a low, thick-set man', in several newspapers, to 'a rather tall man with a fresh complexion and sandy hair' in the *Liverpool Daily Post*. Refusing counsel, Doyle announced that he would be representing himself. His decision — and the rambling, incoherent and boorish way in which he conducted his defence — would do him no favours with the jury.

What both press and public observers found particularly repugnant was his insensitive treatment of the prosecution's chief witness, the woman he almost battered to death on that rainy day in May. Jane Brogine's arrival in court had caused quite a sensation. She did not take the witness stand, but instead was given a seat close to the Judge. The *Macclesfield Courier* (10 August) reported that 'she seemed in an extremely low state'. It was ten weeks since the assault but, the paper stated, 'Her forehead and upper part of her face bore marks of the barbarous treatment she had received. Her skull was indented in many places [and] bore terrible evidence of the cruel punishment her ruffianly paramour inflicted upon her.'

While giving evidence, Mrs Brogine broke down several times and the trial had to be held up for her to receive what were described in the press as 'restoratives'. In her testimony she expanded on her 'dying statement', and was naturally more lucid than when interviewed by JP George Latham. According to the *Courier*, when she awoke in the roadside hollow to find Doyle pressing hard on her head, she now remembered saying to him, 'Take your hand off my head for my head does ache with the weight of it.' And, seemingly still not realising that Doyle intended to do her harm, she added innocently, 'And, another thing, my bonnet will be broken to pieces.'

When he began throttling her, she pleaded, 'For God's sake, spare my life. Or give me a different death from this.' While he was beating her with the sharp-edged stone, she said she could feel it 'cutting into my head and face like an oyster shell.' After one particular blow, she said she cried out, 'Oh, dear, my eye is out of my head.' To which, Doyle replied, 'I don't care for your eye or yourself.'

Reporting the trial on 16 August the *Stockport Advertiser* said of Mrs Brogine, 'Her face still presented a frightful spectacle, and her appearance caused a thrill of horror in the court.' Her evidence was punctuated by 'moans of pain, [which] were perfectly heart-rending';

and afterwards 'the prisoner, who displayed the most callous indifference, cross-examined her at great length as to the origin of their acquaintance, insulting the unhappy woman until at last she fainted dead away and had to be taken out of court'.

The *Macclesfield Courier* seems to have been the only paper to explain in detail what exactly had triggered Mrs Brogine's final collapse, however. It happened when Doyle, in an apparent attempt to show why he was so angry with her, made the shocking claim that she had infected him with syphilis. In the 19th century there was no cure for this or other types of venereal disease, and the most common treatment was massive doses of mercury, administered in various ways, including by mouth. They were designed to induce intense salivation, but also caused side-effects that often brought on more suffering than the disease itself. Syphilis was a particularly awful, potentially deadly, affliction common throughout Europe at this time, and the use of mercury therapy continued into the early 20th century.

Before being carried from the courtroom, Mrs Brogine had denied the sexual allegation. Doyle, however, returned to the theme when he later questioned Dr John Davenport, the medical practitioner who examined her at the Caldwell Arms on the day of the attack. He referred to a conversation he had had with the 27-year-old doctor/surgeon in the cells in Sandbach after his arrest, in which he had first levelled the charge against her. He said that Davenport had asked him whether she had been 'salivated', as he had 'not detected any appearances of the disease'. Doyle's reply was not recorded.

In response to further questioning, however, Dr Davenport admitted that there was 'a taint of the venereal' about Mrs Brogine. He denied asking Doyle whether she had communicated the disease to him, but he revealed that he had found on Doyle's gums 'traces of his having been cured by mercury'. Other side effects of the mercury treatment included mouth ulcers and tooth loss.

Earlier Dr Davenport, whose practice was in Kidsgrove, had told the court of the examination he had carried out at the Caldwell Arms and detailed the extensive injuries suffered by the victim of Martin Doyle's explosive rage. In the *Chester Chronicle*'s trial report (10 August), he was quoted as saying, 'I found her suffering from extreme exhaustion in consequence of great loss of blood and from a severe shock to the nervous system. I thought she was dying.' There were 14 cuts on her head penetrating to the bone and 'seven or eight' on her face.

The most serious blow had caused a three-inch incision on the back of her head and, said the doctor, 'I introduced my finger through the scalp into the wound and found the skull was fractured.' Her lower jaw was broken, her upper lip was cut through and two teeth had been dislodged, he added. The wounds, which 'must have been given with great violence', were, he said, 'of the most dangerous character', insisting, 'Nineteen out of 20 persons would have succumbed to them.'

Jane Brogine, it was obvious, was not your average 'woman as the weaker vessel'. The *Birmingham Gazette* (31 August) described her as 'a somewhat powerful woman'; that was why, said the paper, she managed to escape with her life and, with skilful medical treatment, was able to give evidence at the trial, 'though in a fearful state'.

John Perrin, the 60-year-old carter whose fortuitous arrival at the scene of the crime may well have saved Jane Brogine's life, had been on his way from Alsager to his home town of Tunstall in Staffordshire. He recalled passing through the Linley tollgate and seeing the woman crawling out of the plantation. 'She was saturated in blood', the *Macclesfield Courier* recorded him as saying. Perrin, the paper stated, testified that she called to him to put her in the cart, 'or else . . . she should be murdered'. After climbing into the cart, he said, she asked him to 'wrap her head in her shawl'.

He took the badly injured woman to Linley Hall Lodge, about a quarter-of-a-mile away, to get help. While waiting for the police to arrive, Mrs Brogine seems to have dismounted from the cart and collapsed. For Constable Beckett, 44, of the Staffordshire force based in Talke, said that when he reached the hall entrance, he found her 'lying on the road near the lodge'.

The *Chester Courant* trial report (14 August) went on, "She was badly cut and bruised about the head and face and she was bleeding'. Noticing the loitering Doyle, Beckett grabbed hold of him. Doyle, stated the *Courant*, said, 'You have no cause to take hold of me. It is me that has done it and I am ready to suffer anything for it.' He then told the officer, 'The reason I did it was because she said she would turn again if I did not get work at Newcastle.'

The arrested man told the constable that he had gone to the road to see if it had stopped raining and − without explaining why − he stated matter-of-factly that when he returned 'he took a stone with him'. He said, 'I sat down; she laid her head upon my knee to go to sleep. I commenced beating her head with the stone as long as I could and I left her for dead. I went to a brook and washed the blood from my hands. I then looked for a pond of water to drown myself. I did not care what became of me.'

Doyle showed the constable the scene of his crime, which was about seven yards from the turnpike. It was 'very bloody', said the officer, who found three stones covered with blood, including 'a round one with a sharp edge'. This Doyle indentified as 'the one I did it with'. He even showed Beckett where he had cut his own hand on its sharp edge. A woman's 'back hair comb', which had obviously been knocked off Brogine's head as she tried to fight off her attacker, was also lying on the ground wet with blood.

The prisoner was later handed over to PC Daniel Dale of the Cheshire Constabulary based in Odd Rode. He escorted Doyle to the lock-ups attached to his home in Hall Green. On the way, he told the court, Doyle said to him, 'I did it, and for why I don't know. I suppose the devil tempted me to do it. I wish I was dead.' Cons. Dale, a 36-year-old father-of-five, added, 'His shirt, wristbands and sleeves and his slop were all very bloody.'

Mr Justice Crompton had warned Doyle on a couple of occasions to stick to the subject when questioning witnesses instead of — as the *Macclesfield Courier* put it — 'repeating matters quite irrelevant to the issues of the case'. Examples of his seeming irrelevancies, quoted by the *Courier*, included an exchange with Mrs Brogine, in which she denied saying she was 'uneasy because he had gone away' and that his love for her was 'getting cold', while hers for him was 'as hot as ever'; also that she had ever said of her husband that 'he was so old she was ashamed to own him' (admit he was her husband). Significantly, Doyle at no time questioned the woman about the actual assault.

The Judge seems to have given Doyle a freer rein when making his final statement to the jury. The *Courier* commented, 'He occupied the court with a wearisome harangue [for] nearly an-hour-and-a-half. The gist of his remarks was that she had allured [*sic*] him away and communicated to him the disease alluded to.'

He had been wasting his breath. The jury, on the other hand, were brief and to the point and returned their unanimous guilty verdict after barely a moment's delay. And the Judge gave Doyle short-shrift, too. After his remarks about 'one of the grossest crimes' he had ever tried (as reported in the *Chester Chronicle*), he told the prisoner at the bar, 'There is no doubt in my mind, and there can be no doubt in the minds of those who have heard the evidence, that you intended to murder this woman, who had been living with you as your wife.'

It was, said His Honour, a deliberate and premeditated act; when the woman had fallen asleep on his lap he had picked up the stone and 'began to knock her brains out'. He went on, 'You succeeded in giving her twenty-one wounds and when she became insensible you left her, as you thought, dead. But by skilful treatment her life has been saved. For that murderous assault you must die.'

Doyle was said by the *Chester Courant* to have displayed 'hardened insensibility' throughout his time in court, and received the death sentence 'with stolid indifference'. He seemed reluctant to leave the dock but was eventually led down the steps to the cells below after announcing, 'I am willing to die for what I have done.'

All three Chester papers provided a similar record of Doyle's time in the Castle Gaol awaiting his date with the hangman and of events on the day of his execution. At first the condemned man maintained his 'light and careless manner' (*Courant,* 14 August) and when, the day after his trial, his estranged wife Mary came to visit him, he 'treated her very coolly and scarcely spoke to her'.

However, in the days that followed, due to the ministrations of the local Roman Catholic parish priest, Canon Edward Carberry, and his assistant, the Reverend Henry Hopkins, Doyle (himself a Catholic) was brought to 'some sense of his awful position and during the last week he has listened with marked attention to their exhortations' (*Chronicle,* 31 August).

The *Chronicle*, at this time published on a Saturday, went on, 'He frequently expressed his sorrow to the turnkeys [prisoner warders] for what he had done, but added that he thought it hard that he should be hung while the woman still lived.' Unless stated otherwise, it is the same *Chronicle* edition that is the source of the quoted extracts below.

On Saturday 24 August Mrs Doyle, this time accompanied by one of her female cousins, was at the gaol to bid a final farewell to her cheating husband. 'The interview was of a very affecting character and lasted upwards of two hours. Doyle behaved with much more affection than he had shown on the occasion of her previous visit. He conversed with her freely about their relations and friends and told her to impress upon them that the woman had not died from the effects of the injuries he had inflicted upon her and that, consequently, the disgrace was not so great as if he had murdered her outright.'

The pair, seemingly reconciled at the end, embraced repeatedly, and 'the poor woman, bathed in tears, several times in vain tried to say the parting words'. Doyle eventually persuaded them to leave and, to avoid further distress, advised them not to come to see him again. Likewise, on the following Monday morning after Patrick, one of his brothers, had travelled from Cumberland to visit him, Doyle left instructions with the prison governor not to allow him a further visit.

Patrick Doyle had been especially affected by the meeting, while Doyle himself 'appeared exceedingly cheerful and said to his brother, tapping him on the shoulder, "Oh, Patrick, Patrick, don't put yourself out of the way — I am very happy indeed; it is all for the best."'

At ten o'clock that night, the eve of his execution, he went to bed but did not sleep. He lay on his bed restless until 11.30pm, when the Governor of the county gaol, John Dunstan, told him to get dressed for his transfer to the City Gaol, where the execution was to take place. He rose and put on 'the clothes he had been wearing when he committed the brutal deed'. At midnight, in keeping with ancient tradition, the Sheriff of Chester (James Rowe) arrived at the prison lodge to take charge of the prisoner. Handcuffed to a city turnkey, he was put into a horse-drawn cab and transported the half-mile or so to his final destination. On his way there he sang a hymn and 'remarked to the turnkey that it was a fine morning to go to Heaven'.

Around 4am — in between several courage-fortifying glasses of brandy and water — Doyle ate the customary hearty breakfast of ham, bread and butter and tea; in the course of which he gave the ever-present turnkey, 'a short history of his life'.

This is how the *Chronicle* told the story: 'He said he was born in the county of Mayo but had lived in Ormskirk 13 years. That town he made his home, and learned the trade of a glazier, from seeing pieces of glass being put into windows where he lodged; and he used to get a living by going to the farm-houses in the neighbourhood.'

His father had originally intended to take his family to America, but was persuaded to remain in Ormskirk; so he sent for his wife and children to join him. Son Martin's first job was that of a farm ploughman. After becoming a glazier he met his future wife Mary, who was 'much older than himself'.

'They were married, but lived very unhappily together. He knew Brogine, who had separated from her husband and gone to Ormskirk to reside. An intimacy sprang up between them, he separated from his wife and travelled [all] over the country with [Brogine], until the day on which he attempted to take her life. He loved Brogine, he said, and was very fond of her [*sic*]. He could not tell what made him try to murder her, but it seemed to him as if the devil had taken possession of him for a time, and he had no control over himself. He said he was truly sorry for what he had done, and confessed he deserved the punishment he was going to receive.'

Canon Carberry, who also accompanied Doyle to the City Gaol, had organised a petition to try to save him from the gallows. However, at 5am the 64-year-old priest received a letter from the Home Office with the announcement that almost everyone else seems to have anticipated: Sir George Grey 'regretted' that he could find no justifiable grounds for a reprieve and that the law had to 'take its course'.

At seven o'clock the prisoner, still seemingly in a 'quite cheerful' mood, retired to his cell, where he was again joined by the priest. He had more bread and butter and drank two cups of tea followed by a final glass of diluted brandy, before returning to his 'devotional exercises'. At five minutes to eight his cell door opened and in stepped the Sheriff to lead him to the scaffold. The procession formed up in the press-room (no, not accommodation for the newspaper reporters, but the place in which condemned felons had their prison shackles struck off prior to pinioning); it was headed by the Sheriff, then came the Deputy Sheriff, the Chief Constable, the Governor of the gaol and Canon Carberry and Rev. Hopkins, the prisoner bringing up the rear.

The press-room door was opened and at exactly 8am on Tuesday 27 August 1861 Martin Doyle walked out on to the platform and, 'with a ghastly smile upon his face, he ran up the steps of the scaffold', where the executioner, William Calcraft, waited. The latter placed a white cotton hood over his head, tightened the noose around his neck and within seconds the unfortunate victim was, as the papers loved to put it, 'launched into eternity'. In sharp contrast to what would happen at Calcraft's next visit to Chester in 1863 (see Chapter Eight), Doyle died 'without even the convulsive shivering of a single limb'.

As usual on these occasions, newspaper estimates of the size of the crowd that witnessed the execution varied enormously. The *Liverpool Daily Post* recorded 'considerably under a thousand', the *Courant* reckoned it to have been between 1,000 and 2,000 ('not near so numerous as on previous similar occasions'), while the *Chronicle* put it at 4,000 to 5,000. The latter noted, 'The utmost quiet prevailed, not a sound being heard from the time the culprit appeared on the scaffold till it was all over.'

And the paper added, 'We have been requested to state that the convict Doyle was not hardened, as has been stated in some papers, but on the contrary, from the first attendance upon him by Canon Carberry to his death he was very penitent, and there can be no doubt his repentance was sincere and genuine.'

Morbidly, many people were also drawn to the gaol later that afternoon when, between four and five o'clock, Doyle's body was removed for burial; and the crowd followed the hearse to the old cemetery in Overleigh Road, Handbridge, where the remains were interred in unconsecrated ground close to the main gate. Regulations in force at the time mean there is no memorial stone or marker of any kind to identify the spot where he was buried; indeed, even the cemetery authority no longer appears to have a record of its exact location.

Commenting on the hanging, the *Cheshire Observer*, on 7 September, condemned the whole grim theatricality of public executions and questioned the attitude of many of those who flocked to see them. Of

Somewhere in this corner of the Overleigh Cemetery at Handbridge are the remains of Martin Doyle, buried in an unmarked (and apparently unknown) grave.

Photograph by the author.

the latter, the paper stated, '[The] same morbid feeling which prompts people to go to a low theatre to see a "sensation" [*sic*] drama prompts them to attend a hanging.' Indeed, there was often the same kind of behaviour in the theatre as there was at the foot of the gallows, 'and at the close of each performance the audience departs without having added to their previously scanty stock, one healthy thought or feeling'.

The article went on, 'The execution of Martin Doyle last week cannot, so far as we see, exercise any deterring influence upon those who witnessed it. The crowd gathered in front of the city gaol consisted at first of mere lads, and the lowest class of men, with here and there a sprinkling of girls.'

If Martin Doyle had been laid to rest, the story of the man and the manner of his death certainly had not. In fact, it would be resurrected not once but twice over the next 16 years.

On 14 February 1865, during a sitting of the Royal Commission on Capital Punishment, Sir George Grey, the Home Secretary, was being questioned about a judge's powers to impose a lesser sentence for capital offences. As it was recorded in the official report of the Commission's deliberations, he referred to a statistical return compiled by the Home Office, which showed that in the previous 40 years, during which the use of capital punishment had been extended to many other crimes, the death penalty had been imposed for murder in all but five cases. All of the latter had involved the crime of attempted murder; included among them was the 1861 case of Martin Doyle (though he did not mention him by name), which, he said, was 'scarcely distinguishable from murder'.

Sir George told the Commission, whose members included Horatio Waddington, 'That was a very remarkable case, a case in which a man had cruelly maimed a woman; he had battered her head and face with a stone, and left her, supposing he had murdered her; but she recovered. The medical man who was examined [at the trial] said that scarcely any other person could have recovered; it was like a person rising from the dead to give evidence against the prisoner; and the Judge, who then had the power of recording the sentence ['recording' was a legal procedure by which, under certain circumstances, a judge was able to reduce a capital sentence to transportation for life] thought it so bad a case and that it came so near to murder (in fact really it was the same thing), that he passed the [death] sentence, thinking that it ought to be carried into effect.'

Then, he added, 'But the law was changed immediately after that.' Commissioner John Bright, 46-year-old Liberal MP for Birmingham Central and a leading abolitionist, interjected, 'Was not the change of the law actually in process at the time?' To which the Home Secretary replied, 'Yes, the law had in fact been changed before the man was executed, but not before the conviction, and therefore he was legally executed, and I thought that as the Judge had passed this sentence openly in court — I believe with an entire concurrence of opinion in that part of the country — it would be hazardous to interpose and to say that the sentence of the law should not be carried into effect.'

Mr Bright, 'Are not all attempts to murder practically murder upon the same theory?' Sir George, 'Perhaps they may be, if the intention is not changed during the process of the deed; that is to say, a man may attempt to murder another and may relent and abstain from carrying his intention fully into effect, but in the case to which I refer it was not so.' In the Cheshire case, he commented, 'the man thought that he had murdered the woman'.

Twelve years later, Sir George Grey would be reminded of his evidence to the Commission when Mr Justice Crompton's son Henry released a statement vindicating his father's conduct both during and after Doyle's trial and alleged that it was the fault of the Home Secretary alone that the convicted man had died. Sir George, who served under four Prime Ministers and was Home Secretary three times, had only just returned to the post when the Doyle case crossed his desk. His decision to turn down a reprieve was one of his first acts in his third spell in the job.

Henry Crompton, 41, second son of Sir Charles, was a barrister, political activist and champion of trade unionism who, from 1858 until his retirement in 1901, was Clerk of Assize for the Chester and North Wales Circuit. He was moved to go public when, in February 1877, Mr (later Sir) Joseph Pease (1825-1903) — MP for South Durham and another noted campaigner against the death penalty — announced that he was to introduce into Parliament a private members' bill to abolish capital punishment.

Henry Crompton's statement was not widely reported in the regional press at the time; but the *Cheshire Observer* carried it at some length in its edition of 3 March. It began, 'At the Chester Summer Assizes, 1861, Martin Doyle was tried and convicted before the late Mr Justice Crompton of an attempt to murder a woman, under circumstances of unusual and most extraordinary atrocity. The case was one in which no sensible person could feel pity [for] or sympathy with the accused. The judge, however, was placed in a difficult and painful position. He was himself opposed to the infliction of capital punishment on the ground of policy; but he knew that was not a consideration which a judge ought to entertain in administering the law. He was the administrator not the legislator.

'On a trial for murder a judge has no option as to passing the sentence of death. When the verdict of guilty is found by the jury the judge is bound at once to pronounce the sentence. But in the other capital crimes the judge had power, when there were circumstances of mitigation, not to pass the sentence but simply to record it, and then the capital sentence was invariably commuted by the Secretary of State. Mr Justice Crompton, in this case, acted strictly up to what he believed to be his duty, painful though it was. There was no mitigating circumstance of any sort. Every fact proved on the trial aggravated the guilt of the prisoner and the atrocity of the crime. He [the judge] firmly believed when he passed the sentence of death that the man would be hanged.'

After the assizes, Sir Charles, having learned of the Government's intention to abolish the death penalty for attempted murder, travelled to London to explain to the Home Secretary the reasons for his decision — 'so that there might be no mistake' — only to find Sir George Grey was away from his office.

Henry Crompton's statement went on, 'He saw, however, Mr Waddington, the Permanent Under-Secretary, and said that he had passed the sentences of death because he was ignorant of the intentions of the Government and of Parliament on the subject; that if there was any intention of altering the law and of doing away with capital punishment in such cases, [Doyle's] sentence must be commuted. If, on the other hand, they meant to retain the law, and carry it out [only] in bad instances, then this was one of the worst cases he had ever known. Mr Waddington replied that there was no idea of changing the law and that the Government had resolved to carry it out in the worst cases. Accordingly the man was hanged.'

But, said Mr Crompton, before the sentence was pronounced by the judge 'the Act . . . abolishing the punishment of death in all attempts to murder had received the Royal Assent. The statute did not come into actual operation for some two months after [1 November], and Mr Waddington, meeting Mr Justice Crompton after the vacation, said to him that "It was God's mercy that the man was legally executed."'

Mr Crompton then repeated word for word the Home Secretary's

Judge Crompton: came to believe Doyle should not have been hanged.

Image by permission of
J.J. Heath-Caldwell

evidence before the Royal Commission (see above) and insisted that it was not a true interpretation of the events that had taken place during Sir Charles's visit to the Home Office. He pointed out that his father, who died on 30 October 1865 at the age of 68, had not had the opportunity of 'contradicting and repudiating' the minister's statement, which first appeared in print when the Commission's report was published in January 1866. And he declared, 'The only reason why the man was hanged was Sir George Grey's ignorance and culpable neglect.'

Joseph Pease's 1877 bill, which had its first reading on 21 February, was eventually withdrawn for lack of Parliamentary time. He tried again in 1878 and 1881; but each time the move was rejected by both Houses. In fact, between 1869 and 1881 — encouraged by the passing of the 1868 Capital Punishment Amendment Act, which ended public executions — there were six attempts to have the death penalty abolished in Great Britain. Another Royal Commission on Capital Punishment was set up in 1949 to look at the subject afresh, but four years later the decision once again was to retain the death penalty, both Parliament and the police considering that it deterred offenders from carrying firearms.

Sir George Grey: 'Doyle was legally executed.'

In 1965 Parliament agreed to suspend the death penalty for five years, introducing a mandatory sentence of life imprisonment for murder. However, the 1965 Murder (Abolition of Death Penalty) Act had contained the proviso that the measure could be made permanent before the five years were up, if both Houses resolved to do so. Consequently, since November 1969 capital punishment has been banned in mainland Britain (the ruling didn't take effect in Northern Ireland until 1973).

Thereafter, each year until 1997, a vote was held in the House of Commons to restore the death penalty, but the motion was always defeated. Then, in 1998, in line with the European Convention on Human Rights, MPs voted to prohibit capital punishment 'except in time of war or the imminent threat of war'. This was followed in 2003 by a new protocol in the Convention (to which Britain was a signatory) that since 1 February 2004 has prevented the use of the death penalty under any circumstances.

A year after the 1965 suspension of the death penalty, the eminent barrister and deputy high court judge Mr (later Sir) Louis Blom-Cooper — author, journalist, expert in criminology and penology and an outspoken opponent of capital punishment — summed up the successful conclusion of the abolitionists' long-running campaign thus:

'Given the hypothesis that the death penalty is an irrelevance to the rate of murder in society, few feeling persons will mourn the passing of the hangman's noose, consigned finally to the museum along with the rack, the thumbscrew and scold's bridle. The dismantling of the gallows from our prisons may at least mark an historic event in penal reform, even if the social significance of hanging was far outweighed by the moral heat that it engendered in public and private debate these last forty years.'

He was writing in *The Modern Law Review* of March 1966; but his words were a curious echo of the sentiments expressed by the Editor of the *Cheshire Observer* in the wake of the execution of Martin Doyle. In an editorial in the newspaper's edition of 7 September 1861 he had reflected, 'Men's faith in capital punishment, as corrective or preventive of crime, is not very great [and] is indeed lessening year by year'.

He asserted that the once harsh penal code, which had 'in olden times . . . seemed vindictive and revengeful', had now 'yielded to a kindlier spirit'. He believed that 'the same beneficent spirit, which has worked so powerfully in the history of our civilisation, has also reached to the seat of the judge and the cell of the prisoner'. And he was confident that the day would come when 'this beneficence [would] spread still further and put away from us the great remaining relic of those old barbarous times, the gallows.'

He could scarcely have imagined that it would take more than a hundred years — and the judicial killing of at least another 1,300 people — for his optimistic vision to become reality.

CHAPTER TEN

Curse Of The Demon Drink

By order of the management, the open-air National Theatre of Death was closed; the long-running public execution 'stage shows' were over. Parliament, in a reform hailed by the great and the good as a landmark in the humane treatment of criminals, had decreed that the death penalty would in future be enacted in front of a more exclusive audience hidden away behind prison walls. But those in the cheap seats — the vulgar herd for whom a good, old-fashioned hanging brought a certain vicarious excitement into their humdrum lives — were not going to give up their pleasures lightly. As they demonstrated in Chester, when James Bannister became the first man to be executed in Cheshire under the terms of the 1868 Act, some were prepared to go to great lengths — and heights — for the chance of seeing a fellow creature 'topped'.

Bannister, a 40-year-old weaver from the old Cheshire cotton town of Hyde, was hanged in the Spring of 1877 for the axe murder of his wife. As there had never been an execution at the Castle Gaol, a new gallows had been constructed in the south-east corner of the prison yard in an area that was once part of the 'Castle Ditch', where, in former times, the bodies of many condemned murderers were buried in unmarked graves. The site was hemmed in by the outside wall of the gaol and the main three-storey cell block — one local newspaper described it as being like 'a narrow ravine' — and the natural fall of the land there meant that, by excavating the lower end of the passageway, a brick-lined pit could be created underneath the drop which, unlike the old-style apparatus mounted on a platform 12 steps high, was at ground level.

It was in this gap between St. Mary's Church and the Castle — where once ran the 'Castle Ditch' and the bodies of executed murderers were buried — that the gallows first used at the county gaol in 1877 was erected.

Photograph by the author.

The pit was reported to be 10ft deep but, as it became evident when an unforeseen problem occurred four years later (see the second half of this chapter), it was a couple of feet less

222

than that. Of typical Victorian style, the gallows itself consisted of a single beam, supported by two uprights. 'The arrangement was such', the *Chester Chronicle* explained at the time, 'that when the culprit should drop he would fall into a vault, leaving nothing but the rope visible above ground.'

The old Dee Bridge and, to the right, the Dee Mills, whose roof was seen as a good vantage point from which to witness the hanging taking place in the gaol next door.

Illustration courtesy of Mr Colin Lynch.

But if it offered only a limited view of the proceedings even from close up, it seems there were men so determined to see the Castle gallows claim its first victim that any vantage point, however distant, would do. The county authorities, anxious to ensure there were no uninvited observers at Cheshire's first private execution, had already sealed off the tower of St. Mary's Church, immediately overlooking the gaol. But it was only at the last minute that they realised that some determined individuals had found another elevated position from which to spy on the activity in the prison yard.

The mass of the Dee Mills, which bulked large on the north bank of the river adjacent to the ancient Dee Bridge, was nearly a hundred yards away; but, as it was reported in the *Macclesfield Courier* (7 April), a group of men — mill workers, presumably — made a daredevil attempt to see what was going on over the prison wall by climbing on to the pitched roof of the five-storey building. However, shortly before the execution was due to begin, they were spotted and removed by the police. 'And so,' the *Courier* commented, 'the first private execution in Chester may be said to have passed off with as much privacy as it was possible to secure' (the Dee Mills, originally the manorial mills of the Earls of Chester, whose absolute rule gave them a complete monopoly on flour production in the city, were demolished in 1910 after eight centuries of almost continuous operation).

James Bannister was the first of four men to be executed at the Castle Gaol and one of two convicted murderers who were said to have fallen prey to the major social evil of the day . . . 'the curse of the demon drink'. We shall meet the other alcohol-driven killer, William Stanway — whose method of murder was even more diabolical than Bannister's — later in this chapter.

Chester Castle circa 1909. Between 1877 and 1883 four executions were carried out in the old gaol buildings, to the right of the church tower. The entrance to the Shire Hall, in which the Assizes were held, is in the centre of the picture.

From the author's collection.

Bannister booked his place in the history of Cheshire crime following an argument with his 35-year-old wife Rebecca in the early hours of the morning of Friday 15 December 1876. It was the latest in a series of rows — inevitably caused by Bannister's excessive drinking — between the couple, who, for the past six months, had been living in lodgings at No. 16, Russell Street, Hyde, the home of Elisha and Mary Grayson. The upper storey of the house contained two connecting bedrooms, each with its own entrance. The Graysons occupied one of them, along with their three young children (one only a baby) and Rebecca's 14-year-old illegitimate daughter from a previous relationship; the Bannisters slept in the other. James Bannister had married the former Rebecca Bradley in Halifax towards the end of 1865. It was a marriage beset by tragedy. They had four children together, but they all died in infancy.

About 4.30am, Mr and Mrs Grayson were awakened by the crying of their sick son Joshua, who was about six months old. Mrs Grayson pacified the infant and went back to bed. About ten minutes later, the couple heard a loud bump. They could see under the connecting door that there was a light on in their lodgers' bedroom. Lighting her own candle, Mrs Grayson got up to investigate, followed by her husband. Then they heard a man, in a strange croaky voice, call out 'Elisha'. When they opened the Bannisters' door they were confronted by a gore-drenched chamber of horror.

Rebecca Bannister was on the bed, her head and face a mass of blood. She had a terrible wound over her right eye and gashes on either side of her head. Her husband lay alongside her with his throat cut. Blood soaked the bed and there were spray patterns on the wall behind it. A blood-stained penknife was on the bed between the couple. On a table nearby, also covered in blood, was a small axe. It belonged to the Graysons and was normally kept in the 'coal-place' (part of the cellar) under the stairs.

Though the exact cause of this last, fatal quarrel is unclear, it appears that Bannister, his mind unbalanced by his chronic alcoholism, attacked his wife with the hatchet and then, shocked to his senses, cut his own throat with the knife in a fit of remorse. Mrs Bannister died three days later in Stockport Infirmary.

When Stockport Coroner Francis Johnson opened the inquest into Rebecca Bannister's death in the Infirmary's boardroom on 20 December, Hyde surgeon William Weldon, who had been called to the house by the police, deposed that the injury to her forehead had fractured her skull and he could see 'brain matter escaping through the wound'.

He concluded that it had been caused by the hammer end of the axe-head and was of the opinion that it would have been 'sufficient to cause death'. The woman also had two lacerated wounds on either side of her head and severe contusions about the head and face. 'I considered she was beyond

At the inquest at Stockport Infirmary (above), the details of the horrific injuries sustained by both husband and wife were officially revealed.
Photo courtesy of the I Love Stockport, Stockport Memories *and* Memories of Stockport *websites.*

Right: an axe like the one with which Rebecca Bannister was bludgeoned to death.

recovery,' he stated. Bannister, too, was not expected to survive his suicide bid. The surgeon's deposition, contained within the official court papers, noted that he had a 'large gash' in his throat and his windpipe was 'completely severed'.

According to the *Cheshire Observer* (23 December), the jury also heard that Mrs Bannister had 'complained about her husband using threats to her' and that the couple 'had not lived happily together'. The inquest was adjourned until 28 December.

At the resumed hearing Mr George Turner, 31-year-old house surgeon at the Infirmary, revealed the results of the postmortem he had carried out on Mrs Bannister. In a report in the *Manchester Times* of 30 December, he gave the cause of death as 'inflammation of the brain and its membranes, attendant upon the injuries, combined with exhaustion following the shock to the system'. The jury returned a verdict of wilful murder against James Bannister.

By then, having been admitted to Manchester Royal Infirmary, he had been in hospital for just over two weeks and, against all the odds, was making good progress. Bannister continued to defy his doctors' dire prognosis to make a quite miraculous recovery. He was eventually discharged on 7 February and was taken by train and cab to Hyde Police Station, then in Beeley Street, in the

The old Manchester Royal Infirmary in Piccadilly. After making a miraculous recovery there, Bannister was declared fit . . . to go on trial for his life.

From the author's collection.

custody of Captain John Arrowsmith, Deputy Chief Constable of the Cheshire Constabulary who, the following year, would become the county's chief of police. Later that day he was brought before Coroner Johnson who, along with local JP Thomas Thornely, signed the warrant committing him to Chester Castle Gaol for trial.

On Wednesday 14 March 1877 Bannister was considered fit enough to appear at the Chester Spring Assizes to face a charge of murder. From the outset, however, it was obvious that the defendant was by no means fully recovered. When he came up from the cells the extent of his neck wound was still clearly visible; and, reported the *Chester Chronicle* three days later, he 'appeared in a very depressed condition and swayed himself about in the dock [until he] was at length accommodated with a seat'. Then, when he was asked by the Clerk of Arraigns whether he pleaded guilty or not guilty, he gazed vacantly about him and, in a husky, hesitant voice, said 'I don't know.' When the question was put to him a second time, he made the same reply. The Judge (Mr Justice Lush) ordered a 'not guilty' plea to be entered on the prisoner's behalf.

From the evidence contained in the official court files and press reports of the trial, it is clear that James Bannister had a history of eccentric behaviour. Elisha Grayson, a joiner by trade, said he had known Bannister for about two years before he became his lodger. He told the court that the prisoner was in the habit of absenting himself from work for several days at a time to go on drinking binges. In the same *Chronicle* trial report, he stated that Bannister, a cotton weaver, had lost jobs at 'place after place' because of his drinking, and had been 'on the spree' for three or four days in the week before the murder.

Grayson — his Christian name was given in press reports as 'Elijah', but all the official documentation, including a deposition containing his signature, shows it was 'Elisha' — said he had heard the Bannisters 'quarrel in bed frequently'. And Rebecca Bannister, it seems, was no shrinking violet after she had had a drink or two. About six weeks previously Grayson had to turn her out of the house because of her unruly behaviour; Bannister would have been sent packing, too, had he not left of his own accord. The pair, who were obviously allowed to return to their lodgings afterwards, had been out drinking together on that occasion and, as the *Cheshire Observer* revealed in its trial report (17 March), the row started when Bannister accused her of being 'too familiar with another man'. Said Grayson, 'The deceased appeared to be very much annoyed at the accusation and, as she would not quell her tongue, she was turned out.' He also told the jury, 'At times the prisoner and his wife were not on good terms, even when he was sober.'

Maria Lester, Rebecca's 60-year-old widowed mother, who lived in lodgings two doors away from 16, Russell Street, believed the prisoner was 'addicted to drink' (*Observer*); she had been afraid that he would 'do something to her daughter and it had come at last'. She added, 'This is what I expected.' Some twelve months ago, when he was 'coming off his drink', Bannister had said to her that 'he wished he was in Stockport Workhouse'. She also recalled an occasion five or six years ago when the Bannisters were still living in Yorkshire. The accused, she said, was 'acting out of his mind' and produced a length of rope with which he 'threatened to hang himself'. When she took it off him he 'laughed in her face'.

About a year ago, Mrs Lester added, Bannister had fallen down 'in a fit of giddiness' at the cotton mill in which he was then working and the overlooker had to take him to see a doctor. Bannister and his wife seem to have been lodging with his mother-in-law at the time, for she said she had known him to be 'walking about his room all night, being unable to sleep from the effects of drinking', and he had 'several times asked [her] to forgive him for his drunken habits'.

Bannister's close friend and sometime colleague Henry Harrop, 37, also a weaver, revealed that on 12 December he had had a conversation with Bannister about another incident at his workplace. Where Bannister worked latterly is not recorded (he seems to have had, and then lost, jobs with various firms), but there were six cotton mills within a short distance of Russell Street at this time: Long Meadow and Green Field, on Market Street; the Slack Mills, between Back Lane (modern Lumm Road) and Hyde Lane (modern Market Street); Green Croft Mill, Manchester Road; Springbank Mill in the area of what would become Haughton Street, and Thomas Ashton's Carrfield Mill in Newton Street. They had sprung up during the great industrial expansion that in the early 19th century transformed the tiny hamlet of Gee Cross into the major manufacturing town of Hyde.

Wherever it was he worked, Rebecca Bannister was also employed there and, a few days before, an altercation had taken place between husband and wife which ended with her brandishing a wooden weaving shuttle in his face and threatening to strike him with it. Bannister raised his fists but did not retaliate.

His conversation with Harrop had

Slack Mills viewed from Hyde Lane (modern Market Street). Bannister was said to have lost jobs at a number of local mills due to his drinking.

Image courtesy of hydonian.blogspot.co.uk.

taken place in 'the vaults' (taproom) at The Albion pub in Hyde's Market Place. As the *Chester Chronicle* reported it, father-of-three Harrop, who lived just around the corner from Bannister at 16, Reynard Street, had asked his mate, 'Well, Jim, what's all this trouble about, your fighting the other day with a shuttle?' Bannister replied that 'Becca', as he called his wife, was 'jawing me [scolding him] about being with a married woman'. He seemed 'in deep distress', said Harrop, who thought it was in consequence of the bust-up at the mill and that, to add to his problems, he had just been given notice to quit his lodgings. Bannister, witness said, was 'looking wild during the whole of the conversation'. While they were in the pub, he went three times to the door and announced that his wife was coming, but she never appeared. Harrop commented, 'I thought that he neither knew what he was doing or saying.'

And ('as far as he remembered') Harrop said that, just before he left the Albion, Bannister said casually, 'Something tells me I shall have to kill her.' Harrop replied, 'I don't know. She works very hard.' Bannister retorted, 'Oh, she's a bugger. You don't know her.'

Harrop, who had reluctantly agreed to give evidence at the trial, did not take Bannister's threat seriously; but on 15 December, as soon as he learned what his friend was alleged to have done, he went straight away to his lodgings in Russell Street. In his inquest deposition, he had stated that, as his friend lay on his bed waiting to go to hospital, Harrop said to him, 'Thou hast done what thou said thou would.' Bannister — 'as well as he could' — muttered, 'Yes, yes.'

An old photograph of Market Place, Hyde. The Albion, the pub in which James Bannister made his injudicious comment to his workmate, is marked with a cross.

Image courtesy of hydonian.blogspot.co.uk.

On Thursday 14 December James Bannister had come home from work about 6pm and, after having tea with Rebecca in the Graysons' apartments, he went out again, returning to their lodgings just before 9.30. He had been drinking, though there were conflicting views expressed as to how intoxicated he was when he came back in. Mary Grayson, in her deposition to the Coroner, had said she could not 'perceive from his manner that he had had any drink that day'. Husband Elisha, both in his inquest deposition and in the witness box at the trial, said that he had not seen the accused when he returned to the house but he had heard him conversing with his wife in the kitchen. Bannister, he stated, 'sounded sober' and the couple 'appeared to be on friendly terms' before going to bed. Rebecca went up first and her husband followed about ten minutes later. Bannister had, however, brought a 'jug' of beer home and he took it with him when he eventually retired for the night.

A more telling comment was made by Rebecca Bannister herself, however, in a statement she gave to local JP Edward Hibbert on the afternoon of 15 December, only a few hours after she had been admitted to Stockport Infirmary. Hibbert learned that the medical diagnosis was that she was not going to pull through, so with the doctors' approval, he had rushed to her bedside to interview her. The assistant clerk to the magistrates, Frederick Broadsmith, accompanied him to take notes. At the trial the prosecution attempted to introduce the deposition as evidence, but defence counsel Edward Julyan Dunn argued that the defendant, although present at the hospital interview, had not been physically able to question the witness due to his throat injury. Broadsmith, was quoted in the *Chronicle* trial report as telling the jury that the defendant was at that time 'capable only of making some guttural sounds, which were unintelligible'.

Judge Lush ruled the deposition inadmissible. It survives, however, in the assize court records in the National Archives. It is reproduced here for the first time. The short, disjointed and rather pathetic statement — which obviously reflected the extreme physical and mental effects of the battering Rebecca Bannister had only recently suffered — was as follows:

'I feel that I am in great danger of my life. I went to bed in good time last night. My husband came to bed after me about half-an-hour. He had had some drink, but he was *not very* drunk' [author's italics]. We had a word or two [meaning angry words were exchanged]. My husband has injured me. He said it would be an easily done job. I don't know whether he hit me or what he did. There was no one else did it. He said it is no use your saying anything. I heard him say he had done something. I thought it was his fist, but I don't know what he struck me with.'

Elisha Grayson gave a graphic account of his rude awakening in the early hours of 15 December . . . and the moment he and his wife walked in unsuspectingly on the blood-soaked scene in their back bedroom.

He said the Bannisters were talking until about 2am. Although the two bedrooms were only separated by a thin wall, he could not hear exactly what was being said; but it did not sound as if they were quarrelling. Then, after being disturbed by his baby's crying, he heard a noise which, according to the *Chronicle*, he thought 'sounded something like a blow, which appeared to proceed from the prisoner's room'. Almost immediately Bannister called his name 'in a gurgling manner'. Entering the room, Grayson took in the horrific sight. 'I saw the prisoner lying on the bed with his throat cut,' he said. 'The deceased was sitting up in bed with her hands on each side of her head. She was buried in blood. The prisoner was also bleeding very much.'

He noticed that the hatchet from the coal-place was on the little table beside Bannister. It was 'covered in blood'. In cross-examination, Grayson said he had not heard anyone go into the cellar that night. In the *Observer*'s trial report, he pointed out that Bannister, in going upstairs to bed, would have had to pass the coal-place door, which was 'only fastened by a latch'.

Mary Grayson testified that the axe, which was for both breaking coal and chopping firewood, was in its usual place between 8.30 and nine o'clock that Thursday evening, when she herself had last used it (*Observer*). During a lengthy cross-examination, Mr Dunn questioned her about Bannister's relationship with Rebecca's illegitimate child, a girl called Agnes Anna Hadfield (who, after her mother's death, would go to live with her grandmother, the widow Lester, in the Godley area of Hyde). If he had been seeking to uncover some source of lingering irritation between the couple, he doesn't appear to have pursued it. Mary Grayson's reply was a reticent 'He was not fond of it [*sic*]'.

After the Graysons' shocking discovery, Elisha Grayson had gone next-door-but-one to tell Mrs Lester what had happened to her daughter, then he went to the Beeley Street police station, a walk of about 400 yards. He returned with two officers of the Stockport force, Sergeant Samuel Holme and Constable Thomas Proudlove.

Sgt. Holme said it was around 5am when they reached the house in Russell Street and, climbing the small, winding staircase, he entered

The old Hyde Police Station in Beeley Street. It closed in 1930 and became the headquarters of Hyde Lads Club until the building was demolished in 1993.

Image courtesy of hydonian.blogspot.co.uk.

the back bedroom and found Mrs Bannister 'quite motionless' on the bed, although she was still breathing. 'In a narrow space between the bed and the window,' he stated, 'he found the prisoner, half-sitting and half-kneeling with his legs doubled up under him. He appeared in great pain and was moving his hands and his head about. When he threw his head back he [Holme] noticed a gash in his throat' (*Chester Chronicle*).

PC Proudlove, 26, was sent to get medical help. He returned with the surgeon William Weldon and, said Sgt. Holme, because Bannister was struggling so violently, it had taken all three of them to hold him down while he was examined. Weldon decided to send Bannister for specialist medical care at Manchester Royal Infirmary, which had opened in 1755 on land at the top of Market Street (now known as Piccadilly Gardens), and, said Proudlove, while he waited to go he 'kept beating his hands on the bed, saying "I wonder what made me do it. I think the devil must have been in me."' It was the constable who recovered the bloody penknife from the Bannisters' room; he had missed it earlier as it had been on the floor 'under a lot of rags', which had apparently fallen off the bed. They were on the bed, presumably, to provide extra warmth during the cold winter nights.

At the close of the prosecution's evidence, the Clerk of Arraigns put in the brief statement Bannister had made when first examined by magistrates at Hyde Police Court on 9 February. It stated simply that 'he had no recollection of what took place' that night. It was a claim he continued to express until his death.

Mr Dunn called three witnesses for the defence. The first, Sarah Crabtree, a 52-year-old hatter's wife, formerly of 5, Russell Street, Hyde, said she had known the defendant all his life and had also worked with him at one time. She remembered him complaining to her 'about his head being bad' after he had been in the Cheshire Militia. He had apparently suffered severe sunstroke and had been 'lanced in the back of the neck through his head being affected'. And he once told her, when they were 'coming [home] from the mills', that 'his head felt mazey [dizzy]'.

John Woodcock, 29, of Queen Street, Hyde, was the factory overlooker who witnessed Bannister's 'fit of giddiness' at the mill a year previously. He said that after his fall the weaver was 'throwing his arms about as if he were feeling for something'. He appeared 'very singular' and Woodcock took him to the doctor's. He had seen him looking 'bewildered' while at work before.

William Weldon was the 'doctor' concerned; he had testified earlier that Bannister had arrived at his surgery on 12 March 1876 suffering from 'nervous excitement — a sort of sickness induced by drink'. He had prescribed a sedative; later, he gave him a sleeping draught after the accused had complained of being 'restless and unable to sleep'.

The final defence witness was Victor Wartemberg, 26, senior house surgeon at Manchester Royal Infirmary, who described the condition Bannister was in when he was admitted to the hospital. In his testimony, in the same *Chester Chronicle* report, he said, Bannister 'was faint and exhausted and . . . when he had been in bed some time, and had somewhat regained his powers, he became violent and I had to have the assistance of two policemen to keep him in bed'. The surgeon came to the conclusion that he was suffering from a severe attack of delirium tremens, caused by drink.

'He remained in that condition for several days and it was only by administering a powerful sedative that he was at all kept quiet,' Wartemberg said. 'For some three weeks after he recovered [from] the acute stage of the delirium he was nervous and excitable. He was continually fearing that people were going to do something to him and at times it was difficult to dress his neck, as he objected.' And he concluded, 'I have never known a man to recover from so severe a wound as he suffered. With such a wound it would be impossible for a man to simulate delirium.'

Seizing upon this expert medical opinion, Mr Dunn, in his closing speech for the defence, argued out that the law 'clearly laid down' that, in an indictment for murder, the intoxication of the defendant may be taken into consideration as a circumstance to show that the act was not premeditated'.

The judge interjected, 'That is if a man had lost his mind altogether.' Counsel pressed on, urging the jury that, if they found there had been no premeditation, to 'pause before finding him guilty'. Appealing to them for a verdict of manslaughter, he pointed out that on the night in question the Bannisters had been talking together for several hours 'in the most amiable manner'. So what, he asked, had brought about the sudden change that had left her 'with her head crushed by a hatchet and he with his throat cut in a most shocking manner?'

And he asked them to consider what he described as his 'common-sense theory'. He explained it thus, 'This man, waking up in a state of delirium tremens . . . and fancying that there were people in the room — imaginary beings that troubled and annoyed him — went downstairs and got this axe and, without any intention of killing his wife, did the deed that was done. And then, having as he would think, demolished his enemies, he lit a candle and when he discovered, by the light of it, what he had done, he cut his own throat out of remorse for the crime he had committed'. As well as 'the shakes', the symptoms of delirium tremens can also include hallucinations.

In his summing up, however, Sir Robert Lush, advised the jury that 'there was absolutely no proof that at the time the murder was committed the prisoner was unaccountable for his acts' and, so long as a man knew what he was doing, he was responsible for what he did. The jury was out for about an hour before declaring Bannister guilty of murder. The *Chronicle* reporter observed that the prisoner had his head 'buried in his arms . . . which were folded on the ledge of the dock ' throughout most of the trial; but on hearing the foreman's words he 'raised his face . . . and muttered something which was inaudible to the court'.

Before passing sentence, Sir Robert, who was known to poke fun at the unfortunate connotations associated with his surname, showed he was in no mood for joking on this occasion when he told Bannister, 'You have brought yourself into this wretched position entirely by indulging in drink. You are one of the many miserable examples of that wretched curse which affects the country at the present time. There is not an assize town we visit [where] we don't find that the great majority of the cases in the calendar have arisen from the curse of drink.'

With the capital sentence secured, the charge of attempted suicide, officially an offence in England and Wales until 1961, was not proceeded with.

Two petitions for clemency were organised on Bannister's behalf; their signatories were reported to have included the Mayor and Recorder of Chester, the Chaplain of the Castle Gaol, county magistrates and 'many other influential citizens and professional gentlemen'. But their appeals were turned down by the Home Secretary (the Lancashire-born Viscount Richard Assheton Cross). The man whose life had so recently been saved in the caring confines of a hospital ward was destined to have it snatched from him on the crude, unforgiving stage of the gallows.

The irony of Bannister's situation did not go unnoticed by the press. In its execution report of 4 April, the Editor of the *Chester Courant* remarked intuitively that there was 'something revolting in the idea that a man should, by the exercise of high scientific skill and the tender nursing of benevolent women, be rescued from the jaws of death only that his miserable life may be taken at the hands of the executioner'.

The paper also shared the petitioners' very real concern that, as the prisoner's neck wound had not yet completely healed ('there being a hole in the windpipe, through which the miserable man partly breathes'), the hanging would be 'infallibly invested with peculiar horrors better imagined than described'.

The execution went ahead as scheduled on Monday 2 April 1877 (Easter Monday) in strict conformity with Home Office regulations, which at that time dictated that three Sundays had to elapse before a death sentence was put into effect. It was a tricky one, certainly. Though the appointed hangman, William Marwood, had pioneered the 'long drop' method of execution — which was devised to ensure the prisoner died instantaneously from a broken neck and which largely prevented the hideous struggling and convulsions associated with old-style hangings — decapitations were not unknown. As extra precautions, therefore, he used an unusually thick rope and made a final check to see it was correctly positioned under the angle of the left side of the prisoner's jaw *after* the hood was in place. In another refinement pioneered by Marwood, instead of the traditional thirteen-loop hangman's knot, the rope was fitted with a brass eyelet in a leather collar and the free end of the rope was passed through it to form the noose. By this arrangement the rope was able to run more freely and was more likely to dislocate the victim's neck, producing a speedier death.

The thicker noose, said the *Chester Chronicle* (7 April), was adopted 'to prevent a reopening of the wound in the culprit's neck' (and an untidy blood-letting). It was not entirely successful, but at least there were none of those 'peculiar horrors' that the Editor of the rival *Courant* imagined might happen but could not bring himself to describe. When the hanging was over, the *Chronicle*'s correspondent noticed a red mark on one side of the hood, but 'no palpable extravasation [outflowing] of blood'.

An *Illustrated Police News* depiction of William Marwood conducting a hanging at Wandsworth Gaol in 1879. The culprit was Catherine Webster, a maid who murdered and dismembered her mistress. Marwood carried out all four executions at Chester Castle.

Following a decision by the Visiting Justices, the prisons watchdog group of county magistrates, representatives of the *Chronicle*, the *Courant* and one of the Hyde papers were allowed to attend the execution, and they joined in the formal procession that accompanied the prisoner to the scaffold. The occasion also provided a unique experience for Lieutenant-Colonel Thomas Unett Brocklehurst Esq., a 53-year-old silk manufacturer of Henbury Hall, near Macclesfield, who thus became the first High Sheriff of Cheshire to officiate at a hanging. It was a less-than-pleasant aspect of his official duties he would undertake a second time during his year-long royal appointment (see Chapter 11).

A few days before, Bannister, seemingly acknowledging the cause of his downfall, had a meeting with the prison chaplain, Reverend James Kilner, at which he asked the cleric to write a last letter for him. It was to be sent to the Hyde Temperance Association urging them to 'carry on their good work and God bless them in it'. During their various interviews, Rev. Kilner revealed later, Bannister, in reflecting on his past life, 'had often reverted to the period, not more than a year ago, when he said he and his wife were living together in temperance and comparative happiness, possessed of a good house and furniture, and earning between them fifty shillings a week' — around £250 today.

In contrast to previous executions in Chester, which were regularly attended by thousands of spectators, just 13 people were present to see James Bannister 'launched into eternity' (and, yes, while attitudes towards the death penalty had changed and the practicalities of capital punishment had moved with the times, the local papers still clung to the tired old cliché in their execution coverage).

As the preparations got underway inside the gaol, outside the crowd in the Castle Square was also orderly, the presence nearby of large numbers of soldiers — the Castle had been a military garrison since William the Conqueror fortified the site in the 11th century — possibly keeping a rein on any potential rabble-rousing. It had begun to gather at about 7.30am, half-an-hour before the time appointed for the execution.

Soon there were around 500 people 'gazing at a naked flagstaff', said the *Chronicle*. Its report went on: 'It was a respectable crowd of well-dressed people, and soldiers of the 106th Regiment, stationed in the garrison, together with militiamen who are up for training. Of course, their object was to see the black flag hoisted [communicating to the outside world that the execution was over], and there was nothing to vary the dull monotony of waiting but the shrill bugle-calls for the different squads to fall in, and the sharp words of command of the drill sergeants.'

At 7.45am, however, an ominous new sound rose above the hurly-burly of the parade ground, heightening the sense of expectancy spreading through the Castle precincts. It was the tolling of a muffled, deep-toned bell in the tower of St. Mary's Church next door. Its single doom-laden note rang out for the next 30 minutes. By the time it stopped, the black flag had signalled its deathly message and most of the onlookers had dispersed.

Of the execution itself, the *Chronicle* commented, 'The last dread scene enacted within the walls of the prison was painful in its brevity, but was carried out with a decorum highly creditable to those who had the disagreeable duty of assisting at it.' On the scaffold, Bannister, who appeared in his shirt-sleeves, displayed 'a remarkable fortitude'. Marwood gave him a drop of more than six feet, and the culprit 'appeared to die without a struggle'.

After it was all over the *Courant*'s privileged observer went and looked into the pit where, he wrote, 'The poor man was seen, quite dead, hanging with the left side of his head and neck exposed and, as was expected, the wound on his neck was to a certain extent re-opened.'

Later the 57-year-old executioner announced himself pleased with his handiwork. He was particularly proud of the scaffold, which, said the *Courant*, 'appears to be built on a plan of his, first adopted at Reading [Gaol] and subsequently at Newgate'. He believed that it was only a matter time before the style was adopted throughout the country (he was right). Marwood, a Lincolnshire cobbler who applied his length-of-drop formula according to the weight and strength of each individual prisoner, carried out all four hangings at Chester Castle.

Marwood's scaffold was a portable structure capable, it was reported, of being dismantled and re-erected in half-an-hour. The detail came to light on 28 November 1877, when the *Courant* revealed that it had been loaned to the authorities in Dolgellau, Merionethshire (now Gwynedd), for the execution of convicted murderer Cadwallader Jones. It was the first hanging in that county for more than 60 years and, in a extraordinary train of events, first none of the local carpenters was prepared to build a new scaffold and, with the public at large also expressing their hostility towards the execution, the Under-Sheriff refused to be held responsible for having the Chester gallows delivered to Dolgellau station and, instead, ordered it to be brought to Penmaenpool, the next stop down the line. Then, having been unable to find a carrier willing to transport it the three miles to the gaol, he had to do the job himself, using his own horses and wagons.

Marwood also carried out the execution, which took place on Friday 23 November. 'The scene among the crowd', said the *Chester Chronicle* the following day, 'was heart-rending; on every hand was weeping and anguish.' The newspaper, however, could not understand the extent of the public sympathy for Jones, a 25-year-old farmer who had been convicted at the Chester Assizes in October of murdering a local woman named Sarah Hughes, aged 36 — and, stated the paper disapprovingly, 'not a woman of immaculate character' who had borne two illegitimate children — at his home at Parc Farm, a mile-and-a-half from Dolgellau.

'In spite of the petitions with ten thousand signatures', its editorial stated, 'the public will judge whether there was any one fact in the case to furnish material for a verdict less than that of murder.' Referring to the build-up to the execution, the *Chronicle* put 'the stupid things which both public and officials have done' partly down to 'the superstition of the Welsh people', and added, 'It must not be forgotten that if he was rash and violent at first . . . he was shockingly cold-blooded afterwards.'

The court had heard that Jones, after killing his victim with a blow to the head, dismembered her and dumped the body parts in the nearby River Arran. At the time the river was in flood; but the woman's remains began to come to light six weeks later as the water level receded.

*   *   *

IT WAS Christmas Day 1880. In the famous east Cheshire silk town of Macclesfield, sustained by a steady intake of alcohol, one group of revellers had spun out the celebrations from early morning. Now, as the afternoon faded into evening, in a dingy court in the overcrowded heart of the town, the good natured merry-making took a less than festive turn as a row flared between two of the party, William ('Billy') Stanway and Ann Mellor, the woman with whom he cohabited.

Stanway, a maker and hawker of besoms (the stylised 'witches' broomsticks', sweeping brushes with long handles and heads made from bundles of birch twigs) had been away selling his wares and had walked the 40 miles from Newcastle-under-Lyme to be home in time for Christmas. He had not eaten and, after a lengthy session at the pub, he was hungry. But when the woman refused to prepare a meal for him, he gave her a tongue-lashing that quickly escalated into violence. Maddened by the drink they had both consumed in large quantities, he began punching and kicking her mercilessly.

What had started out as a seemingly minor domestic squabble would develop into a series of bruising quarrels that broke out intermittently throughout the rest of that supposed day of peace and goodwill. At one point he drove her out of the terrace house they shared with their adopted child, a girl called Sarah Ann, and knocked her through a neighbour's front door, the pair of them ending up in a flailing heap on the startled occupant's living-room floor. In another flare-up shortly afterwards, again in the court outside, he resumed the assault and was heard to swear that he was going to 'kick her bloody entrails out'.

Stanway appears to have hurt his shoulder in crashing through his neighbour's door and for a while the situation calmed down. Ann, battered and bruised and nursing a black eye, took the opportunity to escape her tormentor; she grabbed Sarah Ann and they eventually took refuge in the home of a young bachelor friend (a decision that would do nothing to diminish Stanway's seething resentment when she told him where they had been). Yet, just a few hours later, apparently, the couple were back drinking together in a nearby pub.

Around nine o'clock they returned to their mean two-storey tenement in the narrow alley off George Street and Ann and the child went straight to bed. But if she thought her suffering was over, she was seriously mistaken. For her things were about to get hotter. Much hotter.

As he sat beside the kitchen fire, Stanway brooded over her refusal to cook for him, jealousy now heightening his alcohol-induced sense of grievance. Finally, he ordered her downstairs to get him some food, warning that, if she disobeyed him, he would 'bring a red-hot poker to her'. It was no idle threat.

When the scantily-clad woman came into the kitchen and again refused to accede to his demands, he grabbed the poker — whose end was burned away to a point by his habit of heating it in the fire and using it to light his pipe — and plunged it into her abdomen.

Four years after Rebecca Bannister was horrifically bludgeoned to death with an axe following a domestic bust-up, the 'curse of the demon drink' had claimed another Cheshire victim. And, while the preliminaries were similar, this time the booze factor had cast its destructive spell to even more fiendish effect. The *Cheshire Observer* echoed the sentiments expressed in many contemporary press reports when it would later describe the crime as 'one of the most barbarous that criminal history has had to record'.

Incredibly, Ann Mellor's first thought after being stabbed was to protect the man who had inflicted what would turn out to be her fatal wound, refusing medical treatment for fear that, as she explained pathetically, 'the police will lock Billy up'. She did eventually agree to a doctor being called; but by then it was too late. She died as a result of her injury late on Monday 27 December after two days of crippling pain.

The next morning Stanway was arrested and that evening, at Macclesfield Borough Police Station, he was formally charged with Ann's murder. The police station was then located in the Georgian Town Hall in the extension built during 1869-71, which included an imposing new west front facing on to Chestergate; and it was in that grand civic edifice, on Friday the 31st, that the inquest jury inquiring into the dead woman's death returned their inevitable verdict of wilful murder against William Stanway.

By now the case had aroused an immense amount of interest locally and following the hearing the accused was transferred to Belle Vue Prison in Manchester. His removal, revealed the local weekly newspaper the *Macclesfield Courier and Herald* on 8 January 1881, was 'quietly and secretively effected by the Police, who evaded and disappointed the morbid curiosity of a crowd of people who had assembled in the hope of seeing the unfortunate man'.

On 5 January Stanway's appearance before the borough magistrates,

At busy scene in Macclesfield's Market Square around 1900. On 5 January 1881 an even bigger crowd packed the square — not to look for bargains, however, but to try to obtain a seat at the first court appearance of murder suspect William Stanway in the Town Hall. Hundreds were locked out.

From the author's collection.

also in the Town Hall, attracted even more attention. 'From about 10 o'clock a large crowd assembled in the Market Place with the double object of securing places in the court and seeing the prisoner,' reported the *Courier* three days later. 'But there was only limited space in the courtroom and hundreds were unable to gain admission.'

During the proceedings, in which he was committed for trial at the next Chester Assizes, Stanway — not surprisingly, given the amount of alcohol he had consumed — maintained his recollection of the tragic turn of events on Christmas Day was hazy. He claimed he could remember having the poker in his hand, but insisted he had no memory of stabbing his partner with it.

It was the main plank of his defence when, on Tuesday 1 February 1881, at the start of a two-day trial at the county's Winter Assizes, he pleaded not guilty to murder. The *Courier,* in first reporting the murder in its edition of 1 January, had called it 'a wretched tragedy blighting the Christmas season by its horror'. The paper added bitterly that 'the facts leading up to the terrible result are but too commonplace, though none the less lamentable and shocking'.

The 'shocking facts' of this 'terrible' crime, as related here, are mainly extracted from the unusually large number of witness depositions that survive among the assize court papers in the National Archives, the written evidence that formed the core of the prosecution's case at the trial. Where noted, newspaper reports of the trial are used to fill any missing gaps in the official narrative.

The jury heard that Stanway, 31, and 36-year-old Ann Mellor, also a hawker (of tinware), had been living together as man and wife for some time, latterly at an address identified as 'No. 4 House, No. 4 Court, off George Street East, Macclesfield', an impoverished neighbourhood of low, densely-populated terraces, dimly-lit courts and alleyways and insanitary living conditions. Residing with them was their adopted daughter, whose birth name was Sarah Ann Blunt. The nine-year-old was to be the key witness against her 'father' in what was referred to by the *Chester Chronicle* on 5 February as 'this melancholy business'.

In mid-December 1880 Stanway had set out with his self-made besoms on a selling trip to north Staffordshire. He was due back home on Christmas Eve. Ann, eagerly awaiting his return by all accounts, went to Macclesfield railway station to meet him. When he did not arrive, she and Sarah Ann stayed that Friday night at the home of James Williamson just around the corner at 11, Townley Street. She and Stanway had lodged there before setting up home together about the beginning of October.

In his deposition, Williamson, a 40-year-old widower whose occupation was given as labourer (though in the April 1881 census he would describe himself as a hawker), stated that Stanway eventually got back on Christmas morning and came to his house at around eight o'clock. Ann Sutton, with whom Williamson was living, called up to her overnight guest, 'Come downstairs, Billy's come'; and Ann, seemingly, greeted her man warmly. Williamson and Stanway drank half-a-gallon of beer between them, had some more drink at Stanway's and then, at opening time, they adjourned to their 'local', the long-since disappeared Silk Tavern pub in Sunderland Street. Said Williamson, 'We were drinking together off and on all day.'

Ann Mellor and Sutton, a widow in her mid-30s, had gone Christmas shopping together to buy Sarah Ann a new pair of boots, before joining the men-folk about noon. At one time or another there seems to have been as many as seven friends and relations in the group of revellers, which also included Stanway's brother John and his cousin, Ann Smith.

It was approaching 5pm when the party finally broke up. It is likely that the issue of Stanway's missed meal first arose during the afternoon's session at the Silk Tavern. Then, when he and Ann arrived home, he again asked her to get him some food. When she refused he waded into her with fists — and boots — flying.

John Brocklehurst, a 50-year-old bricklayer's labourer and a close neighbour, witnessed what happened next. The accused, he said in his written deposition, 'ran her down the yard [court] and started thrashing her'. He heard the woman shout something about 'clem' and 'vengeance' ('clem' being an old Cheshire dialect word which, in this context, meant 'to make hungry') and Stanway 'called her all sorts of names and told her, "Don't talk to me about clem vengeance when I have walked from Newcastle this morning and had nothing to eat and have given you money to buy some meat [food]."' Ann subsequently spoke to Brocklehurst and, referring to their other drinking companions, explained, 'Was I likely to get meat for a whole household of drunken men.'

The fight in the court quickly spilled over into George Street and a large crowd — which, according to one estimate, numbered between 200 and 300 people — quickly gathered to see what the hoo-hah was all about. Said Brocklehurst, 'I begged the prisoner to be quiet, but he kept on thrashing her and was in a very great rage.' There were shouts of 'murderous villain' directed towards Stanway, though most of the male onlookers evidently saw it as just another bout of the then popular sport of wife-beating (one of the 'too commonplace' facts of life among the working-class poor to which the *Macclesfield Courier* had alluded), and were more inclined to urge the pair on than to interfere.

Brocklehurst, who lived two doors higher up from Stanway, and another man finally managed to separate them and took Stanway back to his house. Ann dutifully followed him home; but five minutes later he turned her out and chased after her into the court. It was then that they ended up crashing into the home of Mrs Mary Holloway, who also lived two doors away lower down the court. In her deposition she said she had heard the disturbance outside and then, at about five o'clock, 'the prisoner and the deceased came bursting in through my door'. She then watched in shocked disbelief as they 'fell on the floor and the prisoner beat her badly'. She went on, 'They got up and she got on the sofa and there he beat her again severely about the face. I said, "Don't beat the woman that way", but he kept on beating her.'

Earlier, she said, she had 'noticed them and others up and down [the court] drinking'. Then after they had dropped in on her so unexpectedly, Mrs Holloway, aged 62, said of Stanway, 'He dragged her out and towards her own house and in about five minutes afterwards I heard her run down the yard screaming and he after her.'

There followed a further outbreak of violence, also witnessed by John Brocklehurst , in which, he said, he heard Stanway swear that he would 'kick her bloody entrails out if she came up the yard again that night'.

After a while, possibly due to his injured shoulder, Stanway appears to have calmed down and Ann, extensively bruised and now nursing a black eye, took Sarah Ann with her to Townley Street, hoping to find safety at the home of James Williamson. There was no one in, however; so, instead, they went across the street to the home of another friend, a young man by the name of Thomas Byrne.

They were together with Byrne, a 22-year-old 'carman' (a driver of a horse-drawn delivery vehicle), for some time, a potentially inflammatory situation that almost certainly contributed to the final fiery event that led to Ann Mellor's excruciating death. The chilling details of the latter were related to the court by the only eye-witness, the child Sarah Ann Blunt. The *Macclesfield Courier*, in its 5 February trial report, commented, 'It was extremely pitiful to hear the story of the dreadful act of the prisoner, as told by the child Blunt who, during her evidence, wept bitterly.'

The girl, in her court deposition, stated that 'she lived with William Stanway and Ann Mellor as long as she could remember and always called them father and mother'; in fact, at his committal hearing, Stanway had explained that she was adopted when she was just six-months old. 'She has no father,' he explained; to which the magistrates' clerk had added, somewhat gratuitously, 'And she says her [birth] mother is nearly always locked up in Newcastle Gaol.'

Recalling that far-from joyful Christmas Day, Sara Ann said her 'parents' were both drinking and that, about tea-time, Stanway 'got angry with Ann because she would not get any tea for him'. She said he had ' beat her and kicked her'; then he 'ran us out of the house and we went to Ann Sutton's and from there to Byrne's'. They were there for about an hour, during which, Sarah Ann said, 'Mr Byrne sent me for some drink three times' (the three quarts of ale she fetched were consumed, apparently, by Ann, Byrne and two of his friends, who were also in the house at the time).

When they eventually returned to their own home was never stated, but it seems that some little time later Stanway and Ann Mellor went out drinking together again. For, in the report of Stanway's committal hearing, published in the *Macclesfield Courier* of 8 January, James Williamson was quoted as saying that, 'Shortly after nine o'clock he saw the deceased and the prisoner coming out of the Silk Tavern.' Ann had a black eye and she said to him, 'See what Billy's done.' Williamson said he admonished Stanway for giving her the injury, which would 'stop her from going out of doors' to earn her living.

Arriving home Ann went straight to bed with her daughter, leaving Stanway downstairs. Sarah Ann's statement continued, 'When [we were] in bed my father . . . shouted to my mother to come downstairs and when she didn't go he said if she did not come down he would bring a red hot poker to her. She got up and put on a petticoat [over the chemise she had been wearing in bed] and went down. I got up and followed her and saw my father hit her in the belly with a poker. My mother fell down and went in[to] a fit. I gave her some water and helped her to get up.'

Stanway, she said, sat down by the fire, having put the poker back in the 'hess-hole' (another local dialect expression meaning ash-hole or fireplace, though in broad Cheshire, with its almost mandatory disregard of the letter 'h', it would have been pronounced 'essole'). Despite her considerable pain, Ann went upstairs and put on a skirt and took her daughter again to the home of James Williamson and Ann Sutton, or 'Daddy Jim' and 'Aunt Ann', as the girl called them.

The first person she saw when she arrived was Elizabeth Blackley, who was also spending the night there. Mrs Blackley, a nail-maker's wife of Cross Street, Macclesfield, stated that when Ann arrived she was clutching her stomach and she said to her, 'Oh, Bessie, Billy has burnt my belly with a poker.' Ann went upstairs and got into bed with Sutton and Mrs Blackley slept in another room. She went on, 'During the night I was awoke by the deceased calling for water. I got up three times to get her some.' On the first occasion, Ann said to her, 'Bessie, look at my belly where Billy has burnt me.' Mrs Blackley, 'I looked and saw a wound as if a red-hot cinder had fallen on the place, and also noticed blood on her chemise. She kept vomiting all night.'

It was a remarkable testimony, because Sutton, who spent the night sleeping in the same bed as Ann, would tell the court that, although she was sober, she could only remember Mrs Blackley entering the room once; that while Ann 'complained of a pain in her right side, she never said anything about a burn' and she 'never showed her [her] bruises' (*Macclesfield Courier*). All she had said to her was "Oh, dear, if I get well after this, I shall never drink rum any more"; and it wasn't until early the following day, Sunday (Boxing Day), that she showed her the poker wound, at which point Sutton said she 'tied a piece of rag soaked in linseed oil round the burn'.

She had been similarly evasive at the inquest into Ann Mellor's death, after which the foreman of the jury called upon the Coroner (the splendidly-named Hercules Campbell Yates) to censure her for 'the unsatisfactory way' in which she had given her evidence. He was happy to do so; like the members of the jury he obviously believed that she knew more about the affair than she was letting on.

James Williamson also learned about Ann Mellor's injury on that Sunday morning. She was sitting up in bed, looking ill and retching and, when he asked her what had happened, she told him, 'Billy has punched me in the belly with a poker.' Williamson went out into the street and there bumped into Stanway who, having slept off the effects of the previous day's carousing, was out looking for Ann. He had his arms folded across his stomach. Williamson asked him what was the matter. Stanway replied, 'I don't know whether I have put my shoulder out or broken it'. Then he confessed, 'The worst of it is I have nearly spoilt her with the poker.'

At Williamson's house, Stanway was confronted by Elizabeth Blackley, who said to him, 'Billy, whatever has't thou been doing to burn Ann's belly with the poker?' He replied, 'Bessie, I don't know. I had the poker but I don't know what I did with it. She wouldn't give me anything to eat and it vexed me.' He then went upstairs to see how Ann was and, Williamson deposed, on coming down he said, 'The bugger (meaning the deceased) has been in Byrne's and she has owned [up] to it.' Despite the obvious seriousness of Ann's injury, he and Stanway were out drinking most of that day, Williamson admitted.

Around 5pm Ann and Sarah Ann returned home. The following day, Monday, Ann's condition was considerably worse; yet, again, Stanway spent most of the day drinking. Williamson caught up with him at the Silk Tavern around noon (*Macclesfield Courier*) and during the whole time they were together 'nothing was said about [the] deceased'.

At about nine o'clock that night, John Brocklehurst visited Stanway and, after looking in on Ann, he urged him to call a doctor; but he was told, 'Hoo [she] won't have one' (*Chester Chronicle*). Asked why, Stanway said that 'she was afraid to do so for fear that [he] should be locked up for giving her the black eye'. Less than two hours later, however, he ran into James Williamson's and, tearful and shaking, he pleaded, 'Some on ye [some of you] get up and fetch a doctor. I think Ann's deein' [dying].'"

Williamson left immediately and, after trying one doctor — who refused to go with him and shut the door in his face — he roused surgeon George Bland from his bed at his home in Park Green. He was at first reluctant to venture out as well, but eventually agreed. This must have been around 10.30pm for by the time he arrived at Stanway's — he fixed it at precisely 10.45 — Ann Mellor was dead.

Catherine Stanway, William Stanway's sister-in-law, who lived next door, was also in the bedroom at the time. Realising how ill Ann was, she had promised her that she would stay with her overnight. But, she said, Ann 'died in the arms of the prisoner, who wept bitterly . . . and asked [this] witness to pray for her' (*Chronicle*).

The following day, Bland, 33-year-old house surgeon at Macclesfield Infirmary, who was also the local Medical Officer of Health and the borough police surgeon, carried out a postmortem examination in the infirmary's mortuary. He noted the extensive bruising around Ann's right eye, also on her face, on both her arms and knees and on her right thigh, all of which he thought 'could have been produced by kicks' (*Chronicle*). In the abdomen, halfway between her navel and the left side of her pelvis, there was 'a punctured wound similar to a burn'.

His deposition went on, 'The direction of the wound was downwards and the walls of the wound had a charred appearance. The wound had passed through the outer margins of the rectus muscle and in the sheath of the muscle I found several scales of a metallic substance.' About three-quarters-of-an-inch of fat covered the abdomen and 'considerable force must have been used to cause the wound.' From the direction of the wound he surmised that the woman had been crouching at the time she was stabbed.

The metallic scales he found 'could have come from a red-hot poker'; the cause of death he diagnosed as 'peritonitis or inflammation of the peritoneum caused by the injury to the abdomen'. Bland, who gave evidence on day two of the trial, was of the opinion that there was 'a very slight chance' that the woman could have survived the injury had she received medical attention immediately; in cross-examination, he estimated the odds to have been a thousand to one. In the *Macclesfield Courier*'s report, Bland explained that 'wounds in the abdomen are always dangerous, but especially when the instrument inflicting them is dirty, as in the present case'.

Inspector Thomas Bullock of Macclesfield Borough Police testified that on Monday evening, after learning of the disturbance in the court, he had gone to Stanway's home, where he found one of Stanway's brothers and Ann Sutton. Stanway was out; but he saw Ann Mellor in bed. He noticed she had a black eye. When, shortly afterwards, Stanway returned home, the officer asked him what had been the matter with his wife. Stanway replied, 'I cannot say.' When questioned as to how she had got her black eye, he said, 'I cannot say, unless she fell when she was drunk.'

Ann Mellor died later that night and at about 7am the next day, Insp. Bullock, 35, arrested Stanway at James Williamson's and took him to his own home, where the deceased still lay. Shown her body and the burn wound in her abdomen, Stanway commented, 'I wonder how she got that. She must have fallen on something.' Told he was being arrested for causing the death of the woman Stanway replied, 'I am the death of no woman.' At Macclesfield Police Station he was formally charged with murder by the Chief Constable of Macclesfield, William Sheasby. The 41-year-old police chief's deposition recorded him as saying, 'I have murdered nobody. I know I was drunk, and she was, too.'

As the final day of the trial drew to a close in the packed courtroom at Chester Castle, Mr Edward Julyan Dunn rose to address the jury on behalf of the prisoner. He faced a daunting challenge, not helped by the fact that he seems to have been handed the task of leading for the defence at very short notice and had only been briefed just before the trial began. He described his situation as 'one of the greatest anxiety and responsibility' (*Chester Chronicle*). He told the jury that he had had 'little or no instruction in this case' but that by 'exercising all his powers' he hoped to demonstrate to them why they need not 'perform the painful task' of convicting the defendant of this 'diabolical offence'.

Quoting case law, he argued that a man's state of intoxication could be cited as evidence to show that his actions were not premeditated. He argued that Stanway 'had been fighting and drinking all day and did not know what he was doing'. When the Judge, Mr Commissioner Brown QC, interrupted him to point out that for such evidence to be taken into account it had to be shown that the man was 'so stupidly drunk that he did not know what he was doing'. Defence counsel replied, 'That is my contention, my Lord.'

Mr Dunn drew the jury's attention to 'some slight discrepancies' in the evidence given by Sarah Ann Blunt, and, according to the *Chronicle*, he urged them to be 'cautious in convicting this man of wilful murder on the testimony of such an infant'. And on the suggestion that Stanway could have sent immediately for the doctor whose medical help might just have saved Ann Mellor's life, he said, 'The fact was that the woman was the elder of the two, and probably had the upper hand, and she would not allow him to do so, while he, being contrite and not wishing to have any further quarrel with her, did not go for one. And again, the fact that the woman, having walked to a neighbour's house and back again, was sufficient to cause him to think that she was not quite so seriously injured as was really the case.'

Summing up, Commissioner Brown told the jury, 'If the prisoner, either because he was angry with her for not getting him the food he had given her money for, or because he was jealous on account of her having gone into Byrne's [house], had in his passion run this red-hot poker into her, he was guilty of the murder, and no amount of provocation would justify the crime.'

If they believed the evidence given by the little girl — whose presence in the witness box 'must have moved them all to compassion' — and, in particular, her reference to her father's shout of 'Come downstairs or I will come up with a red-hot poker', how could they credit the assertion that he was so 'stupidly drunk' that he did not know what he was doing, the only justification for a manslaughter verdict. If they believed he knew what he was doing, said the Judge, 'whether he actually intended to thrust the poker into her or not, their verdict would be wilful murder'.

When, after an absence of 25 minutes, the jury returned with a guilty verdict, Stanway told the judge, 'I never done it, sir, not that I know of.' And dropping to his knees in the dock, he continued, 'If I must die this moment, I know nothing at all about it.' When the death sentence was passed, he touched his forelock in the direction of the Judge and then walked firmly to the far side of the dock. He was still insisting he had no recollection of 'committing the horrible deed' when he eventually did die, three weeks later, at the hands of hangman William Marwood.

In early 1877, when Marwood had unveiled his new gallows at Chester Castle, he believed he had created the perfect killing machine. Four years after it was commissioned, however, he was to discover that it still did not quite measure up. While making the customary calculations in preparation for William Stanway's execution on Monday 21 February, the 'long drop hangman' realised the Castle drop was not quite long enough. He computed that a fall of 8ft 6ins was required. But the pit beneath the Castle Gaol scaffold was no more than 8ft deep.

Contemporary newspaper accounts suggest that it was the veteran hangman's normal practice to arrive in the city the day before an execution. If that were so we must assume that his unexpected discovery caused some degree of panic as prison officials hurriedly sought to arrange the necessary excavation work in order to meet Monday's 8am deadline. However, the job was completed in time and, as a consequence, the overall depth of the pit was increased to 9ft 6ins. Afterwards, Marwood issued a statement in which he said that he now considered the execution facilities at the Castle to be 'excellent'.

Certainly, Stanway's execution, on a bitterly cold winter's morning, was carried out with maximum efficiency. Cheshire's High Sheriff, Cudworth Halsted Poole Esq., of Marbury Hall, near Nantwich, for reasons he apparently felt no obligation to divulge, had given instructions that no Press should be admitted to the hanging. It was a decision that brought forth howls of protest from the local papers, including the *Macclesfield Courier*, which, on 26 February, bemoaned, 'It is a matter of serious complaint on the part of the reporters, as representing the public, that they should have met with supercilious treatment from the High Sheriff downwards, and be obliged to seek out the common hangman to obtain information from him which they are expected to furnish.'

In a more agreeable public relations gesture, Marwood afterwards gave an interview to representatives of three of the papers. As a result, the *Chester Chronicle* was able to state reliably that the victim died instantaneously, with 'not a struggle or movement of any kind'.

Seven years into his tenure as the nation's No. 1 executioner, Marwood had become something of a celebrity. And as if by way of a thank-you for the straight-from-the hangman's-mouth insights he had given the paper, the *Chronicle* devoted much of its 26 February execution report to a flattering personal profile, in which he was portrayed as a kindly old gent (he was aged about 60 by this time) for whom killing criminals was a job like any other.

Referring to his latest official engagement, the article stated, 'That hanging has been reduced by Marwood to a fine art may be judged from the fact that at exactly two minutes past eight the black flag was hoisted above the Castle walls, showing that the dreadful business of the morning had been accomplished with merciful celerity, and without the slightest bungling, the operations, including the procession, having only occupied six minutes.'

The 300 people who had been awaiting the outcome in the Castle Square were there, said the paper, 'mainly with the object of seeing Marwood'; and when the hangman eventually emerged from the gaol he was 'followed by a curious crowd' to the Red Lion Inn in Lower Bridge Street, where he usually stayed on his visits to Chester.

The *Chronicle* article went on, 'On Sunday evening the Red Lion had

William Marwood: 'a cheery, little old man . . . more like a parish clerk than a hangman.'

Below: The old Red Lion, Marwood's lodgings when on 'hanging duty' in Chester.

a great many visitors, and the executioner became the centre of an admiring circle of loungers, who gratified their curiosity and exercised their wits by entering into conversation with him. He is a chatty, cheery, little old man, dressed in rusty black [i.e. shabby], with just the sort of parchment countenance and merry twinkling little eye which could lead one to take him for the parish clerk of a country village — in fact he is the last man you would take to be the hangman.

'It is evident at once that he looks upon hanging a man purely as a matter of business — much in the same way as if it was rate-collecting. Not that he is cold-blooded altogether in

Image courtesy of Steve Howe at www.chesterwalls.info.

his way of speaking about it; on the contrary, he is apparently not without some kindly feeling towards his victims, but his business is to kill them by hanging in the quickest and the most merciful manner possible, and he talks about it in a pleasant matter-of-fact way, which shows he takes a pride in doing his work in a business-like manner.'

The *Chronicle* concluded, 'If death punishments are to be carried out, it is well to perform them without excitement, or unnecessary pain to the victim, and in Marwood we have an executioner who has attained the perfection of his terrible art.' Marwood, who came to the 'profession' late in life — he was 52 when he carried out his first execution — was in office for nine years, during which time he hanged 176 people, including eight women. Officially the hangman of London and Middlesex, he was paid a retainer of £20 a year plus £10 per execution.

In covering the Stanway case, the press had attempted to trace his background, and some interesting details emerged. Most diligent in this respect was the *Macclesfield Courier*, which reported on 1 January that the hanged man was born into a family of hawkers in Macclesfield 'in a row off Gunco Lane'; that his father came from Biddulph in Staffordshire and later moved to Newcastle-under-Lyme, where he died three years ago.

A search among Cheshire's Quarter Sessions files also revealed that Stanway had a prison record. In January 1870 he was sentenced to six months' hard labour in Knutsford Gaol for unlawful wounding and also served two 14-day spells in Stafford Prison, most recently for another assault, in August 1877. In the first mentioned offence, committed on 23 November 1869, he was alleged to have attacked one William *Mellor* at Macclesfield and, according to the *Macclesfield Courier* (27 November), 'violently kicked him in the lower part of his person', i.e. his genitals. There is no evidence to say whether the victim was in any way related to Ann Mellor; but, intriguingly, the date of the offence coincides with a statement made by Stanway — on 29 December 1880, at the inquest into Ann's death — that he had known her for 'very nearly 11 years'.

Census records threw up another curiosity: in the 1871 returns a besom-maker by the name of William Stanway was listed as a boarder at No. 25, Townley Street, Macclesfield, where the head of the household was a certain James Williamson. The ages of the two men — 26 and 27 respectively — don't tally with the official figures published at the time of the trial nine years later; but then it has been shown that personal details on census forms of the period, and especially ages, can be annoyingly unreliable. On the other hand, if it wasn't just another odd coincidence and this really *was* our murderer, in April 1871 William Stanway had a (presumably legal) wife called Sarah and an eight-year-old daughter by the name of Mary living with him at the same address — antecedents that are not to be found in any of the contemporary newspapers or in the court files.

During the trial, James Williamson was reported to have said that he had known Stanway for 'about 14 or 15 years' (*Chester Chronicle*). They were obviously good friends, for in another interesting anecdote discovered among the surviving court documents is an addendum to Williamson's original deposition. In it he revealed that in helping Stanway and Ann set up home together — 'except for a bed, a picture and a few small things' — he had loaned them every other item in their new house . . . including a poker.

CHAPTER ELEVEN

The Wages Of Sin

It was a fine Spring morning in March 1877 when, glancing idly out of an upstairs window, young domestic servant Emma Owen was momentarily distracted from her housework by the sight of two figures walking together along the nearby canal towpath. Although she was more than 200 yards away, and the towpath was on the far side of the canal, from her elevated position she had a clear view across the sloping pasture land in front of her master's house and she could see that one of them was a little girl and the other looked like an older boy. Between them they carried a brown basket; a sister and brother, perhaps, on a shopping errand for their mother.

Emma was able to observe their progress only briefly before they disappeared behind a high wall on the opposite bank of the canal. Having noticed nothing unusual in their appearance or behaviour, she returned to her chores and thought no more about it. Until, that is, she heard the disturbing news that the body of a little girl had been found that day floating in the same stretch of water. She had apparently been attacked, robbed and thrown into the canal and left to drown in its cold, murky depths.

It was then that the 11-year-old house-maid — girls as young as eight were 'in service' in Victorian England — realised that what she had witnessed was something far less innocent than it seemed: the prelude, in fact, to a particularly nasty murder . . . and the final moments of the victim's life.

For, she learned, it was almost immediately after she lost sight of the pair that the girl, eight-year-old Mary Ann Halton, met her cruel death. And the suspected murderer was the companion she had seen with the child on the canalside. He was not Mary Ann's 'big brother', though, but a man of exceptionally small stature, a former neighbour of hers called Harry Leigh, who was just 4ft 8½ins tall.

By the time Emma Owen was able to help police with their inquiries — her important evidence would be heard for the first time at the trial four months later — Leigh, a 23-year-old cotton weaver, had already been charged with the murder, which happened on Saturday 24 March on the section of the Macclesfield Canal that runs through the Sutton area of the town. Mary Anne Halton *had* been on an errand for her mother at the time; not for groceries, however, but to collect Mrs Halton's wages from Bamford's silk mill where she was employed as an 'outdoor worker'.

Murder scene: through the arch of Foden Bank Bridge (Bridge No. 43), the section of towpath on which Mary Ann Halton was attacked, and her body dumped into the canal, is visible.
Photo courtesy of Mr Dave Burdett.

Just beyond the wall buttress on the right is the exact spot where Mary Ann met her cruel death. Her killer waited until reaching this secluded part of the canal before he struck.
Photograph by the author.

It was while she was on her way home with her mother's pay — it amounted to 12s. 3d, worth about £60 today — that Harry Leigh lured the girl on to the canal towpath and, police speculated, after robbing her of the money he silenced her to prevent her from identifying him.

It was a crime that caused outrage well beyond Macclesfield's borders. The mood in the town was said to be approaching 'lynch law' level by the time Leigh was brought before the county magistrates' court. The hearing, at the Cheshire Constabulary's local police headquarters in King Edward Street on Monday 7 April, was conducted in an atmosphere of noisy hostility. It was reported that the officers present had great difficulty in preventing the spectators crowded into the tiny courtroom from breaking down the low wooden barrier that separated the prisoner from the public.

With the justices struggling to keep order, one indignant onlooker — to shouts of approval from his fellows — urged the bench to hand Leigh over to them to deal with. Because of the prisoner's size, the people at the back of the packed courtroom complained they could not see over the heads of those in front of them and called for the chair on which he sat to be placed on a table so everybody could get a good look at him. Both 'suggestions' fell on deaf ears. Harry Leigh was also unmoved by the uproar in court; the *Cheshire Observer* (14 April) noted that he merely sat there with 'a contemptuous smile' on his face.

A detailed description of the murder suspect, however, had been in circulation since 31 March, when the *Macclesfield Courier* reported that he was 'a slimly-built, dwarfish man measuring four feet nine inches [*sic*], light complexioned [with] sharp features and a closely-shaven chin'.

Despite repeated interruptions, the court eventually committed Leigh for trial at the next Cheshire Assizes. Afterwards, hoping to catch a glimpse of the murder suspect — and to give voice to the public's sense of revulsion over the death of an innocent child — crowds of people besieged the police station and also the railway station, from where, it was assumed, he would be conveyed to the county gaol at Chester Castle. But the police out-manoeuvred the mobs by smuggling him into a pony-and-trap and taking him the seven miles to Chelford Station to catch the train there.

Initially, while efforts were being made to sort out a boundary and jurisdiction dispute, Leigh had been brought before the Macclesfield magistrates, as it was then believed the crime had been committed within the borough. However, after the clerk to the county justices consulted the latest Ordnance Survey map, it was established that the boundary between the two authorities ran down the middle of the canal; and, as the towpath at the murder scene was about five yards beyond the borough border, the accused was handed over to the county police.

The *Macclesfield Courier* was quick to point out that the change of command was not hampering the investigation into Mary Ann Halton's murder. The two police forces, the newspaper stated in that same 31 March edition, were 'working amicably and diligently together to garner as much evidence as possible'.

They would discover that the beginnings of what the *Courier* dubbed 'this foul murder', could be traced back to a casual comment made by 37-year-old Mrs Emily Halton during a conversation in the kitchen of the Leigh family home at 54, Fence Street in the Hurdsfield district of Macclesfield during the early evening of Friday 23 March. Mrs Halton, still grieving over the death of her husband Thomas — a silk weaver who had died the previous October at the age of only 33 — lived three doors away at No.60 and was in the habit of dropping in on her friend, Harry Leigh's step-mother Mary Leigh, for a cup of tea and a chat. Fence Street's terrace houses were demolished in the late 1960s to make way for the Victoria Park flats, a development that was also bulldozed in more recent times. Fence Street was approximately where Park View stands today.

On this particular evening, Harry Leigh, recently married and living half-a-mile away in Parsonage Street, was also in the house visiting his 48-year-old silk weaver father Thomas. And he was within earshot when Mrs Halton — whose maiden name, confusingly, was also Leigh, though she was no relation — mentioned to her neighbour that she was not feeling too well and that she wouldn't be going to the mill the next day. Though, by this time in the 19th century, most textile workers had been assimilated into the factory system, both silk and cotton

mills still employed significant numbers of home-based handloom weavers like Emily Halton; usually working in garrets or cellars, they were paid for each piece they produced. In fact, the continued demand for this highly-skilled work ensured that Macclefield's handloom weavers survived well into the 20th century. Joseph Bamford's silk mill (commonly known as the Pool Street Mill) was situated at the junction of Waller Street and Pool

Fence Street, Macclesfield, just before the bulldozers got to work in the 1960s. The Haltons' house was on the extreme left of the picture.
Photo by permission of CALS.

Street, Sutton, and specialised in ladies' scarves and men's ties. Thomas Halton had been a power-loom weaver there up to the time of his premature death.

Mrs Halton, who came originally from Ormskirk in Lancashire, told Mrs Leigh that she would send Mary Ann to collect the pay that was owed to her. The child had done it before and was known to the mill bosses. If Harry Leigh hadn't been taking too much notice of the women's small-talk up to then, this titbit of information plainly caught his attention. And he really pricked up his ears when Mrs Halton let it slip that Mary Ann would be going to the mill around 10.30am.

A female silk handloom weaver at work in her home.
Photo: Nuneaton Hospitals Historical Collection.

A little after ten o'clock on that Saturday morning, three young lads — Harry Gosling and George Whittaker, both aged eight, and seven-year-old Samuel Goodwin, all living in Mill Lane — were playing on the corner of Waller Street and Mill Lane when they were approached by 'a little man' carrying a wicker basket with a broken lid. He inquired whether they knew where Bamford's Mill was. Pointing up Waller Street to the seven-storey building less than 50 yards away, Whittaker said, 'That's it.' The stranger showed them a note and asked them if they would carry it to the mill, and 'bring something back'. The boys agreed. Goodwin took the note and the three of them went first to the mill owner's house at 26, Pool Street, where they saw Mrs Bamford. When they told her about the little man who had given them the note, she sent them to see the mill's 26-year-old manager, Thomas Robinson.

The note, scribbled in pencil in a man's hand, read, 'Mr Robinson, please to pay the bearer my wages, as my daughter is sick in bed and can't come. Wrap it up in paper with a string so as he will not lose it, and oblige yours, E. Halton, 60, Fence-street.' But, suspecting it was bogus, Robinson told the young messengers he would have the money delivered to Mrs Halton later.

When the boys returned empty-handed, they found the man — who they later identified as Harry Leigh — standing outside the butcher-and-general-provisions shop of George Whittaker's father Thomas, just around the corner at 72, Mill Lane. Hearing their news, he made no comment and walked off across the road towards the Wheat Sheaf pub, then located at No.109, Mill Lane. There he remained for some time, leaning against the pub's protruding gable end from where anyone entering Waller Street, about 50 yards away, could be observed. At around 11am he watched as little Mary Ann Halton turned into the street on her way to Bamford's; he waited until she was on her way back from the mill, then he made his move.

Afterwards only Leigh would be able to say exactly what followed, and he never went into the details, by all accounts. But from witnesses' sightings the police were able to piece together a fairly accurate timeline

A 19th century view of Waller Street, with Bamford's Mill at the far end at its junction with Pool Street. The shop of George Whittaker's father Thomas is on the corner on the right.

Photo by permission of the Macclesfield Museums

for the next crucial hour or so, from which it is clear that he somehow persuaded the child to go with him on a journey of about a mile that would eventually take them in the opposite direction from her home and on to the bank of the Macclesfield Canal. They had set out from Mill Lane heading north, along the route Mary Ann would normally have taken to get to Fence Street, but then detoured via Windmill Street, where they joined the towpath at Bridge No. 40, known as Leadbeater's Bridge.

The answer as to how Leigh (who knew Mary Ann, it must be remembered) managed to lead her astray may well lie in the solution to the Mystery of the Wicker Basket. Why he had taken such an unlikely object with him when intending to commit robbery — or worse — has never been explained. He acquired it seemingly from the railway station in nearby Bollington, where he had been earlier in the morning. It belonged to the mother of an 11-year-old boy named Charles Wright of Water Street, Bollington, who, in his haste to catch his train to school in Macclesfield, had left it behind on a bench on the platform. In it was a custard pie in a dish, which his mother had given him to take to his aunt in Macclesfield. The lid of the basket, a type known as a 'Southport', had been repaired with copper wire. Could it be that Leigh told Mary Ann it was a picnic basket (the purloined pie may still have been inside at that time) and, with lunchtime approaching, the prospect of a slice of pastry or some other sweetmeat was too tempting a proposition for her to resist?

Whatever he said to her must have been sufficiently plausible as Mary Ann seems to have followed him without showing any obvious sign of resistance; and once on the canal towpath she allowed herself to be led south for another half-a-mile, going further and further away from her home. Her journey finally ended, and her terrifying ordeal began, shortly after noon at a point about a hundred yards short of Foden Bank Bridge, one of the six ingenious crossings for which the Macclesfield Canal is noted. A 'roving' or 'turn-over' bridge — also known locally as a 'snake' bridge — it was designed to enable horses hauling boats to switch towpaths without having to be unhitched.

It was there, hidden by high walls and banks on both sides of the canal, that Harry Leigh struck. He grabbed the girl and ripped open her frock pocket to snatch her mother's money, which had been put in a leather purse and tied up in a handkerchief for her by Thomas Robinson at Bamford's. Mary Ann was big for her age and put up a brave struggle. One can imagine Leigh, having no doubt been ragged about his lack of inches for years, being determined not to be outdone by an eight-year-old girl and, though there was little difference in their heights, he proved too strong for her and she went tumbling to her death in the water.

But was she pushed or did she fall? It was the vital question that the jury at his trial would be asked to determine in deciding whether Harry Leigh was a deserving candidate for the gallows.

When her daughter had not returned home at her usual time, Emily Halton began to worry. At the opening of the inquest into the child's death at Macclesfield Town Hall on 26 March, Mrs Halton would tell Knutsford Division Coroner Mr William Dunstan that, in going to look for her daughter that afternoon, she had first visited Bamford's mill. There the manager, Mr Robinson, informed her of the three boys who had brought him the note 'sent by a little man'. The inquest was adjourned after the Coroner had heard sufficient evidence for him to release the body for burial.

In reporting the details on 31 March, the *Macclesfield Courier* revealed that when Mrs Halton was returning home 'the thought struck her that the prisoner was a little man and that he was the only one who had heard her say that she was to send her girl for her wages'. So she went to Harry Leigh's home in Parsonage Street, called him outside and, with no more ado, asked him bluntly what he knew about Mary Ann's disappearance. When he denied all knowledge of it, she decided to take her suspicions to the police.

'Shortly afterwards,' the *Courier* added, 'she heard the news that a child had been found in the canal and was then lying at the Railway View [Inn].' She went to the pub, at the junction of Byron's Lane and Gunco Lane, and there 'to her great distress, she identified the dead body of her daughter, when only a few hours ago she had set out full of life and vigour'.

Leigh was arrested that evening after being found hiding in his next-door neighbour's outside privy. Some money discovered concealed in the roof of the building coincided with the coins given to Mary Ann in her mother's wages. He was taken to Macclesfield borough police station — which, since about 1874, had been housed in its own separate premises in an extension to the Town Hall on Churchside — where he was questioned by Inspector George Swindells. Leigh said, 'I know nothing about it. I shall reserve [my defence] at present.'

He was put in the cells and then, when the boundary issue had been resolved, he was transferred to the county police HQ in King Edward Street, in the custody of Superintendent Edward Dale. On Saturday 31 March, about 10.30pm, Superintendent William Sheasby, Chief Constable of Macclesfield Borough Police, visited the station to discuss a new development in the case with Supt. Dale, the senior county investigating officer. When they entered Leigh's cell, they found him stretched out on his bunk with his neckerchief tied tightly around his throat. His face was swollen, his eyes were red and he was unable to speak. Just in time the officers cut the intended ligature and thwarted the obvious suicide bid.

The former Macclesfield county police HQ in King Edward Street (now apartments), where Leigh was held after his arrest and where he attempted suicide.

The *Cheshire Observer* reported on 7 April, 'There is but little doubt that had he been left for a few minutes, life would have been extinct.' The duty constable, said the paper, had looked in on Leigh a short time before and thought he was asleep.

The new lead about which the two police chiefs were conferring was the discovery earlier that day of a two-and-a-half inch length of slate pencil on the canal towpath a few yards from where Mary Ann Halton's body was recovered. These pencils and slate tablets, were the staple writing tools in Victorian schools, the pencil being traditionally made from a softer slate than the writing tablet. It was a significant item of evidence because when Leigh was arrested he had on him, among other things, a slate pencil holder. No weight was attached to it at the time; but since then Mrs

Supt. Edward Dale (pictured when he was an Inspector), the county's chief investigating officer in the child murder case. He helped save Leigh's life when the prisoner tried to kill himself while in custody.

Photos courtesy of the Museum Of Policing In Cheshire

Halton had confirmed that Mary Ann was in the habit of carrying such a pencil in her pocket in an identical holder. The piece of pencil the police found fitted the holder perfectly.

A wicker basket identified as the one left behind at Bollington station had been found behind a low wall close to the crime scene on the day of the murder. And with witnesses coming forward to reveal having seen Leigh and the little girl with it shortly before she was killed, the case against the suspect was getting stronger every day. But the evidence was entirely circumstantial; would it be enough to convince a jury of his guilt?

The answer to that would have to wait until Wednesday 25 July 1877, when Harry Leigh appeared before the county assizes at Chester Castle. Like James Bannister before him (see Chapter Ten), he was accused of both murder and attempted suicide. He pleaded not guilty to both charges. Prosecuting counsel were Mr F. Marshall and the Hon. R. C. Grosvenor, and Mr Burke Wood led for the defence. The latter had undertaken the appointment just two days before the trial at the request of the Judge, Lord Justice (Sir George) Bramwell, after he had learned that Leigh had instructed no one to represent him.

As the prisoner stepped into the dock, the *Chester Chronicle* reporter, seeing him for the first time, noted his unusual size ('he is a very short man') and, in his account of the trial published on 28 July, wrote that he 'looked pale and anxious'. However, the *Macclesfield Courier*, which had been following the case from the time of the murder and throughout the preliminary judicial proceedings, commented on the same day, 'Those who knew the prisoner, and saw him before the magistrates, and were present at the trial, must have been struck with the great improvement in his appearance. At the former tribunal he presented the appearance of a man of dissolute habits . . . who had of late been but scantily fed; at the latter he appeared clean, healthy and cheerful-looking, his more intimate friends and relatives remarking that he had grown considerably stouter during his incarceration.'

An artist's impression on the front page of the more sensationalist *Illustrated Police News* of 4 August showed him sporting a dark and luxuriant goatee beard. How accurate a portrait it was, however, may be judged by the fact that this rather obvious feature went unmentioned in all the other papers covering the case. And, indeed, the *Courier* had remarked about his 'closely-shaven chin'. Unless stated otherwise, it is from the *Courier's* report of the 28th that the quoted passages below are taken.

In a courtroom 'crowded almost to suffocation', it looked like a

The image that appeared in the *Illustrated Police News*, showing Leigh with a goatee. The more local *Macclesfield Courier* described him as having a 'closely-shaven chin'.

calculated move by the prosecution to call Emily Halton as the first witness. The appearance of the doubly tragic widow — who had lost her only child in such harrowing circumstances just months after her husband's untimely death — was bound to have a forceful effect on the all-male members of the jury. The kindly murmur from spectators on the public benches, as she entered the box to give her evidence, reinforced the air of sympathy pervading the Shire Hall.

Harry Leigh was also visibly affected by her presence. Throughout most of the trial he strove to maintain 'a careless and indifferent aspect'; but the mother of the little girl he was alleged to have murdered so heartlessly was 'the one witness who had more effect on his demeanour than any other'. As she went through the formality of identifying the clothing her daughter had worn the day she was killed, Leigh 'coloured and paled alternately'.

Emily first recalled the evening of Friday 23 March when, at about 5.30, she visited the home of her neighbour Mrs Leigh. Harry Leigh was also at the house; Mrs Halton said she had known him 'a good while' and he knew her and her daughter well. During a conversation she had with Mrs Leigh, she complained of having no money. However, her wages were due and, as she was wasn't feeling well, she would send Mary Ann to the mill in the morning to collect them. Mary Ann had done so several times before.

Mrs Halton said that shortly after 10.30 on the Saturday morning, she gave Mary Ann a purse, in which to put the money, and a handkerchief in which to wrap the purse, and she placed them in the new pocket she had recently sewn into her daughter's dress. And, wearing her favourite straw hat (with the brim 'turned up all around'), the little girl waved goodbye to her mother and set off for the mill. The next time Mrs Leigh saw her daughter was when she identified her dead body at the Railway View Inn, which is a little under half-a-mile from the spot on the canal where she perished.

When her daughter had not returned home by 2pm, Mrs Leigh walked the mile or so to Bamford's, where she learned of the visit by the three boys, of the note requesting payment of her wages and of the 'little man' who had sent it. Her fears now intensifying, she was soon knocking on the door of the house in Parsonage Street, where lived a certain 'little man' of her acquaintance, Harry Leigh, and his 26-year-old wife Elizabeth, who had been married less than five months.

She was 'much put about in consequence of her child's absence', she told the court, and she came right out and asked Leigh whether he knew where her daughter was. He said he didn't know. 'She told him no one knew that she had any money to receive but him'. And she

Parsonage Street, Macclesfield, where Harry and Elizabeth Leigh made their marital home, five months before the murder. Right: the rear of houses in the street in the 1960s. At least one of the outside privvies, like the one in which Leigh was found hiding, appears to have survived. *Photos by permission of Macclesfield Library/CALS.*

demanded, 'Never mind the money, where is my child?' When he again insisted he had not seen Mary Ann that day, she told him she was not satisfied and was going to the police. 'I would if I were you,' was Leigh's parting comment.

Mrs Halton did not know for sure whether her daughter had her slate pencil and its holder with her that morning but, in response to a question from the Judge, she said neither item was to be found anywhere in the house afterwards.

All three of the boys who had handed the forged note to mill manager Thomas Robinson identified Leigh as the person who had given it to them. They also recognised the basket produced in court as the one the man had carried. George Whittaker said he knew it 'from the copper wire attached to the lid'. In his summing up later, the Judge was to remark that the way in which the boys had given their evidence did 'great credit to whoever has the teaching of them'.

The court also heard from three witnesses who had seen Leigh and Mary Ann together on the journey that led to the canal towpath . . . and the girl's death.

Charlotte Massey, 30, wife of milk dealer Isaac Massey of 20, Mill Road, Sutton, said she had been crossing Mill Green between 10 and 11 in the morning of Saturday 24 March, when she saw the prisoner standing against the Wheat Sheaf wall, 'from where he could see the street leading to the mill'. He was carrying a brown basket like the one produced. She did not know the man but she took particular notice of him 'because of the smallness of his stature'.

Esther Moore, a 71-year-old silk weaver and wife of Isaac Moore, a brick-maker, of 14, Old Mill Lane, testified to seeing Mary Ann, whom she knew, with Leigh in Mill Lane between 11 and12 that morning. 'The prisoner was about a yard-and-a-half from the deceased and they appeared to be going in company,' she was quoted as saying. 'They turned up towards Windmill Brow [Windmill Street], which leads to the canal.' The man carried a Southport-type basket.

And a 13-year-old boy named George Day observed the pair in Windmill Street. They were passing the end of Calamine Street, a little over 300 yards from Leadbeater's Bridge. It was 'shortly after eleven o'clock'. Day knew Leigh 'very well', as his house in Park Green was just around the corner from the prisoner's home in Parsonage Street. Leigh, he said, was wearing clogs at the time. He did not know the little girl but he noticed she had on a white straw hat 'turned up all around'.

Emma Owen, the last person to see little Mary Ann Halton alive (apart from her murderer), was next into the witness box. She was a live-in servant employed by local grandee Ferdinando Jackson, 72-year-old alderman, JP, silk manufacturer and landowner, of Woodland House, the substantial villa on the west side of Byron's Lane, Sutton, from where she had watched the two distant figures on the canal towpath. Emma said that when she first noticed them she was not sure whether it was a boy or a man with the little girl; the canal could be 'clearly seen' from the front windows of the house, however, and she could tell he was wearing a cap 'like the one produced' and that they were carrying 'something like a basket'. She thought the girl was wearing a straw hat, but could not be sure. It was 'about noon', as she had just heard the house clock chime.

Questioned by the Judge, she stated that the pair were 'going towards Gurnett, away from the town'. She lost sight of them when they 'passed by Stancliffe's wall'. This was the high rear wall of the kitchen garden belonging to Foden Bank House, on the east side of Byron's Lane, which was for many years associated with the noted Stancliffe brewing family, originally of Mirfield in West Yorkshire. Some time before 1850 the property was split into two separate dwellings, though both shared the same name, and Joseph Stancliffe, 'brewer and maltster', occupied the northernmost half, which had the kitchen garden attached. In 1855 his younger brother John Stancliffe established his Sutton Brewery in Byron's Lane and by 1871 he was living there, though the building was then known as Foden Bank Farm.

John Stancliffe died on 20 March 1877 — just four days before Mary Ann Halton was murdered — at the age of 77 and the company passed to his two sons, William Waltham Stancliffe and John Wheatley Stancliffe, eventually becoming known by its more recognisable name of Stancliffe Brothers Ltd. When it was bought out in 1920 by another Macclesfield brewer, Lonsdale and Adshead of Park Green, it had a property portfolio of more than 40 pubs throughout Cheshire, Derbyshire and Staffordshire.

Cross-examined by Mr Burke Wood, Emma said she had not given evidence before the magistrates, nor had she read any newspaper reports of the case. She had heard about a young girl being drowned in the canal from her master's gardener and she said to him, 'I wonder if it is the little girl I saw with the little man' (*Chester Chronicle*). It seems it was only later that she realised the full implications of what she had witnessed that day.

Joseph Jackson, a 37-year-old blacksmith, was the man who found Mary Ann Halton's body floating in the canal. He told the court that about noon he was walking along the towpath towards his smithy, which was close by the Gurnett aqueduct that carries the Macclesfield Canal over the lower end of Byron's Lane, when his attention was drawn to an abandoned wicker basket (he had stated at the inquest earlier that it contained a dish but no custard pie). It was beside the towpath 'about 45 yards from the end of Stancliffe's wall', which ran parallel with the canal on the opposite bank. There was a low wall on the towpath side of the canal and he looked over it to see if anyone was about; there wasn't. 'He thought he would take the basket home, and as he turned round he saw a straw hat and a dress, then a hood and a girl in the canal' (*Chronicle*).

In further cross-examination, he said he had seen no else one on the towpath. The water at this point was 'only a foot from the top of the towing path, which slopes a little toward the water' (*Courier*).

Jackson ran to the smithy for help and then he and his son and one of his workmen returned to the canal bank. They were joined by Thomas Hall, 53, a bricklayer's labourer, of Saville Street, Macclesfield, who volunteered to go into the water to retrieve the body, which was near the middle of the waterway. The canal, he said, was 'rather deep' at this point, so before he went in he insisted that the others should secure a rope to him. It was as well that he did, for almost immediately he got out of his depth and had to be pulled out, along with the body, by the men on the bank. The body was taken to the Railway View to await medical examination. There it was discovered that the pocket, in which Mary Ann had carried the purse containing her mother's wages, had been ripped open.

At the inquest Hall had described Mary Ann as 'a fine girl', who looked more like 12 or 13 than eight; and the trial jury were told by Dr John Rushton, who performed the postmortem on her body, that he took her to be 'about twelve'. He confirmed the findings he had first revealed at the resumed inquest on 5 April, chief of which was that she had been alive when she went into the water. He reported, 'There were six lacerated wounds on the face; they were superficial, such as might be done by a person's finger nails. There were contusions on both cheeks which might have been done by squeezing. There were contusions above and below both elbows, as if they had been gripped.' All of which pointed to her having been grabbed by the arms and pushed into the canal and then having her face forced under water. There was also a scratch on the front of her right thigh, about which the prosecution would offer a theory later in the trial.

The doctor explained, 'Her stomach was about two-thirds filled with water, showing that [she] was conscious when immersed, or she could not have swallowed the water.' And he added that, 'from the condition of the lungs he believed she died from drowning, and that alone'. He saw 'no marks of violence that could have caused her death'.

Thomas Robinson, after recalling the visit to Bamford's by the three boys and the subsequent arrival of Mary Ann, was asked about Emily Halton's stolen wages. He said the 12s 3d was made up of four half-crowns (2s.6d each), two shilling pieces and three pence, making a total of 12s. 3d. He was 'quite certain' as to the coins he gave the girl — 'with the exception of the odd three pence'.

Set against the evidence of other witnesses at the trial, the actual denominations were important to the prosecution's case. For Leigh's sister-in-law Mary Griffith — who was living with Leigh and his wife Elizabeth in Parsonage Street at the time — testified that in the afternoon of the murder the prisoner had given 'Lizzie', as he called her, eight shillings, consisting of three half-crowns and a sixpence (as we shall see, Leigh had changed a shilling at a local pub before returning home). Elizabeth told her she had had no money from him before then; her husband had had no regular job since Christmas, apparently, but he had told them that week that he was working in nearby Bollington. And Inspector George Swindells of Macclesfield Borough Police, who had arrested Leigh in the early evening of the murder after finding him hiding in next door's privy, said he later searched the outbuilding and found a half-crown, a shilling and a three-penny 'bit' 'wrapped up in 'a piece of paper under a broken mug' in the roof space. The prosecution maintained these were coins that had also been in Emily Halton's 'pay packet'.

Mary Griffith, 33, the wife of Robert Griffith, a 29-year-old cotton spinner — who had been one of the witnesses when Leigh married her sister, the former Elizabeth Booth, on 2 October 1876 — spoke of Leigh's movements on the day of the murder and of the moments leading up to his arrest. She said that he had left home at five-past-five in the morning, saying he was going to work at Bollington. This, as we shall see, was a lie. He had been given a job recently by the firm of John Brier and Sons, cotton spinners and calico printers, of Oak Bank Mill, Bollington; but he hadn't reported for work there for over a week. It was not the first time he had deceived his wife and relatives into believing he was gainfully employed.

Mrs Griffith said Leigh arrived home at around 3pm and that at about five o'clock they were having tea, when they noticed 'some policemen in the street'. She had been in earlier when Emily Halton came to the house asking to see her brother-in-law and, although the front door was closed, she overheard Mrs Halton mention she was going to the police. And it was as a result of this comment, that she said to Leigh, "Harry, there's the police, what shall you do?" She stated, 'Prisoner said he would go out at the back and he immediately rose and went outside. She went to look for the prisoner and found him in a petty . . . in the next yard.'

Through the bolted door she challenged him about the police's visit, and he replied, 'I know nothing about it.' She told him to come out, and he said he would 'when all the people had gone away'. Mrs Griffith said he did not return to the house. He had gone 'up the midden' (dunghill or refuse heap) to get into the yard next door, 'where he was apprehended some time afterwards'.

She said she noticed that when Leigh came to the meal table that 'his stockings were wet'. It seems an inescapable fact that, in order to complete his murderous act, Leigh had to have been in the canal himself, though standing at the water's edge where the build-up of mud and silt would have made it considerably shallower than the main channel, to which Thomas Hall had doubtless been referring in his testimony earlier.

Mary Griffith also told the court about a previous incident involving Leigh and some stolen money. It had happened about five weeks before the murder. A sum of £1.1s.6d, belonging to her father, silk winder Joseph Booth, had gone missing and, she alleged, 'Prisoner has since said that he had taken it.'

Inspector Swindells testified that at about 5.00pm on the 24th, acting on the information given to the borough police by a grief-stricken Emily Halton, he visited Parsonage Street and the newly-appointed marital home of Harry Leigh. After discovering him cowering in the 'closet' of an adjoining house, he said he asked the suspect to account for his movements that day. Leigh, he said, told him, 'I have been at work at Brier's Mill, Bollington. I got there about five minutes past six this morning and left about 25 minutes past one.'

Not satisfied with his answer, the officer arrested him on suspicion of murder and hauled him off to the town police station. And when George Whittaker and Samuel Goodwin identified him as the 'little man' who had given them the bogus note to take to Bamford's, he was formally charged with the crime. At about seven o'clock that evening the Inspector returned to Parsonage Street and discovered the 'fourth half-crown' in Leigh's back-yard bolt-hole.

When he was searched, Leigh had in his possession a curious assortment of items, including five handkerchiefs, three pairs of scissors, three half-pence, a black-lead pencil — which, said prosecution counsel, somewhat tenuously, showed that he had the means to write the phoney note — and the slate pencil-holder that was said to be identical to the one Mary Ann Halton always carried with her.

Insp. Swindells was later recalled by the Judge, who asked him about the scene of the crime. He first confirmed that from Ald. Jackson's home, Emma Owen would have had a clear view of the canal towpath. And, as to the exact location of the murder, he replied, 'There could not be a more secluded spot than behind the wall.'

Harry Leigh had chosen well; although there were properties as close as 80 yards from this part of 'the cut', the short and sheltered, gully-like stretch of water in which Mary Ann Halton drowned was screened from them all.

In the witness stand John Dobson, weaving-shed overlooker at Brier's Mill, was questioned about Leigh's claim that he had been working there on the morning of the murder. Dobson said the prisoner had been taken on at the mill 'eight or ten days' previously; that on the first day he had 'started work about a quarter-past two and stopped at five o'clock' and was never seen again.

Harry Leigh had obviously returned to his idle ways, while pretending to be holding down a steady job. For the man who, it would be revealed later, had a history of leaving his employment after disputes with his bosses and who had had only two short spells of work since Christmas, it was a pretence that could only have continued for a short time before his lack of earnings exposed the deception. As each day went by the pressure on him was mounting. Recognising that he needed to find some money soon, the careless talk he had overheard in his father's kitchen that Friday evening must have seemed like a timely stroke of good fortune.

Superintendent Dale, of the county constabulary at Macclesfield, said that on 3 April, after Leigh had been transferred into his custody, he charged him with robbery and murder. Leigh denied the charges and dictated the following statement, which is contained in the official case papers deposited in the National Archives,

'I did not like to say where I had been on the morning of the 24th of March as it was nothing to my credit. I went to the Spinners Arms in Bollington before breakfast and left there about a quarter-past twelve. I met a young man named James Wilson with a huckster's cart near the aqueduct [which carries the Macclesfield Canal over the western end of Palmerston Street, Bollington], and then I came along and across the fields. The next place I stopped at was the Old Ship Inn in Beech Lane [Macclesfield]. I stayed there perhaps half-an-hour or forty minutes. From there I went home and got my dinner. I did not leave the house again until I was arrested.'

It was a statement of half-truths and downright lies. Leigh *had* been in Bollington that morning: he was at the railway station, from where he had made off with the schoolboy's basket. But he was never at the Spinner's Arms. Levi Brown, the licensee, said he had been serving in the pub from nine o'clock in the morning and assured the jury that the prisoner was not in his house that day. And James Wilson, a Macclesfield greengrocer, said he had seen Leigh in Bollington on the previous Wednesday but not on the Saturday.

It was true, however, that he had called at the Old Ship Inn, Macclesfield, which is about three-quarters-of-a-mile from the canal at its nearest point and nearly two miles from the scene of the murder. Landlady Emma Wainwright confirmed the time was about 1.15pm. She said she thought he looked 'rather pale, tired and strange'. The *Macclesfield Courier*'s trial report went on, 'She served him with a glass of beer [half-a-pint] and he put two-pence down.' She didn't have a half-penny to give him as change, but he said he would square things up with her when he had his next glass. He ordered his second drink and gave the landlady a penny.

Later Mrs Wainwright's husband, John, also served him with a glass of beer for which he handed over a shilling and received 10½d in change. The pair got into conversation and Leigh told him he had come from Bollington and, showing him one of his clogs, pointed out where it was broken.

In his closing speech, prosecuting counsel Mr Marshall listed the various facts that, with 'almost absolute clearness', connected Leigh to the murder: the conversation at his parents' home in which he had overheard Mrs Halton speak of sending her daughter to collect her wages; the three boys who had identified him as the 'little man' who had given them the bogus note and of the succession of people who had seen him with Mary Ann either going towards, or on, the canal towpath. 'There was,' he said, 'a great peculiarity in this case — the perfect connectedness of the evidence and the almost providential incidents that brought people to the spot who happened to know the prisoner.'

Having at first walked with the girl as if accompanying her home, Leigh then took her in the opposite direction, leading to the canal. And the prosecutor went on, 'There can be no reasonable doubt he induced her to go with him in order to take her to this secluded part of the canal where he might obtain possession of the money without being seen.'

The fact that Leigh could hand his wife eight shillings later in the day of the murder, after having had no money to give her previously; that he had cash to spend at the pub in the afternoon; the discovery of the money in the privy and the similarity between the total amount involved and the coins in Emily Halton's wages . . . all added up to Leigh having robbed the girl, said Mr Marshall. But how did she end up drowned?

'Conjecturing' that the defence case was that it was because of 'some other circumstance than the prisoner's direct violence', he asked, 'What is the medical evidence? Everything indicated a struggle, and what a most unequal struggle it must have been between that poor little girl and the prisoner.' Pointing to the marks on the girl's face 'as if [caused] by fingernails' and the scratch on her thigh — which he suggested was done by the prisoner 'grasping at the pocket in endeavouring the rob the child' — he postulated, 'Was that not evidence that a struggle had taken place?' And he pointed out that if the girl had fallen in the water and drowned as a result of his attempt to rob her, the law decreed that, as it had happened during the commission of a felony, it was still murder.

Mr Marshall described Leigh's conduct after the murder — the 'tissue of falsehoods' he had told to account for his whereabouts that day, his attempts to evade the police by hiding in a privy, his 'callous indifference' towards the 'heartbroken' Mrs Halton when she questioned him about her daughter's disappearance — as that of a guilty person. And he argued that his attempt to commit suicide while in police custody was 'presumptive evidence of guilt'.

Mr Burke Wood did, indeed, base his defence on the premise that Mary Ann Halton's death had been an accident. He told the jury that he would be 'insulting them if he denied that the prisoner had robbed the child'. But he declared, 'There is, however, a vast difference between admitting that the prisoner planned and carried out the robbery, and admitting that he wilfully carried out the crime of murder.'

He submitted, 'Suppose he had gripped the girl by the arm (and I think it most likely he had), and suppose also that he seized the child's pocket and tore it out; suppose that having done that he ran away with the money. In what condition would a child of tender years be in after all this had happened? In pain for what [the] prisoner had done? In terror of going home, perhaps, without her [mother's] money? In perfect agony of fear and distress, lest the prisoner should commit some further violence, and no doubt blinded by tears, could they [the jury] not imagine the little one running away and stumbling head-first into the canal?' If they found that the child had met her death by accident, he said, then they must acquit the prisoner. And he argued that ('subject to the correction of the Judge') even if the child fell into the canal out of fear of some further ill-treatment by her attacker, he would be guilty of manslaughter only.

Of Leigh's alleged 'guilty behaviour' after the murder, Mr Marshall suggested that at the time he had hidden from the police he was unaware of the child's death and it was his guilt over the the theft of Mrs Halton's money that had driven him to take refuge in his neighbour's privy. And of his suicide attempt, Mr Marshall countered, 'He no doubt felt he had done wrong by meddling with the child at all, and was anxious to get rid of the anxiety and trouble which his own bad conduct had brought about; but that did not prove that he murdered the child.'

Judge Bramwell, in his summing up, advised the jury that if they were satisfied that Leigh had thrown the girl into the canal he was guilty of murder. He added, however, that 'if there was any reason to suppose that she threw herself in, or in running away, she fell in,' he recommended them to acquit the prisoner rather than find him guilty of manslaughter. For, in the circumstances of the case, he said, he could not see how it could be considered manslaughter, 'for it would not be the natural consequence of the unlawful act of which he was guilty'.

His Lordship went on, 'Suppose the prisoner merely robbed the child and then ran away. What would have been the natural conduct of that man? That he might have hid himself to escape the result of the robbery and violence they [might] well understand; but if he did not throw her in how was it that when he heard she was drowned there was no exclamation of surprise or expression of regret?' He might have said something like 'Drowned! I know nothing of that', suggested the Judge;

instead of which the prisoner 'merely said he was not there'.

The Judge also drew attention to several pieces of circumstantial evidence for the jury to consider. He spoke of the witnesses who had seen Leigh with the girl on their journey from Waller Street to the canal and walking along the towpath, and remarked, 'Thus the prisoner was shown to be in the neighbourhood at the time when the child received the wages, standing where he could see her going to the mill, and afterwards traced with reasonable certainty to a few yards from where the body was found.' And he added, 'There can be no doubt that the child and prisoner were traced to the canal bank and that, too, at a time only a quarter-of-an-hour before the body was found.'

Lord Justice Bramwell then referred to Leigh's wet stockings. 'Did not this go to show,' he asked, 'that he had been sufficiently far into the water himself to make sure of throwing the body a sufficient distance?' Of the stolen wicker basket, which several witnesses had seen Leigh carrying when in company with the murder victim, he said it was a 'remarkable fact of the case' that it had been left behind on the canal towpath. 'In addition to this,' Judge Bramwell remarked, 'in the possession of [the] prisoner's wife, in the closet where he was apprehended and on the prisoner, were found, almost to a penny and the very coins almost, [the money] in which the girl was paid.'

Though the full text of the Judge's summary was never published, this was, for Leigh, a fairly devastating recapitulation of the case. Sir George Bramwell was universally regarded as strong and fearless in his conduct of criminal trials; but he was also noted for his fairness. While few guilty men tried before him escaped, it has been said of him that 'to any man in danger of suffering from unfairness, to have Sir George Bramwell on the judgment seat was better than to have enlisted the services of the best advocate at the bar'. For Harry Leigh, however, there was clearly not much he could do to balance the enormous weight of evidence against him.

When, after a trial lasting five hours, the jurors were asked to retire to consider their verdict, the *Macclesfield Courier*'s reporter noticed that most of them seemed inclined to remained seated — 'as if [they] were satisfied and had no desire to retire'. However, it was eventually agreed that they would leave the box. They returned 25 minutes later, at exactly 4.20pm, and, amid 'breathless silence in the crowded court', the foreman announced Leigh guilty of murder. The few who entertained any slight misgivings — presumably over whether the prosecution had proved beyond reasonable doubt that Leigh deliberately drowned the girl — had been fairly quickly persuaded to accept the majority view.

As the verdict was announced 'there was a suppressed exclamation' among the public spectators; then, when asked by the Clerk of the Arraigns whether he had anything to say, the *Courier* reported, 'The prisoner, who was evidently shocked at the verdict, appeared to be quite unable to reply. He stood firmly in his position in the dock; he essayed to say something, but it seemed as if he had lost [the] power of speech.'

Lord Justice Bramwell said he agreed with the jury's verdict; it was his opinion, he told the man in the dock, that 'they could not do otherwise than find you guilty'. He stated, 'It is now my duty to pass on you the sentence of the law, and I do so in the words of the law and, after long experience, I add none of my own.' What was most noticeable in the courtroom, however, were the words he *omitted* from the statutory pronouncement. For, after telling the prisoner he was to hang, he did not end with the customary invocation 'May the Lord have mercy on your soul'. Whether it was because he believed that, by the nature of his crime, Leigh had forfeited the right to compassion — divine as well as secular — or that it was an uncharacteristic oversight, was never explained.

With Leigh capitally convicted, the court did not pursue the suicide charge, and the prisoner was taken next door to the Castle Gaol, where he was placed in a cell close to the gallows (there was no official 'condemned cell' in the prison at this time, apparently). As the prospect of a reprieve had been virtually demolished by the Judge's remarks, he was forced to remain incarcerated there until after the following three Sundays, the minimum time which, since 1868, the law had stipulated must elapse between sentence and execution.

It was during his early days in prison that, no doubt contrary to his and Judge Bramwell's expectations, the diminutive child-killer did receive one offer of forgiveness. And it came from a most unlikely source . . . the mother of the little girl he had murdered.

At the request of the prisoner, the Reverend James Kilner, Chaplain of the Castle Gaol, wrote to Mrs Emily Halton on his behalf. In the letter, date-lined 'County Gaol, Chester Castle, July 29, 1877', and reproduced in several newspapers, the Rev. Kilner revealed for the first time that Leigh had confessed to the murder and also explained why he had done it. The letter stated,

Dear Mrs Halton — Harry Leigh has made a full and particular confession of his crime to me. He meant originally to have deprived you, a poor widow, of your hard-earned money by means of a forged note and, because your poor little girl screamed that she would tell her mother that he had robbed her, he diabolically pushed her into the canal, left her cruelly to drown, and went off to spend the first fruits of his plunder in drink, as in drink he had early in the day maddened his brain for his foul purpose. You have no other child, and your little Mary Ann must have been the comfort of your life. Leigh, who is beside me in his cell while I write, describes her as such a dear, good girl, liked by everybody. I can only say, on behalf of the condemned young man, that he most deeply bewails his crime, and that the first wish he expressed after he had unburdened his oppressed mind to me was that I should write to you. God alone can give you the comfort of which you stand in need, but it would assuredly be some relief to know, as I now assure you, that the unhappy man who has to die for having bereaved you of your beloved child is very sorry, though he can make no reparation, as he gladly would. He hopes that you will, if not at once, still before his execution, in the kindness of your stricken heart, grant him the assurance of your forgiveness, as he hopes in his deep repentance for pardon at God's hand for Christ's sake.

If you can grant the favour asked, it would be a comfort to the culprit, as well as to yours most sympathisingly, The Chaplain.

In the *Chester Chronicle* (18 August), it was reported that, on behalf of the grieving widow, the Rev. Robert Hurst, Curate of Hurdsfield, had replied in 'a kind letter freely forgiving the unhappy man'.

Leigh himself penned two letters to his wife and one to his father and step-mother during his final days in prison. He was by no means illiterate; indeed, he was regarded as being of more than average intelligence. But the poetry and overblown phraseology contained in the letters suggested strongly that he had had a helping hand in writing them: the Rev. Kilner's, most likely.

To his wife Elizabeth, he wrote on 4 August, 'My sentence is pronounced and my death hangeth over me; death which, by my crimes, I have brought upon myself, and which I so richly deserve. What a terrible prospect is now before me; now but a few days — a few short days — are left of that life to which, by my sins, I have thus put an early end, and then I go hither to a more dreadful judgment . . .'

Referring to Mrs Halton's reaction to Rev. Kilner's letter, of which he had just received word, he stated, 'I am thankful to say [she] has heartily forgiven me for having bereaved her of her dear, and only, child. I can assure you it has given me great comfort [during] these last few days, for I now have more hope of having [the] forgiveness of our Heavenly Father . . .'

In a second letter, written on the day before his execution, Leigh told Lizzie, 'I cannot help but think about you; to think of the sorrow I have brought upon you and so many others'. He signed it 'Your truly loving and penitent husband' and closed with this poetic couplet,

'Bright skies will soon be o'er me,
Where the dark clouds have been.'

In reply to a letter he had received from his 'parents', he had responded (6 August), 'You say you are almost broken-hearted; I myself know you cannot be otherwise. To think you have only two sons, and one must soon be led to the gallows to die; but as I have said repeatedly, it is only what I deserve for having taken the life of a fellow creature, and having hurried her unwarned into eternity, vile and miserable sinner that I am . . .'

In compliance with his wishes, on Thursday 9 August, he was visited for the last time by his wife, his father and step-mother, a cousin and his closest friend, James Wright of Bollington. After which, said the *Chronicle*, 'the prisoner affectionately embraced his grief-stricken relatives'.

Harry Leigh was hanged on Monday 13 August. Once again reporters from the Chester papers, as well as the *Macclesfield Courier*, were admitted to the execution, though the reports that appeared in the *Courant* and the *Courier* were largely identical. The *Chronicle* stated, 'The culprit being a little man, Marwood gave him the tremendous drop of seven feet, but a minute or two after he had fallen a few convulsive motions of the legs and head were noticeable. The whole of the sad transaction, from the time of leaving [his] cell up to when the drop fell, only occupied the short space of from three to four minutes.' The cell was a 200-yard walk away from the gallows but, said the paper, it was 'the nearest that can possibly be obtained'.

By the time of this, the second execution at Chester Castle, some improvements had been deemed to be expedient. Most significantly, the gallows was now out of sight of all unauthorised viewers, completely enclosed in a brick building. Owing to the sloping nature of the site, the 'Execution Shed' was constructed on two levels. The main access, from the prison yard, was at ground-floor level, while at the lower level a door led into the vault below the drop. From there a corridor had been created to link directly with the mortuary inside the main prison building. The changes, said the *Chester Courant* on Wednesday 15 August, had been designed to 'entirely remove many ghastly features of the execution'.

It went on, 'Little can now be seen of the instrument of death from the outside, and consequently those whose painful duty it is to be present at the carrying out of the extreme sentence of the law, can discharge that duty with a less degree of discomfort than, when in addition to the knowledge that a human being was about to expiate an awful crime by a violent death, the gallows and all its appendages were full before their eyes.'

At precisely eight o'clock Leigh, accompanied by several warders, and executioner Marwood, had emerged from the cell-block and into a prison yard bathed in bright sunlight shining down from a cloudless sky. And, as the 'mournful procession' was making its way slowly to

By the time Harry Leigh was hanged in August 1877 a brick building, similar to this one at Shepton Mallet Gaol in Somerset, completely enclosed the Chester Castle gallows.

From capitalpunishmentuk.org.
With permission.

the execution shed, the *Observer*'s reporter noticed that 'the diminutive stature of the unhappy man, which formed a strong element in the evidence against him, became more apparent than when he was seen in court — in fact, in contrast to the stalwart warders beside him, he appeared a dwarf, though firmly knit'.

With the execution over, the *Macclesfield Courier* on 18 August published the results of the investigation it had carried out into Leigh's background. It was a detailed biography that told how the life of a young man, who had started out showing every sign of being a good and useful citizen, suddenly descended into idleness, thieving, deceit . . . and, ultimately, murder.

It began, 'As a young man he was well behaved and industrious. Idleness — and that set in only recently — was the forerunner of his ruin; absenting himself from his employment, he became acquainted with a class of companions whom, as a youth, he studiously shunned, and gradually descended the moral scale until he found himself in the extremity which was the temptation to him to perpetrate the crime for which he has just died.'

Leigh was born on 23 December 1853 to Thomas and Sarah Leigh, of Armitt Street, in the Newtown area of Macclesfield. When Thomas had married in March 1853, he was 24 and already a widower; and he was widowed again two-and-a-half years later when Sarah also died, at the age of only 22. Harry, still not yet three, had a half-brother and two half-sisters — 'all of whom now reside away from the neighbourhood', the *Courier* stated .

However, since infancy the young Harry Leigh had been a favourite of his maternal grandfather, Mr George Swanscoe, a coal merchant originally of Macclesfield who had moved to Manchester, and soon afterwards the boy went to live with him there. 'Acting on his father's strict instruction . . . he received an education superior to that given to the majority of lads of his station in life', the *Courier* revealed. A couple of years later — by which time, apparently, his father had married for a third time — he returned to the family home; and this would be the pattern of his transitory lifestyle throughout his childhood and early teenage years.

After only a brief stay in Macclesfield, where he received instruction at the Macclesfield Sunday School, Leigh spent another short period in Manchester living with his grandfather. Back home in Macclesfield again, he was employed at the Pickford Street mill of the renowned Brocklehurst family — one of the pre-eminent companies that helped establish the town's worldwide reputation as a silk manufacturing centre in the 19th century — working part-time while attending the Lord Street School.

No sooner had he settled there, however, than his family moved to Oldham, where he was next employed as a cotton 'piecer' in the same local factory in which his father worked. He was planning to train as a cotton weaver, but he was involved in an accident in which he was caught up in some machinery and sustained a serious foot injury that prevented him from working for some while afterwards.

For a third time he went to live in Manchester and, after recovering from the effects of the accident, worked in his grandfather's coal business for several years as a carter .

Said the *Courier*, 'During the following six or seven years he was a steady, industrious youth, and gave every promise of being an honest, well-behaved man.' He went to temperance meetings, first as a member of the Macclesfield Good Templar Lodge and later the Rechabites friendly society. 'As a result of his active involvement in these various groups, he received a handsome timepiece for the energy displayed in this direction and his excellence in recitation.'

Before leaving Manchester he had been employed for a few months by a draper in Butler Street, off Oldham Road; but left 'after a row with his boss over wages'. It would not be the last time he quit his job under a cloud.

He repaired once more to Oldham intent on reviving his career as a cotton weaver; but he soon tired of that notion and decided to settle down in his home town, where he first worked in the borough's council yard. Again, it was only a brief period of employment. The *Courier* explained, 'While there he was one of the ring-leaders of a dispute between the workers and the bosses, during which he left the job.'

That brought the story up to 1877, when the first signs of Harry Leigh's descent into shiftlessness — and shiftiness — began to appear. Though it was widely reported that he had been out of work since Christmas 1876, the *Courier* stated that in February he was employed at the Lower Heyes cotton mill in Black Lane, Macclesfield. However, said the paper, 'A marked change had been noticed in his manner for months and it was noticed by his parents that he was less careful and industrious than he had hitherto been. He was less frank in his manner and, when interrogated as to his prospects or employment, gave answers which frequently turned out to be either untruthful or a grossly exaggerated statement of the facts.'

The *Courier* went on, 'As we know from the evidence given by his wife . . . and his sister-in-law . . . Leigh had been of idle habits from Christmas up to February, when he started at Lower Heyes, only working there for a short time.' And the paper added, 'Suffice it to say that the period of idleness that immediately preceded the murder was the time when Leigh was . . . systematically deceiving his wife and parents as to his employment. When doubtless conscious that he was not acting the part of a husband in allowing his wife to support both herself and himself [she worked as a silk piecer], he in desperation resolved to possess himself of the pittance of money he knew the girl would receive from the mill, and was thus led to commit the foul deed for which he has suffered.'

Meanwhile, efforts were being made in Macclesfield to raise money to relieve the plight of the murder victim's mother. Again, the *Courier* supplied the details. Mrs Halton, 'though a very delicate woman', had been forced to find a job to support herself and her daughter after the loss of her husband, a 'weakly, ailing man' who had been unable to work for 15 weeks prior to his death. After her daughter's murder, the town's Mayor, silk manufacturer John Birchenough, had visited her home and found that 'she had been left almost destitute', the paper said. He had immediately announced he was launching a public subscription to pay off her debts — which included a bill owing to Dr Rushton for attending to her husband during his illness, amounting to £5 5s. (equivalent to about £450 today), and arrears in food payments — and, generally, to aid her financial recovery.

Author's note: There is some doubt about the real Christian name of Mrs Halton. In Mayor Birchenough's announcement, he referred to her as 'Emma', whereas according to all the newspaper reports of the murder case, and several official documents, she was called Emily (and for consistency's sake she is identified as such here). There is, however, equally compelling evidence that her Christian name *was* Emma. That is the name in the Macclesfield Cemetery register recording the burial of her murdered daughter Mary Ann on 28 March 1877 and also in the 1871 census, in which she, her husband Thomas and Mary Ann, then aged two, were shown to be living at 16, Wellington Street, Hurdsfield, Macclesfield, and her place of birth was stated to be Ormskirk. In the 1841 census she had been listed as 'Emely' (with an 'e'), the daughter of John Leigh of Ormskirk. At that time the confusion might have been explained by the similarity, when spoken, of 'Emily' and 'Emma Leigh'; but 10 years later, now aged 12, she had become 'Emma'. Her marriage lines revealed that 'Emily' Leigh, aged 28, the daughter of the same John Leigh, married Thomas Halton on 3 May 1868 at Prestbury; and it was as Emily Halton that she appeared in the 1881 census, still living at 60, Fence Street. As Mary Ann Halton's poor mother was illiterate, however, the records contain no personal signature that could have settled the matter once and for all.

CHAPTER TWELVE

A Crime That Beggared Belief

The old cottage by the roadside had clearly seen better days. At some time in the past it had been turned into a cheap lodging house and now, like much of its clientele, it had a ragged and forlorn appearance. A tumble-down outbuilding that might once have been a stable, did nothing to dispel the air of neglect; while, inside, the low, dingy apartments displayed a similar lack of care and attention. It was a place where tramps, beggars and various rogues and runaways mingled with more respectable members of the poorer class — labourers and farm hands mostly — and where it cost three pence a night for anyone prepared to share a room (and, more than likely, a bed) with a total stranger.

'Wretched' and 'squalid' would be the most popular terms used to describe the two-storey property by the newspaper reporters who were drawn to the little east Cheshire village of Smallwood by the grisly events of early Spring 1883.

To lodger Edward Sampey it was home. The agricultural labourer had lived there for three years and, as long as he could continue working locally, he was content to stay. All that changed, however, in the afternoon of Friday 9 February when, after visiting several neighbouring farms —with the aim, ironically, of securing the future employment that would enable him to remain at his lodgings — he returned to find the cottage had become a blood-sodden house of death.

He had got back around 3.15. To his surprise, the main entrance door was closed and bolted; normally, though they opened directly on to the highway — now the A50 Newcastle Road and then part of the old turnpike route between Manchester and the Potteries — both front doors were kept unlocked, and often unclosed, during the daytime. But that was nothing compared to the shock awaiting him when he went to try the other door.

It led into the wash-house or 'back'-kitchen (it was actually on the side of the building) and was ajar. As he began to push it open he was met by a heart-stopping sight. On the floor alongside the rear wall of the room, moaning and writhing in agony in a pool of her own blood, was the landlord's 65-year-old Irish housekeeper Mary Moran. Panic-stricken, Sampey turned on his heels and ran about 250 yards up the road to John Dale's smithy to get help.

Accompanied by two of the blacksmiths who were working there at the time — Eugene Ganton, aged 22, and Ambrose Wood, 32 — he back-tracked to the lodging house. With the disturbing image of Mary Moran lying battered and bloody in the back-kitchen still vivid in his mind, he was in no hurry to re-enter the building; so he let the other two lead the way. But, after following the trail of blood from the back-kitchen into the 'house-place' (kitchen-cum-living-room), he was to make a second horrifying discovery. Stretched out on the floor, with his head bashed in, was the landlord himself. Thomas Earlam, aged 64, was dead. His body lay partly in front of the doorway of the little narrow passage that led from the back-kitchen into the living room. And there was blood everywhere. Lots of it.

As well as the pools surrounding the bodies, there was blood spattered about the floor, walls and ceiling of both rooms and in the passageway, indicating the sustained savagery of the attacks and the force of the blows delivered. In the back-kitchen it had even stained the coals red.

It appeared initially that Mary Moran was the first to be struck down. The housekeeper was said to be almost totally blind; yet, despite her disability, she seems to have fought back valiantly. She may possibly have tried to grasp a weapon with which to defend herself, for a crowbar and a bill-hook, both smeared with blood, were on the back-kitchen floor when she was found. There was a large pool of blood under the kitchen's three-legged table and a broken 'pan mug' (earthenware bowl) lay on the floor. It was clear there had been a terrific struggle; then, on hearing the racket, Thomas Earlam had seemingly gone to the aid of his long-time companion. But before he could reach her he was ambushed by the assailant and viciously beaten to death. An opposing theory, however, would emerge later in the rather grander setting of the Shire Hall courtroom at the Chester Assizes.

Earlam was formerly a farmer 'in a small way' and then a potato-dealer; but for more than 20 years the little lodging-house had been his main source of income and Mary Moran his faithful retainer. It would be said of him later that he was known by his neighbours as 'a man of saving habits' and that he 'kept a small store of money by him' in an old box in his 'back pantry', a tiny private cubby-hole off the living room. However, he was secretive about his financial affairs and whenever he had reason to go into his money box — he had his cash 'float' in there and at least one of his neighbours reported that he frequently exchanged gold for silver for him from his secret hoard — he always turned his back to ensure no one could see how much was in it. Both the box and its contents, believed to be about £7 (approximately £650 at today's values), were now missing; Earlam's pockets had been turned inside out and the house had been ransacked.

When he had recovered sufficiently from his nerve-shattering experience, Edward Sampey, a widower who seems to have been aged about 60, discovered that his best suit had also been stolen. It, too, had been in the back-pantry, in the trunk in which he had locked it the previous evening after wearing it on a visit to Sandbach Market earlier in the day. The trunk was now standing in the passageway leading into the back-pantry, its lid open. His bank book had also been taken. As was his usual habit, he had covered the suit with sheets of newspaper to keep the dust off it. They were all that remained in the trunk and they bore the unmistakeable imprint of bloody hands. Whoever had robbed Edward Sampey had clearly been the same person who had attacked Thomas Earlam and Mary Moran.

While Ambrose Wood dashed off to inform the village bobby of the dreadful affair, Eugene Ganton set out for Sandbach to let the police there know what had happened. When it was learned that Dr Charles Latham of Sandbach was that day on duty at the workhouse less than two miles away in Arclid, a message was sent to him by a passing wagoner, asking him to come to the lodging house as soon as possible. He arrived by pony and trap about two hours later and did everything he could to make the elderly housekeeper comfortable.

By then poor Mary, who had also suffered severe head injuries, had been moved into an upstairs room where, according to the *Chester Chronicle* (17 February), her condition alternated between 'raving in delirium' and 'sleeping heavily', her face and head 'a terrible sight to see'. When the doctor saw her she was unconscious and it was his opinion that there was little chance of her recovering from her terrible wounds. Several magistrates called at the lodging house on the Saturday, hoping to take a statement from her before she died; but she was unable to speak. So hopeless was her situation, in fact, that it does not appear that Mary was taken to hospital; certainly there was not a single reference in contemporary press reports to her being admitted. And she died — in the run-down old cottage that had been her home for over three decades — six days later on 16 February at 10am.

When police arrived at the cottage they found near where Mary Moran's body had lain a hammer almost completely covered in fresh blood. It was unquestionably the weapon with which the couple had been attacked. It belonged to another of the lodgers and was usually kept on a stone bench beside the sink in the 'main' pantry, on the right-hand side of the living-room, where the lodgers washed. The pantry also did service as an extra bedroom when demand required, and it was where Thomas Earlam's body was laid out to await the inquest into his death.

News of the unbelievably brutal crime quickly spread around the village, and before long neighbours gathered at the old cottage in large numbers. In the days when the importance of forensic evidence and the preservation of a crime scene were not fully recognised, many people traipsed through the house inspecting the places where the victims were found. Blood-grouping was also a thing of the future, while the system of fingerprint identification and classification was still in its infancy.

As the murder investigation got under way, however, the police did have a significant lead to go on. Like Thomas Earlam's money-pot and the contents of Edward Sampey's trunk, one of the lodgers had also gone missing.

His name was Patrick Carey; though, as was subsequently discovered, he was a man with several known aliases, who was then calling himself White. An itinerant whose only 'occupation' appeared to have been begging, he was said officially to be aged 33, but might have been older. And, generally uncommunicative, he was particularly tight-lipped about his personal life. All the other lodgers could get out of him was that his first name was 'Jack'. Fellow boarder John Stack, a rag-and-bone man, would later tell the *Chester Chronicle* reporter, possibly the first newsman on the scene of the crime, that 'he seldom spoke and only mumbled to himself or whistled'.

'Jack White' (Carey) had arrived at the lodging house — long demolished, it was situated an estimated 220 yards north of the Bulls Head pub on what had been the old coaching road to London — on Friday 2 February. It was his second visit, having stayed there for a short time three years previously. So he would have been familiar with the building's lay-out . . . and, no doubt, with the local gossip about Thomas Earlam's nest-egg.

During the week he was there his begging expeditions had obviously not been very successful, for he was noticeably short of funds. On the Wednesday evening the habitual mumbler was for once speaking more coherently, arguing loudly with the landlord after admitting that he only had two pence for that night's board. Much to his annoyance, Earlam had insisted that he hand over a shirt as security until he could pay the penny he owed. And, talking afterwards to another lodger, a 23-year-old umbrella mender called Isaac Jones, he complained that 'it was very hard of Mr Earlam to take his shirt [for being] short of a penny'. As things turned out, the penniless lodger might have 'lost his shirt', but two days after absconding his financial situation suddenly appeared to have improved. Substantially.

That Friday in Thomas Earlam's lodging house had started out normally enough, as the occupants began their daily routines. Earlam and Mary Moran rose early to lay the table and prepare food for the five boarders staying with them at that time. Edward Sampey, who had been sleeping in the same room as Carey, was the first of them to get up; after eating his breakfast he set out on his work-finding tour of local farms shortly before seven o'clock. Lavinia Shannon, a seamstress and the sole female lodger, left the house for some undisclosed destination at eight. Isaac Jones, who had been sharing a bed with the mysterious 'Jack White', went downstairs at around 7.45; meanwhile John Stack, 47, was outside oiling his handcart in readiness for his day's rag-collecting rounds. By 9.45 they had all departed. Only Carey remained in the house with 'Old Tommy' and 'Old Mary', as they were affectionately known. Jones and Stack would recall that he had been seated by the kitchen fire eating his breakfast when they left.

The scene was set for the explosive events that would propel sleepy little Smallwood — a scattered, largely agricultural community midway between Sandbach and Congleton, whose population in 1881 was 578 — into the national headlines.

What occurred in the intervening period is not known, but at about 11.50am Smallwood collier James Norbury was walking along the turnpike (then known simply as 'The High Road'), when he saw Thomas Earlam hanging out a sheet to dry on the field hedge on the opposite side of the road. Since Mary Moran's eyesight had begun to fail, Earlam had to help her with the laundry and when he went back in he did so via the wash-house door. It was the last time any of his neighbours saw 'Old Tommy' alive.

Two other passers-by that mid-day, however, did see someone in the cottage. A few minutes after noon, 15-year-old farmer's son Joseph Bracegirdle of Moss Bank Farm, Smallwood, rode past in a horse-and-cart, and ten minutes later John Broad, 64, a farmer at Moss End, Smallwood, also went by the house. Both saw a face at the living room window. It was that of a man who, on seeing them, immediately ducked out of sight. Bracegirdle and Broad only had a fleeting glimpse of the man at the window, but it was enough for both of them to identify him later as Patrick Carey.

Blacksmith Eugene Ganton, one of the men who accompanied Edward Sampey on his return to the death-house, had passed the cottage earlier, at around 12.15. He was on his way home for lunch when, as he drew level with the back-kitchen door, he heard 'a very faint groan'. But he attached no great significance to it and continued on his way. What these witness statements showed, however, was that the attack on the defenceless old couple almost certainly occurred between 11.50am and 12.20pm, which agreed with Dr Latham's estimate of Thomas Earlam's time of death. When he arrived at the lodging house at 5.30pm, the doctor would say in evidence later, he judged the man had been dead between four and five hours.

At about 12.40pm wheelwright James Austin was leaving his lodgings near Fourlanes End — the crossroads about 350 yards south of Thomas Earlam's cottage around which the homes of most of the local population were clustered — when he noticed a man, who he had seen around the village the previous day, coming down the road towards him. Austin would testify later that, as he passed the Bulls Head, the man was walking briskly and glancing downwards as if examining his coat and trousers — which, the *Chronicle* suggested, 'a man bespattered with human blood might be expected to do'. Under his left arm was a large bundle wrapped in a distinctive paisley-design 'handkerchief'. In this context the word referred to a large neckerchief or muffler commonly used by travellers to hold their meagre possessions; its dimensions can be gauged from a comment made by Austin at Carey's trial, where he likened it to 'a shawl'. It was definitely big enough to conceal a man's suit of clothes . . .

At the crossroads the man-in-a-hurry turned left into modern Church Lane, the main road to Congleton. Austin would later pick him out in a police identity line-up. It was Patrick Carey.

The last person to see the fleeing Carey in the village that day was William Booth, the 33-year-old village constable. He was on duty near Fourlanes End at around 12.50pm when he also spotted him heading along the Congleton road. Unlike James Austin, however, he observed

The disappearing lodger was seen walking briskly past the Bull's Head pub (right) and examining his clothes (for possible signs of blood?). The lodging house run by double-murder victims Thomas Earlam and Mary Moran was situated just before the white gables seen in the distance in this picture.   *Photograph by the author.*

nothing suspicious in his manner; so, as he explained later, he saw no reason to detain him. It would be another 15 days before the wanted man was finally captured.

The hunt for Carey began in earnest the day after Thomas Earlam's murder when the Chief Constable of Cheshire (Colonel John Hamersley) and the head of the Middlewich Police Division (Superintendent John Hindley) visited Smallwood for an update on the situation from Sergeant Alfred Oldham of Sandbach Police, the officer in charge of the local inquiries.

The presence of such high-ranking officers was intended to send out a clear message to the people of Smallwood, and the public at large, that the police would be directing all their efforts towards solving a crime that would soon be recognised as one of the most cold-blooded and mercenary double-murders ever committed in this country.

In a despatch by-lined 'Our Own Reporter', that 17 February edition of the *Chester Chronicle* provided the most detailed account of the early stages of the investigation — and, indeed, of the entire circumstances surrounding this barbaric crime. It began with a graphic description of the murder house, which, it stated, was 'in a wretched condition'. At one end it had 'a tumble-down shed or stable', while inside was a 'rickety staircase' that led to 'squalid upper rooms'.

The report went on, 'The scene of the crime was on Sunday the centre of attraction to crowds of people from the Potteries, Congleton, Sandbach and other places, many of them coming in gigs, traps and other conveyances. In fact, the village all day long was [as] crowded as a small town on a fair day, whilst the road to Sandbach late in the afternoon had also the appearance of people returning from a gala.'

'Wanted' notices, offering a £100 reward for information leading to the capture of the fugitive, were soon circulating among the major towns of Cheshire and south Lancashire, as well as lodging houses and workhouses in the area. The *Chronicle* carried its own description, which ran, '[He] is about 36 years of age [*sic*], 5ft 7ins or 5ft 8ins high [with a] tanned complexion, black hair, no whiskers or moustache; stout built and supposed to be slightly pock-pitted [as a result of small-pox, presumably], dressed in a hard felt brown hat, long blue 'pilot' overcoat right down to his knees (far worn and with large pockets), a pair of corduroy trousers patched on the right knee and at the bottom with material of a lighter colour, and laced-up boots.' A pilot coat, also known as a pea coat, was double-breasted with square-cut corners like a longer version of the more modern reefer jacket.

Although he was last seen heading in that direction, Patrick Carey does not seem to have continued on into Congleton. He was first sighted in the afternoon of the crime some six miles away in Astbury, to the south of Congleton, and then in the evening of the same day he was reported to have stopped in the village of Eaton, about two miles north-east of the town. At least, a man answering his description called at the Plough Inn there, looking for lodgings. The landlord apparently agreed to put him up, but he never took up the offer. And by the Sunday no further trace of him had been found.

On Monday 12 February the inquest into Thomas Earlam's death was held at the Salamanca Inn (at the time of writing a boarded-up shell of a building awaiting re-development on the A50 close to Fourlanes End). With the public hungry to learn all the gruesome details, the press reports were eagerly awaited. However, as the *Chronicle* reported, East Cheshire Coroner Mr Hercules Campbell Yates, of Macclesfield, announced in opening the inquest that he would be taking only formal evidence and then adjourning the hearing until the police had completed their investigation into this 'abominable and most cruel murder'.

Rag-and-bone man John Stack who, like Edward Sampey, was a long-term lodger, having been at Earlam's for about a year, identified the supposed murder weapon as his property. It had a stock about 14-15ins long and 'a very heavy head' and weighed about 1½lbs. When it was found near Mary Moran's body, he said, it bore 'large and recent blood stains'.

Sampey, known to friends and fellow lodgers as 'Teddy', told of discovering the housekeeper in the wash-house with her head 'swimming in blood' and the scene in the cottage when the old man's body was found. The whole house, he said, was in disorder and appeared to have been ransacked. Of his missing suit, a black worsted three-piece, he said it had been made for him only recently in Sandbach.

PC Booth said he received word of the tragedy at about four o'clock on the Friday afternoon. On arriving at the lodging house, he found the deceased on his back, with his head inclined to the left, between the 'chimney place' and the living-room window. In the wash-house there was 'a great deal of blood' on the floor. By that time Mary Moran had been moved and was lying on a sofa in the living-room.

The most detailed evidence was given by 66-year-old Dr Latham in describing the injuries sustained by the murder victim. Thomas Earlam, he stated, had been 'a strong muscular man but somewhat deformed at the curvature of the spine'. He would, presumably, have had a slightly hunch-backed or stooped posture. Though he was a sturdily-built fellow for his age, he never stood a chance for, said the doctor, his assailant had struck him from behind. The most obvious sign of his injury was a 'large, puffy swelling 12 inches long and four inches wide' on the right side of his head.

In his postmortem report, the doctor reeled off a catalogue of catastrophic injuries: under the puffy swelling the bones on that side of his skull had been 'completely smashed down'; the temporal bone was 'broken into a number of pieces, which were jammed into the brain'; the frontal bone was also fractured; the cheek bone was smashed as were both the upper and lower jaw bones, 'the fractures extending quite to the base of the skull'. And there were gasps around the crowded 'court' room, the *Chronicle* reported, when he stated that he had found 'portions of the brain in the deceased's mouth' and that 'when he inserted his fingers into the mouth they came into contact with the cranium'. The bones, he explained, were technically called 'comminuted' — in other words they were 'in a hundred pieces' — which accounted for the great loss of blood. The flat face of the hammer found in the wash-house, he agreed, could have inflicted the injuries.

Somewhat surprisingly, such devastating results, Dr Latham surmised, could have been caused by a single blow; but if so, he said, 'it must have been a terrific blow given by a strong man'. He had no doubt, however, that, 'due to the nature of the head injuries', death, mercifully, would have been instantaneous. The cause of Thomas Earlam's death, he gave as 'loss of blood and the fracture of the skull'.

The following day, Tuesday the 13th, Thomas Earlam was laid to rest in the graveyard of Smallwood's Parish Church of St. John the Baptist. In compliance with the instructions the old man had left with his solicitors, Messrs Barclay and Henstock of Macclesfield, the time of the funeral was kept secret, and the first the villagers knew about it was when, around 3pm, a horse-drawn hearse pulled up outside the lodging house. However, according to the *Chronicle*, 'a few females left their houses the moment the hearse was passing and formed into a small procession, following the remains to the grave'.

The Vicar, the Reverend Edleston Williams, officiated at the service, but a rather unfortunate incident occurred before he could conduct the committal ceremony. It was discovered that no ropes had been provided with which to lower the coffin into the grave and it was with some relief that a quick-thinking individual, probably one of the undertaker's staff, suggested removing the reins from the funeral horse and using them instead. However, as the *Chronicle* reported, 'It meant that someone had to get a ladder and climb down into the grave to retrieve the reins afterwards.' And the paper commented, 'It is a pity that what was in itself a melancholy affair should have been attended with such an unpleasant and awkward incident.'

Like the private person he was, Thomas Earlam took most of his personal secrets to the grave with him. The *Chronicle*'s extensive despatch had described him as 'a very taciturn man' whose affairs were 'known but little of in the vicinity'. It was said that he came originally from the Macclesfield area (in his census returns he was recorded as being born in both Knutsford *and* Smallwood); and, said the paper, 'he was widely thought to have property in Chester'. In his will, published in June 1884, however, his personal estate amounted to £15 17s 6d — about £1,500 in today's money. It also revealed that he had a half-brother living in Reddish, Stockport.

Mary Moran's inquest was held, also by Coroner Yates at the Salamanca Inn, on the morning of Monday 19 February. The same few witnesses who had given evidence at Thomas Earlam's inquest also testified here. Adding to his previous statement, John Stack (*Chronicle*, 24 February) said that when he saw the housekeeper shortly after she was attacked, one side of her face was 'like a piece of liver'. And his first impression of Patrick Carey when he arrived at the lodging house, was that 'he didn't like the look of him'.

Edward Sampey now recalled the conversation he had overheard in which Carey argued with Earlam about his lodging money. He told the jury he had 'heard Earlam say he would not let Jack [*sic*] stay the whole night for tuppence [two old pence], unless he left a shirt as pledge'. The landlord had a strict rule, apparently, that all strangers had to pay for their lodgings on a daily basis.

Earlier, Sampey had been involved in a curious exchange with solicitor Henry Henstock, of Barclay and Henstock. According to the *Chronicle*, the lawyer asked him to 'account for his own movements' on the day of the bloody double event. Note the significance of the word 'own'. By this time it was commonly acknowledged that Patrick Carey was the police's only real suspect (he would finally be nabbed three days later) and, indeed, there was no evidence to implicate anyone else. Henstock was reported as attending the inquest to keep a watching brief on the case on behalf of, variously, the deceased, the deceased's relatives and the deceased's friends; and it may be that he was simply giving Sampey (a friend of both deceased) the opportunity to confirm the events leading up to his discovery of the dying woman. But by singling out the farm labourer for such questioning, the inescapable impression was that he felt Sampey, alone of the lodger-witnesses, needed to demonstrate that he had an alibi.

As it happened Sampey was not unduly perturbed by the possible insinuation; he answered Henstock unhesitatingly and 'told of a circuitous journey he had undertaken in his search for work, calling at several farms in the Sandbach and Wheelock areas'. And at Carey's trial defence counsel would reject any suggestion that another of the lodgers was involved.

Dr Latham — a highly-qualified and much-loved GP affectionately known at his surgery in Wheelock Road, Sandbach, as 'the old doctor' and who would have a memorial bust erected in his honour in his home town after his death in 1907 — described Mary's appearance when he first saw her on the afternoon of 9 February. On the left side of her head, face and neck, he stated, were extensive wounds; there was 'a frightful swelling on the face' and 'both eyes were closed up'. There was a wound 2½ins long over the left eyebrow, beneath which the skull was fractured. She had a similar wound on the forehead at right angles to the first one, which was 'bleeding very much', and another large wound, also 2½ins long, higher up on the front of her head that had also resulted in a fracture of the skull. When he conducted the postmortem he found that part of the frontal bone had been 'broken into a dozen pieces'. He commented, 'However, the fractures did not extend to the base of the brain, and the bones, although shattered, were not depressed. That accounted for the deceased having survived for a time.' The doctor also noted several bruises and skin lacerations on the left arm, the result, doubtless, of Mary's attempts to fend off her attacker.

Cause of death he gave as 'exhaustion consequent upon concussion of the brain produced by violent blows on the head'. The blows, Dr Latham added, were 'in all probability caused by an instrument like the hammer produced'.

In his summing-up the Coroner strongly condemned the brutality of the attack upon 'an aged couple who could not have done wrong to anyone'. He announced he would not be adjourning the inquest and, at his direction, the jury returned a verdict of 'wilful murder by some person or persons unknown'.

The good doctor: 'Old' Dr Latham whose statue in Sandbach bears the legend 'He was beloved of all and a friend of the poor.'

Mary Moran's funeral took place in the afternoon of the same day, also at the Parish Church. It passed off without incident. Mary, a spinster, was born in Ballinrobe in County Mayo, and had been Thomas Earlam's live-in servant for more than 30 years, from when the cottage was still a private residence. Earlam seems to have started running it as a lodging house some time between 1851 and 1861. His association with the place went back at least 40 years, however; for at the time of the 1841 census, when the owner was a Joseph Newhall and he was a 20-year-old agricultural labourer, he was himself a lodger there.

As the search for Patrick Carey continued, the *Chronicle*, in its extensive coverage of the murder investigation, reported an alleged incident involving the dying woman. The newspaper claimed, 'On Wednesday [14 February] she returned to consciousness for a few moments and the attendants immediately asked her who had inflicted her injuries, and she feebly replied, 'Jack . . . Jack.' However, if the report was correct, the police do not appear to have tried to obtain statements from those concerned in order to corroborate it; and as hearsay it could not have been admitted as evidence in court.

Around this time police hopes were raised when a man matching the description on the wanted posters was arrested at Clatterbridge, near Birkenhead, but it turned out not to be the fugitive. Similarly, it was another case of mistaken identity when a second man was detained at Congleton and he, too, was released.

The police were having more success in building up a picture of Carey and his background. According to the *Chronicle*, they 'ascertained that he was married with two children' (though later press reports indicated it was three, two sons and a daughter). His wife, whose name was never revealed, was traced to Glossop, where she told them that her husband had deserted her 'a long time ago' and that she believed he was 'cohabiting with another woman'.

This 'other woman' was probably Ellen White, who Carey had in tow when he first stayed at Thomas Earlam's lodging house in the summer of 1880. On 22 July, a few days after they arrived, the woman, who claimed she was Carey's wife, was taken ill and the couple were admitted to Arclid Workhouse, where they stayed for an indeterminate period while she recovered. Workhouse records showed they registered as 'John White, aged 35 [*sic*]' and 'Ellen White, aged 30.'

The only other candidate was Mary Murphy, an old flame with whom Carey had cohabited off-and-on during the three years she had been separated from her husband. On the day after the Smallwood atrocity, he fetched up in Manchester, and the pair resumed their relationship after meeting again by chance the following evening in Miller Street. It was to be an ill-fated reunion.

Murphy was officially stated to be a hawker, though some of the papers referred to her as 'a low character' or, worse, 'a woman of ill fame', a Victorian euphemism for a prostitute. After having a drink at a nearby pub, she agreed to spend the night with him. So began two weeks of flitting from one lodging house to another in what was then among the roughest, poorest, most densely-populated areas of the city, where the smoke and grime from its numerous textile mills and factories cast a dark pall over the closely-packed rows of unhygienic, overcrowded dwellings and where running fights between teenaged gangs brought terror to the malodorous streets.

It must have been obvious to Carey on arriving in Manchester that the first thing he needed to do was to dispose of a certain black worsted suit that he had brought with him (and which would later be identified as the one belonging to Edward Sampey). Yet, rather than sell it or dispose of it permanently, he chose to pawn it. On that Saturday he had left it for safe-keeping with a publican friend of his. It was wrapped up in a paisley handkerchief identical to the one he had worn during his week's stay at Thomas Earlam's lodging house. On the Monday, having retrieved the incriminating bundle, he and Mary Murphy visited a pawnbroker's shop, where, while he loitered outside, she handed over the suit and received an advance of twelve shillings. As well as the money, she also gave Carey the pawn ticket, which was found in his possession when he was finally caught. It would lead police directly to the pawnbroker . . . and the stolen suit.

It wasn't that he was desperate for cash, either. For Patrick Carey, who was literally penniless when he left Smallwood, had somehow obtained sufficient funds to go on a spending spree. He paid for the couple's lodgings, for their food and drink; he bought new clothes and gave money to his girlfriend. He even stumped up for a haircut.

His taste of freedom, however, was to be short-lived. It ended on Saturday 24 February, when two local detectives appeared on the doorstep of the couple's latest hide-away. Despite his keeping on the move to lessen the risk of being recognised — and during his second week in the city, at least, he hardly seems to have ventured out during the daylight hours — Carey *had* attracted attention. And the police received a tip-off about the couple who had recently moved into a house off Charter Street.

Armed with the description of Carey/White on the wanted notices that by then had been circulated extensively throughout the region, two officers from the Detective Department of Manchester City Police paid the address a late-morning visit. They found Mary Murphy in the kitchen preparing breakfast, while Carey was still in bed upstairs. It was an alarm call for both of them, as they were quickly arrested and taken into custody at Manchester Town Hall, where the Detective Department was then based. After more than two weeks on the run, Patrick Carey was on his way back to Cheshire to be tried in connection with the Smallwood lodging house murders.

Before then, however, there were some preliminary legal formalities to go through. On the following Monday morning (26th), in the first stage of the judicial process, he was brought up before Stipendiary Magistrate Mr Francis Headlam in the Manchester Police Court. After various witnesses had proved that 'Jack White' was, in reality, Patrick Carey, the prisoner was released into the custody of Superintendent Hindley of the Cheshire Police.

He was brought that afternoon to Sandbach, where the story of the shocking double-murder was still the number-one topic of conversation in the town and the surrounding area nearly a month after the event. The *Chester Chronicle* reported on 3 March, 'Great excitement prevailed in the neighbourhood of Sandbach on Sunday on it becoming known that the man who had been arrested in Manchester, in the name of Patrick Carey, had been identified as the missing lodger, Jack White, who was wanted for the murder of Thomas Earlam and Mary Moran at Smallwood in the early part of February.'

Consequently, the paper added, 'A large crowd of people assembled at the railway station to witness the arrival of the prisoners [Mary Murphy, having sold the missing suit, was facing a charge of receiving stolen goods]. The party, on directly leaving the train, entered a close carriage and drove into the town. In the streets near the police office [station] were not less than 2,000 persons who, as the carriage drove up, indulged in a slight display of ill feeling; but a force of police prevented any further demonstration of hostility.'

Carey, the *Chronicle* noted, was 'wearing a new suit of clothes, which it was said he bought one evening during his nocturnal perambulations in Manchester'. At the police station — situated then in Bold Street — Carey was charged with the murders of first Thomas Earlam and then Mary Moran; each time he said 'I know nowt about it.' To a third charge, of stealing Edward Sampey's suit and bank-book, he made no reply. He was placed in the cells. Murphy who, in answering the receiving charge, had also claimed to be innocent, was granted bail.

Next morning, Tuesday, Carey appeared at Sandbach Police Court before local magistrate Mr George W. Latham (a cousin of Dr Charles Latham). The hearing was apparently due to take place in the 'Sessions Rooms' in the old Town Hall, which was on the south side of Sandbach's ancient Market Square, where the town's war memorial now stands. However, as the *Chronicle* reported, 'About 600 or 800 persons had assembled in the square, evidently hoping to have a peep at the prisoner as he was taken from the cells [located in another part of the Town Hall] to the court, but the magistrate decided to take the evidence in private, and the proceedings were accordingly conducted within the police office . . . With the exception of about a dozen reporters, there were none of the outside public present.'

The *Chronicle*, whose reporter was among the assembled press pack, went on, 'The prisoner is a dark-looking man with heavy-set features and a "hang-dog" look.' In the early part of the hearing he had 'fixed his eyes upon the table' in front of him; but he perked up when one particular witness was giving evidence against him. This was Patrick Shannon, husband of Lavinia, who, until Monday 5 February, had also lodged at Earlam's. He was one of several witnesses to identify Carey as the runaway lodger, who he knew only as 'Jack'. The *Chronicle* reporter observed, 'When the witness Shannon spoke positively as to his identity, and added that the prisoner had sung a song for him called "The Emigrant's Farewell To Ireland" [on the previous Saturday night], he glanced slyly round at him and curled his lip. He, however, made no statement beyond a formal, but feeble, denial of the charge[s].'

He was remanded in custody for a week and moved to Knutsford Gaol. Then, on Tuesday 6 March, he was brought back to the Police Court (forerunner of the Magistrates' Court) for the formal committal hearing. This time-consuming procedure, in which all 27 witnesses appeared and had their pre-trial depositions written down, lasted more than seven hours. It was, to a large extent, a rehearsal for the trial to come and the evidence presented will be detailed later, in the more appropriate context of Carey's Chester Assize Court appearance.

Just as the committal was getting under way, Carey requested permission to make an application to the bench for the return of the money the police had taken from him in Manchester. He said, 'It is my money, all of it; and I should like it to be given to my wife to assist in my defence.' Supt Hindley objected, saying that the money was part of the evidence against the prisoner. Carey persisted, 'But I say it is mine and I shall insist upon it being given up.'

The magistrates decided they were not prepared to grant the application 'at present'. However, at the end of the hearing, the prisoner

A massive crowd gathered in Sandbach's ancient Market Square hoping to witness Carey's appearance at Sanbach Police Court in the old Town Hall, which stood on the site now occupied by the town's war memorial. But the hearing was held in private. *Photograph by the author.*

repeated his request and this time the money was handed over to his wife. It amounted to £1 17s 8½d, the equivalent today of about £170, and was to help pay for counsel to represent him at his trial, he explained. However, as we shall see, it was only at the last minute that he engaged the services of a barrister.

After being committed to appear at the next Chester Assizes, he was transported to Chester Castle and lodged in the county gaol. His trial began on Monday 16 April 1883 and lasted two days. Charged with two murders, he was tried first on the single count of killing Thomas Earlam. He pleaded not guilty. When the prisoner was brought up from the cells, Carey was almost unrecognisable. Gone was the scruffy beggar persona he had previously shown to the world, and in its place was a well-dressed figure who, said the *Chronicle* in its trial report of 21 April, had 'bestowed some care on his toilet preparations'.

The paper's correspondent noted, 'The prisoner is a strongly-built man of the middle height. He wore a well-fitting dark pilot coat and a new kerchief of a somewhat gaudy pattern around his neck. He was clean shaven, his hair was tidily brushed and altogether it was not easy to reconcile his general appearance with the idea of a professional "cadger" and tramp, such as he is stated to have been.' On the court list he was described as a general labourer.

The report added, 'His type of countenance, however, is far from prepossessing, the lines of his face betraying, if not absolute malevolence, certainly a sour and ungenial disposition.'

During the trial, as the jury heard about the terrible events of 9 February, Carey seemed largely unconcerned. 'The only point at which his attention seemed to be particularly aroused,' said the *Chronicle,* 'was that at which the woman Murphy, who cohabited with him in Manchester, gave very damning evidence against him.'

The case had already been described in the *Chronicle* as 'one of the most cold-blooded and mercenary double-murders which have of late years been recorded in the Press'. And in his opening speech, prosecuting counsel Mr F. Marshall remarked that the crime had been committed 'under circumstances . . . of a peculiarly barbarous kind'. Although the jury were being asked to consider the murder of Thomas Earlam alone, he said that they would find it involved 'practically and substantially . . . the murder of two persons'; that they would have no difficulty in arriving at the conclusion that the deaths of those two persons were caused by blows from the bloody hammer found close to the dying Mary Moran; that the blood on the newspaper in Edward Sampey's looted trunk 'left no reasonable doubt' that the person who took the clothes was the person who committed the murders, and that there was 'indubitable evidence' that the person who took the clothes was the person who had them in his possession afterwards.

Counsel argued, 'Unquestionably, the prisoner was the person who took Sampey's clothes, pawned them and received the money advanced upon them. Taking all these facts together, the prisoner at the bar was the man who murdered Thomas Earlam'.

It was a convincing start; and, as each new prosecution witness took the stand, Patrick Carey's situation looked increasingly desperate. The testimonies that follow, though fleshed out with occasional newspaper extracts, are essentially the witness depositions sworn before the Chairman of the Sandbach Police Court bench, F. H. R. Wilbraham Esq. of Alsager, at the 6 March committal hearing. In the absence of a court transcript, the hefty bundle of documents, bound with faded pink cotton tape and preserved in the National Archives, constitutes the only official record of the trial.

Edward Sampey recalled his dreadful discoveries when returning to the lodging house on that Friday afternoon in February. 'I went to the door leading into the kitchen [living room]', he stated. 'It was fastened, so I went to the other door leading into the wash-house. It was a bit open. I looked in [and] saw Mrs Moran on the floor . . . She was bleeding from her head. There was much blood about her head.' When the front door was opened and he went into the living room, he said, 'he saw Thomas Earlam on the floor . . [There was] a large quantity of blood about him and he appeared quite dead'. The *Cheshire Observer* (21 April) quoted Sampey as explaining that he had not entered the house when he first saw Mary Moran lying in the pool of blood in the back-kitchen because 'he was frightened'.

Regarding his stolen suit, he deposed, 'I had been at Sandbach Market on the Thursday and had on my best clothes [at this point his suit was produced in court and he confirmed it was his]. I put them into my box [trunk] when I came home that evening. I put a Post Office Savings Bank book into the box under the clothes [and] locked the box.' His trunk was in 'a little room or place leading out of the kitchen'. He placed sheets of newspaper over the suit and put the key underneath the trunk. Carey had been in at the time he returned from his day out at the market and, stated Sampey, the prisoner commented, 'You look a great swell, like a parson.' His trunk, he added, had been unlocked, not broken into. The key was never found.

Referring to the paisley 'handkerchief' belonging to Carey, which was also shown to the jury, Sampey's deposition went on, 'He had seen the prisoner wearing a handkerchief like the one produced. He used to have his meat [food] in a dish and put his handkerchief over it on the table in the kitchen.' It was an aspect of Carey's behaviour that was also noted by the three other fellow lodgers. The food he brought into the house was acquired from his begging expeditions, seemingly.

Sampey further stated that he had 'seen Thomas Earlam give folks change for a sovereign many a time'. The old man, he added, usually kept his money 'in the place where my box was'.

It was a practice confirmed by John William Dale, the builder son of blacksmith John Dale. The family were near neighbours of Earlam, living three houses higher up the High Road. In his witness statement, he said that at the beginning of January Earlam had given him £3 worth of silver for three sovereigns. 'He went to the second door on the right-hand side in the house [for it],' he deposed. 'I have several times changed gold with him for silver.'

Ambrose Wood who, like Sampey, had witnessed the horrors inside the lodging house, also had some chilling memories to recount. After Eugene Ganton had pushed open the wash-house door, witness followed him into the cottage. 'I saw Mary Moran lying in a heap near the back wall on her right side,' he deposed. 'She appeared to be bleeding from the head very much.' Thomas Earlam was 'lying with his head near to the doorway, partly on his back and partly on his left side. His head was one mass of blood and there was a deal of blood on the floor about his head.' The living-room entrance door had been fastened on the inside with a short bolt at the top and a 'small hook and staple' at the bottom. The door was not locked; neither was there a key in the lock.

Of the lodgers at Earlam's on the day of the murderous assault, Lavinia Shannon provided the most telling evidence. She was immediately able to identify the corduroy trousers Carey wore (also produced in court) during his stay at the lodging house. In her deposition she explained, 'The trousers she knew from the patch on the right knee which she had sewn on for him. She had also mended them at the bottom of the legs.' Mrs Shannon, who was by then said to be living in Buglawton, near Congleton, with her husband Patrick, had been at Earlam's three weeks before Carey arrived.

Eugene Ganton recalled passing the cottage and hearing the 'faint groan' outside the back-kitchen door. He said he 'paused at the door for about two seconds then went on.' It could only have been a matter of minutes since the horrific hammer attack in the cottage; and he had stopped within a few feet of Mary Moran lying close to death, and Thomas Earlam already dead, in the midst of an unimaginable blood-bath. The *Cheshire Observer* reported that Ganton explained his lack of curiosity by saying in cross-examination that he 'took no notice of the groan as he had heard similar noises' at the house before. Pressed by the Judge, Sir Henry Hawkwins, he made the bizarre comment that, 'By similar noises he did not mean that he had heard faint groans before, but he had heard shouting of "Murder" by the lodgers.'

Joseph Bracegirdle, teenaged son of Smallwood farmer Charles Bracegirdle and one of the two witnesses who had seen what they claimed was the face of the murderer at the living room window, said that at the time he was in a horse-drawn cart 'going gently along' the High Road from the direction of the Bull's Head. He had noticed the same man the previous Saturday outside the house and would later identify him as Patrick Carey. The youth stated, 'He appeared to see me looking at him rather earnestly and he put his head back.' In the *Observer*'s report Bracegirdle expanded, 'The prisoner's head was about the middle of the window above a small curtain. I saw his full face, but nothing more.'

Farmer John Broad estimated that it must have been between 12.12 and 12.20 when he passed Earlam's. He deposed, 'I stopped opposite the house. Just as I was passing, a man put his face to the window on the left-hand side of the door going in. The prisoner was that man. When I made a stop he withdrew.' In the *Observer*'s trial report he explained that he had stopped to see if he could spot Edward Sampey, who he knew lodged there and who had worked for him as a thresher 'for many years'.

James Austin, the man who had seen Patrick Carey fleeing the murder scene, said in his signed statement that, although he had noticed Carey 'twice look down at his clothes . . . [and] on to the floor' and had passed within five or six feet of him, he had seen 'no marks of blood upon the prisoner's clothes, nor upon his hands or face'. He had seen Carey in the village the previous day wearing the same coat and the cord trousers patched at the knee that he had on that Friday.

Austin, Stack and Patrick Shannon all picked out Carey in a police line-up in Manchester on 25 February, the day after the absconding lodger was arrested.

Sgt. Alfred Oldham, 39, the Cheshire police officer who headed up the local investigation into the two deaths, told the court of his findings on arriving at the lodging house at around 4.30 that afternoon. Inspecting Thomas Earlam's body in the living room he noticed that his trousers were undone and both pockets turned inside out. He stated, 'His waistcoat was unbuttoned and thrown open. His cap was under his head. There was a large pool of blood around his head on the floor. Blood appeared to be oozing from his mouth, nose and ear.'

His statement went on, 'He found blood on the walls very near the top. There were spots of blood on the wall in the wash-house and also on the ceiling. On the left-hand side of the wash-house there was a large pool of blood under a three-legged table. The legs of the table were also covered with blood and on the top of it was a mark as if someone had had hold of it with a hand.'

The broken pan mug, he observed, was 'covered with blood all around' and contained the remnants of 'some coloured liquid'. This, it was realised later, was a mixture of blood and water. Mary Moran's clothes were saturated in blood *and* water when she was found, leading to the supposition that she had been carrying the fully-laden bowl when her killer struck.

In the back-pantry, where Earlam kept his money, there were obvious signs of a search. 'Shoes were lying about, as were old clothes and rags [the fruits of John Stack's recent labours, presumably]', the officer stated. The lid of Edward Sampey's trunk was open and inside were 'two pieces of [news]paper'. They were marked with blood, which was 'fresh and wet'.

Sgt. Oldham's deposition also revealed that on Monday 26 February he had received from Manchester City Police the £1 17s 8½d that Carey claimed had been taken from him after his arrest, and the pawn ticket for Edward Sampey's suit, which Carey still had in his pocket.

Supt Alfred Olham: as a sergeant based at Sandbach, he led the local inquiries into the Smallwood murders.

Photo courtesy of the Museum Of Policing In Cheshire

Of the large assemblage of witnesses, however, there was one whose evidence would prove the most damaging for Patrick Carey. In her account of the furtive fortnight they spent together in Manchester, Mary Murphy, his occasional lover, supplied the missing details of his last efforts to escape justice . . . and the final nail in his coffin.

In her lengthy deposition she first told of meeting Carey between 8pm and 8.30pm on Sunday 11 February. He was standing near the Gaping Goose, a big semi-circular shaped market pub (also known as The Shudehill Hotel) that then stood on the corner of Shudehill and Miller Street. He was wearing the dark pilot coat and the patched-up trousers, the dark tweed waistcoat and the boots he had had on when he was last seen in Smallwood. But now he also wore a new shirt, new stockings, muffler and pocket handkerchief and a new hat, all of which he told her he had bought the previous day. 'He asked me where I was going,' she deposed. 'I said I was going for a bit of a walk. He asked me to have a drink. I thanked him . . . and we went into the Gaping Goose and had two glasses of beer each, for which he paid. He asked me if I had furnished apartments. I said "No". He said "Come along", and we went down [Miller Street] and took lodgings at Mrs Bennett's in Charter Street.'

This was the lodging house at No.105, Charter Street (modern Dantzic Street) in the parish of St. Michael's, run by 38-year-old widow Mrs Sarah Bennett. In the 1881 census she had been listed as a general labourer and the 'Head Boarder'. It was one of many such establishments in an area of the city that was notorious for its poverty, overcrowding and squalor. It was also on the edge of St. Michael's parish at whose heart was the unlikely-named Angel Meadow, a district that in 1849 had been described by visiting London journalist Angus Reach as 'the lowest, most filthy, most unhealthy and most wicked locality in Manchester'. After conducting an investigation into the conditions of the urban poor throughout the manufacturing districts of England, the *Morning Chronicle* reporter wrote, 'It is full of cellars and inhabited by prostitutes, their bullies, thieves, cadgers, vagrants, tramps and, in the worst sties of filth and darkness, by those unhappy wretches the "low Irish."'

The lodging house at No. 105, Charter Street (on the left of the picture), where Carey spent his first night in the heart of Manchester's teeming slumland.

Image by permission of Manchester Archives and Local Studies.

Once an affluent suburb of the city worthy of its name, the pastoral landscape in and around Angel Meadow was transformed by the all-consuming developments of the 19th century industrial age and the jerry-built back-to-back terraces which housed the huge influx of the predominantly destitute Irish who had fled the Great Famine of 1845-1852 to find work in Manchester's mills and factories. Bounded by Miller Street, Rochdale Road, Gould Street and the heavily polluted River Irk, Angel Meadow covered 33 acres and, at its peak, had a population of 20,000-30,000. By far the largest Irish quarter in the city, it was famously labelled as 'Hell upon earth' by Friedrich Engels (socialist reformer and co-author with Karl Marx of *The Communist*

Manifesto), in his book *The Condition of the Working Class in England in 1844*. And by 1883 a major new social scourge was also bedevilling the lives of the local citizens: 'scuttling'.

'Scuttling', explains Andrew Davies in his authoritative book *The Gangs of Manchester* (2008), was 'the first modern youth cult', a form of street fighting by gangs of youths, usually aged 14-19, distinctively dressed, sometimes in silk mufflers and peaked caps tilted to the left to display their long fringes, and sporting heavy-buckled and decorated belts which, along with their narrow-toed, brass-tipped clogs and stones tied in handkerchiefs, were their main weapons. They also carried knives, though, says Andrew Davies, their purpose was not to kill but to maim and disfigure. Together with scraps with the police, the periodic territorial clashes between the various street gangs — which first broke out in the 1870s — were seen as one of the more extreme ways in which these rootless young men relieved the hard toil of the long working days and the 'dull idleness' of the evenings.

The violence reached a peak in the late 1890s, then gradually died out. One of the scuttlers' regular battle-grounds in Angel Meadow was St. Michael's Flags, a name derived from the flagstones that in 1855 were laid over what had been the city's largest pauper cemetery alongside the Parish Church. Today, wedged between Old Mount Street and Aspin Lane, the award-winning St. Michael's Flags and Angel Meadow Park stands on the reclaimed site, which once again has a green and pleasant aspect.

It was by losing themselves among the area's teeming under-class that Patrick Carey and Mary Murphy hoped to hide from the law. And, in endeavouring to keep one step ahead of the police, they changed their lodgings four times during the next six days.

The following day, Monday, they went to the Crown and Shuttle pub at the junction of Miller Street and Long Millgate (now Corporation Street) to retrieve the bundle he had left with the landlord the previous Saturday. Mary's deposition went on, 'It was tied up in a paisley handkerchief. The one now produced is the same. We then went to our lodgings at Bennett's. There the prisoner opened the bundle. It contained a matching coat, vest [waistcoat] and pair of trousers. He said they were his "Sunday clothes" and had cost him £4. He said he would pawn them and buy a working suit.'

Accompanied by Carey, Murphy took the garments 'under her apron' to the pawn shop of William Hampson at 28, Roger Street, Redbank. Carey had told her to ask for a sovereign for them, but she could get only twelve shillings. The clothes produced, she said, 'were the ones I pawned'. The suit was handed over to the police by the shop's manager,

Ernest Blayney, on 26 February. It was later identified as the one stolen out of Edward Sampey's trunk at Thomas Earlam's lodging house in Smallwood on 9 February. At some point they also visited a clothier's in Great Ancoats Street where, Murphy said, Carey bought a pair of trousers and a sleeved waistcoat for 19s 6d.

That Monday night they moved into new lodgings in Hanover Street, just around the corner from Charter Street. They were in one of the three adjoining properties, Nos 36-40, Hanover Street, that had been converted into the 'model lodging houses' run by Edward Atkinson. In 1881, it is recorded, they were accommodating more than 40 lodgers. The pair remained there until Thursday morning, when they relocated to Samuel Garside's lodging house at 31, Angel Street.

This was the most godless thoroughfare in Angel Meadow. In 1893 an article in *The Spy*, a magazine published in Manchester at the time, commented on 'the dreary wastes of Angel Meadow [and] down Angel Street, with its pestiferous lodging houses, with its bawds and bullies, its thieves and beggars'. The anonymous author wrote, 'One had need to visit such a place when the sun is high in the heavens. When night falls I had [*sic*] rather enter an enemy's camp during the time of war than venture near such dens of infamy and wretchedness . . . but the poor live here and die here, while our city fathers sleep.'

In Charter Street and Angel Street, part of the largest community in the world's first industrial city, the 'trade' that did most business was prostitution. By 1897, as revealed in a survey conducted by local Vicar the Reverend J. E. Mercer, prostitutes were active in 58 of the 79 houses in Charter Street and, of the 54 houses in Angel Street, only eight were 'free of this class of women'.

After spending the night in Angel Street, Carey and Murphy were on the move again the next morning, taking a room at another lodging house in Charter Street. That day, Friday 16 February, they went to a shop in Deansgate, from where Carey — still comfortably in funds — bought a coat. 'He handed over a sovereign and received 4s. 6d change,' Murphy deposed. The following morning, Carey asked her to go out and get him a new toecap fitted to one of his boots, then only five days later, he gave her a half-sovereign to take them back to the shoemaker to get him to put a new matching toecap on the other boot.

Of his seemingly plentiful supply of ready cash, Mary said that when he was going to give her money he turned his back on her, so she couldn't see which pocket he got it from or how much he had.

Towards midday on the 17th they decamped for what would be the final time and took a furnished room at No. 5, Crown Court in Ashley Lane (now Aspin Lane), off Charter Street, where during their last seven days of freedom Carey paid to have his hair cut, gave Mary his old patched-up trousers to sell and decided his old pilot coat was too small and told her that, if she pawned it, she could keep the money. The trousers she sold 'for old rags' for three half-pence and the coat she first took to be repaired. But she never had time to collect the garment for, the next day, she and Carey were arrested.

After keeping on the move for a week, it looked as if the double-murder suspect had begun to relax his hide-and-seek tactics and settle into a state of almost domestic normalcy; it had been his idea to take the furnished room as he would 'rather have a place to himself' (*Cheshire Observer*, 21 April). If he was becoming more confident in his ability to evade the clutches of the law, however, a knock on the door on the morning of Saturday 24 February would have Patrick Carey quaking in his newly-restored boots. The circumstances surrounding his eventual capture were related to the trial jury by Detective Sergeant Joseph Jackson.

The 30-year-old officer said that he and Detective William Fox went to Crown Court tucked away off Charter Street around 11am. In his deposition, he stated, 'Mary Murphy was preparing breakfast. In the top room we found the prisoner. He was in bed. I asked [him] his name and he replied "John Delaney."' Prisoner told him he was from Derbyshire and claimed he had tramped to Manchester via towns such as Handley and Chapel-en-le-Frith. A search of the house revealed that Carey was still in possession of the signature paisley kerchief that would be such a key pointer to his identification. It was hanging on the banister rail of the stairs.

On his arrival at the Town Hall, the prisoner admitted his real name was Patrick Carey. When he was put into an identity parade with 12 other men later that day, the witness John Stack failed to pick him out. But, said Sgt. Jackson, the light in the corridor was at that time 'rather deficient' and, when Carey was placed with three other men in another part of the building, Stack immediately pointed to him. 'On the Sunday evening,' Sgt. Jackson deposed, 'Carey was placed with 13 others then in the yard of the Town Hall and was in my presence identified by the witnesses [Patrick] Shannon and Austin separately.'

The Town Hall corridor was the scene of another revealing incident, a conversation between Carey and Mary Murphy that had allegedly taken place there on the following Monday, 26 February, just before the prisoner was due to go before the Stipendiary magistrate. In her deposition Mary stated that she had passed Carey waiting outside the courtroom and he asked her whether she had 'heard them say anything'. She said 'No.' Then he said, 'Do you think they have found that suit of clothes?' She said, 'Yes, I told them about it last night.' To which, she claimed, he replied, 'Then I'm done.'

At his committal hearing, Carey had suggested to her that what he said was, 'It makes no matter'. But she stood by her testimony. And at the trial, in the face of a challenge from defence counsel Mr Colt Williams, she repeated the claim.

One puzzling aspect of the case involved the pilot coat and cord trousers Carey was wearing on the day of the murder. They were subsequently retrieved by the Manchester Police from the two local dealers and were sent to Cheshire's County Analyst Dr Joseph Carter Bell for examination. But he could find only one tiny spot of mammalian blood — it would be another 17 years before there was a scientific method for distinguishing between human and animal blood — on one of the legs of the trousers. He testified that it was about the size of a pinhead and had been there for about a month. It was a disclosure that was seized upon by the defence.

Mr Marshall had attempted to rationalise this apparent inconsistency when he summed up for the prosecution. He pointed out (*Observer*), '[Carey's] shirt and hat, which, besides his trousers, were probably the only clothes he wore at the time, and which might possibly have contained other marks, had been got rid of.' And he maintained in any case that 'the nature of the blows was not such as to cause a spurting of blood on the prisoner's clothes'.

It was during his final address to the jury that Prosecutor Marshall propounded his theory of how the murders had occurred. He said no-one could be sure of what happened in the Earlam household that day; but he 'suggested as possible that the prisoner, being animated by the desire of plunder, and having seen the lodger Sampey wearing a good suit of clothes, he, when Sampey had gone out, took his clothes from the box and then attempted to possess himself of the money Earlam was supposed to have in the [back] pantry' (*Chronicle*).

He went on, 'It is possible that while so doing he was discovered by Earlam, who endeavoured to prevent the robbery, and that the prisoner, after threatening Earlam, followed him across the floor and, picking up the hammer, dealt him the savage blow on the head which, according to the medical evidence, caused his death. Supposing him to have done this, it is natural to think that the old woman, hearing the noise, shrieked out or tried to give an alarm in some way, and that the prisoner then also struck her with the hammer three or four times and caused the injuries which several days later resulted in her death.'

Colt Williams had a fairly impossible task, not made any easier by the fact that he had had no prior sight of the witness depositions and had 'only just been instructed by the prisoner from the dock' (*Chronicle*). But in his closing speech for the defence he insisted that the miniscule amount of blood on Carey's clothing was 'an important point in favour of the prisoner'. Remarking on the fact that the walls and ceiling in the house were 'bespattered with blood', and pools of it were on the floor, he argued that it was 'impossible for whoever committed the murders to have escaped being splashed with the blood which came from his victims'.

Counsel also questioned whether the two witnesses whose evidence placed Carey in the murder house at just after noon, could have recognised the defendant positively from such a brief glance through a partly-curtained window. In the *Observer*'s trial report (21 April), he further contended that the blood on the newspaper in Edward Sampey's trunk could have been 'conveyed there by the hands of curious people who went to the cottage at the time the murder was discovered'.

He pointed out, 'Old Earlam's ways and where he kept his money [were] known to others more nearly than they were to the prisoner and might have excited their cupidity [greed].' Mr Williams added that he did not suggest the crimes had been committed by one of the other lodgers — the Chronicle quoted Judge Hawkins as saying that he 'rejoiced' when he heard him say so — but he argued that they could have been perpetrated by some other person who had sneaked into the house, after the prisoner had gone, and left without being observed.

At the end of the two-day trial, the jury took just five minutes to arrive at their guilty verdict. Before the Judge passed sentence, Carey was asked if he had anything to say. He replied, 'I admit taking the clothes, but of anything else I am quite innocent.'

His Lordship told him, 'No man who has listened attentively to the evidence that has been offered to the jury can entertain one shadow of a doubt . . . that you are guilty of the wicked and cruel crime.' Mr Justice Hawkins, later the 1st Baron Brampton, had a reputation as a 'hanging judge'; but on this occasion he was left with no choice but to impose the death penalty and to offer the prisoner no hope of any commutation of the sentence . He continued, ''Your crime is of so cruel, so brutal and so barbarous a character that when you leave that dock, and descend to the prison from whence you came, reflect and feel that your days are numbered.'

With one capital offence proved, the court did not proceed with the charge of murdering Mary Moran or of stealing Edward Sampey's suit and bank-book.

After the trial it was revealed that the condemned man had a history of petty crime. It began, curiously enough, when he convinced police

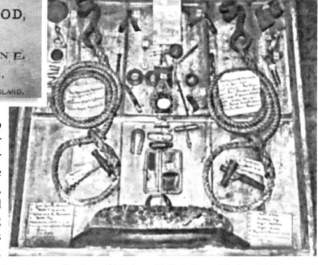

William Marwood, who carried out all four executions at Chester Castle, kept a macabre cabinet of souvenirs, including his ropes and other hanging paraphernalia. Inset: his personal 'business card'.

Images from the private collection of Madame Talbot (www.MadameTalbot.com).

he *was* Patrick Delaney. In that name he was sentenced to one month in Knutsford Gaol in August 1878 for stealing cakes; in July 1879, this time calling himself John Delaney, he served two months, also in Knutsford, for stealing two pairs of boots and, in November 1880, he was back there for a further six months' stay for stealing two pairs of trousers. On that occasion the charge sheet listed him as 'John Price'.

Patrick Carey was hanged at eight o'clock on the morning of Tuesday, 8 May 1883 by William Marwood. As expected there had been no petition for mercy, no reprieve. In the days immediately before his execution — which was switched from its original date of Monday the 7th when it was found that Marwood had a 'booking' in Lincoln that day — he had been visited by his estranged wife, his 16-year-old daughter and two sons, none of whom were named in the press. Once again the newspapers had to rely on second-hand information to compile their execution reports; this time their eye-witness was the Reverend Father Pacificus of the local Franciscan Order, the Castle Gaol's Roman Catholic chaplain, who had attended Carey, himself a Catholic, while he was in prison. The priest gave a statement to the assembled news reporters in which he said that Carey died 'a true penitent sinner' and had 'made over and over again a general confession'.

The *Cheshire Observer* grumbled on 12 May, 'The powers that be followed their usual custom of declining to admit representatives of the Press to the execution and the latter had to be content with joining the small crowd of persons who assembled on St. Mary's Hill to gaze alternatively at the high walls which surround the prison and at the flag-pole.' Since the 1868 Capital Punishment (Amendment) Act, which ended public hangings, the High Sheriff of the county decided who was admitted to the 'indoor' executions.

The paper went on, 'Punctually at eight o'clock a "click" was heard to proceed from within the prison walls and this was rightly conjectured by some of those who stood outside to have been caused by that final operation which sent Patrick Carey to eternity — to wit, the drawing of the bolt, for in two seconds afterwards the black flag was hoisted.' The *Chronicle*'s reporter referred to hearing 'a bang' and identified it as 'the noise of the trapdoors of the scaffold falling'.

Patrick Carey was the last person to be hanged at Chester and his death brought to an end the city's unique history as Cheshire's place of execution, a long and, latterly, a much resented role the city fathers were more than happy to hand over to Knutsford Gaol when, in 1884, the Castle closed as a civilian prison.

Footnote: The boots that Carey was so attached to — and in which he was tried and ultimately died — he had apparently stolen in early February 1883, along with £1 19s 6d in cash, from the lodging-house of John Diskin of Winster, near Matlock, in Derbyshire, according to the *Derbyshire Times*. A Constable Blackney of the Bakewell Police trailed him almost as far as Buxton before losing the scent, discovering later that the suspected thief had made his way into Cheshire (the very journey, possibly, that ended up at Thomas Earlam's front door in Smallwood). The paper reported on 21 April that Carey was still wearing, and would be executed in, the 'borrowed' boots. The robbery victim bemoaned, 'I fear I will not see my £1 19s. 6d again.' As to the stolen boots, there was another claimant to their ownership. Together with the clothes Carey was wearing at the time, they became the possessions of the hangman once the execution was over . . . one of the perks of his singular, solitary profession.

Sources and Bibliography

Chapter One — Part one: Chester Assizes Gaol Files, The National Archives (TNA), CHES24/159/2; Chester Assize Crown Book, Cheshire Archives and Local Studies (CALS), ZCR 580; The will of Margaret Lowe of Sandbach, CALS, WS (1736). Part two: Chester Assizes Gaol Files, TNA, Ches24/162/7; Dee drowning inquisitions, CALS, ZQCI/21/11, ZQCI/22/6 and /22/7.

Chapter Two: Chester Assizes Gaol Files, TNA, Ches24/162/2; *An Account of the robbery of Mr Porter of Raike [sic] Farmhouse, near Chester, by Irish Haymakers*, CALS, DDX 257; Various Rake Farm robbery articles, *Cheshire Sheaf*, February, 1922. CALS.

Chapter Three — Part One: Chester Assizes Gaol Files, TNA, CHES24/163/6. Part Two: Judge's Notes, TNA, HO144/75/A1878; Prison File, TNA, PCOM4/65/20.

Chapter Four — Part One: Coroner's Inquisitions, CALS, ZQCI/26/51; Mayor's File, CALS, ZMF 204. Part Two: Chester Quarter Sessions Order Book, CALS, ZQSO/1; Keeper's Journal, Northgate Gaol, CALS, QAG/3.

Chapter Five — Part One: Chester Assizes Gaol Files, TNA, CHES 24/179/6; Judge's Report and correspondence relating to the Peter Martin case, TNA, HO47/22/32; HMS *Actaeon* Master's Log, TNA, ADM52/2670; *Actaeon* Muster Book, TNA, ADM36/12807. Part Two: Chester Assizes Gaol Files, TNA, CHES24/169/4.

Chapter 6: Execution Warrant, CALS, ZSFE/1/2; Prison Hulk Registers, TNA, HO/9/5; Transportation Records, TNA, HO11/3 (f. 364); Chester Castle Gaol Criminals Book 1818-1823, CALS, D6771/1.

Chapter Seven: Chester Assizes Criminal Depositions, TNA, ASSI 65/1; Cheshire Land Tax Records, CALS.

Chapter Eight — Part One: Chester Assizes Criminal Depositions, TNA, ASSI 65/4; City Gaoler's Journal, CALS, ZQAG/34L. Part Two: Chester Assizes Criminal Depositions, TNA, ASSI 65/7; Quarter Sessions correspondence relating to the execution of Cheshire criminals, 31 May 1866, CALS, QAB 6/31.

Chapter Nine: Minutes of evidence heard by the Capital Punishment Commission, Parliamentary Papers, February 1865. No official Assize Court case records located.

Chapter Ten — Part One: Chester Assizes Criminal Depositions, TNA, ASSI 65/10. Part Two: Chester Assizes Criminal Depositions, TNA,

ASSI 65/12; Cheshire Quarter Sessions Files, CALS, QJF 298/1; Sessions Books, CALS, QJB 5/15; Visiting Magistrates' Minute Book CALS, QAB 3/3.

Chapter Eleven: Chester Assizes Criminal Depositions, TNA, ASSI 65/10.

Chapter Twelve: Chester Assizes Criminal Depositions, TNA, ASSI 65/3; Calendar of Prisoners tried at Chester in 1883, TNA, HO 140/62; Cheshire Quarter Sessions Order Books, CALS, QJB 4/56; Quarter Sessions Files, CALS, QJF 308/4.

Books and Other Printed Materials
Standard histories

Audsley, George Ashdown The Stranger's Handbook to Chester, 1908,

Earwaker, J. P. The History of the Ancient Parish of Sandbach, 1890.

Hanshall, J. H. *The History of the County Palatine of Chester*, 1823.

Hemingway, Joseph *History of the City of Chester*, 1831.

Ormerod, George *The History of the County Palatine and the City of Chester*, 1819 (**G. Helsby** revised edition, 1882).

Other books consulted

Arrowsmith, Peter *Stockport: A History*, Stockport Metropolitan Borough Council, 1997.

Bateson, Charles *The Convict Ships 1787-1868*, Brown, Son and Ferguson Ltd revised edition, 1985

Challoner, W. H. *The Social and Economic Development of Crewe 1780-1923*, Manchester University Press, 1950.

Craig, Robert, and **Jarvis, Rupert**, Liverpool *Registry of Merchant Ships*, Manchester University Press for the Chetham Society, 1967.

Davies, Andrew *The Gangs of Manchester: The Story of the Scuttlers, Britain's First Modern Youth Cult*, Milo Books, 2008.

Davies, Stella *A History of Macclesfield*, Manchester University Press, 1961

Ellison, Norman *The Wirral Peninsula*, Robert Hale Ltd, 1955.

Fiennes, Celia *Through England On A Side Saddle*, 1888.

George, Mary Dorothy *London Life In The Eighteenth Century*, 1925 (Penguin Books edition, 1966).

Hall, M. Clement *A Calendar Of Miseries: Mothers Who Killed Children*, Lulu, 2010.

Hempel, Sandra *The Inheritor's Powder: A Tale of Arsenic,*

Murder and the New Forensic Science, W.W. Norton & Company, 2013.

Hobson, Richard *Richard Hobson of Liverpool, a Faithful Pastor*, his autobiography reprinted by The Banner of Truth Trust, 2003.

Hughes, Robert *The Fatal Shore: A History of the Transportation of Convicts to Australia 1787-1868*, Guild Publishing edition, 1987.

Hutchinson John R. *The Press Gang Afloat and Ashore*, Kessinger Publishing Co., 2004.

Leach, Joan *Knutsford: A History*, Phillimore & Co. Ltd, 2007.

Lynch, Colin James *Colin Lynch's Northwich*, Cheshire Country Publishing, 2004.

Place, Geoffrey *The Rise and Fall of Parkgate: Passenger Port for Ireland, 1686-1815*, Chetham Society, 1994.

Stephens, W. B. (Ed.) *History of Congleton*, Manchester University Press, 1970.

Tomlinson, Richard W. *History of Sandbach and District*, 1899.

Whitfield, Lavinia *The Church At The Ford: The Story of St. Michael's Church, Shotwick*, 1976.

Pamphlets and specialist articles

Barber, the Venerable E. *Parkgate: An Old Cheshire Port*, a paper read to the Chester and North Wales Archaeological Society, 25 October 1910. CALS.

Beazley, F. C. *Notes on Shotwick*, Transactions of the History Society of Lancashire and Cheshire, 1915. CALS.

Boon, Peter *Between The Howty and the Dare in Congleton*, pamphlet 2008; *The Antrobus Family in the 18th and 19th Centuries*, pamphlet 2009. Both published by Congleton Museum.

Bostock, Tony *Local History Notes: Nineteenth Century Davenham*, 2009 (tonybostock.com).

Marino, Dr Gordon S. *The very worst sties of filth and darkness: Exploring the evolving industrial community of Angel Meadow.* In *Patrimonio*, 36-45. San Juan, Puerto Rico: State Historic Preservation Office, 2015.

Marshall, Charles and **Meredith, Gordon** *A History Of Mills In Audlem*, manuscript, 1980, CP/AUDL/M (Ref. 11212), CALS.

Crown copyright material is reproduced with the permission of the Controller of HMSO.

Records in the Cheshire Record Office are reproduced with the permission of Cheshire Archives & Local Studies and the owner/depositor to whom copyright is reserved.

Note: All modern equivalents of historic monetary values given in this book are based on the Bank of England's Inflation Calculator (*www.bankofengland.co.uk*).

ND - #0259 - 270225 - C0 - 234/156/18 - PB - 9781780915531 - Gloss Lamination